GREAT BRITAIN
AND THE
GERMAN TRADE RIVALRY
1875-1914

GREAT BRITAIN
AND THE
GERMAN TRADE RIVALRY

1875-1914

ROSS J. S. HOFFMAN

NEW YORK

RUSSELL & RUSSELL · INC

1964

TO MY MOTHER

PREFACE

THIS volume represents an effort to describe three features of British history in the forty-odd years before the outbreak of war in 1914. They are: first, the inroad made by commercial and industrial Germany upon the far-flung business empire of Great Britain; second, the British national reaction to this German rivalry, and third, the influence of that rivalry upon the shaping of British policy toward Germany. The unity of my study consists in the organic relationship between those three subjects. Although it has been necessary to deal with the decline of Cobdenism in Britain, the general intensification of all international economic rivalries in the pre-war years, and cognate subjects, in order to fit my study into a right setting of historical circumstances, I do not think it will be found that I have stepped beyond the limitations stated above. That is the reason why I chose the title *Great Britain and the German Trade Rivalry* rather than, say, *The Anglo-German Trade Rivalry*. And that is my justification for having composed this book from materials almost exclusively British.

It will, I think, impress the reader that I have sought to track down, order, and compress within a small compass a very large, far-reaching and elusive thing. Whoever does not realize this fact can have little knowledge of the perplexing problems which face the student who seeks to particularize closely the economic rivalries of the modern world, to analyze the effect of these upon the public mind, and to discover the weight of their influence in shaping the policies of governments. These are difficult objects of historical investigation and one who attempts an approach to them can hardly expect to come away without at least a feeling of inadequacy. No one will be more aware than I of the many lacunae in this study, of the matters left untreated, the things left unsaid, the questions unanswered, and the very sketchy handling of many important matters. But in defense I may plead the formless immensity of my subject. If my book has no other value than to throw light here and there upon the less-studied features of the history of the pre-war years, and to draw attention to the deep importance of studying such things as economic rivalries and manifestations of the public mind, I shall feel that I did not write it wholly in vain.

I first conceived the idea of writing this book while a student under Professor William Ezra Lingelbach at the University of Pennsylvania, and it was to the University of Pennsylvania that I presented it last year as a doctoral dissertation. The actual writing of the book was done between the years of 1928 and 1932, during which time I was an instructor in history at New York University; but my connection with Pennsylvania was not broken, nor was the unfailing aid and advice of Professor Lingelbach interrupted. To him and to his university colleagues, especially Professor Edward P. Cheyney, I stand deeply indebted for having been able to complete this study. That, however, does not exhaust the obligations which I have incurred. My wife, Hannah McCruden Hoffman, worked side by side with me through a long summer in the newspaper room of the British Museum in London, copying vast quantities of the material with which my book has been made. My dear friend, Mr. Arthur Ruel Thompson, of Nanuet, N.Y., very kindly drew the figures for the plates which appear in the book. My colleague of New York University, Professor Jonathan French Scott, read the manuscript and offered shrewd and helpful criticism. Finally I would express my gratitude to the library staffs of Columbia University, the New York Public Library, and the British Museum.

Ross J. S. Hoffman

New York, August 1933.

CONTENTS

CHARTS

Chapter I

THE GREAT DIVIDE
1870-1880

THE historian in pursuit of fundamental factors in nineteenth century history could hardly fail to select as one of them the world trade supremacy of Great Britain. Here was the greatest nation of traders the world had yet seen. The British people had built for themselves a new industrial system, an immense merchant navy, and a volume of commerce of such staggering proportions that during the greater part of the century they had no serious business competitors. The fact had the deepest meaning for all the world. It underlay British naval ascendancy and promoted the continued expansion of the Empire; it created a banking power which made London the principal money market of the world and established British investments in all continents. Englishmen thus had an incalculably great influence in the affairs of the world; their country was the only real world power of the nineteenth century, and the sinews of that power were manufacturing, trading, shipping, and investing.

The causes of this supremacy lay rooted in three centuries of energetic commercial activity, and were continuously in operation from the age of Tudor mercantilism, through the empire-building of the seventeenth and eighteenth centuries, to the days of Richard Cobden. The Commercial Revolution of the sixteenth century had placed England in a favorable position to secure a profitable share of overseas trade, and this advantage was turned to good account by Elizabethan merchants. The impetus then given to commercial expansion was followed by a steady growth of trade in the next two centuries, during which British commerce was powerfully assisted by protective legislation, the founding of a colonial empire, and the victorious wars with Spain, Holland, and France, from which Britain emerged with

1

the dominion of the seas. Finally, there came the Industrial Revolution, which launched England into the nineteenth century with a nearly complete monopoly of new machine methods of economic production, against which older systems of manufacturing could not compete successfully. The wars of the French Revolution and Napoleon, supervening at that time, had a fortifying influence on this industrial and commercial leadership; they stimulated the new industrialism at home while arresting its spread abroad, and the closing of European markets encouraged British merchants to seek new ones in remote parts of the world. When the smoke of Waterloo had cleared away and Europe settled down for an era of peace and economic recuperation, the situation was prepared for Great Britain to utilize her factories, her ships, her capital, all the superior advantages of her position, to the utmost, and go forward to a new and more extensive conquest of European and world markets. This was accomplished in the next fifty years in an unparalleled expansion of business, and not until the last quarter of the century did British commercial leadership exhibit signs of weakening.[1]

This remarkable expansion did not, of course, begin immediately after the peace of 1815. Deflation and hard times came in the wake of the wars, much as they did after the last great war. European markets were impoverished and buying power lagged, while numerous governmental restrictions on trade, at home and abroad, retarded commercial progress. An examination of trade statistics reveals no swelling British export trade until the thirties; from 1816 to 1834 the value of exports fluctuated between 31 and 41 millions, but after that the current rose until the figure of 60 millions was attained in the year

[1] Cf. William Cunningham, *Growth of English Industry and Commerce in Modern Times;* H. deB. Gibbins, *Economic and Industrial Progress of the Century;* J. E. T. Rogers, *Industrial and Commercial History of England;* H. H. Bassett, *British Commerce: A Modern Survey;* A. L. Bowley, *A Short Account of England's Foreign Trade in the Nineteenth Century;* L. Levi, *History of British Commerce;* J. Burnley, *Story of British Trade and Industry;* L. L. Price, *Short History of English Commerce and Industry;* William Page, *Commerce and Industry, 1815-1914;* J. H. Clapham, *An Economic History of Modern Britain.*

before the repeal of the Corn Laws. From the middle of the century the ascent of the export trade was very sharp until it reached the swollen figure of 256 millions in 1872.[2] This was the period of the fall of protectionism, and there can be no doubt but that the great fiscal revolution supplied a powerful stimulus to the growth of exports. The British abandonment of the methods and policies of mercantilism was the prelude to a downward revision of European tariffs in the fifties and sixties, which vindicated the prophecies of the Cobdenites and opened the door of Continental markets to the mounting surplus of British wares.[3]

The forward movement of British industry and commerce may be shown best by the use of a few figures. The export trade rose from 97 to 256 millions between 1854 and 1872, while imports over the same period climbed from 152 to 355 millions, and the re-export trade swelled from 19 to 58 millions sterling. These figures dwarf both absolutely and relatively the growth in the foreign trade of other nations. The consumption of raw cotton increased from an annual average in 1851-55 of 750 million pounds to an average of 1228 millions in 1871-75. Coal production rose from an annual average in 1855-58 of 66 millions to 120 millions in 1870-74, and over the same period the pig iron output grew from 3,500,000 to 6,400,000 tons. Steel production, negligible in the fifties, reached an annual average of 200,000 tons in 1865-69 and 500,000 in 1870-74. The widening markets seemed to offer a promise of almost limitless absorption of the products of British industry, and the tide of export manufactures swelled steadily higher.[4] Looking back over this great period of ex-

[2] Unless otherwise indicated, all trade statistics cited in this study are taken from the various official publications of the Board of Trade. For the early nineteenth century the tables in Page's *Commerce and Industry*, vol. 2, have been used.

[3] "How much of the progress was due to one, and how much to another factor, it is impossible to say, but twenty-five years after the change no one could deny that English commerce and industry had prospered under the Free Trade Policy."—W. Cunningham, *The Free Trade Movement*, p. 72.

[4] Tables in British and Foreign Trade and Industry, Cd. 4954, 1909, pp. 154, 166, 168, 170. The Board of Trade occasionally published Blue Books containing vast collections of statistical and other material, selected from

pansive prosperity a writer in *Fraser's Magazine* in 1876 summed
it up:

The nation grew steadily richer and its stores of realized wealth increased with every new enterprise almost that it took up. . . . In
1848 the swelling exports of the country dipped under the weight
of the commercial depression from about £59,000,000 to £53,000,000;
but in 1849 they jumped about 10,000,000 to over 63,000,000. Since
then, with only brief dips, the upward movement of reproductive industries has been continuous up to 1874. Each year the realized
wealth of the one before told, as it were, in swelling the working
power of the nation, and enlarging the business capacities and scope
of its credit.[5]

Shipbuilding and the growth of the shipping trade kept pace
with the mounting volume of exports. The construction of new
merchant vessels for home and colonial use doubled in tonnage
between 1858-59 and 1870-74, while construction for foreigners
showed an even greater relative increase. The tonnage of ships
on register in the United Kingdom grew from an annual average
in 1855-59 of 4,519,192 to 5,728,819 in 1870-74, while the
registry for British possessions gained a half million. Possibly
the best appreciation of the growth of British shipping in this
period can be got from an examination of the percentage of
British and non-British shipping engaged in the foreign trade
of other countries. In 1855-59 British vessels represented 29.4
per cent of all the shipping in the ports of France, and by 1870-

---

the Board's annual or serial publications and from other official or reliable
sources. For the study of British commercial history it is of the greatest
convenience to make frequent use of these handy collections. The one now
cited is referred to hereafter as B F T I, Cd. 4954, 1909, and is to be distinguished from others of similar title published at different times.

[5] A. J. Wilson, *British Trade*, Sept., 1876. The following table from
tables in B F T I, Cd. 1761, 1903, pp. 23-27, showing quantities of several
chief items of export, may give some measure of the growth of foreign trade:

		1850	*1870*
Cotton yarn	lbs.	131,370,000	186,078,000
Cotton goods	yds.	1,358,183,000	3,266,998,000
Wool yarn	lbs.	13,794,000	35,537,000
Linen goods	yds.	122,343,000	226,403,000
Iron & Steel	tons	767,734	2,619,000
Fuel	tons	3,352,000	11,703,000

74 this percentage had risen to 37, while the French portion had sharply declined. Similar figures for American ports show an increase from 20.5 to 46.2 in the British percentage. Comparable figures for Germany are lacking, but it is certain that here also British shipping enlarged its share; at any rate, in 1873-74, of the shipping that entered and cleared in German ports 33.5 per cent was British. In the ports of the United Kingdom 51.7 per cent of the shipping was British in 1855-59, and fifteen years later this percentage was 63. In the trade between Great Britain and her possessions, in this period, foreign-owned ships dropped from 15.2 to 11.5 per cent. These figures tell the story of a growth in British shipping that was far more rapid than, and even at the expense of, the shipping business of other nations. The scrapping of protective legislation for navigation had opened the ports of the world to British ships in the same way that Free Trade had helped to open markets for British manufactures.[6]

The high-water mark of this middle century business expansion was reached in the great inflation of the early seventies. The value of the export trade was then greater than in any previous period and greater, indeed, than it was to be again until almost the end of the century. These were years of rich prosperity, with industrial activity running at record speed. Business profits and wages were high, and industrial unemployment was almost non-existent.[7] Pessimistic prophecies, which were not entirely lacking, passed with scant hearing, for general satisfaction and a spirit of optimism pervaded the country. The *Times* spoke the national voice:

We can . . . look on the present with undisturbed satisfaction. Our commerce is extending and multiplying its world-wide ramifications without much regard for the croaking of any political or scientific Cassandras. . . . Turn where we may, we find in our commerce no traces of decadence.[8]

Competition of a threatening character from the European Continent and America had not yet begun to make itself felt, for the new industrialism beyond England was still in com-

[6] B F T I, Cd. 4954, 1909, pp. 104, 106, 111, 114, 115.
[7] B F T I, Cd. 4954, 1909, p. 223.
[8] Leader of Sept. 26, 1871.

parative infancy. New tariff barriers had not yet become a serious obstruction to the growth of trade; to be sure, duties had been raised to a high level in the United States, but the great Continental protectionist reaction had not yet begun. The numerous factors which were in time to weaken the entrepôt trade were as yet hardly noticeable. Great Britain stood out in the early seventies, perhaps more conspicuously than ever before, as the supreme commercial power of the world. Never again was this position to be so removed from challenge, for when the great depression which began in 1873 had run its course there were clearly in operation all of the great factors which ultimately pulled Britain down from her high estate of trade supremacy and forced her to fight for her life in a new economic world. It is at this point, on the eve of "the great divide,"[9] that this study has its proper beginning; and it will be well, therefore, to enter here into a brief comparative and analytical examination of the extent, nature, and distribution of British commerce.

2

In the five-year period of 1870-74 the average annual value of exports of United Kingdom produce was upward of 230 millions sterling. This represented a relatively gigantic export business: the combined American and German, or French and American export trades fell short of equaling the British sum, while France and Germany together possessed an export trade only a little larger than Great Britain's.[10] Of the total value of British exports of United Kingdom produce nearly ninety per

[9] Cunningham used this phrase in his *Free Trade Movement*.
[10] B F T I, Cd. 4954, 1909, pp. 58-65. If exports are represented per capita, the British figure fell only a little short of equaling the sum of the other three. The following table shows the average annual total and per capita export trade values of the four chief commercial nations in 1870-74:

	Total £	Per capita £— / —d.
France	135,400,000	3 — 13 — 9
Germany	113,700,000	2 — 15 — 0
United States	96,200,000	2 — 7 — 4
Great Britain	234,800,000	7 — 7 — 4

cent represented goods manufactured in whole or in part, exclusive of ships; and it should be emphasized that the vigor of the export trade derived primarily from the activity of the textile, iron, and steel industries, which were the principal representatives of the new industrialism. The chief items of export were cotton yarns and piece goods, woolen and worsted stuffs, linen goods, pig iron, rails and plates, steel, machinery, and coal; and in the markets for these commodities, as well as for many other industrial products, the British had little trouble in outdistancing their competitors. No comparative table of itemized export statistics for the early seventies has been successfully arranged, but the following figures for 1880, when British preeminence was less pronounced, offer a comparison of the iron and steel and textile exports of the four chief commercial nations:[11]

	Great Britain £	France £	Germany £	United States £
Iron & steel	27,200,000	900,000	9,700,000	1,100,000
Machinery	9,200,000	1,000,000	2,100,000	1,700,000
Cotton yarns	11,900,000	100,000	2,500,000	— — —
Cotton Mfres.	62,900,000	3,600,000	3,400,000	2,600,000
Woolen Mfres.	17,300,000	14,800,000	10,800,000	50,000

In examining the distribution of British exports several observations of significance are to be made. The colonies and possessions of the Empire absorbed only 25.6 per cent of the exported produce of the United Kingdom, the rest going into definitely foreign markets. There was, in fact, prior to 1875, a striking tendency in the direction of expanding the export trade in foreign markets, to the neglect of the colonial trade. In the early fifties the markets of the Empire were taking about ten per cent more of total British exports than they received in the early seventies; and this fact, of course, helps to explain the lagging interest in imperialist expansion during the decades just preceding 1875. Later in the century the imperialist revival

[11] B F T I, Cd. 4954, 1909, pp. 79-84.

was accompanied by a notable tendency to cultivate colonial markets. But in the period here under examination Britain's largest and best markets were those of Continental Europe and the United States, the former absorbing about forty per cent of the whole British export trade. Germany was the largest of the Continental markets, France coming next; but in the United States, which in this period took 14.1 per cent of the total exports, Britain had her largest single national market. Latin American markets had not yet assumed a very great importance, although they were dominated largely by the British. Here Brazil was Britain's best customer; but all of Latin America absorbed less than ten per cent of the exported produce of the United Kingdom. The cultivation of African markets had as yet hardly begun, save, of course, in Egypt, which was now buying more British goods than Italy or Belgium. The commercial development of the Far East was still in its infancy, and this great theatre of commercial rivalry had not yet come to be of very great importance in the British export trade. China and Japan absorbed but 2.6 and .9 per cent, respectively, of the goods exported by the United Kingdom. Among the colonial markets the richest by far was India, where more British goods were sold than in all of the Russian and Ottoman Empires. Other colonial markets of growing importance were Australia, New Zealand, and Canada. The following table will show clearly the distribution of the export trade in the early seventies:[12]

Foreign Countries	Per cent of total
Russia	3.4
Germany	11.1
Holland	6.0
Belgium	2.5
France	6.8
Italy	2.6
Ottoman Empire	3.4
Egypt	2.8

[12] B F T I, Cd. 4954, 1909, pp. 33-34.

8

United States 14.1
Brazil 3.0
Chile 1.2
Argentine 2.6
China 2.6
Japan 0.9
Other foreign countries 12.7

    Total 74.4

British Possessions
British North America 3.6
West Indies & Guiana 1.3
Australia & New Zealand 6.0
India 8.5
South Africa 1.4
Other possessions 4.8

    Total 25.6

What has been said so far refers only to the export of the produce of the United Kingdom and has taken no account of the large reëxport trade in foreign and colonial produce, which at this time had an average annual value of some 55 millions, or better than one-fourth the value of domestic exports. This trade was a most important element in British commercial prosperity and leadership. British vessels in great number brought their cargoes of overseas goods chiefly to English warehouses and markets, whence they were distributed amongst Continental buyers; and similarly, goods worth millions annually went from the Continent to England, from there to be scattered over the world in British ships. England was still the chief European entrepôt.

The swollen import trade of this period may also receive attention. Its average annual value was some 290 millions exclusive of reëxports, which, if reckoned in, swelled the figure for imports to 346 millions. The enormous size of this import trade appears only when comparison is made with other countries. French imports for home consumption averaged 136 millions, and the American figure was only 113 millions.[13] Germany's import trade averaged about 180 millions.[14] As in the case of her export trade, Great Britain was importing chiefly from foreign countries rather than her colonies, the proportion being 78 to 22 per cent.[15] About one-sixth of the import trade for home consumption consisted of goods wholly or partly manufactured; the rest represented food and drink, raw materials, and articles mainly unmanufactured. It will, of course, be noted that Great Britain had a large excess of imports over exports, but since the productive energies of the nation as yet showed no decline the extent of this excess could be viewed with satisfaction as a measure of swelling riches.

British preponderance in the selling and buying of goods in these years was accompanied by an even more striking ascendancy in the world's shipping trade. The merchant navy enrolled on the register of the United Kingdom in 1870 exceeded in tonnage the combined mercantile fleets of the next five ranking maritime nations. The German merchant marine, it may be observed, was at this time less than one-sixth as large as the British. These statements concern both sailing and steam tonnage; but a comparative examination of steamships, then displacing sailing vessels, reveals a far greater British supremacy, for the steam tonnage of the British merchant fleet was more than twice the combined tonnage of steam vessels on register in the other five nations.[16] In the early seventies 63 per cent of the shipping

[13] B F T I, Cd. 4954, 1909, pp. 60, 64.
[14] There are no exactly comparable German statistics; this figure is calculated from those given in *Das statistische Jahrbuch für das deutsche Reich.*
[15] B F T I, Cd. 4954, 1909, p. 22.
[16] Figures given in Accounts and Papers on Shipping. The following table gives the comparative figures for 1870:

	Total tonnage	Steam tonnage
United Kingdom	5,617,693	1,111,375
United States	1,516,800	192,544
France	1,072,048	154,414
Norway	1,022,515	13,715
Italy	1,012,164	32,100
Germany	982,355	81,994

trade between the United Kingdom and foreign countries was British; 88.5 per cent of that between the United Kingdom and its possessions was British; more than 97 per cent of the coasting trade of the United Kingdom was British; 37 per cent of the French shipping trade was British; 33.5 of that in German ports was British, and 46.2 of the American ocean shipping trade was British. In the Suez Canal traffic for 1872 more than two-thirds of the tonnage was British. It is needless to go on citing statistics, for the comparative magnitude of British shipping is plain from every angle of approach; and figures of comparative shipbuilding tell a similar story.[17] It would not be easy to exaggerate the importance of this mighty volume of shipping in Great Britain's commercial position. The profits earned by these ships on all the seas of the world represented a vast part of those "invisible exports" which sustained the heavy import trade. Moreover, their established routes and connections with British warehouses constituted a strong factor in maintaining the great entrepôt trade.

It was not to be expected, of course, that Great Britain could maintain unchanged permanently this supreme position in world commerce. Economic development in the western world was proceeding at an accelerated pace, and the speed with which Great Britain climbed to her unique supremacy was to be matched by the speed with which a new economic world, far less agreeable to British business, came into being. In the fifties and sixties British business had been taking on a marked cosmopolitan character.[18] Railroad building and industrial development on the European Continent and in America had attracted British investors, and with the reëstablishment of political stability on the Continent after the mid-century upheavals the flow of British capital there attained very large dimensions.[19] British capitalists, concessionaires, contractors, and technological experts went forth in large numbers to remake the economic life of Western Europe: to build railroads, canals, water and

[17] Cf. tables in B F T I, Cd. 4954, 1909, pp. 97-123.
[18] Cf. L. H. Jenks, *The Migration of British Capital to 1875*, Ch. VI.
[19] C. K. Hobson, *The Export of Capital*, p. 119.

11

gas works, machines, and industries. Business energies everywhere had quickened, while domestic capital was accumulating in France, Germany, Belgium, and America and galvanizing new enterprises into life. The machine economy by 1870 had spread wide over Western Europe and America, although its radiating center was still Great Britain. Under the benign influence of Free Trade and low tariffs the western world might seem to be evolving into a unified economic area with Great Britain as its dynamic center. Great Britain had stood, in the fifties and sixties, in much the same relation to the greater part of Europe that Europe and the United States, fifty years later, bore to the Orient and South America. Her capital, skill, and enterprise were fertilizing richly the growth of Continental industry, and although the Continent would certainly have adopted the new industrialism without this aid, with it the process was more rapid and more intelligent. It is quite important to note that a very heavy part of the British export trade to the Continent and America in the great period of expansion consisted of capital, or producers' goods: iron and steel, rails, hardware, machinery, copper, tin, coal and other materials for the construction and operation of factories and railroads. The value of the chief items of capital goods exported from 1848 to 1877 ran higher than £800,000,000.[20] Thus capitalists, manufacturers, merchants, and contractors, profiting heavily, distributed the sinews of the Industrial Revolution over the western world, and the former British monopoly over the new mechanical methods of production dissipated itself away.

That an era of sharp competition would therefore succeed this comfortable period of British commercial supremacy was apparent in the early seventies, and the warning was not entirely unperceived. But confidence was high and a great many developments of the next decade did come as unpleasant surprises to England. The export of capital goods could hardly go on indefinitely at undiminished rate of increase. The new industries sprung to life in Europe and America were certain to offer

[20] Jenks, *op. cit.*, 174.

a challenge to British production. Presently they were to bid for control of their home markets and resort again to the high tariff weapon, and presently they were to seek foreign markets for their surpluses. A revival of protectionism was to constrict British trade by narrowing some very valuable markets and introducing an unwelcome competition in others. And there were many other factors soon to make themselves injurious to British trade supremacy. Foreign governments were to display a shockingly generous conception of the legitimate role of government in assisting commerce and industry. The extension of rail communications, the development of Continental port facilities, and the new Suez route to the East were to have an unfavorable influence upon the entrepôt trade, much of which was in time to be transferred to the Continent. The progress of new shipping lines connecting Europe directly with the non-European world, shipping subsidies and new navigation restrictions, these too were in the offing and destined to give annoyance to the British carrying trade. The economic nationalism which burst forth in the world after 1875, offering defiance to the cosmopolitan philosophy and enterprise of the age of Cobden, transformed the world for the English business man and inaugurated that furious commercial rivalry which has raged to the present day.

3

The year of 1873, remembered for the collapse of the German post-war inflation, the American panic, and the general snapping of the tentacles of credit, marked the end of the great period of expansive business prosperity in Great Britain and the beginning of an extended period of commercial depression throughout the world. "This epoch of rich commercial progress, pervading all the leading nations of the world," observed a writer in the *Edinburgh Review*, "culminated, and also came to a close with the preëminently prosperous years of 1872 and 1873, ending suddenly when at its height, rocket-like, with an outburst of fresh splendour. Since 1873 the course of events has resembled the 'dissolving' views of the diorama, where a flowing summer landscape is seen to pass swiftly, yet by distinctly marked gradations, into the bleakness and snowy garb of winter."[21] The depression appeared with startling suddenness in the British export trade statistics, which dropped fifteen millions in 1874. During the next five years this fall proceeded without arrest, and its severity may be judged by comparing the 1872 figure of 256 millions with the 1879 figure of 181 millions. There was no recovery until 1880, when exports mounted back to 233 millions. Other statistical data measure similarly the great business slump. Unemployment was at low ebb and almost nonexistent in 1872, but the next seven years witnessed a steady ascent from 0.95 to 10.7 per cent.[22] Statistics of raw cotton consumption, which remained almost stationary during the depression, show the sudden check put to the growth of the chief of British industries.[23] Coal production, of which the average annual total for several decades had been showing a twenty million ton increase from one quinquennial period to another, gained only about thirteen million tons in the 1875-79 period.[24] Pig iron production exhibited no gain at all.[25] Further statistical data, if presented here, would tell the same story of hard times in British trade and industry in the middle and later seventies. The doom of British agriculture, foretold thirty years before by the opponents of Free Trade, also fell at this time. The depression, of course, was world-wide, but it seems a likely fact that, prosperity having been previously most abundant in England, there the general depression was most severely felt.

This sluggish condition of trade led Britain to take stock of her industrial and commercial position. There was no immediate and general loss of confidence in the future; slumps of brief duration had occurred during the previous thirty years, and so it was widely believed that this one would be short and

[21] "Gold and Its Effect on Trade," April, 1879, p. 221.

[22] B F T I, Cd. 4954, 1909, p. 223.

[23] Ibid., p. 154. The increase in the annual average from 1866-70 to 1871-75 had been nearly 250,000,000 lbs.; the next five years showed an increase of barely 25,000,000 lbs.

[24] Ibid., p. 166.

[25] Ibid., p. 168.

that active trade would presently be resumed. Thus the *Times* in early 1874 was reassuring the country against alarm and forecasting a business revival before the year was out.[26] But trade did not improve, and as the depression lengthened, despite the prophets of an imminent return of prosperity, considerable uneasiness over the commercial position of the country appeared. Among the many expressions of this, perhaps no shrewder words were written than the following by Mr. A. J. Wilson:

For the first time almost since the new order of physical progress came to the fore there has been a stoppage of foreign demand. . . . We have no longer the unlimited markets for some of our products that we had formerly. Progress appears to have reached for the time its limit, if by progress we mean the increased production of English mines, English looms and lathes, and the more and more rapid absorption of their products by foreign nations. . . . We may get out of this depression with undiminished prestige; but we can hardly get out of it soon, and, before we do, the trade position of this country towards other countries may be decidedly altered.[27]

"Apprehensions of foreign competition . . . haunt us," observed the *Times* in 1876,[28] and these were not again to pass away. They were, of course, not exactly new. After the panic of 1857 French and Belgian iron manufacturers had entered the foreign field in competition with British ironmasters; a Belgian syndicate in 1859 had captured an important Spanish rail contract against British tenders, and shortly afterward the Belgians had made important conquests in Swiss and Dutch markets; in the sixties some Belgian and German locomotives were supplied to Russia.[29] It had been somewhat startling for Great Britain to fail to command markets which she chose to supply, but the competition which she faced before the middle seventies was not formidable. Now, however, in a glutted world market, this competition became a genuine source of apprehension. The importation of articles formerly manufactured at home began

[26] See leader of Jan. 9, 1874.
[27] *Fraser's Magazine, loc. cit.*, Sept., 1876.
[28] Leader of Dec. 11, 1876.
[29] Jenks, *op. cit.*, p. 192.

15

to draw notice in the press,[30] and a consul in Belgium in 1877 pointed out ominously that "the Belgian manufacturer is enabled to buy pig iron in England, pay for freight, and to deliver the same iron manufactured into beams and girders in the most central parts of England, or even in the heart of the iron districts, at a lower price than it can be made by English firms on the spot."[31]

A combing of the consular reports in the seventies turned to light scattered but significant evidence of this rising competition. A report from Rome on the trade between England and Italy from 1871 to 1875 drew attention to a "serious decrease" in the Italian importation of various British textiles, and this was attributed to French competition. "It appears," wrote the consul, "that the exports from France to Italy under the heads of linen, cotton, and wool, have largely increased. . . . We must acknowledge that French manufacturers are more welcome in Italy than ours. Whether the cause of this change is to be found in a stagnation in the quality of our productions, and an advance in that of the French, in greater celerity in French commercial agents, in the alteration of fashions, in the operation of our labor laws, or in whatever cause, it deserves the anxious consideration of those interested."[32] The consul at Florence, in a report for 1877, pointed to the weakening hold of British railway materials on the Italian market. "From the first introduction of railways in Italy," he wrote, "the rails used were chiefly, if not entirely, imported from Great Britain. . . . Now, however, it would appear that English manufacturers are losing their hold on the Italian market, and that the French, German, and Belgian makers are taking their place. The tenders for steel rails which have been issued within the last few months by the three great Italian railway companies . . . have all been taken up by French, Belgian, and German houses, to the exclusion of English firms. . . . It has been stated that the Germans are

[30] *Vide Times* leader of Jan. 9, 1875.

[31] Accounts and Papers, 1878, vol. 27, pp. 107-8. (Hereafter referred to as A. & P.)

[32] A. & P., 1877, vol. 33, p. 140.

working at a loss; be this as it may, our market is in the mean-time going, and not for rails only, but also, I am informed, for locomotive engines, axles, tires, springs, etc., tools, and the lower qualities of iron. It may be that the quality of foreign steel is inferior; of this there seems no proof as regards French and German manufactures, in any case the article seems to satisfy the purchaser."[33]

The British consul at Santander, Spain, in his report for 1880, wrote of the "preponderance of Belgium in iron exports," attributing it to the fact that some of her leading manufacturers had secured "the exclusive supply of railway material for the north of Spain railways." He also drew attention to "a keen competition going on between Manchester and Harburg-on-the-Elbe in engines."[34] A Belgian report of 1880 observed that "in linen manufacture, and in some descriptions of glass, iron wares, and machinery, Belgian competition is making itself felt as regards British trade."[35] As early as 1875 the Bucharest consul was drawing attention to the growing importation of German and Austrian ploughs into Roumania, while the more expensive English implements were unpopular and ill-adapted to the country.[36] About the same time notice was drawn to the heavy gains the German traders were making on Great Britain in the mar-

[33] A. & P., 1877, vol. 35, p. 1389. Three years later this consul described the establishment of an international goods tariff binding Italy and Germany by closer commercial ties, and expressed his regret that Germany "appears to compete successfully with British manufacturers in supplying the Italian railways with rails, telegraph wire, and machinery."—A. & P., 1881, vol. 33, p. 695. The success of German ironmasters in securing large orders against British competition in Italy, and also in Portugal, was the subject of a letter submitted by the firm of Bolckow, Vaughan & Co. at a meeting of the Board of Management of the British Iron Trade Association in November, 1876.—See account in Times, Nov. 30, 1878. Both interesting and significant is a letter to the Times, signed "Steel" (Nov. 23, 1880), calling public attention to the capture by the German firm of Bochum of an order for 30,000 tons of steel rails for the Alta Italia Railway, in the face of keen competition, and also complaining against the strange and unfair German policy of selling cheaper abroad than at home.
[34] A. & P., 1881, vol. 35, p. 301.
[35] A. & P., 1880, vol. 33, p. 530.
[36] A. & P., 1876, vol. 32, pp. 150-1.

kets of Russia.[37] In early 1881 the Helsingfors consul wrote that "it is my unpleasant duty . . . to state that the German market has completely supplanted us in the delivery of rails and rolling stock required for the Finnish State Railways now in progress of construction." In August 1879 tenders had been solicited for 8,000 steel rails; more than half of the twenty-six tenders received were from British firms, but Krupp, of Essen, was the successful bidder. In December 1880 Krupp captured another 8,000-rail contract against British tenders. The following March, tenders were asked for twelve locomotives; twenty firms, English, Belgium, Austrian, and German, sought the contract, and it was taken by the Mechanische Maschinenbau A.G. of Minden.[38]

The challenge of competition now raised was chiefly but not wholly confined to the European Continent. In his report for 1879-80 the British consul at Teneriffe, in the Canary Islands, sounded a

warning as to the increasing introduction of French, German, and American articles to replace British. . . . That competition is keener these days; that others occupy space where formerly they had none or were little known; that they are elbowing in here and there and everywhere, is worthy of mention as indicating a danger to British commerce.[39]

As early as 1876 a consular official in Venezuela called attention to the lead which Germany had recently taken in exporting to that country.[40] An 1880 report from Berlin mentioned a recent bid by German firms for a Brazilian contract for 4,000 tons of

[37] A. & P., 1877, vol. 33, p. 237. D. M. Wallace was in Russia at this time, composing his famous book, and he observed in it that "the old race of British merchants is rapidly dying out. . . . Every year the conditions alter, and the competition increases. . . . Unless some change takes place . . . the German merchants, who have generally a much better commercial education . . . will, ultimately, I believe, expel their British rivals. Already, it is said, many branches of commerce formerly carried on by Englishmen have passed into their hands."—*Russia,* 1877 ed., p. 181.

[38] A. & P., 1881, vol. 35, pp. 309-10.

[39] A. & P., 1881, vol. 35, pp. 309-10.

[40] A. & P., 1876, vol. 32, p. 137.

steel rails,[41] while another from Ecuador in 1881 described the diversion of orders from Great Britain to the United States.[42] In the same year the consul at San José, Costa Rica, declared that

English manufacturers of cutlery and hardware, as also manufactured cotton stuffs, are being superseded to a large extent by the exporters of the United States, who send their goods to this market with a much better finish and at prices more advantageous to importers.[43]

The consul at Buenos Ayres in 1881 reported that

as regards English enterprise in the interior, I was sorry to find that all the sugar machinery lately sent to Tucuman is French. . . . It was also a matter of painful surprise to find that all the steel rails now being laid on the new Great Andine Railway are French, ordered last year from the Creusot works at a price of about £10 a ton, at a time when similar and better rails might have been obtained from England for less than £7 a ton. I could add similar instances.[44]

An interesting report of 1881 on Mexican railways and trade recommended that English traders should learn a lesson from their German competitors:

There are only six English houses engaged in trade in Mexico. The English goods which are sent from Manchester and Sheffield are ordered chiefly by German and other merchants. The Germans, in fact, appear to have the largest share in trade there, and why? It appears that merchants in Germany establish their various branches in various parts of Mexico, and send their educated youths out to serve an apprenticeship in the business, and afterwards assume the management of the branch house. They become thoroughly familiar with the condition and practices of the country, and master the intricacies of the tariff and interior duties. Nothing disturbs their equanimity; neither forced loans, extraordinary contributions, nor revolutions, nor irregularities of the custom-house officials and the embarrassment of the contraband trade. Now this is a lesson to be

41 A. & P., 1880, vol. 33, pp. 516-17.
42 A. & P., 1880, vol. 34, p. 555.
43 A. & P., 1881, vol. 34, p. 1137.
44 A. & P., 1881, vol. 33, p. 407.

learnt by heart by any British merchants who in the future propose establishing branch houses in Mexico.[45]

A commercial quarrel of some little heat, arising in Australia out of alleged unfair treatment of German goods by British dealers, may also be mentioned here. The Dortmund Chamber of Commerce in 1879 went to the length of soliciting the aid of Bismarck in defense of German trade, charging that the better classes of German goods had been introduced into the Australian market under the names of English firms, while to the cheaper German goods the English merchants had added all the worst products of their own country and then brought them all into the market as "German goods." Thus the wares of German industry were being unfairly damaged in reputation. The Dortmund memorial appealed for an investigation by the Commissioner of the German Empire at the International Exhibition at Sydney, and even suggested the possible advisability of making the matter a subject of diplomatic intervention. The matter was aired in the English press, but quickly disappeared from the news.[46]

It must be emphasized, however, that ominous as this competition might be for the future, it was not a great factor in the trade depression of those years. The instances of competition which have here been given virtually exhaust the evidence yielded up by the consular reports. Strong competition was being felt, therefore, in comparatively few areas, and no serious opinion before 1880 envisaged Great Britain being driven from the markets of the world. Rather the tendency was to scout fears and minimize alarm for the future. "Our manufacturers seem to be losing their hold on foreign markets," asserted the *Times*, but "since nearly all nations . . . make the same complaint, it is probable that the real causes are that . . . markets have been overflooded with goods and that the purchasing power of all countries is lessened by the collapse of an artificial prosperity."[47] Another leader insisted that "the

[45] A. & P., 1881, vol. 33, pp. 397-98.
[46] Account given in the *Times*, Jan. 1, 1880.
[47] Leading article, Oct. 9, 1878.

decline in our export trade . . . is much less than is commonly supposed, and has not yet gone beyond the limits which can be fully accounted for by the ordinary fluctuations of trade."[48]

Thomas Brassey in 1879 denied before an Edinburgh audience that there was any "immediate prospect of a competition which can be injurious to our own manufactures."[49] Leone Levi, in his commercial history published in 1880, characterized the depression as "only a reaction from the excessive speculative excitement of 1872 and 1873," and declared that "foreign competition was not a factor in it."[50] Again and again this note of denial was sounded, but its very frequency suggests a considerable alarm over the loss of markets to competitors.

Another fear discernible in these years was lest British wares had fallen in quality and British methods of trade slumped in effectiveness. The *Morning Post* voiced the apprehension

that a diminution in the quality of the work done, and a slight detraction from what was once the absolute certainty that an article supplied was, if not as good as it could be, as good as it pretended to be, had something to do with the slackness of demand.

Sound evidence to justify this fear is lacking, but as for trade methods and energetic commercial effort, evidence is abundant. Numerous consular reports attest a British reluctance to press for trade vigorously, to study the changing needs of markets, to adjust the qualities of goods to meet the changing tastes of customers, to employ commercial travelers, and to keep abreast generally with the progress of modern business. This criticism of British trade methods is dealt with at length in another part of this study,[51] but it may be observed here that even in the late seventies the story was not an unfamiliar one. "English manufacturers," remarked a *Times* leader of 1880, "are often charged with not adapting themselves as readily as others do to the new requirements of trade. They go on, it has been said, using old methods, which have been superseded and set aside in

[48] Jan. 11, 1879.
[49] Report of lecture in the *Times*, Jan. 25, 1879.
[50] *History of British Commerce*, p. 502.
[51] *Vide* Ch. III.

other countries."[52] In subsequent years this note was to be sounded again and again in the consular reports, ever more widely and with a tireless monotony. The great depression also gave rise to an apprehension of the superiority of foreign over British technical education and skill. In this field of instruction Continental Europe was making rapid progress, while little attention was being paid it in Great Britain.[53] That the last generation of the century had need to rouse itself, if commercial leadership was to be retained, was thus already evident by 1880.

4

By far the most objectionable and confounding development in the changing commercial world was the rising wave of tariff protectionism visible in America and on the Continent. The world was signifying its refusal to continue on the high road toward Free Trade. The United States had launched upon a high tariff policy during the Civil War, and after 1865 American duties became frankly protective. This development had been a nuisance of the first order for British business, and now the same reaction was developing in the Continental countries, where such encouraging progress toward liberal commercial policy had been made in the fifties and sixties. Financial needs of governments, strident nationalism, infant industries, and economic depression were stimulating a revival of protectionist opinion. Italy adopted a new high tariff in 1877; France denounced the Cobden-Chevalier Treaty and gave plain indication of reverting to higher protection, which was partially accomplished by the law of 1881; the commercial policy of Germany, Britain's chief Continental market, was radically altered by Bismarck's tariff of 1879. The swing toward higher duties was manifested also in other countries; the network of commercial treaties was crumbling; and from 1880 onward most European fiscal policies were strongly protectionist.

[52] May 8, 1880.
[53] Cf. Report of C. M. Kennedy, British representative at the International Congress of Commerce and Industry at Brussells, 1880. A. & P., 1880, vol. 33.

The British reaction to this abandonment of the "manifest benefits" of Free Trade may be described as a mixture of amazement and chagrin, coupled with an inclination to lecture foreign countries for their departure from the "true political economy" and to prophesy disaster for such attempts to practise economic fallacies. In England the Cobdenite dogma had become so strongly implanted that protectionist opinion was viewed as the delusion of minds uninstructed in economic science; so that the spectacle of the world renouncing "truth" in pursuit of folly was exasperating in the extreme. The *Times'* leading articles are especially effective in revealing this British point of view:

French manufacturers are deeply committed to Protectionist fallacies, and constantly reproduce them on every occasion. . . . It is strange that public opinion should be thus unenlightened in France, seeing that French writers on Political Economy have been foremost in demonstrating the universal benefits of Free Trade. . . . Prince Bismarck trying to make Germany prosperous by moderate Protection is an example to excite wonder at the follies of the great.[54]

During the debates on the German tariff bill the *Times* declared that

not the least cause of our regret will be that the German Empire should lose the opportunity of associating its development with a principle with which the former policy of Prussia gave it some claim to identify itself, and which all communities will sooner or later come to recognize as essential to their highest public interests.[55]

And again in a sharper vein: "The growth of a strong protectionist party in Germany has been one of the most unsatisfactory signs of the limited political training of that country."[56] In 1879 came the caustic observation that "if Prince Bismarck succeeds in obtaining some increase of duties in Germany the most lasting consequences will be the injury done to his own reputation."[57] Mournful indeed was the outlook in this year:

[54] April 24, 1877.
[55] May 3, 1877.
[56] Dec. 1, 1877.
[57] Jan. 14, 1879.

Russia, Germany, Italy, France have all either moved lately or are moving in this direction. . . . It is discouraging . . . in the highest degree that, after so many years of lowered tariffs, Continental Governments should be so reluctant to acknowledge the great benefits which their subjects have derived from the reductions. A vigorous initiative on our part exposes us to the misconstruction of being supposed to aim at a concealed advantage, for we press on foreign nations what we say will be more for their benefit than it will be for our own.[58]

The revival of protectionism abroad not unnaturally re-awakened similar opinions at home as the seventies wore away. "Are we not ourselves, the very champions of free trade, now debating whether we should not recur to the policy of protection; or are you of the opinion that the flowing speeches at the Cobden Club dinners will set right our balance of trade?" asked a speaker before the Royal Society of Arts.[59] A tariff reform movement arose which, however, did homage to the strength of the Free Trade doctrine by carefully avoiding the word protection.[60] The partisans of the movement affected to speak in favor of the full development of Free Trade principles, and called themselves the advocates of Free and "Fair" Trade. The policy of reciprocity was urged in substitution for that of unrestricted freedom of imports, and propagandist activity toward this end was launched by an organization calling itself the National Fair Trade League. The Fair Traders admitted that Free Trade was very excellent, if adopted by all nations with whom England did business, but they maintained that a nation which scrapped its tariff while others retained theirs placed itself at a great disadvantage. These opinions obtained currency in both agricultural and industrial communities and found nourishment in the widespread depression. Refutations of them were forthcoming from many quarters, but they were not silenced; and reciprocity made its voice heard in Parliament in 1879 when Lord Bateman introduced a resolution asking

[58] April 8, 1879.
[59] E. Leyd, "Causes of Decline in Commerce of Great Britain," April 3, 1878, *Journal of Royal Society of Arts,* vol. 26, p. 401.
[60] *Annual Register,* 1879, I, 82.

that the long continued depressed state of the commercial, manufacturing, and agricultural interests should form the subject of a full
Parliamentary inquiry with a view to . . . counteract the injurious
effects of the excessive tariffs levied by foreign nations against the
produce and manufactures of this country.[61]

Lord Beaconsfield spoke at length against the proposal and
the resolution was negatived without a division. The tariff reform movement made little headway in Parliament or the country during 1879. Influential press opinion was strongly opposed to it. The *Morning Post* remarked that Lord Bateman
"took an exaggerated view of the present distress," and declared the country was far from being in the deplorable condition he had described, "simply because free trade had been
the means of pouring into it abundant supplies of food at low
prices. . . . No doubt," the *Post* went on to say, "it would be a
gain to us, and not more to us than to other countries, if free
trade were to become universal. But we shall not relinquish the
benefits of which we have for thirty years had proof positive
in the enormous increase of the national wealth because other
nations are blind to them."[62] The Liberal *Daily Chronicle* asserted that "the sense of the country is certainly opposed to
a policy of what is termed Reciprocity, and no English statesman could be found to propose a return to protection."[63] John
Bright in a letter to the *Daily News* characterized tariff reform as "heresy or lunacy," and "exactly calculated to catch
the considerable class of simpletons who have no memory and
no logic."[64] The *Times* gave a cautious approval to lifting wine
duties as a retaliatory measure, but "apart from any such
measure we must rely in our fight against protective tariffs on
free trade weapons only."[65] The reciprocity program, in fact,
was commended by no important section of the press, although
the *Evening Globe* expressed an anti-doctrinaire opinion against
"treating as simpletons a class of men in which Prince Bismarck

[61] *Hansard*, vol. 245, p. 1356 *et seq.*, April 29, 1879.
[62] April 30, 1879.
[63] April 14, 1879.
[64] April 3, 1879.
[65] April 8, 1879.

and the late M. Thiers must be included."[66] Fair Trade beat
its head in vain against the wall of orthodox economy, and was
to go on doing so; the overwhelming sentiment of the country
was against any tampering with fiscal policy in retaliation
against foreign tariffs, even though they were admittedly damaging British trade. There was a strong conviction that the
protectionist revival, like the depression itself, would presently
dissolve. "The revival of an exploded economy," asserted the
Times, "was bound to come to pass. . . . Those who have paid
any attention to the subject have long observed how imperfect was the apprehension of the true principles of commercial
policy among the professional rulers of the Continent. . . . It
was morally certain that these things would come, but they will
pass away."[67] Countless expressions of this opinion might be
offered; it is almost astonishing to discover how strong and universal was the conviction.

But if the rise of tariffs against British goods in the valuable
Continental and American markets could not shake the allegiance
of Great Britain to Cobdenism, it did serve to point out the
imperative need for acquiring new markets. "Excluded from the
principal manufacturing countries by a protectionist policy, it
is to the colonies and to the half-civilized countries that we
must look for the expansion of our trade," Mr. Brassey told
his Edinburgh audience. One reads in the newspapers little items
of profound significance: an account of a meeting of Lancashire men at Preston to develop a scheme for opening central
Africa to British trade; an account of another assembly at
Blackburn, with the Mayor in the chair, hearing a letter from
a Manchester industrialist urging that a few millions be spent
on railroads and steamers in Africa so that a market might be
opened which could take double the yardage of cotton cloth annually exported to India.[68] Conviction was being driven home
to British minds that since the old markets were narrowing,
new ones must be found. To Africa, to Asia, to South America,

[66] April 3, 1879.
[67] Jan. 14, 1879.
[68] The *Times*, Jan. 6; March 13, 1879.

26

British eyes were turning, and the search for new markets, one of the great dynamic factors in the imperialist revival, was already under way. In this search Great Britain was forced to compete with formidable rivals, even as in her old markets; but the future was faced with confidence as the long depression faded out in 1880. "The earth is spacious," commented the *Times* lightly as business revived. "For a market closed in one quarter two are opened in another. A regret is pardonable that the neighbours of Great Britain are not very neighbourly in their tariffs. The loss, however, of European custom is redressed as it is, and tends to be redressed more amply still, by new demands from remoter regions."[69]

[69] Oct. 11, 1880.

Chapter II

A NEW COMMERCIAL WORLD

THE new decade opened for England with a welcome delivery from the long depression of the seventies. A business revival, general throughout the western world, began in America, and by the latter part of 1879 had made itself felt in England. In 1880 slumbering furnaces were again in full blast, mills were reopened, and the revival was manifestly in full swing. The optimism of the country returned as the export trade rose from 191 millions in 1879 to 223 millions in 1880, mounting on to 241 millions in 1882; while imports attained new record value levels. Industrial unemployment, which had risen to the distressing figure of 10.7 per cent, receded rapidly until it was down to 2.35 per cent in 1882.[1] Basic industries all displayed restored vigor of activity. But unfortunately the revival did not endure long; by the middle of the decade trade was down again in a bad slump. Export values fell off sharply from 1884 to 1888, unemployment swelled upward, and England experienced a serious renewal of hard times—hard enough, indeed, to move the Crown in 1885 to name a Royal Commission to examine the causes for the "depression of trade and industry." The report of this body contains a vast sum of information for the investigator of commercial history, and much of this chapter is founded upon it.[2]

The great depression of the eighties served to make England very acutely aware of the transformed world in which she had now to carry on her business. Industrial power had increased enormously in the world, and business prosperity depended upon a continuous widening of markets. The chief commercial powers were waging a struggle of increasing intensity for these markets;

[1] B F T I, 1909, Cd. 4954, p. 223.
[2] Reports of Commissioners, 1886, vols. 9, 10, 11. (Hereafter referred to as Rep. Comm.)

and the whole condition was accentuated by the revival of mercantilist policies to protect home markets while stimulating exports. England, alone among the great business nations, maintained a policy of free imports; and this fact made the acquisition of new markets especially necessary for her, because she not only lost her commanding position in many old markets but had now to face the development of competition at home from imported foreign manufactures. How to find those needed markets, and how to capture and hold them in the new competitive mercantilist world, were the pressing questions of the hour for Great Britain.

It is important to observe at once a significant shift in the distribution of British exports in the eighties. There took place a striking recession of British business in certain of the hitherto most valuable markets, especially on the European Continent; not only did the value of exports to these markets decline, but that percentage which they absorbed of the whole trade shrank. The table below will show the measure of this contraction in Russia, Germany, Holland, France, and southeastern Europe; and it was not confined to these countries. A similar contraction may be observed in the Egyptian, American, and certain South American markets. On the other hand, the table exhibits notable gains in the export trade to Australia, New Zealand, and India; and this may be taken to illustrate the reversal of that tendency, previously noted, for British business to neglect colonial in pursuit of definitely foreign markets. Whereas in 1870-74 British possessions absorbed only 25.6 per cent of the exported products of the United Kingdom, in 1885-89 they received 35 per cent. In the new competitive world the value of colonial markets was rising, and new efforts were being put forth to deepen the channels of trade within the Empire. The table follows on the next page.[3]

2

England grew very worried over her commercial position in these years. The nightmare of hostile tariffs and foreign com-

---

[3] Compiled from tables in B F T I, 1909, Cd. 4954, pp. 26-45.

GREAT BRITAIN AND THE GERMAN TRADE RIVALRY

A Table Showing the Changes in the Value of the Exports of the United Kingdom Produce to Certain Countries, and to Foreign Countries and British Possessions Relatively, as Revealed in a Comparison of the Average Annual Values for the Indicated Quinquennial Periods

FOREIGN COUNTRIES

	1870–74 £ 1,000,000	1870–74 % of Total	1880–84 £ 1,000,000	1880–84 % of Total	1885–89 £ 1,000,000	1885–89 % of Total
Russia	8	3.4	6	2.5	4	2.0
Germany	26	11.1	18	7.7	16	7.2
Holland	14	6.0	9	4.0	9	3.9
Belgium	6	2.5	8	3.2	7	3.2
France	16	6.8	17	7.2	15	6.3
Italy	6	2.6	6	2.7	7	3.0
Turkey, Rumania, Servia, Bulgaria	8	3.4	8	3.2	7	3.0
Egypt	7	2.8	3	1.3	3	1.4
United States	33	14.1	28	12.2	28	12.2
Brazil	7	3.0	7	3.0	6	2.6
Chile	3	1.3	2	1.0	2	0.9
Argentine	3	1.3	4	1.7	7	3.1
China	6	2.6	5	2.1	5	2.5
Japan	2	0.9	2	1.0	3	1.4
Other Countries	30	12.7	30	12.7	28	12.3
Total for Foreign Countries	175	74.4	153	65.5	147	65.0

BRITISH COLONIES

	£	%	£	%	£	%
B. North America	9	3.6	9	3.8	8	3.4
W.I.& Guiana	3	1.3	3	1.3	3	1.2
Australia & N.Z.	14	6.0	22	9.4	23	10.2
India	20	8.5	30	12.9	31	13.7
C. of Good Hope & Natal	3	1.4	6	2.6	5	2.4
Other Colonies	11	4.8	11	4.5	9	4.1
Total for Colonies	60	25.6	81	34.5	79	35.0

petition had become a grim reality; and the conviction spread that the new protectionism was stifling British trade in the richest markets while stimulating an unequal competition in others. In no instance was this development felt more keenly than in the valuable American and German markets. As may be seen from the above table, British exports to Germany and the United States declined rather sharply, although imports from these countries increased; contraction of the export trade to other protected countries may also be noted. In 1880, countries classified as protectionist received 41.6 per cent of the exported products of the United Kingdom, while at the end of the decade they took only 38.5 per cent.[4] Tariffs were obviously diverting the export trade toward open markets, a shift which was painful and costly. "We can now-a-days hardly open our *Times* without reading of some new embargo laid on British trade," observed a writer in the *National Review*. " . . . It would be an endless task to trace the restrictions that are killing our trade to the more important foreign markets of the world—to America, to France, to Germany, to Italy, to Austria, to Spain. Their prohibitive tariffs are known to all men; and the disastrous results are felt by all our manufacturers, and by every trade union in the Kingdom."[5] A large majority of the chambers of commerce and commercial associations interrogated by the Royal Commission testified to the injurious effect of the new tariffs on British trade, and the Commissioners in their report emphasized strongly this obstruction to commercial progress.[6] The tariffs, moreover, were not only making themselves felt in the markets which they surrounded, but, as the Royal Commission perceived very clearly, they enabled producers to secure such high prices at home that production was stimulated and surpluses created. "The surplus production which cannnot find a market at home is sent abroad, and in foreign markets undersells the commodities produced under less artificial conditions."[7]

[4] B F T I, 1909, Cd. 4954, pp. 76-77.
[5] Roper Lethbridge, "Is an Imperial Fiscal Policy Possible?" 1885, vol. 5, p. 29.
[6] Section 74 of majority report, and section 58 of minority report.
[7] Majority report, section 67.

Whatever the relation between tariffs and competition, the widespread appearance of the latter was now a serious and enormous fact. Thirty-five chambers of commerce and commercial associations informed the Royal Commission that this was producing an injurious effect upon trade.[8] The warning of the seventies had come true with a vengeance in the eighties, and the products of German, French, Belgian, American, and other national industries were fast penetrating into markets which Great Britain had hitherto dominated. A most elaborate array of evidence for this may be found in the survey secured for the Royal Commission, in 1885-86, through a questionnaire sent out by the Foreign Office to diplomatic and consular officers in the principal countries with which England did business. These officials were requested to report, among other matters, what impediments to British trade existed, and what diversions of this trade to other countries had taken place in their severally respective districts. The replies provide a vivid picture of the new competitive business world, and show the varying fortunes of British trade, in some markets holding its own easily, in others fighting hard for its position and even giving way to rivals.[9]

As may readily be guessed, these reports show England's trade situation most serious on the European Continent, where rival industrialism and the new mercantilism were now grown strong. The Europe pictured in the reports is a Europe rapidly undergoing economic transformation: industrialism, already vigorous and strong in the West, is penetrating fast into Central and even Eastern Europe, and springing to sturdy life south of the Alps. Even in Spain, in Scandinavia, and beyond the Vistula and Niemen, the new industrial processes are taking hold. Railroads are lengthening in every direction, piercing mountains and bridging rivers, multiplying commerce and calling new industries into life. The enlargement of port facilities pro-

[8] Rep. Comm., 1886, vol. 9, pp. 73-113.

[9] An extensive series of selected extracts from these replies, bearing specifically upon the diversion of British trade to rival nations, has been arranged and appears in this study as Appendix I.

32

ceeds, as Mediterranean and Atlantic coasts are bound to the hinterlands by rail and to the overseas world by direct shipping lines. A generation earlier Great Britain had been the center whence this economic revolution radiated out over the Continent, exporting the plant materials, machinery, rails, locomotives, and other capital goods; but now the Continent had its own radiating centers of economic revolution, and was supplying more and more its own capital goods for the construction of factories and railroads. In short, the picture is one of Europe fast shaking off its dependence on Great Britain for both capital goods and finished manufactures.[10]

Especially in the West do the reports tell a story of the wresting of British trade by Belgian, French, and German industry. Spanish and Portuguese markets appeared to be falling steadily under the domination of Continental firms. Similar, if fewer, symptoms of the same shift were discernible in France. The reports from Germany dwelt chiefly upon the relentless displacement of English by native German manufactures, and the Belgian reports described a recession of British trade before the advance of home industry and German commercial penetration. From Holland also came reports of a rising German competition with British wares. In Northern Europe the same tendency was evident: a German invasion of Danish markets, and the shifting of certain Swedish and Norwegian imports from English to German, Belgian, and American producers. In Central Europe the most striking development was to be seen in the conquests made by German industry. A Swiss report declared that the Germans in some branches of trade had "almost completely ousted British manufactures"; and the Italian reports paid eloquent tribute to the vigorous advance of German goods south of the Alps, to the disadvantage of British trade. From Austria came a statement that German, Belgian, Swiss and na-

[10] J. A. Crowe, commercial attaché to British embassies and legations in Europe, was asked by the Royal Commission if "the dependence of Continental countries upon England for machinery is as great as it used to be some years ago," and he replied that it was, up to the beginning of 1885. —Minutes of Evidence, 1056.

33

tive industry had taken over a "considerable proportion of our impórts." In Hungary the competition of Austria and Germany was cited as an important factor in the depression of Britain's Hungarian business. Russia, too, and all of Eastern Europe, were shown now to be the scene of Anglo-Continental and especially Anglo-German commercial rivalry. It is, indeed, somewhat surprising to read in these reports how far German commercial penetration of Balkan and Ottoman Europe had gone before the first Turkish railway concessions were awarded to German financiers.[11]

Beyond Europe the competition now facing British trade, for the most part, was less keen, although it was growing fast. The Royal Commission made a conservative estimate of it from the evidence of the diplomatic and consular reports: "In the neutral markets . . . and especially in the East, we are beginning to feel the effects of foreign competition where our trade formerly enjoyed a practical monopoly."[12] In Asiatic Turkey, German, Austrian, Swiss, French, Russian, and American competition was being met in such lines as textiles, glass, hardware, crockery, steel, coffee, sugar, and spirits; and British trade was "not increasing in due proportion to the trade of foreign countries." The diversion of English cutlery trade in Egypt to Germany was singled out for mention in reports from Cairo and Alexandria; and Tunis reported the recent capture of Britain's iron trade by Belgians. The Moroccan reports drew attention to a German invasion of cloths and hardware, and suggested that Germany might possibly "draw to herself a portion of the trade hitherto in our hands." From the Balearic Islands came information of a "slight competition in the importation of German machinery." In the Canaries the Germans had captured the beer trade from the English. A report from the Azores pointed out the importation of American and German textiles and hardwares, "to the detriment of similar importations from Great Britain." In Madeira Hamburg was now competing "with Eng-

[11] Cf. Appendix I.
[12] Section 74.

land for the supply of various articles . . . which were formerly imported from Great Britain." The small British trade at New Orleans had "dwindled and gone into French and German hands." In Mexico the commercial advance of the United States was excluding "a large proportion of British goods from this market," and it remained to "be proved whether the British commercial world is content to submit quietly and without an effort." In other Central American markets there was also evidence of British trade giving ground to German and American. In Venezuela the successful competition of German and American goods, especially the former, was very marked; while in the Argentine German, Belgian, French, and American imports were growing more promisingly than British. A rather serious challenge, it would appear, had been raised in Britain's South American markets. In the Far East a great struggle for markets had now arisen, and Germans and Americans, as well as Japanese, were competing with England for position in the Chinese trade. Tokyo reported that "there has been for several years past a determined and energetic effort to push German trade all over the East," and the results of this drive figured prominently in the reports of British consuls in Japan. From Siam came information of the entry of competitive Swiss and Indian textiles into the market, the substitution of Continental for English machinery, and the displacement of English by Japanese and Australian coal. Such are some of the fleeting glimpses of the new competitive world afforded by these reports, but they are enough to indicate how vastly the position and outlook for British commerce in the markets of the world had been altered in the course of twenty years.[13]

As ominous as the competition was the apparent weakening in the effectiveness of British methods and equipment for standing against it. Tariffs and cheaper production costs were not the only secrets of England's competitors. A large new class of alert and intelligent business men had arisen on the Continent, and in contrast with these the English business man not

[13] Cf. Appendix I.

infrequently seemed old-fashioned and wedded to obsolete methods of trade. Continental firms, in order to enter foreign markets successfully against British domination, naturally had to
bestir themselves more energetically and devise newer methods
of business; and in doing so they were not without important
advantages. Technical and commercial education were being developed more extensively and intensively on the Continent than
in England, and knowledge of foreign languages was more widely cultivated;[14] so that superior study of markets and superior
ability to exploit them successfully became powerful weapons
for German, French, and Belgian commerce.[15]

It is not surprising, therefore, to encounter the many pessimistic opinions on the future of British trade which became
current in the eighties. England had run her course and was
"done," her trade was going and her industries declining, her
commercial leadership was passing into eclipse—such was the
substance of much doleful forecasting. "There is, perhaps, no
more disquieting sign of the times," asserted the *Daily Telegraph*, decrying this pessimism, "than the readiness of so many
Englishmen in these days to 'give up.' . . . A period of commercial

---

[14] The Royal Commission declared: "In the matter of education we seem
to be particularly deficient as compared with some of our foreign competitors; and this remark applies not only to what is usually called technical
education, but to the ordinary commercial education which is required in
mercantile houses, and especially the knowledge of foreign languages."—
Section 97. The *Spectator* for June 26, 1886, declared: "Educate, educate,
educate, is the burthen of the lesson from Germany,—technical education
for workmen and manufacturers, modern languages and science for commercial men and manufacturers and workers alike." And again July 10:
"The first thing to do is to improve our commercial education. We must
teach our boys the modern languages. Instead of giving them Shakespeare's
learning of a little Latin and less Greek, we must give them, as they do in
Germany, a speaking as well as a grammatical acquaintance with the tongues
of the peoples with whom they are to stand in commercial relations. In
Germany every boy intended for commerce learns English. In England we
should make every boy learn French and German. . . . Our men of commerce are still trained almost entirely in subjects suitable enough for the
professions, but of little value in themselves for manufacturers and traders."
[15] For a contrast between British and German trade methods *vide* Ch. III.

depression sets in, and lasts longer than usual. Straightway our
faint-hearted friends are convinced that the hour of our decline is struck. Solemn homilies are read to us on the mutability
of things and the vanity of all human endeavor. Ill-natured allusions to Tyre and Carthage become common; candid friends remind us that Spain was once the mistress of a world-wide empire; we are bidden to remember that Venice and Holland have
had to learn before us that commercial greatness does not endure forever. . . . So runs the desponding chorus day by day,
until at last, in the good time of the gods, it is suddenly reduced
to humiliated silence by some swift shifting of the scene. Trade's
mysterious breezes set again in the direction of activity, and
the drooping sacks of the merchant fill once more. . . . Pessimism
awakens from its dream to find that for the hundredth time in
human history it has been hastening to embrace evils which
may indeed be coming, but which are still far off upon the
road."[16] This cheerful view in the midst of a severe depression
was all very good, but it was not possible for England to whistle
away the new commercial situation with tariffs and competition
cutting her exports and her own spirit of business enterprise
lagging. England had sound reasons to feel alarmed, and the
Morning Post exaggerated little in asserting that

We no longer possess the advantages that we once held in the past.
Not only by bounties and by hostile tariffs have the United States
and the nations of Europe sought to cripple English trade in the
interests of their own industries, but they have also shown an increasing ability to meet us with our own weapons, and to compete
successfully with us even in open markets. As compared with our
rivals, in short, who have been rapidly advancing, we are distinctly
worse off than we were ten or eleven years ago. . . . The Report of
the Commission shows, in spite of its optimism, that we have fallen
on evil times; that it may well be that still more straitened times are
before us, and that it is only by the most careful public economy
and the most vigorous private enterprise that English industry can
hope to maintain its footing.[17]

[16] Dec. 9, 1887.
[17] Jan. 19, 1887.

3

It is probably true that there was more alarm over the condition of the home market than over the plight of trade abroad. These years were featured by a shrinkage in the demand for British goods within the United Kingdom, which was, of course, the most immediately obvious symptom of trade depression. Doubtless the loss of buying power on the part of the agricultural classes, the slow movement of exports, and the falling off of the entrepôt trade were major causes for the decline of the home market; but stagnant trade made for a growing sensitiveness to the importation of foreign goods,[18] and this appeared to many not only as a cause of the prevalent depression but an ominous portent for the future. The competition of foreign goods in the home market was not, of course, an entirely new development. Part of the sugar industry before 1880 had been conspicuously ruined by foreign imports and had been made the subject of Parliamentary inquiry. Between 1864 and 1875 about thirty loaf-sugar plants had been forced to shut down because of the importation of cheaper loaf sugar from the Continent; so that by the eighties this branch of the sugar trade in Great Britain was virtually extinct. Simultaneously, the millions invested in the West India sugar plantations were endangered by the capture of the British raw-sugar market by the bounty-supported beet-sugar industry of the Continent.[19] The ailing sugar industry was a strong factor in the rise of the Fair Trade movement, and, as will be seen, continued to be a prominent sufferer from unrestricted imports. But apart from the sugar trade, and of course agriculture, the signs of alarm at foreign importations before 1880 were infrequent and insignificant as compared with the alarmist crescendo that went up after that date. The fear that now arose was for the security of the major British industries in the home market; and that there was some ground for this cannot be denied, if the statistics of trade are

[18] As an instance, *vide Times* article on German competition in the Midlands, Jan. 5, 1886.
[19] Report of Select Committee on Sugar Industries, Reps. of Comms., 1880, vol. 5, p. 477 *et seq.*

carefully scrutinized. That percentage of the total imports which represented manufactures increased considerably between 1870 and 1890,[20] and the Royal Commission cited as among the causes for the stagnancy of the home market

the increased competition . . . of manufactured or partly manufactured goods, the importation of which appears to grow at a slightly more rapid rate than the population, having been £1.67 per head in the period 1870-74 and £2.35 per head in the period 1880-84.[21]

How bad the plight of the home market appeared to one member of Parliament, as early as 1880, may be judged from a speech of Mr. Wheelhouse, of Leeds, in a Commons debate on fiscal policy. He ventured to assert that

even in our own country we had lost command of the market. Our watches came from Switzerland, our cambrics and silks from France, and our velvets from Germany. . . . Where now was Spitalfields as an industrial community? The silk trade of Coventry and Macclesfield had been utterly destroyed. It was, perhaps, a grim satisfaction to those who supported these so-called Free Trade doctrines to learn that while the nails came from Belgium our coffins came from abroad also. . . . There was no use saying, as had been said, that England could stand against anything in the shape of manufactures from foreign lands. The broad patent fact was that she was not standing against them. . . . He mentioned some trades which had suffered greatly, and he could name many more. The velvet trade was almost gone; so also was that of lathrending, owing to the great imports from Sweden at a price less than that at which laths could be obtained in this country. England received, duty-free, ships, foreign-made locomotives, implements, furniture, flowers, carpets, clocks, and innumerable other articles, a list of which he held in his hand, but through which it would be wearisome to travel entirely.[22]

Here, indeed, was a sorry outlook for England; but that Mr. Wheelhouse had painted his picture in tones too somber is evident from the absence of any wide concurring opinion and from the

[20] B F T I, 1909, Cd. 4954, pp. 58-59.
[21] Report, Section 73.
[22] Feb. 13, 1880, Hansard, vol. 250, pp. 605-09.

dissent of the Board of Trade from his view. The following year Joseph Chamberlain, President of the Board, in reply to a question from Mr. MacIver of Birkenhead, declared in Parliament that the manufactures imported into Great Britain were largely "articles not manufactured in this country."[23]

But the importation of foreign manufactures went on increasing from year to year in percentage of total imports and exciting more and more attention. The return of slack trade conditions in 1883 helped to focus attention on them and to increase the number of complaints against them. They became, from this time onward, a constant subject of questions in Parliament, allusions in the debates, and notices in the press. On two occasions in 1884 the transfer of the manufacture of paper for Government post cards from Devonshire to Germany was the subject of anxious questions in the House of Commons.[24] The Earl of Dunraven, in support of his Fair Trade motion in the Lords in November, 1884, dwelt upon the dangerous growth of imports in relation to the stagnation of the cotton and iron trades. "We had not far to look for the cause," he declared. "Sir John Brown, the head of a very eminent firm in Sheffield, put the case clearly. He said: 'our former customers have become our competitors, and not only sell against us, but undersell us, not merely in neutral markets, but under our very noses at home.' " The Earl went on to emphasize the suffering of the sugar trade, arguing that cheap sugar was too large a price to pay for the loss of an industry, and to point out how protected foreign firms were able to sell their surpluses in the British free market. "The quantities might be small," he admitted, "but they were increasing, and they were sufficient to bear down our home market to an unwholesome extent." The Earl of Carnarvon, supporting Dunraven's motion, asserted that

there was enormous competition . . . in many trades. That competition existed in large as well as in small trades. It was only the other

[23] April 4, 1881, *ibid.,* vol. 260, p. 558.
[24] July 3, Oct. 27, 1884; *ibid.,* vol. 289, p. 1862; and vol. 293, p. 256.

day that he heard that the whole of the iron work for an enormous railway station in the Midlands had been imported into this country from Belgium, and he knew from his own knowledge that iron for railway bridges had been brought over from abroad. It was precisely the same in smaller industries. When all these matters were put together, they produced an alarming result.[25]

A writer in the *National Review*, in 1885, gave the following view of the condition of the home market:

That we are being rapidly beaten in our own home markets . . . is a fact that seems to me positively to obtrude itself on one's notice at every turn. It is almost impossible to go into any shop without observing it. When the paper for our postcards comes from Germany, and the microscopes in use at Cambridge are obtained there also; when our Government gets its navy-pork from Denmark, and its tinned rations for our troops in the Soudan from Chicago . . . the fact can hardly be denied with decency. . . . Nor can it be honestly said that we only import certain commodities in order to devote the labour of our workingmen to the production of other commodities for which we have greater natural advantage.[26]

War Office purchases of Italian wooden water bottles, which might perhaps have been manufactured at home, were the subject of a question in Parliament in 1888.[27] Navy purchases of tobacco from Continental manufacturers and orders of German slate pencils for Irish schools were also aired in Parliament, likewise a War Office contract for swords from Solingen.[28] The Earl de la Warr declared to the House of Lords in 1888:

It was impossible to walk through the streets of London without noticing the large number of shops filled with foreign goods. Foreign goods were taking the place in a most prominent manner of English goods. The silk industry was almost at an end. The last sugar manufactory in London was closed only a short time ago, and in the manufacture of hats, gloves, lace, and other such articles the French

[25] Nov. 6, 1884, *ibid.*, vol. 293, pp. 1044-82.
[26] Lethbridge article previously cited.
[27] July 2, 1888, Hansard, vol. 328, pp. 74-75.
[28] *Ibid.*, vol. 333, pp. 1010, 1238-40, 1763-64; vol. 332, pp. 230-31; vol. 337, pp. 1145-46.

were driving English goods out of the market. German goods could, also, be seen everywhere. The iron industry had been supplanted by Belgian and German goods, and our swords and bayonets were made abroad, while thousands of Sheffield men were standing idle.[29]

Nothing testifies more eloquently to the alarm raised by the invasion of the home market than the prominent revival of the fiscal question in political debate. Tariff reformers sought persistently in the eighties for a reconsideration of British fiscal policy; and the competition of imported manufactures conspired with agricultural depression and hostile foreign tariffs to supply them with ammunition for argument. Attention has already been drawn to the Dunraven motion in the House of Lords in 1879, and now similar proposals were constantly brought forward in Parliament.[30] In each successive year the fiscal question was agitated, and by the middle of the decade there was a fairly strong demand for a revaluation of the merits of Cobdenism in the light of new world conditions. That the movement was gaining influential support may be judged from the fact that a minority report of the Royal Commission, signed by four members, strongly recommended the Fair Trade scheme for a fiscal policy looking toward imperial tariff union, and from the additional fact that the movement won the approval of an influential section of the press, notably the *Morning Post* and the *National Review*.

The *Post*, which in 1879 had condemned Dunraven's reciprocity idea, now quite abandoned economic orthodoxy. It declared in 1884:

The tide of popular opinion is now flowing so strongly in the direction of Fair Trade that it can no longer be stemmed by the old barriers of prejudice which long ago did service as the most convenient

[29] March 12, 1888, *ibid.*, vol. 323, p. 819.

[30] *Vide* Mr. Wheelhouse's motion, Feb. 3, 1880, *ibid.*, vol. 250, p. 604 *et seq.;* Mr. MacIver's motion, May 23, 1881, vol. 260, p. 1101 *et seq.;* Mr. Ritchie's motion, Aug. 12, 1881, vol. 264, pp. 1728-1816; Mr. Storer's resolution, March 7, 1882, vol. 267, p. 390 *et seq.;* Earl of Rutland's motion, June 3, 1883, vol. 280, p. 3 *et seq.;* Lord Dunraven's motion, Nov. 6, 1884, vol. 293, p. 1044 *et seq.*

obstacles to oppose to it. A time is rapidly approaching when the arguments we have urged in these columns must be met with something more than stale platitudes, partly irrelevant and partly unsound. . . . A big breach has already been made in the huge rampart which for nearly forty years has been raised between the fetish set up by Richard Cobden and all those who have ventured to attack its supreme authority. . . . It will soon be as vain to resist Lord Dunraven's demand as it is already to reinstate Free Trade upon the safe pedestal of sanctity where it seemed to stand twenty years ago.[31]

The *National Review* did yeoman's service for Fair Trade, opening its columns to a number of very powerful attacks upon the existing tariff policy which received wide attention.[32] The assault upon orthodox Cobdenism had got far enough by the end of 1887 for the *Post* to feel warranted in saying:[33]

Not many years ago a distrust of Free Trade was looked upon as a bucolic heresy with which the intelligent artisans of the town would have nothing to do. Under the pressure of bad times, and of increasing foreign competition, the heresy has taken a wider range and its followers are to be found chiefly in the great centers of commerce. Disbelief in Cobden and his theories is no longer a farmer's fad. . . . The extravagant professions made on behalf of Free Trade by its early advocates, and maintained by its later supporters, have naturally had the effect of producing a reaction against it. In France and in the United States, and in our own most flourishing colonies, men who could hardly be regarded as fools deliberately refused to embrace the gospel of Cobden, and prospered in spite of their obduracy. Looking at such instances of successful rebellion against the orthodox creed, English workingmen, having no fear of Cobden before their eyes, have reasonably enough come to ask whether the system of Free Trade is not capable of amendment. . . . At present this movement is in its infancy, and much remains to be done before the leaders of it can place their case fairly under the criticism of the

[31] Nov. 15, 1884.
[32] *Vide,* especially: Roper Lethbridge's article previously cited; Editor W. J. Harris, *A Reply to Lord Randolph Churchill,* vol. 10, p. 441; A. W. Roberts, *Low Prices and Hostile Tariffs,* vol. 6, p. 370; C. A. Cripps, *Competition and Free Trade,* vol. 10, p. 341.
[33] Dec. 9, 1887.

public. . . . The number of those who are ready to examine and, if need be, amend our present fiscal system is daily growing.

But in spite of the cry against foreign tariffs and competition England was not to be budged from her allegiance to economic orthodoxy; and the return of a period of renewed trade prosperity at the end of the decade temporarily cut some of the ground beneath tariff reform. No major party leader as yet had dared to embrace any program which might be stigmatized as protectionist. Staunch Cobdenites, indeed, were inclined to minimize the damaging effects of foreign tariffs and to scout the alarms which they raised, while arguing that free imports provided the best weapon with which to combat hostile tariffs. As for foreign competition, the Cobdenite remedies were more technical and commercial education and more active individual business enterprise.[34] The merits of the fiscal question in this period constitute no question to be answered by this study, but it may be remarked that the continued strength of the Free Trade conviction was very eloquent of the pragmatic conservatism of the British temper of mind. Cobdenism had brought wealth and prosperity in past years; therefore it was the right system, and he who attacked it was simply committing folly. What boldness it required to lay hands upon the sacred dogma, even as late as 1890, was suggested by a writer in the *Nineteenth Century*:

To criticise the principle on which our entire system of trade is based —that is to say, free imports as against hostile tariffs—is a very hazardous enterprise. The man who launches out upon it is instantly attacked by all the "statisticians" and political economists with the

[34] A very representative Cobdenite view of Great Britain's position in the commercial world was that of Robert Giffen, head of the Commercial Department of the Board of Trade and a high authority for the orthodox. "Our welfare," he asserted in 1885, "does not depend on any external causes or on any injury which it is in the power of foreign governments to inflict, but on our own industry and energy. If trade is diverted at all by external causes, it will find other channels so long as the will and determination to use our great resources of capital and organized labour exist."—"Trade Depression and Low Prices," *Contemporary Review*, 1885, vol. 47, p. 800.

biggest bludgeons they can find, and it will be a lucky thing for him if it is not soon proved that he is not only destitute of reason and common sense, but that his moral character has some ugly flaws in it, and that it is exceedingly doubtful whether he ought to be at large.[35]

4

There were several features of the trade competition which seemed very unfair to Englishmen, and one may read a good deal in the eighties about the unorthodox and unfair commercial practices and methods resorted to by foreign rivals. The practice of selling goods cheaper abroad than in the protected home market of course seemed to staunch free traders as of very doubtful commercial morality; but far less defensible was the fraudulent use of British marks and place names on "cheap foreign goods," which gave rise to the legend that the Germans captured the trade of England by sending into world markets imitation wares stamped with forged British trade marks.

This grievance of British business appears to have been of long standing. Joseph Rodgers and Sons, the Sheffield cutlers, for example, were almost continuously in litigation to restrain the fraudulent imitation of their trade marks from 1826 onward.[36] But no great attention was directed to the dishonest business until 1859, when Professor Leone Levi read a paper on the subject before the Royal Society of Arts. He found the Germans to be the chief offenders, and said it was a common practice with their manufacturers "to produce a low priced and inferior article, wretchedly bad, upon which they unscrupulously impress the trade marks of the most celebrated Sheffield and other English makers." Nor was this the limit of their dishonesty; they imitated English parcel labels, "and as if to fill up the sum of their imposture, the Sheffield manufacturer having enclosed in such parcel of goods a printed notice of the deception thus practiced . . . the German immediately had the effrontery to copy this also."[37] Professor Levi's revelations were largely

[35] L. J. Jennings, *Trade League Against England*, vol. 28, p. 901 *et seq.*
[36] The *Times*, Dec. 20, 1871.
[37] *Journal of Society of Arts*, vol. 7, p. 262 *et seq.*

the cause for passing the Merchandise Marks Act of 1862, which aimed at the suppression of trade mark frauds. One hears a good deal about trade marks in succeeding years.[38] There was an extensive development of registry and protective legislation throughout the world, and by 1880 nearly every country in Europe was possessed at least of a trade marks registration law.[39] In 1883 an important step toward international protection of trade marks was taken in the signing of the Convention of the Industrial Property Union, the members of which agreed to a common basis for legislation; but, unfortunately, several important states, notably the United States and Germany, did not immediately become parties to the Convention.

Nevertheless, the fraudulent and deceptive use of marks was not entirely put down, and the Germans especially were still complained against in England. Their refusal to adhere to the 1883 Convention was one reason for this; and there was also the fact that from the passage of the German trade marks registry law in 1874 down to 1887 a large number of British trade marks were refused registration in Germany on the ground that they could not be shown to have been universally recognized as distinctive trade marks at the time the 1874 law became operative.[40] Now in the middle eighties British complaints against foreign, and especially German, trade-mark frauds became rather heated. A demand for additional legislation led to the naming of a Select Committee for investigation and to the passage of the famous Merchandise Marks Act of 1887.[41] The agitation seems to have been started by a complaint to the

[38] See *ibid.*: E. M. Anderson, *Piracy of Trade Marks,* vol. 14, p. 370; W. W. Robertson, *Trade Marks,* vol. 17, p. 414; H. T. Wood, *Registration of Trade Marks,* vol. 24, pp. 17, 49.

[39] J. S. Salaman, solicitor for Trade Marks Protection Society, in the *Times,* Oct. 23, 1880.

[40] Edmund Johnson, manager of Trade Marks Protection Society, in the *Times,* Jan. 5, 1887.

[41] The Special Report from the Select Committee on the Merchandise Marks Act (1862) Amendment Bill, in Reps. of Comms., 1887, vol. 4, is the most valuable source of information on the false trade marks question in the eighties.

Board of Trade in 1883, from the Cutlers Company of Sheffield, against "an increasing practice, especially in Germany, of putting the word 'Sheffield' upon articles of inferior cutlery," which were being sent "to the foreign and colonial markets and even to the English markets, and thereby the Sheffield trade was very much injured and the good name of English goods was imperilled."[42] Presently there was a customs seizure of German goods bearing false trade marks,[43] and by 1886, when other grievances had been added to those of Sheffield, a loud complaint against these frauds was heard in Parliament and the press. "This nefarious business," declared the *Daily Telegraph* bitterly, "wounds honest British commerce like a two-edged dagger; it robs us of business which belonged to us, and it damages the very reputation which obtained that business."[44]

That the grievance was not ill founded seems incontestably proved by the testimony of witnesses examined by the Select Committee. This evidence also showed that the Germans were the prominent offenders; and it is worth observing that almost all complaints about this nuisance sent home by British consuls were against Germans, although such consular complaints were by no means frequent or conspicuous. A careful search of the returns of the Foreign Office questionnaire of 1885 and of the diplomatic and consular reports in the later eighties revealed complaints from Warsaw, St. Petersburg, Odessa, Munich, Belgrade, Nisch, Christiania, Barcelona, Cairo, and Shanghai.[45] Doubtless there were trade-mark frauds in other places, too, but the reports ignored them. Even the complaints made were not all charges of actual trade-mark forgery, but most of them simply pointed to the use of English words and place names to make goods appear as having come from Great Britain. Nor were the offenders all foreigners. Mr. Mundella, President of the Board of Trade, when questioned in Parliament about the

[42] Testimony of Sir Courtenay Boyle, of Board of Trade, Evidence taken by Committee, 4-6.
[43] Appendix to Report, p. 238.
[44] Sept. 1, 1886.
[45] See Appendix I; also Annual Series, 14, 130, 176, 274, 447, 534.

importation of falsely marked goods, said he had heard that Sheffield men had been likewise guilty of this;[46] and Herbert Hughes, solicitor for the Cutlers Company, admitted to the Select Committee that "there are home sinners as well as foreign sinners."[47] The Royal Commission on the Depression of Trade stated regretfully "that the practice of fraudulent marking appears from the evidence before us to be not unknown in this country."[48] The *Times*, in a leader complaining against falsely marked Solingen goods and "impudent imitation of English trade marks," confessed that English manufacturers also had been guilty of exporting foreign-made goods under English stamps, and of sending out imitations of foreign wares—but "better than the originals," and hence, although a fraud, yet "a pious fraud."[49] Indeed, it is not unlikely that most of the fraudulently marked German wares that were going out into world markets were going by way of England, with English merchants' names stamped on them as dealers' advertisements. But the frauds perpetrated by the Germans themselves appeared much more heinous.

In the Spring of 1886 the Board of Trade informed the Foreign Office of its "regret that the German Government have not, up to the present time, deemed it desirable to become a party to the Industrial Property Convention," and stated the opinion that the international arrangements for the suppression of falsely marked goods "will be very imperfect so long as the German Government are unwilling to enter the Industrial Property Union."[50] About the same time the Foreign Office instructed its Berlin ambassador, Sir Edward Malet, to represent to the German Government the

hardship caused to British trade and manufacture by the production in Germany of goods falsely bearing indications of British origin, and that it was the desire of Her Majesty's Government to come to

[46] Hansard, 3rd. Series, vol. 302, p. 1543.
[47] Evidence, 1951.
[48] Report, section 78.
[49] Aug. 16, 1887.
[50] Appendix to Report, p. 238.

an arrangement with that of Germany for the purpose of putting a stop to such proceedings.[51]

To these representations no definite reply was elicited, but the British Government drew some encouragement from the presence of German representatives at the Conference of the Industrial Union at Rome that year. The British delegates at this meeting proposed and secured the adoption of an amendment to the 1883 Convention, to prohibit false marks of origin as well as piracy in trade marks. The operation of the amendment depended upon internal legislation in the signatory countries, and it was in pursuance of this that the British Act of 1887 was carried through Parliament. Germany, however, continued to remain outside the Union, adhering neither to the 1883 nor 1886 Convention.

The Merchandise Marks Act of 1887 substituted much more stringent legislation for the 1862 law.[52] Going beyond the safeguarding of trade marks of individual firms, it forbade misrepresentation of place or country of origin, thus striking at such frauds as German cutlery marked "Sheffield" or hosiery marked "Balbriggan." Not all imported goods, of course, were required to bear a mark of origin, but only such goods as were sold with the mark of an English dealer or an English place name. "The Act," observed the *Chamber of Commerce Journal*, "is clearly intended to reëstablish the reputation of British manufactures, and, acting as it must, on both our exports and our imports, there is little doubt that it will, in the long run, produce this effect in both home and neutral markets. It will also tend to encourage the consumption at home of English rather than foreign articles, and will act as a guarantee to customers abroad and in our colonies, that they are receiving real British-made produce and not foreign imitations thereof."[53]

Some of the consequences of this act will be noticed in the following chapter, but it will not be amiss here to observe that

[51] *Ibid.*, p. 240.
[52] Public General Statutes, XXIV, 1887, Ch. 28.
[53] Oct. 5, 1887.

the law was conceived in greater honesty than commercial sagacity. Its practical effect was to put the stamp "made in Germany" on countless imported wares throughout the United Kingdom and the Empire, to awaken the British to a realization of the surprisingly large quantity of goods that came from Germany, and thus to give a stimulus to the German trade hysteria of the succeeding years. One of the witnesses before the Select Committee had prophesied that the law would have the effect of advertising the foreign producer, thus informing purchasers where they might secure desired articles directly and more cheaply, to the damage of British business;[54] and he did not prophesy falsely. In Germany the immediate effect was to produce considerable dissatisfaction in industrial circles,[55] but in 1889 the Frankfort Chamber of Commerce could express this view of the law:[56]

The Merchandise Marks Act of 1887, of which such decisive results were anticipated in Great Britain, has injured German industry in some respects but slightly; while, in others, it has benefited it, and should this law be applied in India and other British Colonies, it would soon be found out there that many articles, and perhaps the best among them brought into the market by British shipping houses, are not of English origin, but bear the words "Made in Germany."

English opinions respecting this Act . . . have been discussed at length in the English press. It is established that many abuses have been removed, although its primary object, a protective and partly prohibitive duty against Germany, has not been accomplished. The Act . . . is calculated to further honesty and integrity in trade. The provision, however, requiring the Customs officials to search all goods entering the United Kingdom, even those in transit, has most seriously affected the interests of British shipowners. The injury caused by searching carefully packed goods, the seizure, the delay incident on claims, the careless repacking of the goods, often rendering the same unfit for sea voyage, is so great that the exporter will certainly give the preference to any foreign port. . . .

[54] Testimony of Louis Blumfeld, Evidence 2627-2759.
[55] Annual Series 379.
[56] Quoted in report of Sir Charles Oppenheimer at Frankfort for 1889, Annual Series 573.

Increased facilities and profits will thus be afforded to German shipowners.

5

Another factor in the struggle for markets which impressed British opinion as hardly in keeping with sound ethics of commerce was the exercise by foreign governments of diplomatic or official pressure to secure special trade favors for their nationals. England's allegiance to the economics of laissez faire was yet too unshaken for her to regard this phase of neo-mercantilism without a self-righteous anger and contempt. The prevailing English view was that although the agents of the Foreign Office had a duty to secure and protect fair conditions of trade for English merchants wherever possible, the actual promotion of commerce was the business of traders themselves. Consuls, of course, were required to supply commercial information of a rather general character, perform certain services neutrally for businessmen, and "to protect and to promote the lawful trade of Great Britain by every fair and proper means";[57] but diplomatic representatives were engaged in *haute politique,* which touched commerce only in protecting the security of conditions for carrying it on.

Some symptoms of a change in the attitude of the Foreign Office toward trade, it is true, can be discerned prior to the eighties. In 1857, when reports at regular intervals from missions abroad were originated, a circular recommended that embassy and legation secretaries occasionally visit ports and manufacturing centers to witness the course of business, and, if necessary, suggest the adoption of measures by which British trade might obtain facilities or be relieved from burdens and obstructions. In 1865 the Commercial Department of the Foreign Office was established, and in 1872 the Queen's representatives were called upon to report on the general question of British trade with the countries to which they were accredited and to suggest means for its further development. In 1878 they were instructed

[57] Correspondence Respecting Diplomatic and Consular Assistance to Trade. Commercial No. 16, 1886. Appendix: Instructions to Her Majesty's Diplomatic Representatives and Consuls.

to forward home "*précis* of Parliamentary debates or proceedings, or the proceedings of public bodies, on matters affecting British commercial interests." In 1881 a circular confessed the difficulty in enforcing strictly and universally the

> general rule . . . that the Secretary of State should decline to give letters of introduction or recommendation to Her Majesty's Diplomatic and Consular Agents abroad in favour of gentlemen proceeding to foreign countries for the purpose of promoting any specific commercial or industrial undertaking, or of obtaining Concessions from a Foreign Government.[58]

These facts doubtless have their significance in showing a growing attentiveness to commercial matters in the Foreign Office, but the *haute politique* tradition was nevertheless still strong in the eighties. England's great volume of commerce had been developed by private enterprise, and only by the continued vigor of this could it be sustained. Such was the orthodox view, and such was the theory, if not always the consistent practice, of the Foreign Office.

By the middle of the eighties a less zealous allegiance to this orthodoxy had become manifest among some of England's commercial rivals, who entertained less doctrinaire views of the correct functions of the state in its relation to trade. Lord Granville, in early 1885, was induced to query diplomatic representatives in the United States, Belgium, France, Germany, and Italy on the extent to which these governments lent their aid to foreign commerce. The replies showed no radical divergence in policy from Great Britain—certainly not any with respect to the stated limits of consular activity. Contrary to a very widespread belief in England, the consular agents of these countries, like the British, were forbidden to act as agents for exporting firms, save in the case of certain unpaid Belgian and low-paid American consuls.[59] Nevertheless British commercial circles were complaining against the official support given to trade by the diplomatic and consular services of foreign governments, and the complaints derived chiefly from those regions of the world where political

[58] *Ibid.*, Appendix.
[59] *Ibid.*, Documents 31, 32, 33, 34, 41, 42.

and commercial life, if not corrupt or unstable, yet differed most from the standards of Western Europe. Such regions afforded a greater elasticity in the scope of effective support which diplomatic and consular officials might lend to trade, with the result that alert and energetic consuls did something more than draft reports and answer inquiries. The following excerpt from a dispatch of Sir E. Thornton, at Constantinople, in 1886, may illustrate this:[60]

. . . since my arrival, complaints, verbal and in writing, have been made of the scant protection given by Her Majesty's Diplomatic and Consular officers to British subjects.

A leading merchant of this city lately called on me and used very plain language in this sense, especially in comparison with the protection enjoyed by German subjects. I asked him to give me an instance. He put forward what he considered to be the strongest proof of his assertion. He said that English merchants would sell their goods at one month's credit on much easier terms than German merchants would sell on six months' credit. The natives, however, always preferred to deal with the latter, who dared to give such long credit, because, in the event of their debtors not paying for the goods purchased, the German consul would interfere to force them to pay their debts, and, in fact, would act as the agent of the merchants. Englishmen did not venture to give the same credit because they would not receive the same support from Her Majesty's Consuls, and, therefore, lost much of the custom of the natives.

Moreover, in such regions as the Ottoman Empire and the Far East, official influence was not uncommonly rewarded with commercial favors, and the temptation to exert it was, therefore, quite strong. When foreign governments did exert it, the policy of the British Foreign Office was to intervene as a neutralizing force. For example, in 1885 there were British complaints against the exercise of official influence to promote German commercial interests in Japan, resulting in the award of government contracts to German firms,[61] and Lord Salisbury authorized the

---

[60] *Ibid.*, Document 46.
[61] *Vide* Tokyo report in Appendix I.

Tokyo Embassy to lend its aid to British interests in cases where they were threatened by the interference of agents of foreign governments.[62] Similar complaints arose out of the struggle for commercial position in China, and in early 1886 the London Chamber of Commerce appealed to the Foreign Office for support at Peking, because Germans, French, Americans, and others enjoyed "the privilege and the advantage of being supported in their trade negotiations by the Ministers of their several countries." To counteract this it was of "the utmost importance" that British merchants should have the "firm support and assistance of Her Majesty's Representatives at Peking," without which there was "great risk of one of our most valuable trades, at a time of special activity, passing to a large extent into the hands of Germans and Americans."[63] Ten days earlier, however, Salisbury had dispatched an authorization to Peking to give support to British commercial interests "where the interference of the Representatives of foreign powers is exercised to their detriment";[64] and the London Chamber was presently notified of this action.[65]

It was the situation in China which gave rise to the first loud public outcry in England against these unorthodox tactics of foreign governments. The *Times*, early in January 1886, published sensational news of a scheme taken up by a German syndicate for placing a huge loan with the Chinese government, chiefly for the purchasing of war materials and railway stocks. The loan was characterized as a "bait" to secure control of the expenditure and thus to place the orders among members of the syndicate. Prince Bismarck, it was alleged, was so desirous for the success of the project that he had "put the services of the German diplomatic and consular officers at the disposal of the syndicate." The *Times* writer then went on to say that of late "bitter complaints" had been publicly made both in China and Japan against the adoption of a "wholly new method" by

[62] Commercial No. 16, Document 36.
[63] *Ibid.*, No. 1.
[64] *Ibid.*, No. 38.
[65] The *Times*, Feb. 24, 1886.

German officials, who had made themselves the "agents of their countrymen with native officials" and were scandalously "touting for orders."[66]

A wave of excitement and protest was stirred in commercial circles and the press by the *Times* article, the substance of which occasioned leading articles and numerous letters in the chief newspapers; and alarm over the danger to British trade was mingled with strong disapproval of "systems of procedure, hitherto . . . unknown to diplomatic and political life among ourselves."[67] The ambitious German enterprise fell through, but the affair helped to direct attention to the question of how the British foreign service might properly give more effective support to commerce.[68] The consuls, who were habitually pointing out the shortcomings of British merchants and their antiquated methods of trade, were now called upon to defend their own position with respect to commercial matters. There appeared considerable press comment suggesting that British consuls and diplomats might be less squeamish in the business of assisting trade. "We are far from asking," remarked the *Times*, "that the services of English diplomacy shall be used as Prince Bismarck uses those of Herr von Brandt in China, or those of other German representatives elsewhere, for securing contracts for English firms. . . . No one wishes, or expects, that the Government should supply the country with trade . . . but . . . we may fairly expect it to help trade, especially by stimulating the Consuls to greater activity and furnishing fuller reports of the trade and requirements of the different countries of the world. . . . And as regards the semi-civilized powers, which are just now awakening after the sleep of centuries . . . there is no reason why information should not be given to them as well as to ourselves. The efforts of British merchants and manufacturers to prove to the Chinese

[66] "A Danger to British Manufacturers," Jan. 2, 1886.

[67] J. E. C.'s letter in *Morning Post*, Jan. 5, 1886.

[68] The demand in commercial circles for more vigorous support of Commerce by the Foreign and Colonial Offices and the Board of Trade, at this time, may be seen in a strongly worded leader, "Government and Trade," in the *Chamber of Commerce Journal* for March 10, 1886.

that we can make ships and rails better and cheaper than the Germans may well be seconded from official quarters. To abstain from so doing, in the face of the desperate efforts of Germany and France, is magnificent, but it is not business."[69] A general demand, in fact, was raised, if not for the outright adoption of the tactics attributed to German officials, at least for what the *Pall Mall Gazette* called a *via media* between the "clouds" of *haute politique* and the "mud of official assistance to private enterprise."[70]

The whole question was brought up in Parliament on April 2, when Mr. McLaren, of Stafford, moved for the Government to consider the advisability of appointing special diplomatic agents in all foreign capitals "for the express purpose of promoting the extension of British commerce." British traders, he asserted, "were met in every market by what he could not help calling unfair competition by foreigners, assisted by the representatives of the countries to which they belong." He said it was notorious that the diplomatic and consular agents of other nations left no stone unturned in their endeavors to assist the industries of their respective countries, while British consuls did nothing of the kind to aid British industries.

If the existing state of things went on we should soon have a new "Continental System" raised up against us, which would be dangerous, if not fatal, to our trade. Occult German and other foreign influences were now at work all over the world for the purpose of diverting trade into their channels. France and Germany both took care that their foreign trade should be fostered as far as possible partly through their consuls abroad and partly through their higher placed officials. They did not hesitate to use the money of the tax payer in backsheesh in order to smooth the way for contracts with firms of their own nation. In many places that sort of diplomatic pressure was easily put on, and Governments like those of China, Japan, or Servia were quite willing to pay a higher price to please the minister of a particular nation. A great many instances of that kind of thing might have been seen in the newspapers in the last

[69] March 1, 1886, leading article.
[70] Jan. 4, 1886.

two or three months. The influences he had mentioned were at work all over the world, and the energy and ability of Prince Bismarck had even brought England within his toils. Instances had come under his observation of English consumers being influenced by means of consular influence to obtain their goods from German manufacturers. He also knew of an instance in which Prince Bismarck had actually written to a large importer in the United States to ask him if he would not see his way to purchase some of the goods he required from German firms. The same state of things existed in Eastern Europe, where the interests of German firms were being worked through the Consuls. He did not for a moment contend that the trade of this country be carried on by means of our Consuls abroad; but he asked that some means should be taken by which, at all events, our own manufacturers might be placed in as good a position as those of other countries. . . . From local inquiries which he had made with respect to Sweden, Norway, and Denmark, he found that English trade with these countries was entirely falling off. Every week boats came in from Germany laden with every class of goods which we used to supply. Agricultural machinery and everything in the way of machinery came from Germany to Scandinavia. Then as to ships. Two or three years ago China required two iron-clads. At that time there was only one Chinese Foreign Minister in Europe—the Minister at Berlin. One of our largest ship-building firms applied to the Chinese Minister at Berlin to be allowed to tender. They were allowed to tender for one, but heard nothing more about it. They were not allowed to tender for the other at all. The building of the iron-clads went to Germany, procured, beyond the shadow of a doubt, for Germany by the Berlin Foreign Office. . . . Not long since the *Times* Berlin Correspondent stated that two new belted cruisers were to be built for China by Germany, so that two new vessels which could be easily built on the Tyne, the Clyde, or the Mersey, had gone to Germany without any English firms having had a chance to compete for them. It was the same with regard to Japan. Two or three years ago Austria was building three iron-clads. It was thought that an English firm would have the armour-plating; but just as the contract was about to be signed they received an intimation that it would be supplied by a German house. In order to please the Sister Country of Germany the contract was snatched from English firms and given to an unknown competitor.

57

Formerly we had contracted for all the railways in Europe; but he had lately received a letter from a leading firm of railway contractors, showing how a contract in one of the Eastern States of Europe had been lost. The moment it was known that an English firm was likely to obtain the contract, the Austrian Consul . . . complained to our Foreign Office that their representative on the spot was interfering with foreign trade. The Foreign Office instantly recalled him . . . informing him that it was a most dangerous thing for the Representative of the English Foreign Office to interfere with foreign trade.[71]

Thus did Mr. McLaren paint his cheerless picture of English business being captured through the "unfair" tactics of foreign governments, while the Foreign Office almost supinely watched it go; and in the debate which followed other voices were raised in criticism of diplomacy's attitude toward trade. Mr. C. Palmer said Germany "was running England so close in regard to manufactures and commerce that he feared, unless we took a lesson from it in the assistance offered to industry and commerce, we should certainly see ourselves behind in the race." Mr. Hutton, of Manchester, said that for the last ten years, and especially during the last two years, he had, as president of the Manchester Chamber of Commerce, "impressed upon the Foreign Office the necessity of taking more interest in the manufactures and trade of this country." He held it to be a ground of complaint that in so able a body as the foreign service "there were many men who were so useless as regards commerce." The consuls, he felt, should not be blamed as they were trying to do their duty abroad, but they met with little support and encouragement from home; what was clearly required was a "greater amount of earnestness and determination on the part of those who were charged with the administration of this country." Mr. Lawrence, of Liverpool, drew attention to the Cameroons and Zanzibar as instances of Germans capturing trade through the inaction of the Foreign Office. The German acquisitions in the Cameroons, he said, had caused the city of Liverpool to suffer to the extent of a million pounds a year, although he admitted this "might be exaggerated." As

[71] Hansard, 3rd. S., vol. 304, pp. 609-13.

for Zanzibar, here the Germans had been allowed to steal a march, and the "trade of Africa and the great central places there through the activity of Prince Bismarck had gone to Germany. What was wanted was energy, pluck, courage, and resource at the Foreign Office." Mr. Sutherland, of Greenock, declared that the fault lay "with the spirit which prevailed at the Foreign Office in regard to commercial affairs." No voice, however, was raised in defense of using diplomats and consuls as actual "touters" for trade. Mr. Goschen, of Edinburgh, warned against the dangers of embarking upon "a new system totally contrary to the traditions of diplomacy," and defended the Foreign Office against its critics. The time had passed, he asserted, when the Foreign Office regarded British merchants as "troublesome people." Within proper limits he favored improvement of diplomatic and consular aid to commerce, but he hoped the House would not encourage

the idea that either Prince Bismarck, . . . or any French, or Belgian, or Austrian Ministers ought to be the guides of this country or of our diplomacy abroad—our diplomacy which is looked to to promote British interests, but at the same time to hold as high as possible the standard of British honour.

Mr. Bourke, of Lyn Regis, formerly in the Foreign Office, "could not imagine anything more inconvenient and derogatory to the character of the diplomatic service than that our Consuls and Diplomats abroad should be turned into commercial agents." Under-Secretary Bryce, speaking for the Government, told the House that the Foreign Office had already taken the subject of assistance to trade under advisement and investigation, and, while minimizing the importance of diplomatic aid in commercial success, he denied that there existed any longer in the Foreign Office a desire on the part of anyone to "snub" commerce.

If there were any traces of it yet lingering among our Diplomatists, such traces were fast disappearing; and it was now acknowledged within the Foreign Office that one of its clearest duties was to promote the interests of British commerce to the best of its power by all legitimate means.

These words of Mr. Bryce are of capital interest, for in spite of the strong feeling for diplomatic propriety, they announced a further departure from the mid-century *haute politique* tradition toward the commercial diplomacy of the neo-mercantilist age.[72]

The debate in the House of Commons occasioned additional press discussion of the subject of diplomatic and consular assistance to trade. While disdaining any suggestion for adopting the "new methods" of rival nations, the *Times* declared that the legitimate extension of British commerce was

an object which no representative of this country should be suffered by the Foreign Office to neglect. . . . Diplomatists must not be allowed to think that commercial interests are beneath their notice. . . . The Foreign Office should be required to take commercial and industrial interests as seriously as it has hitherto taken purely diplomatic and political interests. . . . Without disparaging *haute politique,* we are safe in saying that there are hardly any affairs of England in foreign countries which are more important than commercial affairs.[73]

The *Morning Post* observed that, although the new procedure of foreign diplomatists and consuls was incompatible with the "dignity and independence" of the British foreign service, yet there existed a "wide margin between the reserve and the indifference of our agents and what was termed last night the 'touting' of the agents of foreign states"; it was, therefore,

a matter for serious consideration whether further efforts should not be made by the Foreign Office to secure for British traders a better acquaintance with the various markets of the world. We have been taunted since the days of the First Napoleon with being a nation of shopkeepers, so we could hardly be reproached if we acted, to some extent at least, in conformity with the character assigned to us.[74]

The Cobdenite *Daily News* not unnaturally rather deprecated the McLaren motion, although welcoming any means which Parlia-

[72] Hansard, 3rd. S., vol. 304, pp. 613-43.
[73] Leader of April 3, 1886.
[74] Leader of April 3, 1886.

ment might suggest for the improvement of trade. The German "pushing" of trade was characterized as the "crude policy of beginners and ... not to be imitated by the first commercial country of the world."[75]

The prominence which had thus been given to this question had contributed to stimulating action at the Foreign Office early in the year. In February Lord Rosebery began a general inquiry into it, soliciting opinion widely from leading business men, commercial associations, chambers of commerce, and Foreign Office representatives abroad.[76] The sum of opinions received embodied complaints which were reducible to two: first, that the traditions of British diplomacy were unfriendly or, at best, indifferent to the promotion of commercial interests, and that there existed a certain disposition to snub traders; second, that the information regarding commercial matters which was transmitted from abroad was not of the right kind, arrived too late, and was not published in an accessible and attractive form. The first of these complaints the Foreign Office presumed to deny; for the second some foundation was admitted. As for the suggestions elicited for the better promotion of commerce by the foreign service, these were found to be more numerous than acceptable and fruitful. Mr. Bryce was able to draft a list of some twenty-eight specific recommendations, taken not only from solicited sources but also from the press and Parliamentary speeches. Some of these he characterized as obviously useful, others as obviously inapplicable, while others had already been acted upon. In a circular letter to the chambers of commerce he then defined the views of the Government respecting the extent to which the various proposals could be adopted; and in an elaborate memorandum, circularized among diplomats and consuls, he dealt at length with the proposals and sought to redefine the proper scope of action for Foreign Office agents in commercial matters.[77] The tenor of both documents was in defense of established policies, and it

[75] *Ibid.*
[76] Documents in Commercial No. 16, 1886.
[77] These two documents appear as Appendices 1 & 4 in Commercial No. 5, 1897.

was asserted that there were "very few possible lines of action" which had not already been opened up; but it is easy to detect, in the memorandum especially, the approval of a more generous latitude of discretion in introducing and recommending merchants to foreigners, and in using exceptional pressure to secure "equal favour and open competition" for British business. Greater promptness in transmitting from abroad current commercial news was ordered, as well as increased activity by diplomats and consuls in affording information and help to Englishmen seeking to do business in foreign lands. Certain consuls were specifically requested to send home full and detailed descriptions, with accompanying samples for exhibition, of manufactured goods for which a special demand existed in their respective districts; and this practice was recommended to all. Moreover, greater encouragement was promised to members of the foreign service who mastered commercial questions and acquired special usefulness to the trading community.

Viewed in the large, the Rosebery-Bryce inquiry of 1886 was not sterile of important results. The Foreign Office undertook to clear itself of the charge of inattention to trade by an effective reorganization of the system of publishing commercial reports, so as to eliminate tardiness, uselessness, and inaccessibility.[78] It also coöperated with the Board of Trade to launch the *Board of Trade Journal,* a useful organ for supplying timely and adequate commercial information. Thus steps were taken to redress one of the chief complaints of the trading community. But more significant was the clear and emphatic acknowledgment by the Foreign Office of the duty of looking after commercial interests with resourcefulness and alacrity. The new business world was fashioning a new diplomacy, and the *haute politique* tradition of Whitehall was going down.

[78] The *Times,* March 5, 1887, observed: "It is impossible to examine the two series of reports on commercial questions from our diplomatic and consular officers which are now being published without being convinced that the discussions in Parliament and the press last year on the duties which these officers owe to trade have been productive of benefit to the community."

6

Several other circumstances in the new world of commercial rivalry remain to receive attention. They relate to Great Britain's leadership in shipping and to the state of her valuable entrepôt trade. With respect to the former there was little ground for apprehension: British ship-owners could view the world with an assurance of secure leadership which was no longer possible for mercantile and industrial interests. It is true that foreign shipping was going forward, but as yet not fast enough to present a serious challenge to the mercantile marine of Great Britain. An examination of comparative tonnages of the principal merchant navies of the world, over the twenty years from 1870 to 1890, certainly suggests no weakening of British supremacy in the ocean carrying trade. Rather do the statistics indicate the opposite.[79]

Nevertheless, the horizon was not unclouded, and British shipping had some worries and grievances other than the inevitable scarcity of traffic in periods of commercial depression. The merchant fleets of other nations, if still far behind the British in development, were growing fast enough to promise a real competition in the future. "Without a doubt," a representative of the North of England Steamship Owners Association told the Royal

[79] In this connection the statistics of Suez Canal traffic are particularly interesting, for whereas in 1870-74 British ships represented 72.11 per cent of the total tonnage of ships passing through the Canal, in 1885-89 British vessels represented 76.82 per cent of the total traffic. Moreover, there was a continued increase in Great Britain's percentage of the shipping which entered and cleared in the ports of France, Germany, and the United States; while in the foreign shipping of the United Kingdom the British percentage of the whole rose from 63 per cent in 1870-74 to 70.4 per cent in 1885-89. In the trade with the colonies and dominions British ships held their grip on nearly ninety per cent of the traffic, and the same was true of the United Kingdom coasting trade, barely more than two per cent of which was carried in foreign bottoms until after 1890. (B F T I, Cd. 4954, 1909, pp. 96-101, 108-113, 123.) Yet both the British coasting and colonial trades, in contrast with the policies of other powers, were open to foreign ships on equal terms with British. Well might the Royal Commission state "that British shipping has as large a share as formerly of the carrying trade of the world." (Report, Section 22.) The export trade might languish and the entrepôt trade dissolve, but British ships continued to transport a vastly preponderant share of the world's exchangeable commodities.

Commission, "foreign nations are increasing their tonnage more
and more, . . . so that whilst in the past, we may not have suffered
much, it looks very much as though from now forward we are
going to do so."[80] Nothing was plainer than the fact that other
nations were bending great efforts towards this end, and with
generous government assistance. Subsidized shipping was characteristic of the revived mercantilism, and the eirhties witnessed
an extensive development of it. France, in 1881, enacted a law
granting substantial construction and navigation bounties, and
between 1860 and 1887 steadily increased postal subventions to
shipping companies from six to twenty-seven million francs. An
Italian law of 1886 inaugurated generous construction bounties;
and other maritime powers, if they did not offer bounties, gave
aid to shipping by enlarged postal or admiralty subventions,
which usually operated as concealed subsidies. The case of Germany commands special notice. Here shipping received its first
big favor from the Government when shipbuilding materials were
placed on the free list of the 1879 tariff. Two years later Bismarck memorialized the German parliament on the French law of
1881, raising the question "whether, under the given conditions,
Germany's shipping and commerce will be able to continue their
prosperous development in the face of the state-aided competition
of other nations." Four years later, in 1885, he carried through
a bill designed to secure the establishment of direct steamer service between Germany and the Far East. Contracts for the carrying of mails to Australia and Eastern Asia, as well as for a branch
line from Trieste to Alexandria, were let to the North German
Lloyd, which was able, through the generous postal subventions,
to open the new services.[81]

It is thus evident the British shipping interests were on the
threshold of a competition with subsidized foreign vessels. W. R.
Price, an underwriter for Lloyds, told the Royal Commission that

[80] Evidence of Mr. A. Scholefield, 10,830.

[81] This whole subject of subsidized shipping is competently treated in
Royal Mecker's *History of Shipping Subsidies,* 1905. Great Britain, it may
be noted, paid no navigation or construction bounties, but granted postal and
admiralty subventions, which were, however, considerably lower at this
time than in the middle of the century.—Meeker, pp. 1-42.

foreign shipping bounties would "unquestionably" work to the prejudice of British owners. The Italian bounties, he said, were bound to have a detrimental effect on British shipbuilding "for the simple reason that a ship built in Italy gets a bounty . . . which is more than equivalent to the difference in cost between building in this country and building in Italy"; and as for the German subsidizing of direct lines to China and Australia, this, he held, "must be manifestly to injure British shipping very materially."[82] Richard Cattarns, manager of the General Steam Navigation Company, testified to "an increasing competition, especially with Germany"; and although, like other witnesses, he was inclined to minimize the effectiveness of the bounty system for promoting commercial navies, he said that "with Germany it may be a different thing. They are a more pushing and business-like and enterprising people, and it remains to be seen whether it will seriously affect our carrying trade." In another connection Mr. Cattarns characterized the German competition as "a more serious affair than had yet happened."[83]

An additional complaint of shipowners arose from the circumstance that foreign vessels loading in British ports were not subjected to the Plimsoll load-line and other regulations of the Board of Trade, which, being imposed on British ships, caused special expense and trouble for their owners. "Owners of foreign ships," declared some of the Royal Commissioners, "thus not only obtain the bounties or subsidies . . . but also enjoy in our ports a latitude in regard to loading, and an exemption from other troublesome regulations, which give them an unfair advantage in competition."[84] The testimony of witnesses from the shipping trade was eloquent of the deep resentment which shipping

[82] Evidence, 10,087, 10,108.

[83] Evidence, 11,326-11,333, 11,436. On the whole, it does not appear that as yet much damage had been done to British shipping by new mercantilist navigation policies, but there was point to a statement in the minority report of the Royal Commission: "The bounties and subsidies now given by several foreign nations . . . have probably not yet produced their full effect on the interests of our shipbuilders and shipowners. It is clear, however, that they cannot but suffer by being exposed to subsidized foreign competition."— Section 126.

[84] *Ibid.*

65

circles bore towards the supervising regulations of the Board of Trade. "Benevolent but very mischievous in practice" were the words Mr. Price, of Lloyd's, used to describe it.[85] The Board's authority to impose a limit to loading, to stop or condemn unseaworthy craft, and to impose light dues on merchant vessels appeared to work an advantage to foreign ships which were free from these burdens. Thus Mr. Cattarns declared that the Germans were deriving an advantage from these regulations in the North Sea traffic.[86] G. Renwick, of the North of England S. S. Owners' Association, said his firm was "seriously considering the question of placing all our steamers under the Turkish flag" because of the Board of Trade.[87] Another member of the same group stated:

I can assure you that it is a subject under serious contemplation amongst a great many shipowners whether it is not better for them to pack up bag and baggage, and to go and register their ships abroad and to go and live abroad to manage them; that is to say, to go and naturalize themselves as foreign subjects in order to manage them free abroad instead of here.[88]

John Burke, a Belfast shipbroker, drew attention to the capture by Norwegian ships of most of the trade in carrying Canadian timber to the United Kingdom, due chiefly to the transfer of British vessels to Norwegian ownership to escape the Plimsoll line and Board of Trade supervision.[89] How far the Board's regulations actually handicapped British shippers it would be hard to say, but probably the resentment against government supervision of business was rather out of proportion to any disadvantage imposed upon the shipowners. The unweakened preponderance of British ships in the foreign, colonial, and coasting trades, despite the progress of state-aided competition, certainly points that way.

Developments in the shipping world and the weakening of Brit-

[85] Evidence, 10,128.
[86] Ibid., 11,430.
[87] Ibid., 10,916.
[88] Ibid., 13,902.
[89] Ibid., 10,439-40.

ain's entrepôt trade were closely related. Diminishing reëxports, although probably not yet cutting British shipping, did increase foreign rivalry, for to use the words of one of the witnesses quoted above, "directly the trade gets into the course of going direct to destinations to particular countries, naturally the foreign flag competes with us."[90] And on the other hand, the more foreign nations developed their shipping, and the more British ocean steamers called at Continental ports, the more European countries tended to supply themselves with overseas goods directly instead of buying through British middlemen. Trade statistics, consular reports, and the testimony of witnesses before the Royal Commission make it very clear that England's entrepôt trade was in a state of partial dissolution. Especially was there a decline in the export of foreign and colonial goods to European countries. Between 1875 and 1885 the value of reëxports to Belgium fell from eight to six millions, to France from twelve to eight millions, to Russia from three to two millions; the Spanish trade fell off about fifteen per cent, the Italian forty per cent, and the Greek and Roumanian trades were halved. Part of this fall in the value of reëxports to Europe is accounted for by declining prices, but much was due to the steady progress of direct trade between places of production and consumption and to the inevitable tendency of entrepôt trade to seek its way toward the great centers of manufacture.[91]

Evidence of the eating away of British reëxport trade by the growth of direct commerce abounds in the consular reports. A Stockholm report, for example, drew attention to recent importations of cotton and pork direct from America, "thus diminishing the transit trade of Great Britain in these articles." From Gothenburg it was reported that

lines of Swedish steamers now regularly ply between this port direct to the principal ports in Holland, Belgium, France, Spain, and Portugal, all such trade having previously passed through British ports, while the Germans have lately opened up a direct line of steamers

[90] Mr. Cattarns. Evidence, 11,341.
[91] Mr. C. E. Collyer's testimony. Evidence, 10,736-39.

between this port and German ports to the United States of America, taking and bringing back passengers and produce which likewise hitherto passed through British ports.

A dispatch from Norway pointed out the establishment of a regular line of steamers between Christiania and New York which had "diverted some of the trade which formerly went through England." An Antwerp report dwelt upon a direct trade "springing up of late between Belgium and various British colonies," a movement so marked that "some of the principal steamship companies have found it to their interest to send their large ocean steamers to Antwerp to compete for Belgian and other Continental produce for export." The consul-general at Hamburg drew attention to the fact that British colonial goods were now coming in large quantities direct to Hamburg, instead of by way of England, a movement which he thought was likely to increase; and an Ecuador report pointed out a diversion of the cocoa and ivory nut markets from London to Hamburg.[92] Thirteen important steamship companies trading to all parts of the world had come into existence at Hamburg by 1890, and a consular report of 1891 from here declared:

The produce of Brazil and South America, east and west coasts, Africa, China and Japan, Australia, formerly brought by British ships are now brought direct to Hamburg through the enterprise of these lines, an enterprise which it must be remembered has sprung up almost in a decade.[93]

Other similar illustrations, touching many of the chief ports of Europe, might be offered to show how railways and harbor developments were conspiring with steamship lines to link Continental Europe by direct ties to the overseas world, and thus to undermine the position of the British middleman. The *Chamber of Commerce Journal* remarked as early as 1884:

After having succeeded . . . in producing their own manufactures, our European customers are endeavoring, with much prospect of suc-

[92] *Vide* Appendix I.
[93] Misc. Series 237. Report on Progress of Trade of Hamburg, 1841-1890.

cess, to become the carriers of their own raw materials and of the goods which they export in competition with our own. The development of railway and banking facilities on the Continent has contributed considerably to the means of working this change; the opening of the Suez Canal and the Alpine tunnels has facilitated the diversion of traffic from British ports, and today the simultaneous efforts of the French, Belgians, Germans, Italians, and Austrians to carry their own trade under their own flags direct to their own quays, have become successful to a degree which is, for us, of the most serious moment.[94]

One of the most striking examples of diverted entrepôt trade was that in raw silk. In 1872 Great Britain reëxported more than 3,000,000 lbs. of this commodity. She sent nearly 200,000 lbs. to Belgium, almost 2,500,000 lbs. to France, about 72,000 lbs. to Spain, and some 158,000 lbs. to the United States. By 1886 her total entrepôt trade in raw silk had dwindled to barely half a million lbs., a decline of more than eighty per cent. The Belgian trade had dropped to 26,000, the French to less than 450,000, the Spanish to 17,000, and the American to 19,000 lbs.[95] "London," wrote the Tokyo consul, "has ceased to be the distributing center of the silk trade."[96] Among other branches of the reëxport trade which diminished conspicuously were: spirits, which between 1872 and 1886 fell from 3,663,107 to 2,361,434 gallons; wine, which dropped from 2,036,277 to 1,142,287 gallons; coffee, which dropped from 1,416,694 to 786,709 cwt.; raw cotton, which sank from 2,437,545 to 1,766,590 cwt.; cocoanut oil, which fell from 251,627 to 98,450 cwt., and unmanufactured tobacco, which dwindled from 15,553,326 to 5,840,084 lbs. British consignments of coffee to Russia dropped from eleven to three mil-

[94] Oct. 10, 1884.
[95] Annual Statement of Trade of United Kingdom.
[96] *Vide* Appendix I. Mr. Price, of Lloyd's, who had formerly been connected with a large eastern silk concern, told the Royal Commission that the firm's silk used invariably to come to London to be sold in the London market. "Some of it was transferred to the Continent, again to Lyons, and those places, but in the last three or four years that I was connected with it the silk went direct either to Marseilles or to Venice, and was then distributed over the Continent, and never came here at all."—Evidence, 10,072.

lion lbs., to Sweden from five to three and a half million, to Germany from thirty-five to less than two million, to Holland from sixty-one to less than three million, to Belgium from nine to four million, to France from seven to four and a half million, and to Italy from ten to three million. Plainly the British middleman in the coffee trade had lost nearly all his business. A better grip on the reëxport trade in raw cotton was retained, although French purchases of raw cotton in the British market fell off about eight per cent and Dutch purchases dropped about seventy-five per cent. As for unmanufactured tobacco, it is a striking fact that Great Britain, in 1886, sent less than ten per cent as much to Germany as she had sent in 1872, while her export of this commodity to Holland dropped eighty per cent and to Belgium more than fifty per cent.[97]

Among the several causes operating to diminish the British entrepôt trade one of decisive importance was the Suez Canal. Down to 1869, when this highway was opened, most of the trade between the Orient and Western Europe toiled slowly and uncertainly around the Cape of Good Hope, at an expenditure in time of from six to eight months for the round voyage. The contingencies attendant upon such lengthened voyages and service, such as the possible interruption of commerce by war, or failure of crops in remote countries, which could not easily be anticipated, required that vast stores of Eastern products should be always kept on hand at one spot in Europe where the consumers of such commodities could speedily supply themselves. That spot, by reason of its geographical position, shipping supremacy, and leadership in Eastern commerce, was England; and out of this situation came naturally a vast system of warehousing in and distribution from England. Then came the Canal, opening a new (or better, reviving an old) and shorter sea route to the Far East. It synchronized with the displacement of sailing vessels by steamers, and a tremendous stimulus was thus given to direct commerce between Eastern Asia and the ports of Southern and Eastern Europe. The Commercial Revolution was reversed. The Canal did

---

[97] Annual Statement of Trade of United Kingdom.

to nineteenth-century England what Vasco da Gama's voyage did to sixteenth-century Italy: it cut much of the ground from under the position of the British middleman. Trieste, Venice, Genoa, Marseilles, Odessa, and other south European ports were enabled to increase greatly their direct trade with distant lands, and instead of buying Asiatic goods in the British market they imported more and more directly from the places of origin. At the same time there took place the establishment of telegraphic communication between India and China and the markets of the West. This made it possible for dealers and consumers

to adjust to a nicety their supplies of commodities to varying demand, and with the reduction of the time of the voyage to thirty days or less, there was no longer any necessity of laying up great stores of Eastern commodities in Europe; and with the termination of this necessity the India warehouse and distribution system, with all the labour and all the capital and banking incident to it, substantially passed away. Europe, and to some extent the United States, ceased to go to England for its supplies. If Austria wanted anything of Indian product, it arrived en route, by the Suez Canal, at Trieste; if Italy, at Venice or Genoa; if France, at Marseilles; if Spain, at Cadiz.[98]

This was the state of affairs as it appeared to an observer in 1888:[99]

Formerly we were the great . . . distributors and the great warehousemen of the world. Our country was the point on which the great passenger traffic impinged from America and from our Colonies, and from which passengers distributed themselves over the Continent of Europe. The products of the world as a general rule came to English ports, and from English ports were distributed to their various markets. All this has much changed. . . . About twenty years ago all the silk that was manufactured or consumed in Europe was brought

[98] David A. Wells, "The Great Depression," *Contemporary Review*, Aug., 1887, vol. 52, p. 295 *et seq*. The effect of the Canal on British entrepôt trade is here very well discussed. This significant shift in trade was discerned by the Royal Commission: "There was a general agreement . . . that owing to the Suez Canal our entrepôt trade had fallen off."—Section 22 of Report.

[99] H. M. Hozier, "England's Real Peril," *Macmillan's Magazine*, June, 1888, pp. 179-183.

to England from the East, mostly in a raw state, and was thence distributed to continental mills. Notwithstanding the increased consumption in Europe, silk now coming to England for distribution is only about one-eighth of the quantity that came here some twelve years ago. This is one single example of an Oriental product. The same diversion in our distributing trade can be traced in almost every other commodity. Many people believe that the opening of the Suez Canal has caused this diminution of our distributing trade, and it cannot be denied that the Suez Canal has done much to divert Oriental trade from their country, and to send goods direct through the Canal to the Continental ports, where they are consumed, or where they can be placed on railways and forwarded without break of bulk to their destinations. But whatever the Suez Canal may have done to divert trade in Oriental goods such as tea or silk, it cannot account for the diversion of the trade coming from America. Yet we find the same diversion of American products which formerly came to England for distribution. With cotton the same result is found, and with coffee from Brazil. Nor does the diversion of these articles merely demonstrate that our distributing trade is being lost to us: it also shows that the manufacturers of England now permit the raw material of their industries to be sent straight to the factories of their competitors on the Continent. It shows that the great manufactures of the world are being transferred from England to Belgium, France, Germany, and even to Portugal and Spain. In the train of these manufactures are rapidly following all the complex and complicated businesses which are the handmaidens of commerce. For instance, the financial business which used to centre in London is being transferred to Paris, Antwerp, and Germany, mainly because the goods to which this business relates are now consigned to continental countries instead of as formerly being brought to England to be distributed therefrom. It is impossible to calculate in pounds, shillings and pence how much wealth is being lost to the country by this diversion of trade.

Chapter III
BRITAIN FALTERS AND
GERMANY ADVANCES

TO THOSE who seek causes for political estrangements between modern nations in the development of commercial antagonism there must appear a high significance in the fact that the first serious disturbance of cordial relations between England and Germany was coincident with the dawning realization in Great Britain that her most formidable competitor in the struggle for markets was her "cousin" across the North Sea. Englishmen and Germans had not been wasting much affection on each other since the refounding of the German Empire, but official relations were excellent until the Bismarck-Granville quarrel over African colonies in 1884-85, the first spectacular clash of economic rivals who had begun to crowd and jostle one another in many parts of the world. It must have been discerned in the preceding chapters that the Germans were, of all Great Britain's trade rivals, the most frequently encountered, especially in the old world. The Royal Commission found that the severity of competition was "especially notable in the case of Germany," that German business enterprise and perseverance were being felt in every part of the world, and that in the actual production of commodities the British had now but few, if any, advantages over them; while in knowledge of markets, desire to meet the tastes of consumers, determination and tenacity in gaining and maintaining a foothold, they appeared to be gaining ground on British business.[1]

The German was beginning, indeed, to be a very conspicuous and annoying person in British eyes. He was touring the world

[1] Report, section 75. For an interesting contemporary British view of Germany's recent climb to industrial prominence, her ability to compete with England, her superior education and boundless energy, etc., vide *Saturday Review* article, "Germany's Industrial Progress," Dec. 19, 1885, vol. 60, pp. 805-6.

with his sample case, his accommodating manners, his earnest zeal, his resourceful methods of trade, and his extraordinary knowledge of languages. He was gathering desirable orders even in England and throughout the Empire, under Britain's very nose, and the fact was being noticed with rising apprehension in the United Kingdom. Germany's upward climb in industry and commerce was a prominent topic of public discussion in England by 1885; it was being noticed in Parliamentary debates and forming the subject of leading articles in the press. The newspapers began about 1885 to carry a great deal of news about German commercial progress and to publish numerous extracts from consular reports contrasting British and German trade.[2] In 1885 German imports into Holland for the first time exceeded those of the United Kingdom, and this lead was held for several years. Swedish imports from Germany, likewise for the first time, surpassed the value of purchases from Great Britain; and in Roumania German trade leaped ahead of British. In Spain and Italy the years of 1885-86, years of acute depression in England, saw a sharp forward movement of German trade simultaneous with a serious drop in the imports from Great Britain.[3] In 1885 the Reichstag passed the ship-subsidy legislation for steamer lines to the Far East, and early in 1886 occurred the sensational bid of the German syndicate for a loan to China. In 1886, too, came the agitation over trade marks, directed chiefly against Germany, and almost simultaneously the outcry against German diplomatic and consular methods of aiding commerce. The Germans were directly charged, in fact, with responsibility for the economic depression in Great Britain. "Apart from general causes," the *Spectator* declared, "which may or may not have their day and cease to be, there can be little doubt that the salient fact of the industrial world . . . is the commercial uprising of the German people; and to this is due, perhaps as much as to any more general or recondite cause, the continued depression of British industry. For it would seem that had it not been that the new or

[2] For example, *vide* four columns of extracts from consular reports in *Times*, Oct. 12, 1886, and two columns, May 4, 1887.

[3] Cf. tables in Statistical Abstract for Foreign Countries.

neutral markets of the world had been violently attacked and al-most taken by storm by German competition in the last half dozen years the depression would ere now have passed away."[4]

A British workman wrote to the *Times* that one could hardly pick up a newspaper without seeing something about "this Ger-man craze," and that "we are constantly being told that they are supplanting us in everything."[5] Nor was the intrusion of his goods, his ships, and his flag the only transgression of the Ger-man; he was coming himself to take the job of the Englishman at home. The German clerk in the English commercial house was only less conspicuous than the cutlery, paper, and woolens sent over from his native land. A writer in the *National Review* in 1885 declared that the Germans in England were underestimated at 250,000, and that by common saying, although absurdly ex-aggerated, half the members of the Stock Exchange were Ger-mans.[6] The London Chamber of Commerce in 1887 collected evi-dence to show that 35 per cent of the leading city firms employed foreigners who were almost invariably Germans, the reasons be-ing their knowledge of languages, superior commercial usefulness and willingness to work for a pittance salary with a chance to learn the business.[7] Walter Besant pictured such a German clerk in one of his novels. "We are cheap, we German clerks," says Dittmer Bock, "You say so. Mein Gott! You will find us dear. We are learning your trade; we will find out all your customers and your correspondents; we learn your profits and we undersell you." The *Morning Post* in a leading article declared that the growing practice of employing these clerks had "awakened an anxiety approaching to alarm."[8]

[4] "English, German and Chinese Trade," Aug. 14, 1886, vol. 59, pt. 2, pp. 1077-79.
[5] Oct. 14, 1887.
[6] Vol. 5, p. 259, C. E. Dawkins, "The German Abroad." The Germans evidently seemed much more numerous than they actually were, for the estimate of 250,000 was grossly exaggerated. There were only 53,591 Germans in the United Kingdom, according to the 1891 Census.
[7] The *Times,* July 13, 1887; see especially the leader.
[8] November 24, 1887. The German clerks were also discussed in an in-teresting leader in the *Daily Telegraph,* Nov. 25, 1887.

Thus in a multitude of directions, the vigorous new Germany was quietly encroaching on the business empire of Great Britain when the first imperialist collision between these powers took place in the middle eighties. A thousand British and German paths were crossing. The German trade peril was rising before England's gaze, and the succeeding years, which witnessed the increase of political differences and a growing coolness between the nations, saw also a commercial duel of mounting intensity. From Hamburg, in the year of the accession of William II to the German imperial crown, the British Consul-General surveyed the rising position of Germany in world trade:[9]

In every quarter of the globe Germany is extending with steady and successful persistence its commercial activity. . . . German cloth finds its way now to the markets of Morocco; the Japanese are becoming good customers for German cloth and buckskin; the markets of Yokohama reveal the fact that one-sixth of the trade in grey shirtings . . . and 60 to 75 per cent respectively of that in half-silk satins and Italian cloth is German, to say nothing of flannels and printed cotton stuffs; to Hiogo-Osaka go cotton velvets; Tunis takes German jewellery, lamps, and other manufactured and cotton goods find their way to Port Elizabeth in South Africa; and Manila takes cheap cotton goods. The value of the exchange of goods between the United States and Germany has increased within 10 years from 32,000,000 dol. to 69,000,000 dol., and Germany now claims the second place in the trade of that country. Similarly in Porto Alegre the French importation has been reduced from 30 to 7 per cent of the total import, and Germany claims to have added to this extent to her trade there. It is asserted that in Venezuela German influence is spreading, and a company is about to construct a railway from Caraccas to Victoria. In Europe the exportation has risen, especially to Norway and Denmark.

All these facts go to show that, notwithstanding British manufacturers and merchants may pooh-pooh the possibility of their being cut out by German trade, it is nevertheless slowly but surely making its way, and attaining proportions the more alarming from its silent and undemonstrative progress. . . . If Great Britain still holds, as she undoubtedly does, the larger share of the world's commerce,

[9] Report from Hamburg, 1888; Annual Series No. 729.

her merchants and manufacturers must not despise small beginnings; and if they allow their competitors to outdo them in small markets, the total results may prove more disastrous than they could ever think possible.

2

The emergence of Germany as a serious commercial rival of Great Britain was relatively sudden. While the foundations of German industry had been extensively laid down in the fifties and sixties, and German merchants had been silently working many of their wares into foreign markets before 1870, the great impetus to economic progress came with political unification. But even this was cut short quickly by the deflation of 1873, and German business was retarded in the seventies; so that there were few auspicious stars on the commercial horizon of the new Empire before 1880. At Philadelphia in 1876 German products made a poor showing and were even denounced by the chief German commissioner to the Centennial Exposition.[10] In 1877 a British consul at Danzig drew a most unpromising picture of the outlook for German commerce, expressing the view that "the prospect of exporting German manufactured goods at remunerative prices has become a poor one, or at least one that cannot be relied upon in future."[11] How shortsighted was this view the world was soon to learn. Before the seventies were out Germany had armed herself with Bismarck's tariff, emerged from the great depression, and begun to draw notice to herself in the fight for markets. An impetus was given to trade expansion which brought the Germans swiftly into second rank among modern business nations and enabled them to challenge some of the strongest branches of British trade.

The German industrial advance toward the level of the United Kingdom was almost sensationally rapid. Germany's pig iron output, during the last twenty years of the century, rose from 40 to 78 per cent of that of Great Britain, while her consumption of this commodity climbed from 48 to 91 per cent. Producing less than half as much steel as Britain in 1880-84, Germany soared

[10] *Vide Times* for July 24, 1876.
[11] A. & P., 1877, vol. 34, p. 429.

ahead of her rival by 20 per cent before the end of the century. Her coal production, as compared with that of British mines, rose in this period from 33 to 44 per cent, her coal consumption from 22 to 39 per cent, her wool consumption from 65 to 80 per cent, and her cotton consumption from 22 to 39 per cent. British industry appears almost stationary as compared with this German rate of growth. An expanding export trade resulted inevitably from this accumulated manufacturing power, and the idea of worldwide commerce began to take hold of the German mind. "A few years ago," wrote the British consul at Frankfort in 1899, German opinion troubled little about the great questions of international economics. Today the idea of a commercial policy for the conquest of the world completely holds the masses."[12] The value of German exports in 1880-84 was 65 per cent of that of United Kingdom exports, and in 1895-99 this figure had risen to 78.[13] Similarly, exported manufactures climbed from 44 to 59 per cent, exported iron and steel goods from 42 to 61 per cent, exported machinery from 23 to 36 per cent, exported cotton yarns and manufactures from 7 to 15 per cent, and exported woolens from 61 to 64 per cent of British figures for these branches of trade.[14] This forward movement of German exports was exhibited chiefly in the conquest of those Continental markets to which German producers had advantageous access, but overseas markets were also vigorously attacked; and this gave a strong impetus to German shipping. The merchant marine increased in size proportionately with the swelling of exports. Germany's sea traffic to Black Sea ports more than doubled between 1885 and 1895, while over the same period the increase to Atlantic ports of the United States was 70 per cent, and to Brazil 75 per cent; traffic to South American Pacific ports grew more than 100 per cent, while to the Atlantic ports of Africa the increase was almost threefold; traffic to Cape Colony more than tripled; to

[12] Annual Series 2122.

[13] For an interesting comparison of British and German export trade in 1897 see Annual Series 2040, Report by Mr. H. Gastrell, Comm. Attaché at Berlin.

[14] B F T I, Cd. 4954, pp. 8, 9.

the East Indies, Australia, and the Pacific Islands there was an equal increase, while to the Asiatic Far East the growth was nearly fourfold. The major shipping companies of Hamburg increased in number from four to ten between 1886 and 1896, and their total share capital mounted from £1,462,500 to £3,273,750.[15] The following table will show roughly the comparative industrial, commercial, and shipping advance of Germany and Great Britain between 1880 and 1900 :[16]

Annual average of:	UNITED KINGDOM		GERMANY	
	1880–84	1895–99	1880–84	1895–99
Domestic exports......	£ 234,300,000	237,800,000	152,800,000	181,000,000
Exported mfres........	£ 206,400,000	199,600,000	91,200,000	116,400,000
Exported iron, steel and mfres. thereof.......	£ 27,600,000	25,200,000	11,500,000	15,300,000
Exported machinery...	£ 11,500,000	17,300,000	2,700,000	6,200,000
Exported cotton yarn and mfres........	£ 75,900,000	65,900,000	5,000,000	10,000,000
Exported woolens.....	£ 18,500,000	16,500,000	11,300,000	10,500,000
Coal production.......	T.156,400,000	201,900,000	51,300,000	89,300,000
Steel output.........	T. 1,800,000	4,200,000	800,000	5,100,000
Pig iron output.......	T. 8,100,000	8,600,000	3,200,000	6,700,000
Shipping tonnage on register............	T. 6,937,000	9,026,000	1,233,000	1,584,000
Shipping entered and cleared in ports.....	T. 61,482,000	88,989,000	14,519,000	25,904,000
Pig iron consumption..	T. 6,700,000	7,700,000	3,200,000	7,000,000
Coal consumption.....	T.129,300,000	153,900,000	45,100,000	79,600,000
Cotton consumption cwts..............	12,900,000	15,000,000	2,900,000	5,900,000
Wool consumption lbs..	336,000,000	493,800,000	219,800,000	394,700,000

3

The strongest branches of British industry and trade, metals and textiles, as well as a host of smaller businesses, were attacked by this forward German movement, in markets new and

[15] Report on Maritime Interests of German Empire, 1897, Misc. Series 443. See also Misc. Series 237, Report on Progress of Trade of Hamburg, 1841-1890.

[16] B F T I, Cd. 4954, pp. 4, 5.

old; and the damage done was not merely the result of German sagacity at commerce, but due also to a vulnerability which was, perhaps, an inevitable accompaniment of the vast strength of British trade. There is an overwhelming mass of evidence exhibiting British business weighted down by complacent apathy, arrogance, conservatism, and antiquated commercial practices.[17] Back in the seventies this evidence had begun to accumulate in the consular reports, and during the following decade it became more prominent. The Royal Commission on the Depression of Trade, after an elaborate survey of foreign markets in 1885-86, reached the conclusion that "there is some falling off among the trading classes of this country from the more energetic practices of former periods. Less trouble appears to be taken to discover new markets for our produce, and to maintain a hold upon those which we already possess; and we feel confident that, if our commercial position is to be maintained in the face of the severe competition to which it is now exposed, much more attention to these points must be given by our mercantile classes."[18] The press repeatedly in the eighties drew attention to this commercial "backwardness" of England by publishing extracts from consular reports and referring to it in leading articles. "The Germans," declared a *Times* leader of 1886, "are beginning to beat us in many of the qualities which are the factors of commercial success. They are content with smaller profits; their clerks work for lower salaries; they speak all languages; they are bound by no hard and fast traditions. . . . If we are to hold our own against them we must be content to adopt once more the methods which we used to practice when our trade was in its infancy, but which we seem to have largely forgotten."[19] The *Daily Telegraph* called for "a

[17] The best view of this is to be obtained from (1) the Blue Book. *Foreign Trade Competition*, C.-9078, published by the Board of Trade in 1898, and containing excerpts from consular reports on British methods of trade (*vide* article, "Neglecting Our Customers," by Agnes Lambert, in *Nineteenth Century*, 1898, vol. 44), and (2) the Blue Book, *Trade of the British Empire and Foreign Competition*, C.-8449, published in 1897 by the Colonial Office, and containing reports in answer to a questionnaire on trade competition sent out by the Colonial Secretary.

[18] Section 76.

[19] Aug. 6, 1886.

new leaf from the enterprise and activity of the Germans";[20] but
this summons, which was echoed throughout the press, met with
little response, for the chorus of consular criticism of British
trade methods grew louder in the nineties. "There is . . . an un-
accountable slowness on the part of many men engaged in the
home industries to accommodate themselves . . . to the conditions
of successful trade abroad," remarked the *Daily News* in 1895,
". . . and the only possible conclusion is that past success in trade
has puffed us up in our insular pride . . . and that it is not for
Englishmen to take lessons from foreigners in businesses which so
many of them learned from us. But that is just where the mischief lies."[21] "There is no time for delay," said the *Hardware
Trade Journal*, "no room . . . for any indulgence in optimism. We
must go to school and learn of our neighbours. It is humiliating,
but it is also undeniably true."[22] In October 1898 the Board of
Trade issued a Blue Book consisting of a large collection of excerpts bearing upon British trade methods from recent consular
reports from all parts of the world. Altogether, 171 reports from
116 officials were quoted, and with scarcely an exception the reports lamented and condemned the shortcomings and supineness
of the British trader. The *Times* described the book as "not pleasant reading," but hoped it would be widely circulated: "Let the
young Englishman take a hint from the German traders described
in this report, and there need be no fear for the future. . . . There
could not be more wholesome reading for a large number of persons."[23] A special article in the *Daily Mail* asserted that "when
the warnings and denunciations . . . are gathered in one volume
the accumulative effect of the indictment makes a stirring and
artistic performance which should compel the attention of our
peccant traders."[24]

It may have been that Englishmen long accepted without much
perturbation this criticism of their trade conservatism as an inevitable reflection of their national character, but in the last

[20] Sept. 1, 1886.
[21] Dec. 5, 1895.
[22] "The German Rival," July 31, 1896.
[23] Oct. 14, 1898.
[24] "Why We March Backward," Oct. 14, 1898.

81

decade of the century the condition became acute by contrast with Continental and American business, and the surprised chagrin of the eighties passed into the panic and alarm of the nineties. Slackened initiative and a sense of superiority and overconfidence made England seem a drowsy giant resting on the laurels won in the middle of the century, while the sleepless German carried off the prizes of trade. "The commercial Barbarossa is awake at last," warned the *Times*, "and his methods, according to the consuls, are in almost every respect exactly the opposite of his still slumbering rival. In a single word, he exports more mind than his rival . . . and this is the secret of his success. Indeed, if the consuls are to be trusted, Barbarossa is not only awake but wide awake, while the British merchant still tosses uneasily and only half awake on his monopolist pillow—with the stuffing out."[25]

The "conservatism of the British manufacturer, who does not move with the times or . . . understand that he is no longer the 'boss,' so to speak, of the manufactory industries of the world," was one of the chief reasons pointed out by the British consul at Athens, in 1886, for trade losses to Germany. At the same time the Tokyo consul remarked the many British merchants who "are content to work along the old lines, and do not seem to keep up with all the progressive movements in Japan, and thus find themselves at a disadvantage in business transactions with the Japanese."[26] Ten years later the Düsseldorf consul was lamenting that "British men of industry and commerce seem to think that the old lines they worked on 50 or 60 years ago are good enough for the present day."[27] A consular opinion from Warsaw held that trade losses were due "absolutely and undoubtedly" to the "apathy and arrogance of the British manufacturers themselves."[28] From Samoa came a warning that British trade "will suffer far more severely during the next five years from German competition than it has done already unless British manufacturers attack the colonial and foreign markets in the energetic,

[25] Nov. 14, 1898.
[26] These reports are printed in part in Appendix I.
[27] Foreign Trade Competition, C.-9078, p. 27.
[28] *Ibid.*, p. 15.

well-organized, up-to-date manner adopted by the Germans."[29]
In the view of the Queensland Secretary of Agriculture, in 1896,
until the conservatism of the British yielded "they could not hope
to compete with those manufacturers who are keeping pace with
the march of progress in the 19th century."[30] It was the accumulated force of this sort of testimony which led Sir Michael Hicks
Beach to declare in a speech at the Mansion House that "the
secret of the success of our most active competitors in the development of foreign trade is their promptitude in seizing opportunities. We have been too leisurely in our methods, and we
must rise to the occasion a little more alertly."[31]

This conservatism was the source of most of the weaknesses of
British commerce when the German rivalry became really acute.
It helps to explain the reluctance of manufacturers to accept
small orders, at low profits but with the possibility of creating
new lines of trade. In the 1886 report from Tokyo quoted above,
the consul observed that

manufacturers in England are accustomed to large orders, to established markets, and to no very marked change in the tastes of consumers. German manufacturers, on the other hand, do not disregard
small orders; they are eager to meet the tastes of the market and
adapt themselves with greater readiness to the varying needs of the
Japanese . . . than do the mill owners of Great Britain, who rather
despise a small trade and will not alter their productions to suit a
demand that does not offer a certainty of extensive future business.

Such criticism of British trade was repeated again and again in
the consular reports. "The Briton does not care to sell unless he
gets large orders," remarked a consul in Spain in 1897; while from
the Argentine it was reported that the mounting success of the
Germans was due to their willingness to work for a small return
and the "trouble they will take to secure even a small order."[32]
British conservatism likewise explains the strong disinclination
to go in for the cheaper grades of manufactures required by

[29] *Ibid.*, p. 102.
[30] Trade of the British Empire, C.-8449, p. 450.
[31] *Pall Mall Gazette*, Nov. 11, 1899.
[32] Foreign Trade Competition, C.-9078, pp. 52, 89.

most newly opened markets. Accustomed for so long to supply standard articles for established markets, British business seemed unable to supply, or even to realize adequately the importance of supplying the class of goods most readily salable among the impecunious populations of Russia, Eastern Europe, Asia, Africa, Latin America, and the less advanced colonies of the Empire. Again and again in the trade reports this note was sounded: Britain must offer cheaper goods if she is to keep her position in world commerce. From Stockholm and Archangel to Aleppo, from Panama to Cape Town, from Zanzibar to Ceylon and Queensland, came repeated warnings that trade would go unless this condition were complied with.[33] Other shortcomings frequently cited in the trade reports, and deriving from this deep-seated conservatism, were failure to improve methods of packing, reluctance to compete with foreign makers in giving a good finish to low-class commodities, and refusal to depart from the use of English weights, measures, and money in dealing with countries where the metric system obtained.[34] The reports also testify to a marked reluctance on the part of British manufacturers to share risks with commercial agents,[35] or to extend credit terms as generous as those granted by Germans and others. This was singled out as an important cause for trade losses in Roumania in 1885,[36] and in the nineties it was a trite observation in the consular reports. Where British firms demanded cash against bills of lading or, at the most, three months' credit, German firms commonly gave four, six, nine months, or longer, and this was undoubtedly an important secret of the deflection of trade into German hands.[37] The Odessa con-

[33] Instances of this are very numerous throughout the reports quoted in C.-9078 and C.-8448; vide summaries of them in pp. 1-3 of former, and pp. 8, 9 of latter.

[34] Observations on these weaknesses are also very numerous; vide C.-9078, pp. 4-6, and C.-8449, pp. 9, 172, 356, 460-1; also Times article, "An Obstacle to Our Trade," Sept. 30, 1891.

[35] For example, the consul at Nagasaki wrote in 1898: "British trade suffers from reluctance of manufacturers to take any part of the risk in introducing a new article, . . . forcing the commission agent to shoulder all of it." C.-9078, p. 99.

[36] Extract from Bucharest report in Appendix I.

[37] C.-9078, pp. 4-5, and excerpts from reports from Nagasaki, Rio Grande

sul in 1898 stated that "the success realized by German machines over English is due to the long terms of credit given by German firms, in some instances amounting to three and four years."[38]

But the most widespread and fundamental weakness of British business was its failure to study adequately the needs of markets and to adapt goods to changing tastes and demands. A certain contempt for the customer's wishes and a stubborn insistence on putting old styles and patterns on the market were very characteristic of British commerce all over the world. This criticism was not unfamiliar even before 1880,[39] and in the late eighties and nineties it was to be encountered with a wearisome frequency in the consular reports; in nearly every instance it was the contrast with German adaptability and study of markets which provoked the observation.[40]

One of the important reasons for this unresponsiveness to changing currents of demand was the glaring scarcity of British commercial travelers, and the ineffective endeavors to supply their place by lavish distribution of price lists and catalogues—generally printed only in English. The day when even world-famous British goods could sell themselves, without having to be pushed in the markets by drummers, passed when the period of acute competition dawned. Vigorous salesmanship, carried on by commercial agents canvassing the world with alert and attentive eyes, became one of the great decisive factors in trade competition, and British business was very slow in responding to the new set of conditions. Back in 1881 the Teneriffe consul was observing that "we do not pay equal attention ... with others to the importance in these days of the system of traveling,"[41] and this observation

---

do sul, Braila, Piraeus, Berne, Odessa, Cairo, pp. 99, 88, 63, 60, 38, 11, 73; also C. 8449, p. 10, and reports from Singapore, Melbourne and Malta, pp. 277, 354-5, 549.

[38] C.-9078, p. 11.

[39] The consul at Florence wrote in 1877: "A readiness to adapt themselves to the wants of others may be among the causes which give foreign a preference on the Italian market over English manufacturers." A. & P., 1877, vol. 35, p. 1389.

[40] C.-9078, pp. 14, 24, 29, 39-40, 46, 77, 81, 91, 96, 98-99; C.-8449, pp. 91-92, 545.

[41] A. & P., 1881, vol. 35, p. 310.

became increasingly apposite as the years passed. Without a well trained army of traveling commercial agents it was no longer possible for an industrial-mercantile people to go forward successfully in the new business world. "All the consular reports," wrote the Secretary of the Embassy at Rome in 1885, "in speaking of foreign and especially of German competition draw attention to the absence in Italy of British commercial travelers. Surprise has constantly been expressed to me during my inquiries, by Government officials, professional men, merchants and shopkeepers that Italy and Rome should be so neglected by British commercial travelers, whilst German travelers are everywhere, and by their intelligence, activity and pertinacity secure quantities of orders no matter how small."[42] In 1896, only four English as compared with twenty-nine German commercial travelers visited Palestine.[43] Switzerland, in 1894, issued permits to only sixty-nine British travelers, while 154 were issued to Austrians, 175 to Italians, 633 to French, and 3,310 to Germans.[44] An Ecuador consul wrote in 1898 that not a single British commercial traveler had visited Quito during the year just passed. "The British commercial traveler," declared a consul in the Azores in 1897, "is conspicuous by his absence, our merchants at home evidently thinking his services can be dispensed with, and in his place send out by every mail well got-up and well-written trade circulars, pamphlets and journals. These find a place on my table in the Consulate, but I cannot compel merchants, traders, engineers, etc., to come and read them. And if anyone happens to look into them and finds some article . . . which he would like to obtain, in all probability he goes to his friend the German commercial traveler or agent and shows him the description or drawing and gives him the order, the British trade journal or circular having been the means, by a sort of irony, of getting an order for Germany."[45]

Even the travelers and agents whom British firms did employ

---

[42] *Vide* Appendix I.
[43] C.-9078, p. 67.
[44] *Ibid.*, p. 38.
[45] *Ibid.*, p. 92.

were quite commonly inferior to their competitors in certain important respects. In the first place, they carried their English standard of living with them and hence it cost relatively more to hire them. The Barcelona consul in 1886 found the chief impediments to British trade in Spain in "the peculiar character and habits of these foreigners as opposed to Englishmen. Take the Germans, for example, who are by far the most numerous," he wrote, "these men live in a style incredibly economical; their salaries for the most part are mere pittances, and, in fact, many of them devote their time and labour in behalf of commercial houses without any remuneration at all, content with having obtained a footing in the business. . . . The little money they save never melts away in the cafes or theatres, as the Englishman's does. It is this thrifty, self-denying life they lead which spares expenses by their employers."[46] This picture of the German commercial agents in Barcelona, and the contrast which they offered to their British rivals, was probably true for all parts of the world. "The youths who go from Germany . . . to push their fortunes abroad," wrote James Bryce in a Foreign Office Memorandum of 1886, ". . . are willing to live more plainly than Englishmen do, to work for smaller profits, to allow themselves fewer amusements. If they have less dash and enterprise than our countrymen, they have a steady tenacity and habits of systematic application not less valuable in the long run."[47] Inadequate commercial education, as compared with their competitors, was another handicap to British commercial agents and travelers; and this is evidenced not only in the consular reports, which abound in discussions of it, but also in the great prominence given to the commercial education question by press and platform towards the close of the century. This, asserted the *Westminster Gazette*, was "the basis of the success of the Germans in pushing their commerce. And until we learn the wisdom of giving an equally efficient training to our commercial clerks and the pioneers of our trade, we shall continue

[46] Report on Openings for British Enterprise in Catalonia, Misc. Series 8, p. 1.
[47] Memorandum on Diplomatic and Consular Assistance to Trade. Appendix No. 1 in Commercial No. 5 of 1897.

to play second fiddle in an increasing number of markets."[48] An even more serious handicap was British inferiority to Germans in acquaintance with foreign languages. One may read often in the consular reports of the British traveler's ignorance of the languages and customs of the countries he visited and his consequent poverty of equipment for successfully studying market needs and opening new lines of trade. "I often hear of commercial travelers from England arriving in Moscow unable to speak anything but English," wrote the Moscow consul in 1896, "whereas Germans invariably speak a little Russian."[49] There is abundant testimony showing German superiority in this respect. Not only was commercial education more advanced among them, but far more attention was paid to language study, and German houses had adopted more extensively the practice of sending young men all over the world to acquire knowledge of languages and business habits. "There are in this town," wrote the Warsaw consul in 1898, "a fair number of German clerks who are studying the language and the local way of doing business, who will render valuable assistance when they return to their fatherland. Cannot young Englishmen be found to study the market in this way?"[50] Evidently not enough of them could be found. British business was apparently not training up a class of men from which to recruit sufficient first-class commercial travelers; indeed, many of the representatives employed by British firms were of necessity Germans. "It will therefore be obvious," asserted the Düsseldorf consul in 1898, "that the English firm requires English travelers with the necessary knowledge of languages, countries, and peoples, which the German who goes out as a salesman possesses. . . . The ground lost has got to be rewon by travelers especially educated and trained. The millions of elaborately got-up advertisements in the English language, although well, very well done, are simply consigned to the waste paper basket, used to light the foreigner's fire, or sold to the mills. There is nothing

[48] Nov. 12, 1898.
[49] C.-9078, p. 10.
[50] Ibid., p. 16.

new in these statements; based as they are on facts beyond dispute; it appears passing strange that it should be necessary to drive them home to those who work in the counting houses of their grandfathers."[51]

High freight costs were another burden under which British foreign commerce labored against German competition. Subsidies to foreign shipping, notably for the Far East carrying trade, were one factor in this, but not the most important one. The Shipping Conference, consisting chiefly of British owners, was maintaining freights from British ports at higher levels than from Continental and American ports, thus giving a virtual subsidy to foreign goods in their competition with British products —a practice which the *Daily Mail* called "unpatriotic and shortsighted."[52] For example, the rates on cotton piece goods and machinery, carried by Conference steamers in 1896 from New York to Hongkong and Shanghai, were only about half as high as those charged from British ports.[53] "German firms," observed a *Times* writer, "can ship to Australian ports at 5s per ton less than English firms can ship from English ports, and this fact has greatly assisted the Germans in their competition with the English iron trade in Indian and Colonial markets."[54] A natural result of this was an increasing tendency for British manufacturers to send their goods to foreign ports, especially Hamburg, for transshipment to overseas markets. The difference in freight costs on biscuits shipped from London and Hamburg to Singapore was the difference between 20 shillings and 12 and 6 pence, with the result that Singapore had begun to import not only German biscuits but Scotch biscuits shipped from Hamburg."[55]

Closely related to the matter of freight rates were the cheaper railway facilities on the Continent. A delegation from the British

[51] *Ibid.*, p. 27.

[52] "Our Eastern Trade," Aug. 31, 1896; *vide* also leading article in *Times*, "Shipping Rings and the Iron Trade," June 12, 1899.

[53] Report of Hongkong Governor's Committee to Colonial Office, 1896. C.-8449, p. 323.

[54] "Decay of the Iron Industry," Sept. 18, 1894.

[55] Report of Singapore Registrar of Imports and Exports, 1896, C.-8449, p. 276.

Iron Trade Association, visiting Belgium and Germany in 1895, learned that one of the largest works in Germany, 150 miles inland, could reach Antwerp by rail for 3s 6d per ton of finished iron or steel, whereas similar produce transported from works in the Midlands, over the same distance, was charged about three times as much by the English railways.[56] There was also the close coöperation developed abroad between railways and shipping companies, making possible the advantageous quotation of through rates from interior places of manufacture to ultimate destinations overseas.[57] In Great Britain, where railway and steamship companies worked quite independently, no such arrangement existed; but in Germany the state railways operated in close union with manufactures and shippers to swell the export trade. The Germans were the chief masters of this principle of collective effort in promoting exports, and this was perhaps shown best in their adoption of special railway tariffs on goods marked for export.[58] A comparison of the railway portion of the through-tariffs quoted by the German Levant and East African lines with rates for similar freight hauling to British ports reveals a powerful advantage conferred upon German wares.[59]

Another important weakness in Britain's commercial empire at the close of the nineteenth century was the absence of consular assistance to trade in the British colonies. Foreign consuls, active in fostering the trade of their nationals, were established through the Empire but the United Kingdom had no corresponding officials. Colonial governors and administrators were not always business men, and were in no position to send the minute information to the Government or to private inquirers such as foreign consuls gathered and dispatched. "The result . . .," wrote the Melbourne Commissioner of Trade and Customs in 1896, "is twofold; first, the British Government is not so well

[56] The *Daily Telegraph*, Jan. 20, 1896.

[57] Cf. reports from Lorenzo Marques and Tokyo quoted in C.-9078, pp. 49, 98.

[58] Cf. Report on Prussian Railways by Commercial Attaché at Berlin, 1902. Misc. Series 574.

[59] *Vide* tables in Appendix No. 17 of Report of Select Committee on Steamship Subsidies, 1902, pp. 246-47.

informed of the trade of Victoria as it is of that of foreign countries; and, second, foreign nations are better acquainted with the trade of Victoria than is the British nation."[60] The Customs Collector at Adelaide, South Australia, at the same time urged the appointment of consuls or trade representatives "in some at least of the more important British possessions." In support of the proposal he said the Council of the Sheffield Chamber of Commerce had issued a statement to the effect that three-quarters of the barbers' cutlery used in Australia was supplied by Germany, and that when it was proposed to obtain samples of the goods preferred in the Colonies nothing could be done because there were "no consuls in the Colonies, and therefore no official representative of the Mother country to communicate with."[61]

Another adverse factor in British commerce, which was the subject of much public controversy in the nineties, was the operation of the Merchandise Marks Act, designed in 1887, as has been seen, to check the importation of falsely marked goods into the United Kingdom. The Act was serving to advertise the foreign manufacturer whose goods had long been going into world markets through the British entrepôt, and thus promoting the growth of direct dealing between foreign maker and consumer. "General opinion," declared a committee of the Trinidad Chamber of Commerce in 1896, "is that the Merchandise Marks Act has had a very contrary effect to that which was intended or expected. Far from assisting British trade it has opened the eyes of importers to the true origin of goods imported, and these are, now, in many instances, imported direct, instead of, as heretofore, through a British agent."[62] The Canadian Minister of Trade and Commerce reported at the same time that "the trade of the United Kingdom must unquestionably suffer" from the operations of the Act;[63] and it was officially stated from Singapore that "the effect has been not only to encourage direct dealing from Hamburg and Antwerp, but to extend trade in other

[60] C.-8449, p. 357.
[61] Ibid., pp. 54-55.
[62] Ibid., p. 184.
[63] Ibid., p. 24.

lines; thus if cotton singlets were from the Continent, why not thread and buttons? and if steel were cheaper from Antwerp, why not needles?"[64] This law had been enacted chiefly to defend the Sheffield cutlery makers, and the provision requiring marks of origin on all goods made abroad but sold under British firm names was highly unpopular throughout many business circles, especially among export merchants and manufacturers who secured abroad partly manufactured goods for finishing. The *Pall Mall Gazette* declared the act had struck the wrong target and urged the erasure of a "gratuitous advertisement of German goods";[65] while the *Manchester Guardian* pronounced the following judgment on the law, nine years after its enactment:

It is a simple fact of experience that one important effect of the compulsory marking of foreign goods imported into the United Kingdom prescribed by the Act of 1887 was that it led to a diversion of demand from Great Britain to the countries of origin, which they found plainly indicated on the goods they had bought here. Buyers abroad naturally thought that they could obtain such foreign merchandise on better terms by going direct to the original sources of supply. Thus the Merchandise Marks Act was the means of establishing, in many cases for the first time, direct commercial intercourse with these sources, not only in respect of the articles originally sought there, but also of others.[66]

This suggests the question of how far British trade, at the close of the century, was suffering from the nuisance of fictitious trade marks. The answer is that one reads less about these in the nineties than in the eighties; references to them in the consular reports became much rarer, and they may be dismissed as an important factor in trade rivalry. Trade-marks legislation was strengthened generally throughout the world,'[67] and in the

---

[64] *Ibid.*, p. 276, Report of Registrar of Imports and Exports.
[65] Leader of Jan. 28, 1897.
[66] Nov. 16, 1896.
[67] Germany, too, adopted more stringent trade mark legislation. *Vide* discussion of 1894 imperial law by Sir Charles Oppenheimer, Frankfurt Consul General, Misc. Series 340. "The Imperial Government," wrote Sir Charles, "is of opinion that Germany ought not to be behindhand in this respect, if her industry is not to risk the high position it has gained in the com-

British Empire practically all the colonies copied the English statute of 1887. The Colonial Office, in 1896, after an elaborate survey of trade competition in the Empire, found that "the competition which British goods have to face is on the whole a fair one."[68] Accusations against German "unfairness" consequently fall to the ground. "Germany, no doubt, has done this country much harm commercially," wrote E. J. Dillon, "and bids fair to inflict still greater losses upon the British Empire. But the competition, however keen, is fair; the methods, however we may dislike some of them, are expressly allowed by the rules of the game. It is the bitter truth, however much it may be gainsaid by optimistic Ministers, that our commercial defeat is the result of commercial inferiority, and that we shall never manage to hold our own against our continental cousins unless we humbly confess that fact, and seriously seek to remedy it. The sooner we go to school to Germany, instead of preaching morality to her, the better for ourselves."[69]

4

From what has been said here it may seem that the outlook for British commerce at the dawn of the twentieth century was almost hopelessly dark. Harried by competitors more progressive in their methods and less encumbered by tradition, in a business world moving at quickening tempo, what could the future hold for Great Britain save defeat after defeat in one market after another? She was no longer "the workshop of the world"; indeed, her industrial plant was growing antiquated as compared with that of Germany, where business men were less given to putting the profits of industry into deer forests and hunting lodges. Those strong British convictions in the rightness of Free Trade and economic individualism, which had carried Great Brit-

---

petition of nations." The *Hardware Trade Journal,* discussing the new German law, pointed out (Oct. 31, 1894) that "now that the defect of the old law as regards effective protection has been remedied, there will be less likelihood of foreign representatives of German firms undertaking to supply goods bearing the same marks as those of English firms."

[68] C.-8449, p. 11.

[69] "Germany's Foreign Policy," *Fortnightly Review,* Dec. 1, 1896, p. 769.

ain to the peak of her prosperity, had been successfully challenged, mocked, and rejected.[70] Her commercial and technical education lagged behind that of her great Continental rival, and many of her established methods of doing business were rendered obsolete. How could a people of insular conservatism, tenaciously individualist, wedded to the outworn ways of doing things, their manufacturing leadership passing, continue even to hold their own against another people of superior genius for methodical exactness and laborious energy, of better education, of higher talents in collective organization of national economic life, in such an age as had dawned? Contemporary English opinion saw the darkness on the horizon and expressed itself in a vast literature of pessimism and alarm.

The pessimists saw all that has been written in this chapter, wherein attention has been pointedly concentrated upon British commercial weaknesses rather than upon the sources of continued strength. But there was another and very different side of the picture, which one may see by turning from a consideration of these dissipating tendencies to assess the continued immensity of British commerce. If the export trade appeared to have stopped growing in the nineties, it was still by far the world's largest national volume of exportation. The skill and sagacity of rivals would need to be almost infinitely superior to dislodge such a massive sum of established trade, and geographical position alone guaranteed that England would go on being an important commercial power. If her industries were declining, no nation possessed such vast quantities of capital for modernizing old and founding new ones. In the growing specialization of industry the prospect of inevitable decline because of dissolved monopolies gave way to the prospect of continued and perhaps renewed leadership in more narrowly specialized trades well

[70] "We grew to be the greatest commercial nation in the world because individually our merchants and manufacturers had more energy, more capital, and more knowledge than their rivals. Now we are in commerce individualists still, and our rivals have the advantage of all that modern collectivism can do for them in education, knowledge of markets, and combined resources."—*Daily Mail* leader, Jan. 27, 1898.

adapted to the country. Moreover, British financial leadership and merchant shipping supremacy were still virtually undisputed. The *Daily Telegraph* in 1901 declared:

"Those who are bewailing the supposititious retrogression of the country ignore everything in favour of British manufacturers, and sedulously advertise the slightest success of foreign competition. ... Every incident of American or German progress is shown in the limelight, while the whole vast and steady process of British trade is left in the shade. ... What is gone is our monopoly. What is not gone is our supremacy. There is no decadence. The total volume of our trade is still twice as much as that of the United States, and one and one-half times as great as that of Germany.... If America and Germany were blotted from the industrial map and foreign competition were to disappear, that would not enable us to take their place, to add their foreign trade to our own. ... Absolutely, nothing could be sounder or more enviable than our position. ... The industrial activities of our Transatlantic and Continental competitors have only displaced former British trade in a very minor and incidental degree.[71]

If this view seemed too optimistic in the light of British commercial history in the eighties and nineties, it was nevertheless borne out largely by the trade expansion down to 1914; for as world commerce expanded and competition intensified, British commercial power surely did not founder. The figure[72] shown here comparing the expansion of British and German export trade until the eve of the war certainly does not suggest any decay of England's export capacities. There was a tremendous expansion of world business in the decade before the war, and Great Britain participated most profitably in it; indeed, the growth of her export trade was not demonstrably less prosperous than that of Germany. Free Traders steadily maintained that the more the industries of the rest of the world prospered, the richer the world became and the greater was its capacity for buying British goods. This argument, by no means specious,

[71] Leader of May 30, 1901.
[72] Based on figures in Statistical Abstract of United Kingdom and Statistisches Jahrbuch für das deutsche Reich.

nevertheless appeared rather thin and unconsoling in times of slack trade, which were not wanting in the pre-war years. Severe business depression obtained from late 1900 to 1904, again from 1907 to 1909, and on the very eve of the war another slump had begun.[73] In these periods it was evident enough that the industrial foundations of British commercial prosperity were weakening. Much was written and heard of England's industrial decay, and the country rang with the cry for tariff reform; but in the

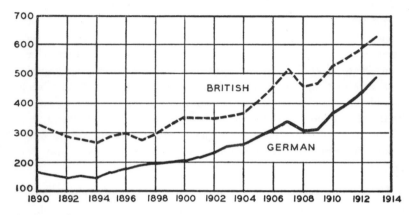

CHART 1. COMPARATIVE VALUE OF BRITISH AND GERMAN EXPORT TRADE, 1890-1913, EXPRESSED IN MILLION POUNDS STERLING. THE BRITISH SUM INCLUDES REËXPORTED FOREIGN AND COLONIAL GOODS AS WELL AS UNITED KINGDOM DOMESTIC PRODUCE.

prosperous years British business went on complacently enough, slowly adjusting itself to the exigencies of world competition, and the record trade levels of 1913 seemed to justify a pragmatic optimism.[74]

[73] It is of interest to compare German with British business cycles. In Germany the depression of 1900 began earlier than in England, but recovery came a year earlier; then in 1904-05, while Britain was on the upgrade, Germany fell into a short slump. The depression of 1907-09 began earlier and lasted longer in Germany than England, and the slump on the eve of the war was noticed in Germany before it was in England.—*vide* conspectus of business cycles given in W. L. Thorp's *Business Annals*.

[74] Mr. Lloyd George said in the House of Commons on May 4, 1914. "Last year was an exceptionally prosperous year. I had based my estimates of revenue on the assumption that the trade boom would surpass anything

This optimism was maintained chiefly by Free Traders, who generally pointed to the swelling import trade as a proof that English prosperity was still of sound foundation. Tariff reformers, however, continued to worry about the failure of the export trade to grow more rapidly. They knew well enough that so long as England held her leadership in banking and shipping she could pay for her unfavorable trade balance. British capital held the world in tribute and British ships kept an immense superiority over others down to 1914, but evidence that productive industry at home was rapidly forming fresh capital was doubtful. Indications of crumbling in the industrial foundations of British business were abundant, and it became a commonplace to contrast the antiquated industrial plant of England with the progressive, up-to-date character of German industry. After all, as William Cunningham and other able tariff reformers contended, it was on the active elements in economic life—creative labor and productive enterprise—that continued prosperity depended, and it was evident to scores of observers, at home and abroad, that British industries were being outstripped more and more by those of Germany. Albert Ballin, for example, expressed the view in 1910 that the "British can really no longer compete with us, and if it were not for the large funds they have invested, and for the sums of money which reach the small mother-country from her great dominions, their saturated and conservative habits of life would soon make them a 'quantité négligeable' as far as their competition with us in the world's markets is concerned."[75]

Although national alarm over German industrial competition swept the British nation, and many new industries sprang up in

we had experienced in this country. I was charged with over-sanguine estimates. However, I think I am entitled to point out that all those estimates were more than justified by the results. The trade of this country reached the highest point it has ever reached. Unemployment touched the lowest point it has ever touched in the history of this country, and it is all the more gratifying inasmuch as there is hardly any other country in the world which could put forward the same claim. . . . I think that is a story which must be a source of encouragement to all those who feel any doubt as to the future of British industry."—Hansard, 5th S., vol. 62, pp. 56-57.

[75] Huldermann, *Life of Albert Ballin*, p. 161.

the place of old ones, it cannot be said that the British Government did very much to keep alive industrial prosperity. It is true that Great Britain, like Germany, became increasingly mercantilist in her economic policies, and that the Government used its influence more and more to secure economic favors and privileges for British business abroad. But it is not true that much legislation was enacted to help domestic industry, and there was much bitter criticism of the Government by industrial interests alleging that the whole British system was sacrificing the productive to the commercial and foreign investing interests.[76] A survey of Parliamentary legislation in the years before 1914 certainly reveals very few measures enacted in behalf of manufacturing interests. The fight for tariff reform was abortive, and the record shows plainly that shipping, financial, and commercial interests received first consideration from Parliament. Other than the temporary coal-export tax, there was only one significant piece of producers' legislation enacted: the Patent Act of 1907.

This measure, sponsored by Mr. Lloyd George, struck a blow at foreign patent holders in Great Britain for the benefit of certain home industries. Thousands of patents were being taken out in Britain every year, especially by Germans, not for the purpose of working them there, but to prevent them from being worked there. This circumstance became a matter of grievance especially for the chemical industries, and for perhaps ten years the need for reform of the patent laws had been urged upon the Board of Trade.[77] The principle of compulsory working in Great Britain of patents held there was now brought forward to end what the

[76] The following complaint of the authors of a book on the status of the fire arms industry is characteristic: "The industrial interests, the interests of the humble toiler who produces wealth, have been sacrificed to all other interests. The financiers, the minor capitalists, the bankers, the merchants, the international traders, all have been admitted to a voice in the direct government of the country before any of the industrial class were admitted to its secret councils. That is a reason of decay in British industry."— Opifex and Artifex: *The Causes of Decay in a British Industry,* 1907, pp. 269-70.

[77] *Vide* leading article in *Chemical Trades Journal,* Feb. 2, 1907.

President of the Associated Chambers of Commerce characterized as "that insane practice in this country of conferring a monopoly on foreign labour to supply our markets."[78]

That the agitation for the measure was aimed primarily at Germany was evident enough. "It is no secret," remarked the *Chemical Trades Journal*, "that it is directed against the coal-tar industry of Germany."[79] And this is further borne out by a speech of a Lancashire Member in the House of Commons:

We were the only country in Europe that allowed a patentee to take his grant away and work it where he liked, or sell it to whom he liked. The result of this careless liberality was that foreigners came here and got patents granted them without ever having the slightest intention of working them in this country. They not only did this, but, aided by powerful associations and syndicates, particularly in Germany, they use these patents to filch our trade away, and in this . . . they had often been successful. . . . Some of these patents were only taken out for blocking purposes, and were unscrupulously used when our manufacturers wished to make any article which would compete with a German production. Others which were of importance were taken abroad and were used to start industries there by new and improved processes, and so superseded industries carried on in this country. Thus our manufacturers suffered great injury and our work people lost their employment. . . . That Germany had made enormous strides could not be denied, and in his opinion the advantages that she had enjoyed through our

[78] *Chamber of Commerce Journal,* April, 1907. Mr. Lloyd George, in announcing his bill, summarized the industrialists' complaint in these words: "Big foreign syndicates have one very effective way of destroying British industries. They first of all apply for patents on a very considerable scale. They suggest every possible combination—for instance in chemicals—which human ingenuity can think of. These combinations the syndicates have not tried themselves. They are not in operation, say, in Germany or elsewhere. But the syndicates put them in their patents in obscure and vague terms so as to cover any possible invention that may be discovered afterwards in this country. . . . At the present moment many British industries have been completely wiped out by privileges conceded by British institutions to foreigners. I propose that these bonds shall be cut, and that the British industry shall be made perfectly free to engage on equal terms in the severe struggle with its competitors."—Hansard, 4th S., vol. 172, p. 683.

[79] March 16, 1907.

absurd leniency in regard to patents had been one great factor in the success which she had attained, in some degree at our expense. . . . It was a well-known fact that the foundation of the aniline colour industry in Germany had been laid by the manufacture of alizarine, for which a number of patents for working it commercially had been obtained in this country, with the result that every one was able to make and sell in that country, whilst in this country it was a close monopoly, and our dyers were charged an enormous price for an article which could be just as well made by us as by Germans. . . . By our patent laws, as they were at present, we were benevolently fostering great industries in Germany, to the detriment of the manufacturers, consumers, and working classes of this country.[80]

The 1907 law gave foreigners holding patents in Great Britain one year in which to begin manufacturing, partially at least, or show some exceptional cause why protection of their patent rights should not be lifted. That the act caused a good deal of chagrin in Germany goes almost without saying. In June, 1908, on the eve of the law becoming operative, a group of German industrialists petitioned the Imperial Government to exert diplomatic efforts for an extension of the time limit, asked for retaliatory measures against English patent holders in Germany, and urged the opening of negotiations with a view to establishing between the two countries a reciprocity of patent protection, such as existed between Germany and Switzerland.[81] The move occasioned a large crop of leading articles in the British press strongly opposing any such extension of time.[82] and the law came into operation on the scheduled date of August 28, 1908.

There were high hopes in England that the measure would inaugurate an industrial revival of considerable proportions.

[80] Hansard, 4th S., vol. 172, pp. 1012-16.

[81] *Vide* especially the *Daily Chronicle* and the *Times,* June 26, 1908; also the views of the *Berlin Morgenpost* quoted in the *Chronicle,* and a long article in the *Daily Mail* for June 27; German chagrin is likewise described in the consular reports from Dusseldorf and Frankfort, Annual Series 4283, 4325.

[82] *Vide* especially the *Times,* the *Daily Telegraph,* and the *Daily Mail* for *June* 29; also the *Hardware Trade Journal,* July 3; the *Chemical Trades Journal,* July 4, and the *Shipping World,* July 1.

"Trade and employment," the *Daily Telegraph* prophesied, "will be transferred wholesale from foreign countries to our own soil. A vast capital will be sunk here that would otherwise be invested abroad. Factories will be built on British soil by British labour, and to a very large extent at least out of British material. . . . When these establishments are in full swing their consumption of raw materials, their sales of finished products, will bring more business to British ships, railways, banks. It is believed that in a very short time all the new operations, represented by a total capital of £25,000,000 will be set up in this country instead of being carried abroad. The nation as a whole will benefit and the Patents Act is the one measure of constructive patriotism passed during recent years upon which the Government, the Opposition, and the Country are to be equally congratulated."[83] How far this optimistic outlook was borne out by the actual results it would be very difficult to say. Certainly some new industries came to England because of the modified law. The *Chemical Trades Journal* declared in the fall of 1908 that already no less than eighteen German and American firms had made arrangements for the erection of works in the United Kingdom.[84] And the *Times* said about the same time that

although the foreign factories so far established are not numerous, it is the opinion of experts in patent matters that the next two or three years will witness a considerable increase in the number of these branch manufactories. . . . The ultimate benefits derived by this country, directly or indirectly, from the passing of the Act last year may, therefore, be very considerable.[85]

Probably British industry profited less from the erection of new plants in the United Kingdom than from the acquisition by British manufacturers of licenses from foreign patentees to produce for the English market;[86] but in any case the change in the patent laws undoubtedly made some contribution to the revival of British industrial activity in the five years prior to the war.

[83] June 29, 1908.
[84] Nov. 7, 1908.
[85] Nov. 26, 1908.
[86] *Vide Chemical Trades Journal,* Nov. 28, 1908.

Chapter IV
HOME AND CONTINENTAL MARKETS

A N ADEQUATE detailed and quantitative view of the Anglo-German trade rivalry when it had become the most conspicuous feature of the globe-encircling fight for markets can only be got by a painstaking inquiry into the several trading communities of the world. Such an inquiry, pursued chiefly through the reports of British consuls, will now be attempted, beginning in this chapter with a view of the rivalry in the markets of the United Kingdom and Continental Europe between, roughly, the decade of the eighties and 1914.

The eighties had seen the rise of a Continental industrialism less dependent on Great Britain for capital goods, the consequent retarding of the British advance in European markets, and the emergence of German business to Continental leadership. By 1890 Germany had taken first place among the nations exporting to Russia, Sweden, Denmark, Switzerland, Austria-Hungary, and Roumania; she was a close second to Great Britain in Norway, Holland, and Belgium, and her exports to France had three-fourths the value of Britain's; in exporting to the United Kingdom France alone among Continental nations surpassed her.[1] Now the period between 1890 and 1914 witnessed a very heavy growth of European commerce and a large expansion in the capacity of markets to absorb the export surpluses of Great Britain and Germany. Competition became very keen and in no part of the European trading community did German firms fail to gain at the expense of some British commercial interests. It was here, indeed, that the German merchants and industrialists scored their most substantial victories over British rivals. The advantage of geographical position was, of course, largely on their side, especially in their easier access to the mar-

[1] Cf. tables in Statistical Abstract for Foreign Countries, and for United Kingdom.

kets of Poland and Western Russia, Hapsburg lands, Italy, and the Balkans. Germany had an advantage in many Continental markets very much like the advantage which the United States enjoyed over Great Britain in Canadian markets: they were right at her door, and she could get her goods into them generally at the cost of one handling and one train journey at very cheap rates. Britain, on the other hand, in most cases had to entrain goods in England, re-handle them at the port of shipment and again at the port of discharge, where they were commonly en trained a second time before reaching their ultimate destination. "It is manifest," observed a writer in 1910, "that under such conditions as these our rivals have a marked advantage over us, and as regards some of the European markets the advantage has proved to be quite overwhelming."[2]

Germany's Continental trade leaped forward strongly in the middle nineties in response to the stimulus of a modified fiscal policy. A reaction from the high protectionism of the previous decade was inaugurated by Chancellor Caprivi's acceptance and extension of the conventional tariff system. The needs of German industry for enlarged markets conspired with the country's shrinking ability to raise its own food supply to dictate this "new course" in tariff policy. It began with a series of commercial treaties concluded in 1891 with Austria-Hungary, Italy, Belgium, and Switzerland; was continued in 1893 by similar conventions with Spain, Roumania, and Serbia, and reached a climax with the Russo-German commercial treaty of 1894.[3] "The four first-named treaties," wrote Sir Charles Oppenheimer, consul-general at Frankfort, "may be regarded as the fundamental basis or ground floor, the three next (the so-called 'small' commercial treaties) as the second story, and the Russian treaty as the crowning stone of a monumental work."[4] The Caprivi treaties

[2] G. Durham, "The Foreign Trade of Great Britain and Germany," *Contemporary Review*, Oct., 1910, p. 396.

[3] *Vide* the excellent reports of Sir Charles Oppenheimer from Frankfort-am-Main, especially Annual Series 1082, of May, 1892, and Misc. Series 340, of July, 1894.

[4] Report on Germany's Commercial Relations with Foreign Countries, Misc. Series 340.

103

opened the door of many protected markets to German industry and enlarged considerably the liberty of commerce in Europe. Great Britain, of course, benefited from the reduced duties, through her most-favored-nation conventions with Continental states, but the Germans were better equipped by geographical position and commercial methods to exploit the widened trade opportunities.

Some consequences of this veering toward liberal commercial policy were reflected clearly in the statistics of trade. The early nineties had been slack years, with British and German exports both languishing; but 1895, by which time the new treaties were all operative, saw a sharp recovery in the German export trade, which attained record levels in the following two years. Sir Charles Oppenheimer attributed this revival of German prosperity directly to the new security afforded by the tariff conventions, coming as they did to terminate a period of successive tariff increases and general uncertainty in the permanence of existing duties. "Now the exporter or manufacturer," he wrote, "knows for certain that until the end of the contract period he will not need to fear any increased customs for certain goods; he is quite safe and can calculate with absolute confidence. . . . These fixed customs rates have strengthened the hands and enterprises of German exporters to a great extent, and can naturally be seen not only in the states with which treaties have been concluded, but also everywhere."[5] Although there occurred a simultaneous recovery of British exports to the Continent, it was neither as strong nor as enduring as the spurt made by Germany; and it seems conclusive, from a reading of consular reports and trade statistics, that the conventional tariffs conferred much greater advantage on Germany than on Great Britain. It will presently be seen that the loudest outcry against German competition yet heard in England was raised at this time,[6] and Sir Charles Oppenheimer wrote in 1897: "If last year so many complaints were made about the German competition in trade, this [the modified Continental tariff system] is the ex-

[5] Annual Series 1942.
[6] *Vide* Ch. VI.

104

planation."[7] In the main, the conventional tariff system worked out by Germany and her Continental neighbors underwent little change down to 1914. The conventions of the nineties were renewed, with modifications, in the twentieth century and remained in force until the war. Although tariff levels rose higher after 1900, there occurred no revolutionary changes in European fiscal policy comparable to the protectionist revival of the early eighties; so that in the twenty years before the war, in the general security afforded by commercial treaties, Germany was able to pour her surpluses with swelling volume into all parts of the Continent. A *Fortnightly Review* contributor, regarding this German conquest of Continental markets, wrote the following in 1905:

Germany has, by the conclusion of commercial treaties with many Powers, secured for the German industries an immense outlet, almost the monopoly in many countries on the Continent of Europe to the disadvantage of our own industries, and she is now assiduously working for a Central European Customs Union of States to which Union she means to be the most favoured, and almost the sole, purveyor of manufactured articles. Thus Germany is striving to recreate in time of peace Napoleon's Continental System against this country, whereby English goods were excluded from all Continental countries under his sway. Through Germany's action our markets on the Continent of Europe have been completely spoiled, and before long they may be almost closed against British manufacturers unless Great Britain meets force with force and violence with violence instead of meeting it with polite and perfectly useless remonstrances.[8]

2

It will be convenient to examine first the direct trade between the United Kingdom and Germany and to discover the measure of competition which went on within the home markets of the rival nations. The balance in this exchange trade was strongly in Germany's favor during the whole period of 1885 to 1914;

[7] Annual Series 1942.
[8] "The Foreign Policy of Germany" by . . ., vol. 78, 1905. *Vide* also "The Influence of the New German Commercial Treaties on British Industries," by W. A. S. Hewins, in *National Review*, vol. 45, 1905.

that is to say, Great Britain was a more valuable market for German business than Germany was for British business.[9] Despite England's alarm over the invasion of goods "made in Germany," there was no significant strengthening of this favorable German balance in the nineties; it seems, in fact, to have remained fairly stable down to the last few years before the war, when heavy German selling in England greatly enlarged it.

But the character of this exchange traffic underwent a noteworthy change. Before the era of sharp competition Germany had been a very good market for the finished products of British industry, but now raw materials and partly manufactured goods bulked larger in the British exports across the North Sea; while imports from Germany became increasingly goods of finished production. The German industrial tariff had begun early in the eighties to discourage the importation of finished goods while keeping raw materials on the free list, and consular reports of that decade frequently drew attention to the decline in Germany's importation of completely manufactured products from Great Britain.[10] By 1896 Sir Charles Oppenheimer could write:

Germany receives in the main from Great Britain raw materials and half-finished goods, which in Germany are either not manufactured at all or only in quantities not sufficient for the demands. . . . The German export to England embraces, on the other hand, principally manufactures of the zinc, textile, leather, iron, and chemical industries, while the export of raw materials and half-finished goods is of minor importance.[11]

[9] The Board of Trade statistics can easily mislead one here, for prior to 1904 they do not show how much Anglo-German trade passed through other countries. The strictly direct trade showed a strong balance in Great Britain's favor, but at least one third of German exports to England went through the Low Countries, and reference to these must be made to show that the balance was the other way.

[10] *Vide* reports from Berlin and Munich in Appendix No. I. The *Spectator* pointed out in 1886 that "in German markets, in all articles of great bulk, of simple manufacture, and daily household use . . . German goods have ousted English goods. . . . In pig iron, agricultural machinery, cement, in the lower qualities of yarns, in shoddy, 'mungo,' jute, even in cloth, the English producer is being driven out of the German market."—"The Depression of Trade Abroad," June 26, 1886. Vol. 59, pt. 1.

[11] Annual Series 1752, p. 38.

Such a transformation in the German trade, the *Times* declared in 1906 (somewhat belatedly), was "calculated to give rise to serious reflections" in the first business nation of the world, for "we stand today, in our trade with Germany, in the position of an industrially undeveloped country trading with another country on a far higher level of industrial efficiency."[12] J. Ellis Barker, about the same time, wrote that "we have become hewers of wood and drawers of water to Germany."[13]

It does not appear, however, that this transformation became more accentuated in the last ten years or so before 1914; rather a new equilibrium was reached and sustained by the exchange of more specialized manufactures. Thus British textiles, iron and steel goods, and machinery held up fairly well in the German market until the outbreak of the war, despite the great expansion of similar German exports to the United Kingdom. A mutual dependence was especially to be seen in the case of machinery. "Even today," wrote Sir Francis Oppenheimer from Frankfort in 1909, "Germany receives from the United Kingdom machines for such branches of industry in which mechanical working has already been for some time introduced, e.g., agricultural and textile machines. On the other hand, the United Kingdom receives from Germany machines for the newer branches of manufacture, e.g., electro-technical machines, and mining machines, etc., in which the technical development of Germany strives to excel."[14] The trade statistics show that Great Britain bought £2,167,797 worth of machinery from Germany in 1913 while selling her British machinery worth £1,887,397. That Germany remained a good market for British industrial manufactures at the end of this period is indeed evident enough. Half of the sixty millions of British exports to Germany in 1913 were classified as manufactured goods, and this proportion had been fairly constant since the early years of the century.[15]

[12] Leader of Oct. 4.
[13] "The Future of Anglo-German Relations," in *Nineteenth Century*, vol. 59, 1906.
[14] Annual Series 4325.
[15] But the preponderance of German over British manufactures in the

The enormous volume of commerce which developed between Great Britain and Germany in the thirty-odd years before the war created a powerful economic bond between the two countries. Countless business houses in each land were dependent for their stocks upon firms in the other land. By 1913 these countries were linked together by 140 million pounds of trade annually, which, it might seem, should have been a source of satisfaction on both sides of the North Sea. But a considerable portion of this trade was highly competitive, and it follows from what has been said above that the principal manifestations of competition appeared in the sale of rival manufactures in the markets of the United Kingdom. Doubtless there were many German concerns which suffered from competitive imports from Britain, but on the whole Germany's tariff policy confined Anglo-German competition to the free commercial area of the United Kingdom.

The nineties saw heavy German blows struck at British producers in their home market. The value of the importation from Germany rose about twenty per cent between 1890 and 1902, and the largest increases were in such lines as iron and steel goods, sugar, chemicals, textiles, paper, glass, china, and earthenware. All these fall into the classification of manufactured goods and therefore permit the generalization that in the nineties the healthiest lines of German trade in the world's still leading industrial community were in just those manufactured commodities in which Great Britain herself had long specialized. Since 1860 no ten-year period had shown so large an increase in Great Britain's importation of foreign manufactured goods as the decade of 1890-1900;[16] and the German commercial invasion

---

exchange traffic was nevertheless very great. In 1913 there were very few lines of goods ready for the consumer in which Germany's sales to Great Britain did not far exceed her purchases. *Vide* detailed analysis of Anglo-German traffic for 1913 in Annual Series 5404, Report of British Commercial Attache at Berlin (Sir F. Oppenheimer), pp. 44-102.

[16] *Vide* tables in B F T I, Cd. 4954, 1909, pp. 66-67. An international comparison here is instructive, for it shows Great Britain receiving a greater increase of foreign manufactures than any of the other leading industrial nations. The following figures give the value of imported manufactures into

was plainly the chief explanation for this fact. The following table showing imports from Germany in several important branches of manufacture will give some measure of the invasion:[17]

	Cotton Mfres. £	Woolen Mfres. £	Iron & Steel Mfres. £
1890	253,381	670,444	353,887
1891	235,547	767,284	361,886
1892	266,094	774,483	379,551
1893	272,599	741,776	431,109
1894	462,801	907,569	567,142
1895	536,471	1,016,694	510,662
1896	659,291	1,252,225	650,068
1897	566,639	1,126,336	691,260
1898	664,435	974,717	825,743
1899	679,117	955,136	917,587
1900	818,808	932,325	1,123,527
1901	902,872	1,029,182	1,362,306
1902	1,121,065	1,483,577	1,379,744

This table might be extended to include other important items, but it is enough to show substantial ground for the anxiety of the nineties and to refute the view that Britain was merely awakened by the Merchandise Marks Act to a full realization of the extent of her purchases from Germany.[18] German manufactures of the widest variety and in impressively mounting volume were coming to her from across the North Sea. E. E. Williams, in his well-known book, drew attention particularly to the swelling imports of German cottons, linens, woolens, embroidery and needle work, leather goods, gloves, iron and steel wares, chemi-

---

the United Kingdom, Germany, France, and the United States, expressed in millions sterling:

	U.K.	Germany	France	U.S.
1890	73.5	44.0	24.6	67.3
1900	94.3	49.1	25.6	59.3

[17] Annual Statement of Trade of United Kingdom. These figures do not include the large importations via the Low Countries.

[18] J. B. C. Kershaw advanced this argument in "The Future of British Trade," *Fortnightly Review*, 1897, vol. 68, p. 732 ff.

cals, toys, musical instruments, china, glass, and earthenware, all of which competed with important English manufactures. Williams advised his readers to take observation of their own surroundings. They would find that their own clothes and their servants' clothes were probably woven in Germany, that the toys, dolls, and fairy books of the nursery, as well as the governess's fiancé, were "made in Germany." "Roam the house over," he said, "and the fateful mark will greet you at every turn, from the piano in the drawing room to the mug on your kitchen dresser. . . . Descend to your domestic depths, and you will find the very drain pipes German made. You pick out of the grate the paper wrappings from a book consignment, and they also are 'made in Germany.' You stuff them into the fire and reflect that the poker in your hand was forged in Germany. As you rise from your hearth rug you knock over an ornament on your mantelpiece; picking up the pieces you read, on that bit that formed the base, 'manufactured in Germany.' And you jot your reflections down with a pencil that was made in Germany."[19]

It would be an endless task to follow the growth of each line of competitive goods sent from Germany into United Kingdom markets in this period, but something may be said of the more important ones. The largest of all was beet sugar, raw and refined. A great expansion of the German sugar industry had come in the eighties, with a resultant overflow into the open British market; so that for several years before 1890 German sugar was driving West India cane from Great Britain and cutting under the position of British refiners.[20] The succeeding decade then saw the strengthening of Germany's hold on the British sugar market, and the West India planters were reduced to imminent ruin in the midst of a vast world over-production, which was intensified by the inability of sugar-producing countries to suppress the bounty system.[21] The tide of German sugar

[19] *Made in Germany,* pp. 10-11.
[20] Sir Robert Giffen's Report to Board of Trade on Progress of the Sugar Trade, 1889, pp. 27-29.
[21] *Times* article, "Twenty Years of the German Beet Sugar Industry," Sept. 8, 1899; E. E. Williams, "Beet Root and Bounties," *Saturday Review,*

which swept into the United Kingdom may be measured in the rise from five million hundredweight in 1890 to nearly twelve million in 1900, without including the quantities imported indirectly through Holland.

The invasion of German iron and steel goods in the nineties was less overwhelming than sugar, but of more serious consequence for the national industrial life. These wares approximately doubled between 1890 and 1900, attaining an annual value of probably two millions sterling by the new century.[22] In these years the iron and steel industries of the United Kingdom seemed to have ceased expanding, so that the German inroad in the home market was very unwelcome. Competition grew very acute in the first years of the new century, when, in a period of slack business, large German surpluses were disposed of in Great Britain.[23] This occasioned a special report in 1902 from the British commercial attaché at Berlin, in which he emphasized that the condition of the iron and steel trade between the two countries was "improving from the German point of view and deteriorating from that of the British manufacturer."[24]

Other branches of trade in which German competition flourished conspicuously in the nineties were textiles and chemicals. By 1890 Great Britain had been eclipsed by Continental Europe in raw cotton consumption, and about one-third of the Continental industry was German.[25] After 1890 the absolute expansion of the German cotton industry was about equal to that of the British, and one of the results was that Manchester had to face at home a German competition which may be measured in

Aug. 15, 1896; G. Baden-Powell, "The Doom of Cane Sugar," *Fortnightly Review,* vol. 37, 1897; Brooks Adams, "The International Struggle for Life," *Fortnightly Review,* vol. 71, 1899; E. E. Williams, "The Case for Sugar," *New Review,* vol. 15, 1896; Harold Cox, "West Indian Sugar," *Economic Journal,* vol. 7, 1897.

[22] Approximate because of the impossibility of determining the exact quantity imported via the Low Countries.

[23] Cf. detailed statement of German iron and steel goods competition in British home market, 1900-03, in B F T I, 1903, Cd. 1761, pp. 343-53.

[24] Memorandum by W. S. Gastrell on German Iron Trade for 1900-01, Misc. Series 575.

[25] Tables in B F T I, 1909, Cd. 4954, pp. 152-59.

the table given above. As for competing German woolens, the increase in which is also shown there, by the early years of the twentieth century Great Britain was taking from Germany about ten per cent as much as she herself exported to all the world. In the chemical trades the Germans were at this time forging to world leadership and dealing severe blows to British producers. "It is no exaggeration," wrote Mr. Williams, "to say that Germany is a more formidable rival, and has already given us a sounder beating in chemicals than in any other field of trade, not even excepting iron and steel."[26]

The German commercial invasion of Great Britain continued strong down to 1914, the annual value of the trade rising from 49 to 80 million sterling between 1904 and 1913. The latter figure was better than ten per cent of the whole British import trade. Moreover, 52 of the 80 millions in 1913 represented finished manufactures, exclusive of refined sugar, which, amounting to six millions, was still the largest item of German trade in the United Kingdom; Germany, in fact, on the eve of the war, was supplying England with about one quarter of all her imported manufactures. Whereas in 1890 Britain had bought more from France than from Germany, by 1913, despite the progress of French commerce, she bought almost as much from Germany as from all France, Belgium, and Holland combined.

It does not follow, however, that the British industries challenged in the nineties were steadily defeated in their home markets, nor that British industry generally suffered more acutely in proportion to the growth of German imports. In the case of the sugar industry some help came with the abolition of bounties by the Brussels Convention of 1902 and with the placing of a duty on imported sugar. The import of raw sugar, both beet and cane, held up fairly well and even showed a strong rise just before 1914; moreover, the export of domestically refined sugar lost no ground after the turn of the century. While the tide of

[26] *Made in Germany,* p. 90. A *Times* leader, Jan. 7, 1899, called attention to the suffering of the chemical trades: "The successful competition of late years carried on by German houses in this important trade, which was formerly in our hands to a large extent, is striking."

112

German sugar was not rolled back, and the Germans did not cease to offer rivalry both to the planters of the Empire and the refiners and confectioners of the United Kingdom, yet the British sugar trade kept a place for itself among the national industries. Competition in iron and steel manufactures was periodically noticeable, and the value of these imports from Germany continued to grow, especially from 1910 to 1913; but it is important to notice on the other hand the remarkable growth of importation from Germany of pig iron and steel ingots and the continued export to Germany of iron and steel manufactures. The situation in these trades illustrates that equilibrium in Anglo-German commerce which was attained in the early years of the twentieth century. As for textiles, with the exception of a strong increase in German cotton piece goods, the trade statistics bear no testimony to any conquest of the United Kingdom market by German products. In chemicals, on the other hand, the Germans continued their capture of the market. Writing in 1911, J. D. Whelpley pointed out that the men who formerly traveled in Germany selling English chemicals now traveled in England selling German chemicals.[27] But it is probable that in chemicals as in machinery and electrical goods, which Britain imported very heavily after 1900, specialization had done much to blunt competition. It is thus very difficult to make a certain generalization on German competition in the United Kingdom markets in the decade before the war. That a good measure of it continued is probably true, but it does not seem to have been agitated publicly as much as in the nineties. Apprehension of Germany as a world rival capturing British trade on all continents did not abate, but of complaints about the displacement of British by German goods in the home market one reads little; and where competition is not complained against it is difficult to discern. Indeed, in 1913, a *Times* article concerning the textile trade declared that the number of complaints had been reduced, that "materially less has been heard of the destructive effects of foreign efforts since the expansion of world business began." Prob-

[27] *Trade of the World*, p. 77.

ably the significant fact is that British business gradually adjusted itself more and more to greater specialization and to the handling of ever larger quantities of German goods for industrial uses, thus relaxing in some degree the strain of competition in the home market.

3

The scene may now be shifted to the markets of Continental Europe, where some of the most acute phases of Anglo-German rivalry are to be discovered. The statistics of commerce, from which the figures produced in this chapter have been prepared, indicate very plainly these facts: (1) that German trade gained very rapidly on British in Continental markets generally from 1880 to about 1885, when the first serious apprehensions of Germany were felt in England, (2) that this gaining either ceased or slowed down from 1885 to about 1895, and (3) that it became evident again in the later nineties and absolutely sensational after 1900. The figures below for the Low Countries, France, Italy, the Balkan states, and Russia show this movement especially.

Let us look first at the chief facts about Anglo-German trade in the Belgian and Dutch Netherlands, through which so large a part of the exchange traffic passed. The figure[28] here represents the comparative value of German and British goods imported *for domestic consumption* by these small but wealthy countries. The figure indicates a certain stability in the relative extent of British and German commerce in this trading community until after the turn of the new century; then the upward shoot of the German line tells the whole significant story. What may be said, however, of the Netherlands as a whole is less true of each of the countries considered separately. The supremacy attained by the Germans in Belgium was much less marked than in Holland. Germany, although forging ahead of Britain temporarily between 1882 and 1885, had a smaller trade than Britain enjoyed in Bel-

[28] This and similar figures shown in this chapter have been prepared from the tables given in the annual Statistical Abstract for Foreign Countries.

gium during the next ten years ; and even in 1898 Belgian imports from Britain and Germany stood, respectively, at 284 and 245 million francs. After the beginning of the new century the annual value of the German trade here was continuously larger than the British, although the comparative totals for 1912 were 703 to 506 millions, which was a far less remarkable margin in Ger-

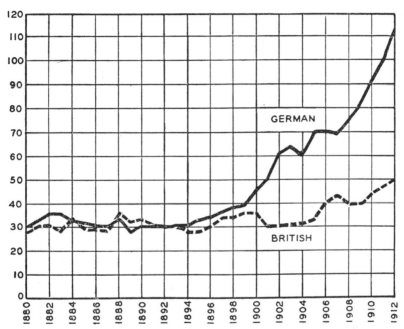

CHART 2. COMPARATIVE VALUE OF BRITISH AND GERMAN GOODS IMPORTED BY BELGIUM AND HOLLAND FOR HOME CONSUMPTION, 1880-1912, EXPRESSED IN MILLION POUNDS STERLING.

many's favor than she had secured in Dutch markets. Belgium, of course, was a powerful industrial competitor of both Britain and Germany and stood in lesser need than her sister state of Anglo-German industrial exports.

As for Holland, imports from Britain and Germany for home consumption alternated in greater total values during the eighties, but from 1891 onward the German advance grew steadily heavier. The British consul at Amsterdam in 1897 drafted a special report on the German rivalry, but owing to the insufficiency of available statistical detail he could form no certain conclusions. He pointed to "considerable fluctuation from time to time, in which articles of one country have been partially displaced by those of the other," but he could not discern for a surety any great change in the general volume of trade of both countries with the Dutch consumer.[29] There was taking place, however, under his very eyes, a most significant shift in the relative extent of British and German trade in Holland. Whereas in 1888 Dutch purchases from Britain had exceeded those from Germany by 20 million gulden, in 1901 the German trade was greater by 221 million gulden. That this became conspicuous enough by 1900 is quite evident from the following words of the British commercial attaché at The Hague:[30]

German and Belgian firms appear, in many cases, to have been able to obtain important contracts in Holland, such as the gas and water works of Amsterdam, the gas works of Rotterdam and Haarlem, though British firms were first in the field with tenders. . . . In late years the imports from Great Britain, especially in iron goods and materials for ship-building, have considerably fallen off as compared with those from Germany. German manufacturers have rapidly acquired a solid reputation for their work, which was formerly looked upon with suspicion, and their products are now accepted as good without remark or query. It is only quite recently that the Dutch Admiralty and the more important ship-builders in Holland have taken to accepting the tenders of almost any German firm for materials. A few years ago it was only the best known German firms that could tender with any chance of success. So great is the reputation of German building yards at the present time, that a certain number of freight steamers are now ordered in Germany, whereas the orders used to go to the United Kingdom. These are changes that have come about in recent times.

The superior export facilities of the German kartel were severely felt by British business in the Dutch market for iron and steel goods and coal, especially in periods of overproduction. A

[29] Misc. Series 419.
[30] Memorandum of W. S. H. Gastrell, Misc. Series 543.

report on the trade of Amsterdam for the depressed year of 1900 dwelt at length on the blows struck at English iron wares in Holland by the great extension of the German principle of syndication. "British manufactured iron," it was asserted, "finds it impossible to compete with the German product under these abnormal circumstances, and can only await the return of a healthier condition of trade."[31] But the Dutch market continued to fall more and more under the domination of German iron-masters. Similarly, Holland bought increasingly German rather than British coal, the respective quantities taken in 1906 being 8,331,000 and 2,381,000 tons. The Amsterdam gas works in this year consumed twice as much German as British coal, and the Dutch steamers were now obtaining their supplies chiefly from Westphalia.[32] By 1913 Germany was sending into Holland more than five times the quantity of coal exported there from Great Britain.[33]

By the eve of the war the commercial struggle between England and Germany in Dutch markets had in most lines been settled decisively in the latter's favor. Imports from Germany in 1913 totaled 1,051 million gulden, those from Britain 356 million gulden. Holland became, indeed, virtually an integral part of the German economic community. Great Britain's position here may be seen fairly well in the following words of the vice-consul at The Hague in 1914:[34]

My connection of many years with the engineering industry in the United Kingdom and the Continent has given me experience of the constant loss of ground of British industry in the Netherlands, which I desire to put on record. I have, therefore, tried to obtain some idea from various buyers as to the extent of the competition to be faced by British goods in the Netherlands, and the most specific and striking information I received from the manager of a large warehouse or bazaar at The Hague. I believe it to be quite trustworthy. In this warehouse nearly all articles in use, except finished clothing,

---

[31] Annual Series 2577.
[32] Annual Series 3948.
[33] Annual Series 5315.
[34] Annual Series 5315, Mr. Barger's Report for 1913.

are sold to the number of more than 10,000 separate articles. About 4000 firms in all parts of the world supply that bazaar with goods, and as against 1000 German makers there are but ten British firms. ... On the first Monday in March the manager of this bazaar will go with three of his buyers to the annual market in Leipzig. ... From Leipzig he will proceed to Berlin, and he also visits Paris. ... But he never goes to the United Kingdom because he does not know of any place he could profitably visit. At present he buys only about a dozen British articles, such as some kinds of paper, leather wares, travelling and photographic requirements, some perfumes, faïence, oilcloth and armchairs.

Let us move rapidly to the commercial scene in France. As in the Netherlands, there was here a certain constancy in the relative proportions of British and German commerce down to 1900, with Great Britain leading by a good margin. The comparative figures in 1888 were 529 and 333 million francs, and these sums were almost exactly the same in 1898. Nevertheless, as it has been shown in the second chapter, British traders had felt the force of German competition in France since the early and middle eighties.[35] There were abundant symptoms long before 1900, especially in southeastern France, of a quietly increasing German commercial penetration, although neither statistics nor trade reports indicate any sharp Anglo-German duel. Protectionist France was striving to keep her home market for her home industries and was not disposed to open her door wide to either Britain or Germany. In fact, she bought from both less during the nineties than the eighties.

Even so, British business suffered in a degree from German encroachment. At La Rochelle in 1895 it was noted that "amongst the things still required from abroad, the Germans are cutting out the English manufacturer."[36] Similarly, at Cherbourg in 1896 it was observed that the Germans were profiting from "the unconscious antagonism and dislike which British methods and British manners on the Continent have earned for our countrymen"; and the consul at Havre in 1898 reported that Sheffield cutlery had "to a considerable extent been ex-

[35] Vide 1887 Report from Nice, Annual Series 189.
[36] Annual Series 1683.

cluded from the Havre market by German competition."[37] A report for 1900 from La Rochelle dwelt at length upon British losses of trade and German gains: "Generally speaking, . . . British manufactures are being less sold year by year. . . . At the same time that our imports are diminishing German goods seem on the increase, although the same custom rates are levied in both cases."[38] At the same time a Marseilles report described recent blows struck at Indian natural indigo by the competition of Germany's new artificial product.[39]

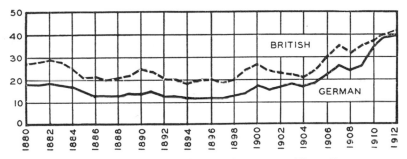

CHART 3. COMPARATIVE VALUE OF FRENCH IMPORTS FOR HOME CONSUMPTION FROM GREAT BRITAIN AND GERMANY, 1880-1912, EXPRESSED IN MILLION POUNDS STERLING.

These consular observations point to a quickening competition in the last years of the century, which were followed, as the above figure indicates, by a striking change in the relative proportions of British and German trade. At the Paris Exhibition of 1900 the German section scored a brilliant triumph,[40] and from that time onward the Germans gained hard on the British. In 1901-03 French imports from Britain declined sharply, while those from Germany rose almost as sharply; and although this movement did not continue, by the eve of the war the two trades were almost equal.[41]

[37] Annual Series 1699, 2034.
[38] Annual Series 2569.
[39] Annual Series 2668.
[40] Annual Series 2680.
[41] German coal became competitive in France from about 1907 onward.— A. S. 4659.

Crossing the Pyrenees, we find the Iberian Peninsula a scene of very active Anglo-German rivalry from the early eighties onward. By 1885 the Germans were reported to be underselling English manufacturers in the markets of Lisbon in many lines, chiefly woolens, hardware, refined sugar, and rice; a considerable transfer of long-established British trade was there taking place, partly to France and Belgium, but especially to Germany.[42] As for Spain, unfavorable tariff relations with England were at this time opening advantages to German commerce, which leaped forward almost sensationally in 1885-86. A relatively poor coun-

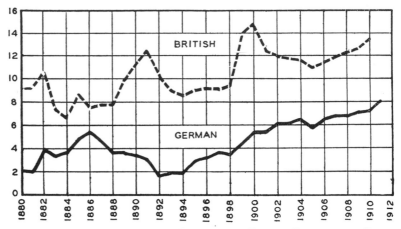

CHART 4. COMPARATIVE VALUE OF BRITISH AND GERMAN IMPORTS INTO SPAIN AND PORTUGAL, 1880-1911, EXPRESSED IN MILLION POUNDS STERLING (PORTUGAL NOT INCLUDED BEFORE 1884).

try, Spain offered good trade opportunities in those cheaper manufactured wares which German industry was better able and less reluctant to produce than was Great Britain. "The poorer the markets," wrote the Barcelona consul, "the better for the Germans, which explains the success of their sales in the Spanish towns and villages."[43] That the rising competition was peninsula-wide is evident from the fact that as early as 1885 serious diversions of British trade to Germany were mentioned in reports

[42] Vide Appendix I.
[43] Annual Series 274.

from Corunna, Bilbao, Cadiz, Malaga, and Barcelona.[44] In certain northern Spanish ports the growth of German imports in the eighties was exceptionally remarkable. "Germany," wrote the Gijon vice-consul in 1887, "now sends us nearly the whole of our imports of nitrate of soda, sulphuric acid, alkali, machinery, rice paper and bricks, besides miscellaneous products unenumerated, and she may now be considered the largest importer."[45] At Corunna, a year later, it was observed that British manufacturers were "losing ground, both in bulk and in value. . . . We are, in fact, losing our chemical trade from Newcastle, pig-iron from Glasgow, and machinery and iron trade from Liverpool, whilst Germany is coming to the front in all these manufactures."[46]

But by the late eighties the German advance in Portuguese and Spanish markets began to recede, as the above figure very plainly shows. In relative value, British commerce in Portugal in 1888 was almost thrice as great as German. "The extent of the commercial relations between Portugal and England," declared a consular report of 1889, "is so very much greater than between Portugal and other countries that it is difficult to see how these conditions can be readily altered."[47] As for Spain, by this time the inequality of tariff treatment had been ironed out, and the value of German goods imported there was barely half that of imports from Britain. The years of 1888 to 1892, indeed, witnessed a German fall and a British gain in the trade of the Iberian peninsula. The retreat of the Germans, during those years when the new imperial fiscal policy was being shaped, was especially marked in Spain; and although the lost ground was fully recovered in the trade revival of 1895-96, at the opening of the new century the value of German imports into Spain stood in about the same proportion to British imports as in 1888. Portugal, in these years, afforded a somewhat better welcome to German goods. Anti-English sentiments there, arising out of colonial troubles and the Delagoa Bay Railway dispute, hampered Brit-

---

[44] *Vide* Appendix I.
[45] Annual Series 152.
[46] Annual Series 329.
[47] Annual Series 700.

ish trade to Germany's advantage; and although Germany, like England, was denied most-favored-nation treatment by the Portuguese differential tariff, her total trade gained sharply on the British. "It will be noticed," declared a report for 1902 on the trade of Northern Portugal, " . . . how the imports from Germany are increasing at the expense of those from the United Kingdom."[48] Heavy losses in the cutlery and textile trades were being suffered, and the valuable rice trade, once almost exclusively in British hands and the backbone of London's Portuguese commerce, was moving to Germany. Rice had bulked very large in the British trade of the eighties, but in 1902 Northern Portugal bought four times as much German as British rice. The British sugar trade in Portugal was similarly almost extinguished in Germany's favor.[49] But of course not all branches of British trade suffered in the competition, and losses in one line were commonly being recouped in others; so that early in the twentieth century Great Britain was still exporting to Portugal more than twice as much as the Germans sent there—was retaining, in fact, nearly one-third of the whole Portuguese import trade.[50]

In the remaining years before the war, the story of Anglo-German commerce in the Iberian peninsula is one of increasingly active rivalry, with the Germans steadily gaining on Great Britain. In Spain both trades exhibited a healthy growth, but in most competitive manufactures the Germans undoubtedly made many inroads upon British markets; and their sales were assisted by a much larger capital investment in Spanish enterprises. In the Portuguese market, British and German trade underwent little change in relative position; each expanded, the German slightly more than the other.[51] But that altered character of the trade which showed itself in the nineties became more striking: that is to say, Great Britain yielded to Germany as Portugal's chief

[48] *Ibid.*
[49] Annual Series 1308.
[50] *Ibid.*, also 3064 and 3183.
[51] A long discussion of growth of German trade and stationary condition of British trade at Oporto in *Times*, Dec. 28, 1908.

source of imported finished manufactures. Raw materials, foodstuffs, and coal sustained the growth of British trade, and even English coal faced a rising competition from the Westphalian product after 1908.[52]

Taking the Iberian peninsula as a whole, it was a significant arena of Anglo-German competition and a fair field for rivalry. Neither England nor Germany held any great natural advantage of geographical access to the markets. The Continental railways may have given a slight advantage to the Germans, but the major part of the trade was carried by sea, which gave an equal advantage to Great Britain. The two trades had to cross the same tariff walls, and they both underwent considerable expansion. But their history was very like the history of Anglo-German commerce throughout Europe generally: a more rapid German advance accompanied by a large displacement of British by German finished manufactures.

The scene may now shift to Italy, where perhaps the sharpest phase of Anglo-German rivalry in Continental Europe took place. In 1881 Britain's export trade to this country was five times as large as Germany's; but already German business men were beginning to cross the Alps in large numbers to bid for trade in many lines hitherto almost exclusively British. And at the same time German capital investments in Italy began to grow.[53] By 1885 the Secretary of the Rome Embassy could write that the German firms were offering "the most serious competition" which England faced, especially in crockery, glass, cutlery, hardware, chemicals, surgical instruments, earthenware, and other finished products. German iron and coal, too, were becoming competitive, notably in North Italy; and in Sicily a strong German competition in chemical products and textiles had sprung up.[54] This peninsula-wide rivalry grew steadily

[52] Annual Series 4643, 4689, 5265.

[53] The Deutsche Bank undertook a government loan in 1882 and a large Roman bond issue in 1883; and in 1885 a syndicate headed by the Disconto Gesellschaft took over an Italian railway loan, which was extended in 1887. —Cf. Herbert Feis, *Europe: The World's Banker*, p. 235 *et seq.*

[54] *Vide* Appendix I; also Annual Series 239.

keener in the succeeding years. In 1887 a consular report from Venice emphasized the supplanting of British by German goods ;[55] while from Genoa, in the next year, the consul wrote:

In a great many departments of the iron and steel trade, I am sorry to have to report that . . . the German firms . . . are still steadily supplanting us in this market. This observation applies to steel as well as to iron. . . . I find that in all the iron works along this coast, the greater part of the steel employed is German. I learn also that boilers, complete with all their tubes and fittings, are imported in considerable numbers from Germany, as well as locomotive springs, engine and wagon wheels and other railway materials.[56]

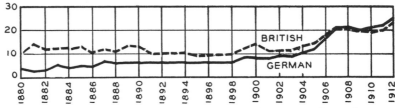

CHART 5. COMPARATIVE VALUE OF IMPORTS INTO ITALY FROM GREAT BRITAIN AND GERMANY, 1880-1912, EXPRESSED IN MILLION POUNDS STERLING.

The consular reports of the nineties dwelt much upon the growing mastery of Italian markets by Germany, although, as the above figure shows, the value of Germany's export trade here remained virtually constant between 1888 and 1898. British trade, during the same period, however, fell in value. At the close of the century they both rose sharply, and when the British fell off heavily again in 1901 the German did not; so that, whereas in 1888 the two trades had stood at 263 and 144 million lire, in 1901 the margin had shrunk to the difference between 279 and 205 millions. "The expansion of German trade with Italy," wrote the Naples consul in 1900, "is notable and interesting, notable because the figures show a persistent progression over a series of years, and interesting because this trade has come to a great extent out of British pockets."[57]

[55] Annual Series 245.
[56] Annual Series 308
[57] Annual Series 2524.

Germany's Italian trade was served by a number of important advantages. The enlargement of the Italian railway system increased German ability to deliver goods in Italy with speed and regularity.[58] Italy's tariff war with France from 1887 to 1896 cut French imports and opened opportunities to German firms, and the extensive growth of German investments south of the Alps strengthened business ties and directed orders to Germany. During a severe economic crisis of the late eighties, when the French attacked Italian credit, German banks came to Italy's financial rescue. Large sums of German capital found their way into many fields of private enterprise, also, the most striking feature of this development being the creation in 1894 of the famous Banca Commerciale Italiano of Milan, which founded numerous industrial enterprises under German ownership or management.[59] Still another highly important factor in the growth of Germany's Italian commerce was the large number of young Italians who went to Germany in these years to secure the requisite training and knowledge for managing industrial establishments. That they went to Germany for this rather than to England may be partially accounted for by the constant visits to Italy of intelligent German commercial travelers, and even professors, who, speaking Italian, were able to instill into young men the advantages of a German industrial education. Upon returning to their native land many of these Italians became factory managers and proprietors, and, being familiar with the German language and industrial methods, they naturally turned to Germany for their supplies of industrial machinery. Had England taken the same part in the industrial education of Italy, English machinery and plant would certainly have been less extensively displaced.[60]

Despite all this, at the opening of the new century Great Britain still led all other nations in selling to Italy, Germany

[58] Misc. Series 417 (Rome, 1897) pointed out: "Great complaints are made concerning the slowness, and still worse, the want of certainty in the date of delivery of goods ordered in England."

[59] Feis, pp. 237-39.

[60] Annual Series 1700.

125

following in the second position. The export of coal explains this leadership.[61] German coal, it is true, had become competitive, but even in 1913 Italy was buying ten times as much British as German coal.[62] Save for this item, the Germans had the best of the trade in Italian markets, and from 1907 onward not even the coal trade could maintain Britain in the first position, as the above figure indicates. The German trade shot upward almost continuously from 1901 onward, breasted and passed the total value of Italian imports from the United Kingdom.[63] In virtually all competitive lines, chemical products, iron and steel goods, copper, brass and nickel wares, tools, machinery, scientific instruments and rubber products, the Germans either defeated or gained hard on their English rivals.[64] In 1912 German and British trade in Italy stood at 626 and 577 million lire, respectively, although a drop in the former and a rise in the latter made the 1913 totals almost even.[65]

It has been commonly alleged that the success of German business in Italy before the war reduced that country to "an economic vassal of the Empire."[66] This has been much exaggerated. The British consular reports reveal no such condition, and indeed after 1900 cease to dwell much upon Germany's commercial advance in Italy. The investment of German capital there shrank rather than increased in the twentieth century; by 1906 Paris had become again the chief foreign money market to which Italy resorted, and in 1914 both the French and the British had far heavier investments in Italy than had the Germans.[67] The

[61] *The Times,* April 9, 1900 quoted the British consul at Rome as follows: "Although British imports to Italy are still greater than those of any other country, the position is not altogether satisfactory, because their pre-eminence is due to large imports of coal and raw materials, rather than to increasing imports of manufactured goods."

[62] Annual Series 5310.

[63] *Vide* an interesting letter to the *Times,* Sept. 24, 1904, from "Anglo-Italian" at Florence, describing German winning of Italian markets.

[64] *Vide* list of competitive trades, Annual Series 4836.

[65] Annual Series 5310.

[66] For example, H. Hauser, *Germany's Commercial Grip on the World,* p. 62.

[67] Feis, Ch. X.

lion's share of the industrial import trade of Italy was without doubt in German hands, but effective competition from British, French, and home industry had by no means been crushed.

Before continuing this survey of Continental markets into Central and Eastern Europe, it will be convenient here to regard briefly the situation in the Scandinavian lands, where a remarkable economic progress in the thirty years before the Great War vastly increased the absorbing capacity of markets. The Scandinavian lands grew in wealth and bought increasingly from their chief customers, England and Germany, who vied with each other for the leading position during the eighties. At no time during the whole period here under survey did British trade in Denmark bulk larger than German, but there was considerable see-sawing in the comparative value of the two trades in Norway and Sweden. Thus in 1887 Great Britain forged ahead of Germany in Norway, after the latter had held the front position for five years, and the consul at Christiana could write: "At a time when the trade of Germany is being pushed to the utmost, and the competition with England is so great, it is satisfactory to find that the trade of Great Britain and Ireland more than holds its own."[68] In Sweden, Germany had assumed a lead over Britain as early as 1881, and from this place she was temporarily dislodged in 1884, regaining it, however, in the following year.

The figure shown here indicates a certain constancy in the relative position of the two trades in Scandinavia as a whole down to the very end of the century, but after that the Germans greatly enlarged their superiority. In Norway a swarm of persevering German commercial travelers, speaking a fluent Norwegian and not infrequently offering skillful imitations of the more salable English wares, eventually delivered the larger share of competitive trade to their own home industries; while British trade exhibited its familiar insufficiency of zeal.[69] Especially marked was the German success in the years following 1908. As for Sweden, Germany's hold on the import trade here grew steadily firmer through the hotly competitive nineties, and, as in

[68] Annual Series 440.
[69] Annual Series 2569, 5081.

Norway, the consular evidence is eloquent of German superiority in exploiting the market. "The efficiency of the work done for German firms by their commercial travelers," declared a report of 1898, "is especially exemplified by their activity in Sweden. Probably ten German commercial travelers visit Stockholm for every one British."[70] By 1909 German woolens, hides, skins, coffee, and iron and steel rails had virtually driven similar British goods from Swedish markets, although Great Britain continued to maintain a strong trade in less competitive wares.[71] This displacement was conspicuous also in shipping. "As regards the carrying trade of Sweden," lamented a Stockholm consul in

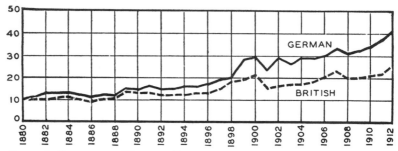

CHART 6. COMPARATIVE VALUE OF BRITISH AND GERMAN GOODS IMPORTED INTO DENMARK, NORWAY, AND SWEDEN, FOR HOME CONSUMPTION, 1880-1912, EXPRESSED IN MILLION POUNDS STERLING.

1907, "the same sad fact that statistics prove concerning the percentage of articles exported and imported is evident, namely, that the British percentage has decreased."[72] Indeed, by 1910 German shipping in the port of Stockholm had secured a very strong lead over British tonnage.[73] Consular reports from Denmark did not bristle so much with observations on Anglo-German rivalry, although German imports there increased much more heavily than did purchases from Britain. The Danish market appears to have been large enough for both trades to expand, and, of course, a very large portion of German importations were for

[70] Annual Series 2062.
[71] Annual Series 4786.
[72] Annual Series 4126.
[73] Annual Series 4786.

128

re-export. Indeed, taking the Scandinavian lands as a whole, the rivalry of the English and Germans from the eighties to 1914 was less sharp and conspicuous than in other parts of Europe. Both peoples had strongly established trades at the opening of the competitive era, and neither had any significant geographical advantage over the other. Moreover, the markets were rich enough to afford extensive growth for both British and German business, and the increasing specialization of industrial production doubtless had a blunting influence on competition. Finally, in Norway and Sweden at least, no spectre of German economic subjugation arose before British eyes.

Turning now to Central Europe, there is no need to linger over the trading communities of Switzerland and Austria-Hungary, for these lands stood in the closest economic relations with Germany throughout the whole period under survey, and imports into them from Germany preponderated heavily over imports from all other countries. Switzerland steadily bought six times as much from Germany as from Britain, and despite continuous appeals from British consuls for a more effective exploitation of Swiss markets there was no change at all in the relative proportions of the two trades. As for Austria-Hungary, the German and British trades stood at 19 and 5 millions sterling respectively in 1891 and at 59 and 10 millions in 1912. Geography, railroads, and similarity of civilization alone are sufficient to explain this German monopolizing of the widening markets of Central European lands.

But continuing on into the Balkan peninsula, we enter an area of very active Anglo-German rivalry. Our figure here indicates a rather considerable trade victory for the Germans over the British in the countries of Roumania, Bulgaria, Serbia, and Greece, for it will be seen at once that the British preponderance of the later eighties gave way to a powerful German command of these markets on the eve of the War. The enlarged facilities of railroad transport into these lands gave to German (and also Austrian) exporters powerful advantages of rapid access to the markets, while direct importation from Great Britain continued by way of maritime routes. German traders also profited from the through-tariff system for goods shipped from Hamburg via the Levant Line from 1889 onward.[74]

Only in Greece, where the railroad revolution had rather less effect upon British trade, did the British export business keep its long lead over the German, although that is not to say a keen rivalry failed to develop.[75] Anglo-German competition became

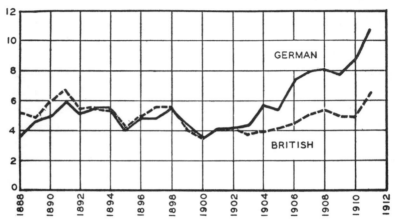

CHART 7. COMPARATIVE VALUE OF BRITISH AND GERMAN IMPORTS INTO ROU-MANIA, BULGARIA, SERBIA, AND GREECE (FOR HOME CONSUMPTION), 1888-1911 (SERBIAN IMPORTS NOT INCLUDED BEFORE 1895).

marked here as early as the eighties, the Athens consul writing of Germany in 1886 as "our greatest rival in Greece."[76] A general report on the trade of Greece at this time, indeed, painted a dark picture of the British position:

The whole of the iron rails, carriages, locomotives and plant of the Piraeus and Patras narrow gauge railway, as well as of the similar railway from Athens to Laurium, etc., came from Germany. . . . Again as regards war materials, the artillery of the Greek army and navy is entirely supplied by the firm of Messrs. Krupp. . . . Six large first-class torpedo launches were lately purchased by the Greek

[74] *Vide* Report from Frankfort, Annual series 2851.

[75] *Vide* Annual Series 50, 56, 1362, 1591, 1682, 1720, 1763, 2068, 2857, 4668, 4530.

[76] *Vide* Appendix I.

Government from Germany. . . . As regards hardware and articles of this description, English goods are nowhere: they are seldom imported; the German goods are cheaper, and . . . answer every purpose. . . . In fact, judging from what is taking place . . ., the trade appears to have passed from Englishmen to foreigners. The old English Levant houses have disappeared, and British enterprise with them.[77]

Despite this doleful outlook, German and English imports into Greece stood in 1888, respectively, at 3 and 31 million drachmas; and although consuls went on citing trade losses to Germany, the respective figures in 1911 were 13 and 41 millions. British losses in one line must, therefore, have been constantly made up in others.

But in the countries of Serbia, Bulgaria, and Roumania, there took place a complete reversal in the preponderance of trade. Serbian import statistics are lacking in the Board of Trade tables before 1895, but by 1901 purchases from Germany had come to exceed those from Britain by 7 to 4 million dinars, and by 1912 the respective figures were about 31 to 9 millions. In Bulgaria imports from Great Britain exceeded those from Germany by 20 to 4 million lei; by 1911 the figures stood in Germany's favor by 40 to 30 millions.[78] In Roumania British and German imports were about equal in value during the eighties, but from about 1890 onward the German figure soared, while the British failed to gain at all. The two trades stood at 184 and 86 million lei, respectively, in 1911. Consular reports from all these countries contained frequent references to the steady capture of British markets by German agents, so that there can be no doubt but that a great part of the German expansion was accomplished at British expense. And some of the principal reasons for this were also continually cited—the familiar reasons: the larger number of German commercial travelers, the greater facility and elasticity of German credit arrange-

[77] Annual Series 50.

[78] "In the year 1909," declared a consular Report (A. S. 4609), "the value of imports from Germany into Bulgaria surpassed those from the United Kingdom for the first time."

ments, the more extensive German knowledge of the needs and capacities of markets and of the Balkan languages, the cheaper cost of German goods, plus cheaper freights and more prompt delivery. Charges of apathy and lack of effort on the part of the British in Balkan markets abounded with more than usual frequency in the trade reports from this part of the world, which constantly compared British business unfavorably with German in respect of methods and intelligent effort. But whatever may have been the reasons, the central fact of importance here is that German commercial power in Balkan Europe, especially after 1900, soared far beyond that of Great Britain. The statistics of trade show the Balkan peoples being drawn ever more closely into the Central European economic community, the heart of which was industrial Germany.[79]

Attention may now be turned to Russia. Here, in the late nineteenth century, was one of the great world areas whose markets, if adequately opened, offered the prospect of almost limitless cultivation by western business. Railroad building, agricultural and industrial progress quickened their pace, but on the other hand the eighties saw a rather premature Russian attempt to gain greater economic independence of the West.[80] A mounting tariff and a declining import trade featured Russian commercial history in this decade, with depressing results for both British and German exports to Russia. Great Britain, if her export of foreign and colonial wares be reckoned in with United Kingdom produce, at this time held the first place among nations trading with Russia; but the Germans were not far behind, and they maintained their business against the Russian tariff more successfully than did the British. The latter, indeed, labored against formidable difficulties. Political hostility, which drew England and Russia so often to the verge of war, retarded commercial relations and steered British capital away

[79] *Vide* Annual Series 70, 176, 1448, 1609, 1775, 1826, 2029, 2100, 2493, 2553, 3329, 4609, 4677, 4797, 4817, 5326; also report of address of Serbian Consul-General for Scotland at London C. of C. on British commercial relations with Balkan countries in *Times,* Dec. 6, 1905.

[80] Cf. Misc. Series 37, Report on Development of the Industries and Manufactures of European Russia.

from Russian investments.[81] Moreover, there existed in Great Britain a vast ignorance of the great Muscovite Empire. Englishmen traveled very little in Russia, and few were acquainted with the language. The consular reports are full of references to the dearth of English commercial agents and the consequent dependence of British business on native or German agents.

The Germans faced fewer obstacles. They knew better both the country and the language, and because of their proximity derived special advantages from the development of overland transportation. With the cheaper wares they had to offer and their superior sales methods and study of the market, they were better able to maintain their trade and even to secure much that was lost by British firms. "It is the comparative cheapness of German hardware that drives our own nearly out of the Russian market," wrote the St. Petersburg Consul-General in 1887, and this was generally true for most goods in which Anglo-German competition existed. Often the cheaper German article paid homage to the established reputation of its British rival by bearing to it a striking resemblance in shape, finish, and packing, but there does not appear to have been much German piracy in British trade marks.[82] Russia, moreover, was honeycombed with German agents and drummers, especially in the western provinces, and these often acted for British as well as German firms. The Odessa Consul-General in 1886 found Kieff swarming with German commercial travelers, and he wrote significantly: "I hear that several English houses have employed Germans as travelers, and that these persons have by degrees transferred the business they have collected together to their own countrymen."[83]

The early nineties afforded Great Britain a favorable opportunity to recoup some of her losses at German expense. Russo-German tariff reprisals developed into a bitter customs war in 1891, and Germany found herself temporarily almost shut out of Russian markets. Her exports there declined sharply,

[81] *Vide Times* article, Sept. 4, 1877; "British Capital and Russian Industries."
[82] Annual Series 447.
[83] Misc. Series 1.

while Great Britain's Russian trade for 1890-95 increased fifty per cent over the previous five-year period. But the tariff war ended in the convention of 1894, by which Russian duties on manufactured goods were scaled downward and the former differential rates favoring goods imported by sea, which had worked beneficially for Great Britain, were abolished.[84] The British chance to gain on the Germans in this market thus passed, and the slight extent to which it had been capitalized may be seen in the following words of the Odessa consul in 1894:

That the tariff war with Germany was an opportunity for British manufacturers to step in and bid for the immense trade held by Germany formerly is patent to every one acquainted with this country, and that the British manufacturers utterly failed to reap any permanent benefit is also well known to every one acquainted with Russia. . . . Now that the tariff war with Germany is over, it is safe to say that Russia is inundated with travelers and offers from Germany, and the spirit of enterprise shown by Germany in being willing to adapt her manufactures to the requirements of Russia bids fair to ensure the largest proportion of Russia's requirements for the next ten years being supplied by Germany.[85]

This forecast was entirely accurate. Although the British, through most-favored-nation treatment, secured the benefits of the lowered rates in the 1894 convention and their exports to Russia rose encouragingly, Germany's Russian trade in the next ten years shot up to double the value of United Kingdom exports. The German recovery was so sudden and strong that the Berlin correspondent of the *Times* early in 1896 drew "public attention to the growing danger with which German competition [in Russia] threatens English trade—a danger, perhaps, more urgent and real than any which is likely to arise out of political friction between the two countries."[86] By 1897

---

[84] *Vide* reports of Secretary of Berlin Embassy and Frankfort Consul-General on Russo-German tariff convention of 1894. Misc. Series 328, 329.

[85] Annual Series 1439.

[86] "German Trade Competition," Feb. 5, 1896. *Vide* also leading article, "English and German Trade with Russia," in *Iron and Steel Trades Journal*, Dec. 28, 1895, and another leader of same title in same journal for March 7, 1896.

the German trade exceeded the combined value of British exports of both domestic and foreign and colonial goods. Hundreds of significant facts might be set forth to illustrate the commanding position which German business now assumed. For example, at Odessa in 1903, when British shipping was still twelve times as heavy as German, a large tinning industry employing eight hundred hands had secured all of its new machinery from Germany. Another Odessa plant for the manufacture of cocoanut oil at this time had twenty presses in use, of which the four original ones were made in England and the remaining

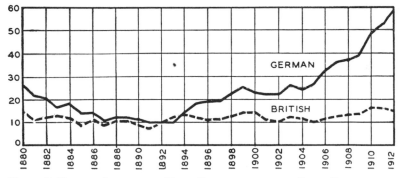

CHART 8. RUSSIAN IMPORTS FOR HOME CONSUMPTION FROM GREAT BRITAIN AND GERMANY, 1880-1912, EXPRESSED IN MILLION POUNDS STERLING.

sixteen came from Germany.[87] Of the total Russian importation of electrical plant and appliances, well over three-fourths was coming from Germany and only a very small fraction from Great Britain. "The employment of electricity," wrote the Moscow Consul in 1905, "is rapidly increasing in Russia, and Germany . . . seems to have quite the lion's share of the market, both as regards getting the big contracts for electrifying tramways, etc., and for supplying all sorts of plants. The installation of electric lighting in towns, the conversion of tramway systems to electric traction, etc., is taking place in various towns, but everywhere I hear of it being done by Germans."[88] The advertisements of German firms in the Russian press had become

[87] Annual Series 3277.
[88] Annual Series 3441.

common, although British advertisements were rarely seen.[89]
The following Russian import statistics for 1904 will exhibit
the measure of Germany's superiority in several important lines
of competitive trade:[90]

	From Great Britain (rubles)	From Germany (rubles)
Mill machinery	7,967,000	22,966,000
Chemicals	1,687,000	7,853,000
Iron & steel goods	1,138,000	5,021,000
Leather goods	910,000	3,947,000
Wire	653,000	3,231,000
Agricultural machinery	590,000	3,626,000
China ware	159,000	735,000

The expiration of the 1894 tariff convention did not check
the German commercial advance in Russia, for a new treaty,
without serious disadvantage to German industry, was negotiated for the regulation of Russo-German commerce until 1916.
The decade following 1904 thus saw no important changes in
the relative position of British and German trade in Russia,
save the strengthening of the latter's commanding leadership,[91]
as the figure given here clearly shows. Among the forty-seven
leading classifications of Russian imports from Great Britain
and Germany in 1913, British sales exceeded German in only
five: tea, fish, coal, tallow, and ships; so that of all the manufactures of the "workshop of the world," ships alone maintained
their supremacy in the Russian market. Even the 41 million tons
of British coal were almost matched by the German shipment of
36 millions, and in coke the Germans actually led. On the eve
of the war the German export trade to Russia was almost four
times as large as Britain's in value. Certainly in none of the
other great areas of the world was the victory of German over
British commerce more emphatically complete. A comparative
examination of itemized competitive imports shows this much

[89] *Ibid.*

[90] *Ibid.,* figures taken from different parts of report.

[91] Cf. leading article on British and German trade with Russia in *Chamber of Commerce Journal,* June, 1910.

136

more effectively than the round figures of total trade. In iron and steel goods the German superiority was 15 to 2 million rubles, in bricks and tiles 3 million to 400 thousand, in dye stuffs and paints 11 million to 600 thousand, in wool yarn 10 to 7 million, in cotton yarn 5 to 4 million, in hardware and cutlery 8 to 1 million, in machinery 86 to 15 million, in chemicals 19 to 2 million, and in woolen manufactures 12 to 2 million. These branches of trade represent, for the most part, the output of plants and factories situated in the United Kingdom and Germany, but even in the business of transshipping overseas commodities to Russia Germany had now far surpassed England. This is shown by the fact that in 1913 Germany sent Russia raw cotton to the value of 30 million rubles as compared with a British delivery of less than 10 million rubles. For coffee the respective values were 5 million and 601 thousand rubles, for spices 1 million and half a million, for rice 2 million and half a million, and for tobacco 1 million and 142 thousand rubles.[92] Although a very great proportion of Germany's enormous trade entered Russia by overland transport, its preponderance naturally contributed to the vast increase of German shipping in Russian ports, especially on the Baltic. In St. Petersburg-Cronstadt, Russia's chief seaport, British shipping on the eve of the War exceeded Germany's by only ten per cent, and at Riga, the second port in size, the German tonnage in 1912 surpassed the British by 394 to 322 thousand tons; while a much greater German superiority obtained at Reval and Helsingfors.[93]

In considering the many reasons for Germany's extensive commercial victory over Great Britain in this part of Europe, it ought to be noted that by no means all of the special advantages were in Germany's favor. The capital investments of Germany in Russia were by no means proportionate to her commercial penetration, for by 1914 both France and Great Britain possessed larger Russian investments than Germany. Large sums of British money poured into Russian industries, banks, oil-

[92] Annual Series 5328. Report for 1913 of foreign commerce of European Russia.

[93] Figures in Annual Series 5227, 5328, 5354.

fields, and mines, after 1906, and these undoubtedly stimulated Anglo-Russian trade.[94] Moreover, British superiority in ships conferred an important advantage on England in the approach to the Black Sea region markets—an advantage comparable to Germany's geographic nearness to western Russia.[95] And even in Poland the German advantage of proximity was partly offset by anti-German feeling and a consequent widespread preference for British instead of German goods; the consular evidence indicates that if British business had bestirred itself more actively in Polish markets it might have secured a much larger share of the trade.[96]

[94] Cf. Feis, *op. cit.*

[95] British shipping at Odessa in 1913 was eight times as great as German.

[96] *Vide* leading article, "English and German Trade with Poland," in *Chamber of Commerce Journal,* Jan., 1911; also consular reports from Warsaw, Annual Series 5233, 5329.

Chapter V

OVERSEAS MARKETS AND SHIPPING

THE pressure of German commerce on Great Britain's business empire extended to so many parts of the world that it does not seem possible, within the limits of this study, to pursue all of its manifestations. Therefore, if its almost universal spread be remembered, it will be enough here to show its approximate measure in the more important areas of competition beyond Europe: to wit, the lands of western Asia (especially those of Ottoman dominion), the Far East, Latin America, and the scattered dominions of the British Empire.

1

The Ottoman Empire, one of the great pre-war arenas of clashing political, financial, and commercial imperialism, may well command attention first. Although partly European, it was largely Asiatic in territorial extent, and we may proceed through it as a gateway to the markets of the East. The high features of Anglo-German rivalry in this sprawling and decadent empire were, of course, not purely commercial. The opening up of Asiatic railways revolutionized avenues of communication and brought to the front important considerations of British imperial strategy; but what is said here will be confined as far as possible to the purely economic and commercial aspects of conflicting British and German interests.

The long-standing friendship between England and Turkey which had been especially marked between 1840 and 1880, was cemented by strong economic ties. A great deal of British money went into Turkish investments and a preponderant share of the Ottoman import trade was of British origin. The English Ambassador enjoyed the Sultan's ear, and British business men supplied the greater part of the trade of his dominions. Economic favors for Englishmen came easy in Turkey. But this pleasant situation was radically altered in the closing years of the century. Anglo-Turk friendship underwent a cooling, simultaneously with the advent of German business in Turkish markets; the German Ambassador captured the Sultan's ear, and Germans began to secure most unusual economic favors. Out of this alteration of circumstances arose one of the most acute issues between England and Germany that the pre-war years witnessed.

The emergence of a German rivalry for the trade of the Sultan's dominions was, as it has been already noted, a development of the middle eighties.[1] For several years before the world began to take much notice of German interests in Turkey, news of energetic German bidding for trade in lines cultivated chiefly by Great Britain was appearing in reports from British consuls in the Ottoman Empire. Statistical records do not permit an accurate gauging of changes in relative trade totals, but it seems probable that in those early years no significant shift of British trade into German hands occurred. During the eighties Great Britain certainly kept her hold on better than forty per cent of the Ottoman import trade. The Consul-General at Constantinople in 1892 would not even admit that since 1884 German trade had made any special progress as compared with British trade; although he acknowledged that German subjects by this time were perhaps enjoying some advantage "in the greater influence possessed ... by their Government," and that German military prestige was sending Government war material contracts to Krupp instead of Armstrong. There had been for some years, he stated, "a panic among British merchants here, with regards to German trade, which, they maintain, is beating the British import trade out of the country"; but for this alarm he could discover no adequate grounds.[2] The following year the same official again analyzed the comparative position of British and

[1] *Vide* reports from Crete, Philippopolis, Salonica, Constantinople, Angora, Beirut, Trebizond, Alexandria, Cairo, Tripoli, Tunis, which are quoted in Appendix I.

[2] Report for 1889-91 by Consul-General at Constantinople, Annual Series 1099.

German commerce, this time noting that the increase in German imports since 1890 had been greater than that for any other country trading with Turkey, in spite of the fact that a large amount of German goods came from non-German ports and consequently failed to be credited to Germany in official statistics. The hold which Germans had obtained on Turkish railways, he found, was doing much to spread their trade; the German colony in Constantinople had increased visibly and "with it, naturally, the demand for German goods." Further, he drew attention to large quantities of imported German railway materials which, being exempt from duty, escaped notice in the import statistics, and also to the fact that "German beer is largely drunk and cheap German goods and stuffs find favour with the natives." Competition was evidently growing keener, but the Consul-General remained of the opinion that German trade had not yet "succeeded in ousting British to any appreciable extent."[3]

The nineties were indeed years of remarkable German business activity in Turkey.[4] The signal for the advance had been given in 1888 when a Turkish loan of £1,500,000 was sold in the German market and the Deutsche Bank took over the Anatolian Railway Company, inaugurating German railway construction enterprise in the Ottoman Empire. The following year a group of Hamburg men, foreseeing an enlargement in the Turkish trade, established the German Levant Line running from Hamburg-Bremen-Antwerp to Constantinople; and this line, from its inception, operated on a system of through tariffs from interior towns in Germany to inland towns in Turkey, arranged by collaboration with German railways at home and in Turkey. The line, therefore, not only largely freed Germany's export trade to Turkey from dependence on British vessels, but conferred a decided advantage on such German goods as competed with British products in Ottoman markets. Thus the early nine-

---

[3] Annual Series 1384.
[4] For a good discussion of Germany's growing interests in Turkey at this time vide Ch. III of E. M. Earle's *Turkey, the Great Powers and the Bagdad Railway*, 1923.

ties, years when British exports to Turkey were falling off somewhat, witnessed a very striking rise in the statistics of German shipments to Turkey.[5] The sharp ascent was checked in the middle of the decade, doubtless because of a lull in railway building, but taking the nineties as a whole German business underwent a very remarkable enlargement in this part of the world; while British trade remained almost stationary. An excellent British summary and view of all this may be seen in a long article in the *Times* for October 28, 1898, written by a special correspondent from Berlin.[6] Until very recently, the writer declared, German commercial relations with the Ottoman Empire had been of "comparatively little importance. England was in a position of unchallenged preëminence in this sphere, and what remained of the Western export trade to the Levant was mostly in the hands of France." But of late, and especially during the last three years, a great change had taken place, and the influence of German finance and German commerce had "mightily increased." Far more important than the direct participation of German capital in Turkish ventures, it was asserted, were the indirect consequences for German industry and commerce. The transaction of business by industrialists and merchants was facilitated, and German traders had leaped to their opportunity. German bicycles, furniture, metal wares, cloth, Solingen hardware, machinery, and electrical appliances were gaining in the competition with similar British articles. But in spite of this seemingly formidable growth of German business, the close of the century still did not find the British much alarmed over the new trade situation in the Ottoman Empire. The author of this *Times* article stated that "British trade still

[5] Cf. tables in Statistical Abstracts for United Kingdom and for Foreign Countries, and Statistisches Jahrbuch für das deutsche Reich. The Consul-General at Constantinople, in Annual Series 2813, gave a table of Hamburg shipments to Turkey which showed a rise from £66,000 in 1890 to £520,250 in 1898. The tonnage of German sea traffic to Asiatic ports on the Mediterranean and Black Seas increased from 1,800 in 1881-85 to 42,500 in 1891-95.—Misc. Series 443, Report on Maritime Interests of the German Empire.

[6] Article occasioned by Kaiser's visit to Jerusalem.

142

holds a firm grip on the Eastern markets, that it has by no means been ousted by German competition, and that . . . it might assuredly achieve success proportionate to its existing extent and past record." Such a view was also given by the Constantinople Consul-General in his report for 1899-1900. To him the most remarkable feature of the Turkish trade was that "in spite of all the numerous artificial appliances for overcoming British competition," the United Kingdom continued to hold its supremacy.[7]

The British reaction to the Sultan's decision in 1899 to award the Bagdad Railway concession to German financiers testified very well to the absence as yet of any serious fears of German commercial domination in Turkey. Influential British opinion was at that time inclined to see in the projected enterprise a promise of great benefit to British commerce. "There is no power," remarked the *Times*, "into whose hands Englishmen would more gladly see the enterprise fall, because there is none which has made such substantial advance in the direction of our liberal economic policy. Both the establishment of flourishing German settlements and the general amelioration of the conditions of life among the peoples of the country . . . are distinct advantages to a great trading nation like ourselves."[8] To whatever extent such a view may have been a reflection of that temporary British flirtation with Germany signalized by Mr. Chamberlain's famous invitation to alliance, the important fact here is that Great Britain, at the time, seemed able to view the Bagdad Railway enterprise projected by her greatest trade rival without alarm. Professor Earle has judged rightly in saying that "British opinion, on the whole was well disposed to Teutonic penetration in the Near East."[9]

The next few years heard the sounding of a very different note. National irritation and anger toward Germany rose to new heights as a result of the 1900 Navy Bill, the South African War, the Boxer War, and the joint intervention in Venezuela.

[7] Annual Series 2650.
[8] Leading article of Nov. 30, 1899.
[9] *Op. cit.*, p. 178.

The idea of Germany as a dangerously aggressive world power took firmer hold upon the British mind, and this cast a different light upon the Bagdad Railway project. The specter of a German strangle-hold on Turkish commerce and a German-controlled highway to India loomed up; a political menace to the Empire began to be read into German railways in Western Asia.[10] By 1902 there were many indications of a rising British apprehension of the German peril in the Ottoman Empire; and if imperial security in Asia (threatened by Germany, perhaps in coöperation with Russia) was uppermost in British minds, the commercial aspect of the danger was none the less plainly pointed out. The following excerpt from a *Pall Mall Gazette* article may be taken as illustrative of the manner in which the German trade peril in this part of the world was being represented:

The German Anatolian Railway Company and the Austrian Oriental Railway Company are at the present moment trying to come to an agreement with the Ottoman Government to obtain special tariffs for the transport of goods from Central Europe into Asiatic Turkey at a rate 50 per cent lower than that actually in force. The reduction, however, would not apply to goods from other countries. . . . This new operation is another move in Germany's ambitious project of capturing the trade of Asia Minor, the importance of which, from the point of view of British interests, should not be overlooked. As Germany's colonial ventures in Africa, Asia and the Pacific have hitherto proved anything but satisfactory, she has for some years past been trying to obtain a footing in Asia Minor by means of commercial concessions at the expense of British trade and the trade of all other countries. The German companies to whom these concessions are granted are all more or less intimately connected with the German Government which backs up their claims. . . . The Germans are not making much noise about their schemes in Asia Minor, but those who are in the know are confident of success. A distinguished German, who is in the confidence of the highest personages in the Empire, has declared that Germany will gradually obtain an almost exclusive commercial monopoly throughout Asiatic Turkey.[11]

[10] *Vide* "The Focus of Asiatic Policy," by 'X,' *National Review*, June, 1901, and "Russia, Germany, and Britain," by Malcolm MacColl, *Fortnightly Review*, Jan. 1, 1902.
[11] June 18, 1902.

Press articles of this sort foreshadowed the great cry of protest which arose in 1903 when German financiers sought the participation of British capital in making the Bagdad Railway.

The construction of this railway, it need hardly be said, came in time to appear to British eyes as a spearhead of German imperialism threatening the subversion of British dominion in Asia, and the opposition which Great Britain offered to its progress, from 1903 to the eve of the war, was motivated largely by considerations of high imperial strategy: protection of India and Suez and maintenance of British control over the Persian Gulf. But the great German enterprise also promised economic and commercial readjustments in the Ottoman Empire affecting British business most importantly, so that purely commercial interests contributed a good deal to Britain's policy of blocking the path of the German engineers.

The British Government's abrupt change of attitude toward the railway in 1903 is well known. Premier Balfour and his Foreign Secretary, Lord Lansdowne, were not opposed to the line if British participation in construction, supply of materials, and management could be secured. Lansdowne, in fact, encouraged a group of London financiers to attempt such an agreement with the German concessionaires, virtually promising that if the line were effectively internationalized Great Britain would approve a needed increase in Turkish customs,[12] aid in securing a Persian Gulf terminus, and grant a subsidy for carrying the Indian mails. The British and German financiers then, early in April, arranged a tentative plan for internationalizing the railway which both Lansdowne and Balfour regarded as satisfying the conditions of the British Government. But rumors of a deal with Germany got into circulation, a stormy attack upon the enterprise arose in press and Parliament, and both the financiers and the Foreign Office beat a retreat.[13]

[12] Owing to a partial foreign control of Turkish revenues, the Sultan did not possess full control of his customs and Britain was in a position to block increased tariff rates.
[13] For a full discussion of the British attitude in 1903 *vide* Earle's chapter VIII; also a review of British policy by A. Parker in the *Quarterly Review,*

The cry was raised that England had "coöperated" enough with Germany in China and Venezuela, that the Germans were not to be trusted, that British participation would create more friction with Russia, that a road to India under virtual German control would be opened, that British trade would suffer to Germany's profit, that the enterprise was a wildcat scheme anyway. To borrow the words of Professor Earle, there was "let loose a torrent of vituperation against German imperialist activities in general and the Bagdad Railway in particular." Although the high political considerations touching Russian relations and imperial security in Asia were chiefly emphasized in this storm of opposition, the commercial arguments against British participation were much exploited. The *Daily Mail*, for example, contended that the railway would compete with the Suez Canal, injure British shipping, and (if Turkish customs were increased to secure funds for construction) choke British trade in Ottoman markets. This last objection was put forward by organs of the most diverse views: The *Times, Morning Post, Pall Mall Gazette, Spectator, Daily Chronicle, Westminster Gazette*, and *Manchester Guardian*. They all thought that an increase in Turkish customs to pay a kilometric guarantee to the German concessionaires would mean "financing the line straight out of the pockets of the British merchant and manufacturer."[14] One of the strongest statements of the commercial argument against the railway may be seen in the following excerpt from an unsigned leading article in the *Fortnightly Review*:

From Central Europe to the heart of Asia Minor where the sphere of the nominally cosmopolitan company begins, German trade will possess a through route in almost exclusively German hands. . . .

October, 1917. Herbert Feis, in *Europe, the World's Banker*, pp. 348-53, discusses the British attitude in the light of the *British Documents on the Origins of the War* (II, 174-197), which were published after Earle wrote and therefore necessitate slight modifications in his excellent account. For discussion in Parliament *vide* Hansard, 4th S., vol. 120, pp. 1247-48, and vol. 121, p. 122.

[14] *Pall Mall Gazette*, April 14, 1903.

Nothing can prevent German trade under these circumstances from occupying a preferential position. . . . Nothing can prevent the whole railway system between the Bosphorus and the Persian Gulf from being used for the favoured treatment of German trade, and to the prejudice of British. From the point of view of our national commerce there is not one sound word to be said for our participation in this scheme. . . . Under any conditions . . . the line will be manipulated to serve the purposes of our industrial competitors in Central Europe. But to promote this purpose, it is proposed . . . that we should give our consent to the elevation of the customs duties in the Ottoman Empire. . . . In other words, British trade, which is sea borne, will be handicapped at the outset in order to provide the kilometric guarantee for a railway which has been designed from the first to support German competition. There has not often been a nearer parallel in real life to the case of being made to pay for the razor to cut one's own throat.[15]

That this press outcry was partly inspired by threatened vested interests seems highly probable. Professor Earle has listed the special interests which became alarmed and consequently made themselves heard at Downing Street. The British-owned Smyrna-Aidin Railway Company feared the development of other ports at the expense of Smyrna. The Lynch Brothers' Euphrates and Tigris Navigation Company, which operated a practical monopoly of the river carrying trade between Bagdad and Basra, also took alarm; and so did larger shipping interests, fearing railway absorption of some of the through traffic to the East, depression of freight rates by locomotive competition, and loss of the Indian mails subsidy. These interests, according to Earle, warned the British public that the railway "would bring with it all sorts of German interference in the Near East and undermine British commercial and maritime interests in that region." He does not show clearly, however, in what manner these interests made their influence felt, nor how great that influence was; and, indeed, it does not seem possible to show this. Since the railway certainly promised some general commercial benefits to Great Britain by enlarging and enriching

[15] "The Latin Rapprochement and the Bagdad Embroglio," May 1, 1903.

Turkish markets, it may seem likely that the threatened special interests conspired with the press to misrepresent the enterprise before the British public. Dr. Arthur von Gwinner, of the Deutsche Bank, who had conducted the financial negotiations with the British group, expressed the opinion some months later that "if the question had been fully explained to the British public, and they had been made aware of the conditions offered by the Deutsche Bank, their views would have been considerably altered."[16] But, on the other hand, it must be remembered that it was not at all clear to British publicists that genuine equality of treatment over the railway for British and German goods could be secured. All the attacks on British participation in the project assumed that there could be no guarantee against special favors being granted to Germans but withheld from the British. In the light of what can now be known of the German proposals in 1903, there is no good reason to doubt the sincerity of the cry that the railway would establish German trade in a privileged position in Turkey.

The reason for the Lansdowne-Balfour change of attitude has never been clearly explained. Professor Earle declared that the Government yielded to the hostile press; but it is also possible that a change of attitude on the part of the British bankers may have had something to do with the Government's about-face, for they too evidently retreated before the ebullition of hostile sentiment.[17] Whether the shipping and other specially threatened interests influenced the Government in any other way than through the press is a question that must remain unanswered; but as for the anticipated influence of the railway on British trading interests generally, the force of this in determining the Government's attitude can at least be conjectured. An international railway from the Bosphorus to the Persian Gulf, with Britain enjoying equal participation, and with guarantees against preferential treatment for the goods of any one nation, probably excited no commercial apprehensions whatever

[16] *British Documents on the Origins of the War,* II, 195.
[17] *Ibid.,* II, p. 196.

on the part of the Government.[18] But if the railway was not effectively internationalized and the guarantees against preferential treatment were inadequate, the commercial effects of the line might be very disagreeable to Great Britain.[19] Neither Professor Earle nor anybody else has proved that the terms offered by the Germans *were entirely satisfactory* to the British Government. A recent writer, reviewing the evidence, states that "About the affair there still remains, after close examination, a suspicion that though the German Government was willing to have the façade international, it held to the retention of having the internal organization German."[20] The real stumbling

[18] Sir Nicolas O'Conor, Ambassador to Turkey, strongly favored the project and deplored the decision against participation. *Vide* his long despatch of April 28, 1903, in *British Documents*, VI, 325-27. The argument that an increase in Turkish customs would damage British trade carried little weight. "I am told," Lansdowne wrote on April 14, "that, in the opinion of the Board of Trade, such an increase would not, if fairly levied, materially hamper the more important branches of British trade." *Ibid.*, p. 187.

[19] In a report drafted just about the time the 1903 Concession was granted, the Consul-General at Constantinople wrote: "I hear that, although an agreement was made that no preferential rates should be charged, the Company proposes to exempt from quay dues at its newly constructed quay at Haidar-Pasha goods which do not break bulk. The effect of this would be to place at a disadvantage British goods arriving by sea at Constantinople, and forwarded by rail from Haidar-Pasha to the interior, as compared with goods conveyed from the Continent by rail, and transferred from the Oriental Railway System across the Bosphorus to the Anatolian Railway at through rates. . . . All goods sent into the interior by this line must pass over the Haidar-Pasha quay, and a tariff of through rates from inland towns in Germany to inland towns in Asia Minor might easily be framed in such a manner as heavily to handicap British goods."—Annual Series 2950. The following year, 1904, this Consul dwelt at length on the many minor and subordinate features of the 1903 Concession, which, " in the hands of a powerful railway company, backed by an energetic Foreign Office, may in future possess great importance." Turkey, he thought, might some day become westernized and progressive, and then the Germans would be economically in the saddle. "Preferential rates over the Bagdad Railway are forbidden by the terms of the Concession. But in spite of all self-denying articles it is difficult to believe that, if the country were seriously developed and a large market for foreign imports were created, advantage would not be taken of a combination of the German Levant Line and the German Bagdad Railway Company to convey goods by an all-German route at specially favorable rates."—Annual Series 3140.

[20] Feis, *op. cit.*, 351-52.

block was probably the German-owned Anatolian Railway from Haidar-Pasha to Konia, which the British Government wished to have included in the internationalized line. The representatives of this line were ready to vest its control in the international company at some future date, but this was evidently disapproved by the German Government.[21] Failure to bring that line into the international scheme would leave the Germans in exclusive possession of the Anatolian door through which traffic to the East over the internationalized section would pass. There is, consequently, no good reason to doubt Balfour's sincerity when he announced in the House of Commons the reason for the Government's decision to withhold its support from the financiers' plan:

The arrangements which have lately been under consideration were . . . designed to place the railway . . . throughout its whole length from sea to sea, under international control, and to prevent the possibility of preferential treatment for the goods or subjects of any one country. . . . After careful consideration of these proposals, His Majesty's Government have come to the conclusion that they do not give to this country sufficient security for the application of the principles above referred to.

Probably the truth is that Balfour and Lansdowne personally had been willing to accept the German terms, but were overruled by the more commercially minded Chamberlain and other members of the Cabinet who did not regard the German offer as a satisfactory one.

In the years following 1903 the economic progress of the Germans in Turkey[22] created more and more uneasiness in Great Britain, and British diplomacy in the Bagdad Railway question was powerfully affected by high commercial interests. The For-

[21] There is the following significant statement in a memorandum of the Committee of Imperial Defense, drafted July 31, 1905: "It is clear from the former negotiations that the German Government is strongly averse from the internationalization of the Anatolian Railway." *British Documents,* VI, 333.

[22] *Vide* "German Finance in Turkey," by "Constantinople" *National Review,* vol. 48, 1906-07.

eign Office, especially after Sir Edward Grey went there, displayed an increasing solicitude for British interests in Mesopotamia and the Persian Gulf.[23] A memorandum handed by Sir Edward Grey to the French and Russian Ambassadors in 1907 shows this most clearly:

Apart from the political aspects of the question, the commercial position of Great Britain in the Mesopotamian delta is altogether exceptional. This position has been steadily consolidated since the foundation, upwards of two-and-a-half centuries ago, of the first English factory at Bussorah (Basra): in 1776 a British resident was appointed at Bagdad; at Bussorah there has long been a British Consul, charged with the care of British trade, represented by 96 per cent of the shipping coming into the port, and by the Euphrates and Tigris Steam Navigation Company, who are the principal carriers of merchandise between Bussorah and Bagdad, and who are subsidized by the Government of India for the carriage of mails. Such is now the nature of these commercial interests that the trade of Bagdad and Bussorah, valued at £2,500,000 in 1903, is predominantly in the hands of British and Indian merchants. . . . In these circumstances, His Majesty's Government may justly consider, both on political and commercial grounds, that their attitude towards the Bagdad Railway should not be disregarded by the promoters of the undertaking. They have concluded that this attitude cannot be actively favourable, unless British participation in the scheme were assured and rendered permanent on equitable terms; and they are persuaded that such participation can only be arranged if Great Britain secures the construction and control of the railway from a point north of Bagdad to the Persian Gulf. . . . His Majesty's Government are further of the opinion that the predominant position of British trade would justify the concession to British contractors of such harbour works as might be required at Bagdad, Bussorah, and Koweit.[24]

[23] The *Times* observed, March 13, 1907: "It is satisfactory to note signs, since Sir Edward Grey has been at the Foreign Office, that our Government seemed at last to have awakened to the necessity of doing something to save our commercial and political interests from eclipse in a region where they are so old, and where they are naturally so great."

[24] *British Documents*, VI, 356. *Vide* also the memoranda of the Board of Trade and the Committee of Imperial Defense, upon which Grey's policy was founded. *Ibid.*, 328, 331-34.

It was in Mesopotamia, of course, that the Bagdad Railway could prove most dangerous to British interests. This part of the Ottoman Empire was virtually considered to be a British sphere of influence into which the intrusion of German-constructed railways was not to be tolerated; and the principal key to British policy was to keep the Germans out of this special preserve. As yet German business interests in Mesopotamia were negligible, but they would not be so when the railway arrived. Already some unpleasant things were happening. In 1906 there was sent into Mesopotamia what Earle called "an advance guard and reconnaissance expedition on behalf of German trade." The Hamburg-American Line broke into the British shipping monopoly on the Persian Gulf by establishing a direct line of steamers, running on fixed schedule, between European ports and Mesopotamia, and inaugurated a rate war with British lines which did not end until 1913. Two years later a German consul took up residence at Bagdad. The services of this consulate, supplementing the pioneer work of the Hamburg-American Line, had immediate results in the development of commercial relationships with the Land of the Two Rivers. The value of exports from Basra to Germany increased from about half a million dollars in 1906 to slightly more than a million dollars in 1913; German goods received at Basra during the same period increased from about half a million dollars to almost nine million dollars.[25]

Keeping out the Germans was only the negative side of British policy in Mesopotamia; the positive side was a forward imperialism greatly distrusted by the Turks. Very strong suspicions of British aims in Mesopotamia were entertained in Turkish official circles, which were consequently most reluctant to grant increased privileges to the British in this region.[26]

[25] Earle, pp. 108-9.
[26] The British investor, too, prior to 1908, was distrustful of Turkish investments. "Turkey," wrote the Consul-General at Constantinople in 1906, "is, in German and French eyes, by no means the 'quantité négligeable' which it seems to have become in those of the British investor. As we diminish our holdings in Turkey they are eagerly snapped up by others; and it seems a

Great Britain's assertion of control on the Persian Gulf, especially, had appeared to the Turks as a policy of arrogant aggression. This lack of cordiality in her relations with Turkey was, of course, a serious embarrassment to Britain in her Bagdad Railway diplomacy, but opportunity struck in 1908 when the Young Turk Revolution broke out. Prospects brightened for a revival of high British influence in Turkey as the new Ottoman régime veered temporarily away from Germany; and moreover, the new Government's financial stringency, which led it to seek the consent of the Powers for another customs increase, placed one more useful bargaining lever in British hands. Sir Edward Grey refused his consent to the new tariff schedule unless British wishes were met; and conspicuous among these wishes were (1) that no part of the new revenues be paid out to the Bagdad Railway Company for kilometric guarantees, and (2) that the Turkish Government grant to a British syndicate the right to build a rival Mesopotamian railway coursing the Tigris valley from Bagdad to Basra, with an option for prolonging the line westward through the Euphrates valley to the Mediterranean. As Grey explained to the German Ambassador in London, it was impossible

to agree to the increase of the Turkish Customs Duties unless we had proper safeguards against the use of the additional revenue for the purpose of displacing British trade in Mesopotamia. We felt that we must either have a part in the Bagdad Railway itself, or else we must have a concession by which we could trade with Mesopotamia on equal terms.[27]

This position Great Britain maintained substantially until the famous striking of bargains in 1913-14. "Everything," wrote Grey in 1909, "points to its being our objective to induce the Turks and the Germans to eliminate from the Bagdad conces-

serious question whether we are not making a mistake in letting go all hold in this country. . . . The Germans are, year by year, investing more money in this country. . . . There is apparently no difficulty in finding German money for enterprise in Turkey. The only railway in Turkey left to-day in British hands is the Smyrna-Aidin."—Annual Series 3533.

[27] *British Documents,* VI, 373-378.

sion all interest in any line south of Bagdad and to promise us a concession to make a railway from Bagdad to the Gulf. The *quid pro quo* for this would be an unconditional consent on our part to the four per cent increase of Customs dues. We must also consider how far our interest should be secured in a line west from Bagdad to the Mediterranean." Mistress of the Persian Gulf and with a powerful trading foothold in Mesopotamia, Britain needed only this opportunity of blocking the customs increase to put the screws on Turkey and bring the Germans to a satisfactory agreement. "Our position," observed Sir Charles Harding, "is a very strong one and we must now take care to get all that we want."[28]

In this situation, the Turks, although drawing back somewhat suspiciously from British demands, induced the German concessionaires to seek again for an arrangement that would make the British partners in the Bagdad Railway and thus bring their opposition to an end. Dr. von Gwinner reopened financial negotiations with the British bankers, offering them the section from Bagdad southward. But although this was just what Grey's policy had been aiming at the negotiations resulted in no agreement, owing to a number of circumstances. Differences of opinion over the principle of kilometric guarantees (which the British Government strongly disapproved), the dedesire of the German government to make the deal part of a general and wider Anglo-German understanding, British fears lest Russia should also come to a separate agreement with Germany which would give the Germans commercial entry into Persia, and Turkish reluctance to enlarge the British foothold in Mesopotamia—all these conspired to defeat an Anglo-German settlement of the Bagdad Railway question in 1909-10.[29]

But the way to a settlement was partly opened in 1911 when the German concessionaires accepted a revision of the 1903 concession. Under this the Bagdad Railway Company abandoned its claims to further commitments from the Ottoman Treasury and agreed to surrender, at the pleasure of the Turkish Govern-

[28] *British Documents*, VI, minutes of Grey and Hardinge, p. 385.
[29] *Ibid.*, pp. 380-576.

ment, to an Ottoman company internationally owned and controlled, the construction and operation rights for the Bagdad-Persian Gulf section. Thereupon the Turks opened negotiations with Great Britain to remove British objections to the completion of the railway and to the customs increase. Sir Edward Grey's position and objectives during these negotiations may be seen in the report of his address before the Committee of Imperial Defense, May 26, 1911:[30]

We have only got two objects as regards the Bagdad Railway. One is to secure that when the railway is made British trade shall not be at a disadvantage in the rates which are levied on goods transported, by the railway; and we should like to have some say in the management of the line which would enable us to know exactly how the rates on goods were being fixed, so as to make sure that the rates fixed on British goods were not higher than the rates fixed on goods in which Germany was more interested than we were, and so forth. That is one object. The other object is that the situation in the Persian Gulf—the strategic situation—should not be altered in any way which would damage our prestige or damage our strategic position. . . . I think we shall be able to arrange all these things, but what makes them acute at the present moment is this: Turkey wants an increase of customs dues. That increase of dues will fall on the trade, and, though it will eventually be paid by the Turkish consumer, it will fall in the first instance on trade in which we are more interested than any other Power. The increased duties cannot be imposed without our consent. Turkey asks for our consent, and when

[30] *Ibid.*, pp. 786-87. A good sample of the view of the commercial community on the question of equal rate treatment was the following: "With regard to the preservation of our trade in the regions served by the Bagdad Railway, if equal trading rights are not recognized, or if the demand that preferential rights should not be given is unsuccessful, there would be no remedy, unless other concessions for railway construction could be secured. In railway rating, as in commercial treaties, goods may be graded in such a way that grades which appear equal may nevertheless press with unequal severity upon the manufacturing industry of one or other of two countries. Thus, alternative classes of goods, slightly differing, are produced in two countries and a division is made in the classification so that one class goes at one rate and the other at another. The possibility of discrimination of this sort makes it essential that equal rights for British trade upon the Baghdad Railway should be insisted upon."—Leading article, "The Baghdad Railway," in *Chamber of Commerce Journal*, April, 1911.

she has got the money she is going to use it directly or indirectly to make the Bagdad Railway, and we have said to her we will agree to this burden on our trade if it is necessary to increase your revenue; but we cannot agree to it if the money is going to be used to make a railway in which we shall have no share, and which possibly may be found to be to the disadvantage of British trade.

It will be noticed that Grey now made no mention of his former demand for a British syndicate to have the construction and management of the southern section of the railway, and in the final settlement of the whole problem Britain did not take this. But she got things equally good. The Anglo-Turkish negotiations ultimately came to fruition in a series of agreements in 1913, which were supplemented by an Anglo-German accord and, with the latter, constituted a complete settlement of the major issues raised in the economic rivalry between England and Germany in the Ottoman Empire.

The principal points of the 1913-14 settlement can be summarized briefly. The German railway concessionaires were permitted to build the line from Bagdad to Basra, but without an extension to the Persian Gulf, over which the Turkish Government now acknowledged Britain's special position. The Germans gave a guarantee, fortified by the appointment of two Englishmen to the Board of Directors of the Bagdad Railway Company, against any discriminatory or preferential rates for goods or passengers. How well British shipping interests were taken care of in the bargaining may be seen in the fact that Lord Inchcape, head of the Peninsular and Oriental and the British India Steam Navigation companies, secured exclusive rights for sixty years to operate barges and steamers on the Mesopotamian rivers. With these rights in his possession, Inchcape organized the Ottoman Navigation Company (into which the Lynch Brothers were absorbed) and secured a guarantee from the Bagdad Railway Company for the freight carriage of railway construction materials. Inchcape and Mr. John Lynch also got a forty per cent participation in a newly organized Ottoman Ports Company, which received all rights for the construction of port and terminal facilities at Bagdad and Basra;

twenty per cent of the shares in this company were assigned to the Bagdad Railway Company. Irrigation and oil rights also figured prominently in the bargain making. German irrigation interests in Cilicia and British irrigation interests in lower Mesopotamia received recognition. Also, the German Government recognized southern Mesopotamia and central and south Persia as an exclusive field for the operations of the British Government-controlled Anglo-Persian Oil Company; while an Anglo-German syndicate formed the Turkish Petroleum Company, which received exclusive rights for the exploitation of oil resources in the Mosul and Bagdad vilayets. This concern was actually under British control, since half the shares were assigned to the National Bank of Turkey (controlled by Sir Ernest Cassel) and another financial group in which Lord Inchcape was included; while a quarter interest went to the Royal Dutch Shell and the remainder to the Deutsche Bank. Other features of the exchange of bargains were the extension of the British-owned Smyrna-Aidin line and its junction with the Bagdad line, and the granting of valuable navigation rights on Asia Minor lakes to British interests. It is not difficult to perceive in all this the high price which Great Britain exacted for approving the Turkish Customs increase and abandoning her opposition to the Bagdad Railway. In Professor Earle's opinion, England gained more than Germany in the bargain making. She secured guarantees of equality for British citizens and British goods on the German railway lines in Turkey. In addition, English capitalists received a monopoly of navigation on the Tigris and Euphrates, a forty per cent interest in the port and terminal facilities at Bagdad and Basra, control of the oil resources of the Mesopotamian valley, extensions to British owned railways in Southern Anatolia, and other valuable economic concessions. British political control was recognized as dominant in southern Mesopotamia; therefore the Bagdad Railway no longer could be said to be a menace to the safety of India.[31]

[31] *Vide* Earle, pp. 252-70, for full account of bargain making. For text of Anglo-German Convention of June 15, 1914, which brought all to a conclusion, *vide Political Science Quarterly*, 1923, pp. 29-44.

If it is true (and it certainly seems to have been true from 1908 to 1914) that Great Britain held her own fairly well against German rivalry for economic privileges in Turkey, the same can hardly be said for competition in the sale of goods. The

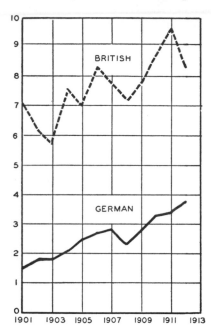

CHART 9. COMPARATIVE VALUE OF BRITISH AND GERMAN EXPORTS TO TURKEY IN EUROPE AND ASIA, 1901-1912, EXPRESSED IN MILLION POUNDS STERLING.

figure given here,[32] showing the comparative value of British and German exports to Turkey from 1901 to 1912 indicates a steadier and more consistent expansion of German sales; moreover, in 1902, 1905, 1907, and 1912 a rise of the German figures occurred simultaneously with a fall in the British. "Our percentage of the total trade," wrote the Consul-General at Constantinople in 1906, "is not as high as it was, but our sales have increased. We do not get so big a share of the new business as we did."[33] These words would have been equally true if written in 1913. Britain held her leadership in Turkish markets down to the outbreak of the war, but if the 1901 and 1912 figures are compared it is seen that not only the percentage but the absolute increase was greater in the German than in the British trade. The regions in which German commerce flourished chiefly were, naturally, the Turkish Mediterranean littoral and Anatolia. A remarkable advantage was enjoyed by the Germans here in their system of through rates by

[32] Compiled from Statistical Abstracts for United Kingdom and for Foreign Countries, and Statistisches Jahrbuch für das deutsche Reich.

[33] *Vide* Annual Series 3533.

rail and sea, a method which the British failed to employ.[34] Although severe trade competition in Turkey came also from Austria, Italy, France, Russia, and America, it is impossible to escape the conclusion that the Germans captured a large quantity of business that otherwise would have remained or gone into British hands. It was in Mesopotamia that British business prospered chiefly. Some sixty-five per cent of Bagdad's import trade in 1912, for example, was of British or Indian origin, while only fifteen per cent came from Germany; and in 1913 the tonnage of German shipping at Basra was only 55,149 as compared with 254,714 tons of British shipping.[35] Commercially the Germans certainly got into this British preserve, but not very far.

Anglo-German rivalry in Persia was so closely related to the competitive situation in the Ottoman Empire that this section may properly conclude with some account of it. The Bagdad Railway concession drew German interests farther on into the Middle East, for in addition to bringing railways through Mesopotamia to the Persian Gulf it included a project for a branch line from a point on the Tigris, north of Bagdad, to Khanikin, on the Persian frontier. So that very early it became the hope of German business that such a line would eventually be linked with Persian railways to give German trade direct overland access to Persian markets. As early, indeed, as 1899 the disturbing prospect of German economic penetration of Persia was taken under consideration by the British authorities in India. The famous "Curzon Despatch" of September 21, 1899, drafted by the Indian Government, contained the following observations:[36]

In recent years Germany has begun to display a positive and increasing interest in Persia and also in the Persian Gulf. This interest has been the historical and perhaps the natural sequel of a commercial policy that has for some time aimed at securing the control of the principal railways in the Turkish dominions in Asia Minor,

[34] *Vide* Annual Series 3776; also article entitled "German Through Railway and Shipping Rates," *Times Commercial Supplement,* March 18, 1908.
[35] *Vide* Annual Series 5225, 5369.
[36] *British Documents,* IV, 357.

and of a political ambition, that more recently still, would appear to aim at the protection of the Ottoman Empire, alike in Europe and Asia. The obvious corollary to a system of German railways in Asia Minor, would be similar railroads to the Persian border and through Mesopotamia to the Persian Gulf. Already . . . the Germans have procured a concession for the construction of a road from Khanikin, on the Turko-Persian frontier, to Teheran, and have apparently only abstained from pressing for a railroad in the same quarter because of the violent opposition with which the Russian Minister met the proposal at Teheran. The second son of the Shah, Prince Malik Mansur, has been spending several months in 1898-99 in Germany, where his education and proclivities are reported as having acquired a marked philo-Teutonic tinge. German military instructors have been proffered for the reorganization of the Persian Army. Prolongations of the Turko-German railways to Bagdad and to the Persian Gulf have been and are still being freely discussed. . . . In the Gulf itself a German Consulate was established in 1897 at Bushire, to safeguard the interests of six German subjects in the entire ports of that sea. A Bremen firm opened business at Bushire, but the specially chartered steamers which were sent out from Germany appear to have been a failure. At Basrah a more resolute attempt is being made to capture the local market. Quite recently a number of Germans have for some time been engaged in a study of the situation at Bunder Abbas. During the spring of the present year, a German man-of-war, the "Arcona," visited Muskat, Lingah, and Bushire, and reports have reached us of the likely appearance, at no distant date, of a German line of merchant steamers in the Gulf.

While we regard these symptoms of increasing German interest in the Persian Gulf as emphasizing the international aspect which the Persian question appears more and more destined to assume, and therefore as adding to the complexities of an already sufficiently difficult situation, we do not question the bona fide commercial enterprise which is carrying German trade there, as to so many other open seas and ports of the world, and we can conceive that we may even find, in the existence of German political interests, an occasional ally or safeguard for our own. German interests, however, have a tendency to grow with some rapidity, and by steps which are not always acceptable to their neighbours: and we think that the need for an early decision upon the future policy to be adopted by

160

Her Majesty's Government is not diminished, but is enhanced, by the appearance of so active a competitor upon the scene.

This despatch was a landmark in the history of Britain's policy in Persia, and it pointed ahead toward the famous Anglo-Russian Convention of 1907. The authors plainly thought that an accord with Russia was worth seeking, and an important reason for their view was this appearance of the German on the horizon. Commercially and politically Persia at this time was virtually an Anglo-Russian imperialist preserve, into which the Germans were soon to introduce complications. Russia preponderated commercially and carried on an aggressive imperialist action in North Persia, while Great Britain, with a volume of trade second only to Russia's, had political interests in South Persia connected importantly with defense of the Indian Empire.[37] When Great Powers are extending their influence over "backward nations" it is very difficult to distinguish sharply between what are political and what are purely commercial or economic interests, for the one interest serves the other.[38] Political influence wins economic privilege and economic privilege invites further extensions of political dictation. So it was in the case of Anglo-Russian encroachment upon Persia, and therefore the intrusion of German business into that country created one more source of imperialist antagonism between Great Britain and Germany.

In 1907 Russia and England signed the famous St. Petersburg Convention dividing Persia into Russian, British, and neutral spheres of interest. By this instrument their long-standing rivalry gave way to a partnership in the task of "reforming" and coaching the acts and policies of the Persian state. Published documents showing the progress of the Anglo-Russian

[37] For survey of British position in Persia (1905) *vide British Documents*, IV, 365-74, especially Foreign Office Memorandum of Oct. 31, 1905, on British policy in Persia.
[38] ". . . concessions for railways and other enterprises in countries such as Persia carried more with them than appeared on the surface," wrote Sir Arthur Nicolson to Sir Edward Grey, Nov. 4, 1906, *British Documents*, IV, 409.

rapprochement make it very plain that Germany's arrival in Persia constituted one of Great Britain's most pressing reasons for entering into this engagement.[39] The Germans, to be sure, were claiming no political interests which the 1907 Convention might have thwarted, but their commercial penetration was progressing significantly. It has already been noticed that in 1906 the Hamburg-American Line opened a direct line of steamers to Persian Gulf ports; and now a British Consular report from Bushire for 1906-07 for the first time gave prominent notice to goods believed to be coming from Germany.[40] The press in England also began to take cognizance of this. The *Times*, for example, on June 19, 1906, published a report stating

that the Germans are showing the greatest activity in the Middle East . . . increasing their prestige and fortifying their economic position. Their agents are working methodically according to pre-arranged and systematic plans. Thus while the Hamburg-American Steamship Company is organizing a regular and well-combined service between the Baltic and the principal ports of the Persian Gulf, the Imperial Government is creating a new consulate in Persia and Mesopotamia.

Another despatch published November 2 described the progress of the new German steamer line which, it was stated, "hopes to get all the cargo in the Persian Gulf from the English and Russian steamship companies." On December 17 the *Times* printed a report to the effect that there was reason to fear that before long the Germans would be masters of the maritime traffic with Persian Gulf Ports. Germany had a most-favored-nation treaty with Persia, and her exports there (quite negligible in 1900) had tripled in value between 1901-02 and 1906-07. A concession for establishing a German commercial bank at Teheran was granted in 1906, and about the same time a German

[39] *British Documents*, IV, gives detailed account of 1906-07 negotiations.
[40] Annual Series 3951. An elaborate view of Persian trade early in the twentieth century may be seen in a Report on the Conditions and Prospects of British Trade with Persia, by H. W. MacLean, Special Commissioner of the Board of Trade, 1904. Parliamentary Papers, Cd. 2146. This gave almost no attention to German business in Persia.

application was made for a concession to build a railway from Khanikin to Kermanshah. There were also disturbing rumors of possible German financial assistance for the Persian Government, and of German efforts to secure a coaling station somewhere on the Persian Gulf.[41] A capital significance attached to the fact that Herr Stemrich, who had held the important post of German Consul-General at Constantinople, was sent as Minister to Teheran in 1906. "The appointment of a tried and able official like Monsieur Stemrich to the post of German Minister at Teheran," Sir Nicolas O'Conor informed Grey, "is . . . sufficiently indicative in itself of a more active policy in Persia, and unless I am very much mistaken, the new German Envoy will play a much more important rôle in Persia than did his predecessor. . . ."[42] In the light of these developments it is easy to understand why the Germans, although disclaiming all political interests in Persia, were somewhat apprehensive of the possible commercial effects of Anglo-Russian action, lest the door be closed against them. Even though outright inequality of treatment was not inflicted upon German goods, the fact that no clear line could be drawn between commercial and political interests meant that the Anglo-Russian preponderance of influence might be used to thwart the acquisition by German capital of

---

[41] *British Documents*, IV, 382 ff., 396, 401, 418, 453-54. *Vide* also leading article, "German Enterprise in Persia, British Trade Seriously Threatened," in *Pall Mall Gazette,* April 3, 1907. This journal on the same day declared editorially that Germany was taking a political preponderance at Teheran: "Her first step will be the foundation of the German Orient Bank, which is heavily financed and enjoys the active support of the German Government. That institution—and much more—will have to be carefully watched by the Power which is, and must remain, predominant in the Persian Gulf. The safety of our Indian Empire may ultimately depend upon the vigilance and firmness of our policy in Persia." For other interesting surveys of the German trade threat in Persia, *vide* Lovat Fraser, " The Position in the Persian Gulf," in *National Review,* 1907, vol. 50, and "The Question of Persia," by Angus Hamilton, *Fortnightly Review,* 1907, vol. 82. "It is impossible," observed the latter, "to avoid the conclusion that before many years have elapsed our commercial supremacy in the Middle East no longer will be able to prevail against the flood of Continental articles carried to Persia by German steamers or over the metals of the German railway."

[42] *Ibid.,* p. 381.

economic opportunities and privileges. Thus in 1910 Stemrich, now under-secretary in the Berlin Foreign Office, complained to the British Ambassador that "it was very trying" for the Germans to be told, whenever they applied for the smallest commercial concession, "that it could not be granted because it affected British or Russian political interests." Such was always the answer he had got from the British and Russian Ministers at Teheran.[43]

The Germans refused to consider themselves maneuvered out of Persia by the Anglo-Russian Convention, and continued their efforts to secure economic opportunities there, much to the annoyance and embarrassment of the British Government. "The Germans, as you know," wrote "Our Persian Correspondent" to the *Times*, "are extremely clever at coming on the stage when the audience does not expect them, and at adding life and movement to the play by giving scenes not on the original program, such as the Morocco Crisis, Adventures in China, and Wanderings in Mesopotamia."[44] At length in 1910, during the Anglo-German negotiations over the Bagdad Railway, the navy question, and other sources of disagreement, the German Government raised questions concerning Persia, partly no doubt as a lever for use in the larger negotiations. The German Chargé in London told Sir Edward Grey that "Germany did not wish to be made to feel that a monopoly was being established against her in Persia," to which Grey replied that although England had to watch her strategic and political interests very carefully she "had no desire to exclude foreign commerce by establishing a commercial monopoly."[45] A little later, Chancellor Bethmann-Hollweg, discussing German commercial aims in Persia with Sir Edward Goschen, said that all Germany wanted was an assurance of the open door. With Russia, he said, Germany was seeking an agreement by which, in return for a renunciation in Russia's favor of all efforts for railway, road, and telegraph concessions in North Persia, Germany should secure equal rights in all other

[43] *British Documents*, VI, 464-5.
[44] March 30, 1908.
[45] *British Documents*, VI, 443.

economic questions, the linking up of Russian railways in Persia with the projected German line to Khanikin, and an assurance that Russia would not prejudice international traffic on this line by hostile tariff measures. A corresponding agreement with Great Britain in South Persia Bethmann-Hollweg said he would like to have, and for this he hinted that Great Britain might guarantee to German business a percentage of participation in British concessions as well as recognize Germany's equality with all other third Powers in loan questions and questions affecting the reorganization of Persia's financial administration.[46]

The British reaction to these proposals was very cool. Grey was distinctly apprehensive of a possible Russo-German agreement admitting Germany to a special status in Persia, and as for the idea of bargaining with Germany in the British sphere of influence he expressed his views as follows:

The German Government are prepared to renounce railway and other Concessions in the British sphere, in return for a share in any concession we may obtain there. The only railway project which has been seriously considered is a line from Bundar Abbas to the interior, and, under the German proposal, the Germans would be free to obtain concessions, say, from Bushire to the frontier of the Russian sphere, or along the Gulf in continuation of the Bagdad line. No corresponding share is offered in such concessions, and we should be jeopardising our position in the Persian Gulf, if we allowed such concessions to go to Germany. . . . For these reasons we are not attracted by the German offer.[47]

The Foreign Office was, in fact, absolutely determined to keep the Germans from obtaining any special influence whatever in Persia. The nationalist Government in Persia at this time was struggling to free itself from Anglo-Russian dictation and consequently was inclined to look elsewhere than to Britain and Russia for financial aid; which raised the possibility that it might be secured from Germany, a Power not suspected of cherishing political aspirations in Persia. To prevent this, Great Britain was willing to go to almost any lengths. "As regards

[46] *Ibid.*, pp. 458-9.
[47] *Ibid.*, 461.

Persia," wrote Sir Charles Hardinge to the British Ambassador at Berlin, "if we and the Russians present a solid front and coöperate very closely in that country, I think we shall be able in the end to defeat the Germans, as we are the two Powers on the spot, who are in a position to exert pressure. . . . I will even go so far as to say that I should be ready to advise the exercise of the severest form of coercion upon the Persians, if there were any question of their yielding privileges to Germany which could in any way injure our political and strategic interests. We think that our best policy now is to say no more to the Germans, and we do not intend to send you any instructions as regards a reply to the Chancellor."[48]

All the while Germany was pressing Britain for an agreement, the British and Russian Governments were engaged in extracting from Persia a commitment against granting to any third Power any concessions having a strategic or political character;[49] and that considerable tension was created is well known. The German Ambassador at Vienna was reported in May to have said that if Great Britain and Russia were not more conciliatory the Persian question would cause a crisis more dangerous than that brought about by Morocco and by the Bosnian annexation.[50] And the German Ambassador in London told Grey that in the event England and Russia applied pressure to Persia the German Government would be "compelled to resort to a protest against a breech of most-favoured-nation treatment by the Persians."[51]

Germany continued throughout 1910 to seek an understanding in Persia with both Russia and Great Britain, and Sir Edward Grey continued to be reluctant to approach the question. It is true he considered meeting German wishes in Persia, if

[48] *Ibid.*, 468.
[49] The following observation in a minute by the Eastern Department of the Foreign Office, Oct. 20, 1910, is significant: "The fact is that such concessions in Persia cannot in many cases be considered purely commercial, especially if they involve an extension of such an enterprise as the Bagdad Railway." *Ibid.*, p. 527.
[50] *Ibid.*, p. 481.
[51] *Ibid.*, p. 485.

Germany accommodated Great Britain in the Bagdad Railway question, but the German Government had no wish for such a bargain.[52] So the situation remained unchanged until the end of the year. In October Bethmann-Hollweg complained to Goschen that the British Government had ignored Germany's "most self-denying and considerate proposals" and had stood side by side with Russia, exercising pressure on the weak Persian Government and endeavoring "to reduce German commercial relations with that country to the narrowest possible limits."[53] The Anglo-Russian front against Germany soon afterward was weakened somewhat by the famous Russo-German Potsdam agreement, which opened the door a little wider for German commerce in North Persia. But Great Britain never made a similar agreement for those regions in which her influence was paramount, although the Persian question kept intruding itself in the search for a general formula of rapprochement between Great Britain and Germany down to the eve of the War.[54]

The Germans were thus effectively prevented by Britain from gaining any important economic privileges in Persia, but it is worth noting that their commercial penetration was not slackened. They made a very effective use of the parcel post shipment system and in 1911-12 forged above France into fourth position among the nations trading with Persia, while their shipping in the Persian Gulf came to be second only to that of Great Britain.[55] In his report for 1912-13 the Secretary of the British Legation at Teheran sounded a note of warning on the progress of German commerce, which, in a year that showed a considerable fall in British exports to Persia, had made a sharp gain. "It is important to note," he stated, "that no steps are being spared by German representatives throughout Persia to push forward German commercial interests, and if British trad-

[52] *Ibid.*, pp. 490-91.
[53] *Ibid.*, p. 523.
[54] Haldane, on his famous mission to Berlin in 1912, hinted to Bethmann-Hollweg that some enterprises in Persia might be thrown open to German participation, if an accord were reached on the problem of naval competition. *Ibid.*, p. 679.
[55] Annual Series 5307.

167

ers are to maintain their position they must use every effort to, that purpose."[56]

2

Another great area of Anglo-German trade rivalry was the Far East, to certain regions of which attention may now be directed. In China this rivalry was already fairly active even before the fateful last decade of the nineteenth century. But all over the Far East, in fact, it was springing up: in Japan, in Siam, the East Indies, the Pacific islands, and Australia, observers had begun to notice it. The whole Pacific Orient, by the nineties, was a theatre of sharpening commercial rivalry in which the British and the Germans, although undoubtedly the leading, were by no means the only important contestants. French and other Continental European firms, along with the Americans, were pushing their interests actively, and the world was witnessing the portentous emergence of a modern commercial and industrial Japan. The Far East was becoming a maelstrom of international trading and imperialist competition, soon to precipitate one world crisis after another. These events were to have a profound influence upon the commercial position of Great Britain, which, despite the Germans, Japanese, and Americans, continued through the nineties to be very commanding all over the Orient. To defend that strong position was fundamental in all British policy in this part of the world, and the efforts toward that end were at times crossed by the energetic activity of German business and the acts of the German Government.

It would be difficult to exaggerate the commercial preponderance of Great Britain in the Far East during the eighties and nineties of the last century. A few striking facts may indicate how immense it was. Japan, for example, in 1883, obtained more than half her total imports from the United Kingdom, but only about one-twentieth of them from Germany.[57] In 1888, of the 2,983 westerners resident in Tokio and the open ports of Japan, 1,324 were British, 640 were Americans, and 357 were Germans;

[56] Annual Series 5261.
[57] Misc. Series 564. Notes on Trade of Japan, 1872-1900.

while of the 234 western business firms established there, 103 were British, 46 American, and 36 German. Japan in this year bought goods from the United Kingdom to the value of £5,130,353, as compared with imports from Germany worth only £886,458; and these figures included none of the goods brought from the East Indies, China, and Hongkong, many of which were of British origin. British ships to the number of 846, and totaling 1,319,438 tons, entered Japanese ports in 1888, as compared with German shipping (which stood second) of 342 vessels weighing 312,711 tons.[58] The Tokio Consul-General could write as follows in 1895:

That, in the import trade to Japan, Great Britain, notwithstanding all that has been written about declining trade and the results of German competition, is still far in advance of any other country is shown by the facts that the imports from Great Britain were nearly fourfold those from any western country, and from the British Empire nearly four-fold those from China, which stands next in the list as a supplier of Japan's requirements. So far, experience affords not a particle of justification for the fears so often expressed in late years that either Great Britain or the British Empire will fall behind in the race as far as the aggregate values of imports to Japan are concerned.[59]

In China British commerce was equally preponderating. Most of the trade that passed through the busy entrepôt of British-owned Hongkong was of British origin, and the foreign trade of the Yangtze valley was almost entirely in British hands. Tonnage figures for shipping entered at Shanghai in 1889 show that the British share was twice as large as the Chinese and eight times as great as the German. Six years later the Chinese figures had dropped sharply, while the German rose from 193,724 to 420,284 tons and the British mounted from 1,334,927 to 2,301,184 tons.[60] A similar preponderance of British shipping was to be noticed, in greater or lesser degree, at most of the open ports of China. Satisfactory import statistics for the whole

[58] Annual Series 614.
[59] Annual Series 1632.
[60] Annual Series 765 and 1740.

of China are not to be found, but a good idea of Great Britain's command of Chinese markets may be got from regarding the situation at Shanghai. Here, in 1895, the direct imports from the United Kingdom (exclusive of all goods brought via Hongkong, Straits Settlements, India, etc.) were one and a half times as great in value as all the other goods brought from the United States, Japan, Continental Europe and the rest of the world. The statistics, in the opinion of the Consul-General at Shanghai, afforded

little countenance to the idea that has been disseminated in various quarters, viz., that our trade is being driven out of the neutral markets of the world by German and other foreign competition. . . . From all I can gather here there is not the faintest reason to suppose that in ordinary mercantile business we are in any more danger from German competition that we were 20 years ago.[61]

The British supremacy in all the great marts of the Orient might similarly be indicated. Writing in 1893, George N. Curzon (the future Marquess and Foreign Secretary) declared:

The commercial position of Great Britain in the Far East stands unassailed and unassailable. Of the trade of Japan, more than one half of the imports and more than one quarter of the exports, are in British hands. Out of 570 foreign firms engaged in business in Japan, 120 are English. There are 1,380 English residents in the country, as compared with 720 Americans, 430 Germans, and 320 French; nearly as many as those of the three rival nations combined. Three-fourths of the entire foreign trade of China falls to the share of the British Empire. The trade with the United Kingdom, including that passing through Hongkong, exceeds £15,000,000 in the year. In the Treaty Ports of China 65 per cent of the total tonnage is British; 17,720 British vessels, with a burden of 17,440,000 tons, entered them in 1891; Germany was next on the list, with 2,520 vessels and 1,900,000 tons. At Saigon, the center of French influence, British trade, in spite of prohibitive tariffs, leaves the French far in arrears. At Bangkok there is the same British predominance. In the commercial competition Germany comes second and never loses ground.[62]

[61] Annual Series 1740.
[62] "Destinies of the Far East," *National Review*, May, 1893.

Manifestations of strong trading competition from Germany in the Far East first attained prominent notice about ten years before Curzon made the above observations. German merchants and shipping firms, by the middle eighties, had acquired in the Western Pacific islands interests sufficiently extensive to launch their Government on a program of colonial annexations,[63] and throughout this region there were coming into existence innumerable sources of Anglo-German friction which this study must perforce ignore. Simultaneously the Germans were becoming very interested in the much more promising markets of China and Japan. Both of these lands were becoming more valuable to the expanding business of the west, not only because of the general intensification of international trade rivalry, but because they were awakening under the western stimulus; China especially seemed to offer the prospect of almost limitless absorption of Occidental goods. By 1885 there were abundant signs that the Germans intended to gain a strong foothold, side by side with Britain, in the Chinese trade, and that their Government aimed to help them get it. The *Iron Trade Exchange* observed editorially in late 1885 that

The German manufacturers are determined to establish connexions with China in view of the probable introduction of railways in the Celestial Empire. Already from the great works at Essen a commercial ambassador has gone forth to make an opening for the production of Herr Krupp's work in China, and it is stated that the Deutsche Bank has arranged a syndicate of the principal German rail works to negotiate with the Chinese Government for railway concessions, construction and the supply of materials.[64]

About the same time a writer in *The National Review* asserted that this German rivalry was being "severely felt," that it had "cut down profits at Hongkong to a minimum," and that the coasting trade of China was "rapidly passing into German hands."[65]

[63] Cf. M. H. Townsend, *The Origins of Modern German Colonialism* and *The Rise and Fall of the German Colonial Empire*.

[64] Issue of Nov. 28, 1885.

[65] C. E. Dawkins, *The German Abroad*, vol. 5, 1885.

The attempt of a German financial syndicate to float a large loan at Pekin, the opening of a subsidized North German Lloyd steamer line to Hongkong, and a loud outcry in England against Germany's mercantilist diplomacy in China have already been noticed as occurring in 1886.[66] In July of the same year a British representative at Coburg reported to Foreign Secretary Lord Rosebery

a new departure in the sense of pushing German commerce in the Far East . . . the practical value of which appears to justify my calling Your Lordship's attention to it. . . . With the view of ascertaining the class of European articles most in favour, and commanding the readiest sale in Chinese markets, the German Consular authorities in Canton and elsewhere were instructed to purchase on the spot, and sent home specimens of European goods of every nature, forming the staple commodities most in vogue, together with observations based on local knowledge as to the marks, mode of packing, and other minutiae which specially induced the Chinese purchaser to favour one class of goods more than another. An exhibition of these goods has been opened in Gotha by the Ducal Ministry, at the request of the Saxon Chambers of Commerce, with the express object of showing practically to German manufacturers the objects to which they should devote their attention, with the view of increasing their export trade to China—a trade which they consider capable of almost unlimited expansion.[67]

The interest of the Foreign Office in this development is attested by the fact that the Berlin Ambassador was at once requested to make a full inquiry, which revealed that several similar exhibitions for business men interested in the Chinese trade had also been set up in Berlin, Stuttgart, and Frankfort.[68] Several ironclads were built for China about the same time by the Vulcan Company at Stettin, and early in 1887 a Chinese loan for five million marks was taken up by a German syndicate. "The Germans," declared a *Times* despatch from Berlin, "now think, of course, that they have begun to succeed in their scheme for fi-

[66] *Vide* Chapter II.
[67] Misc. Series 4.
[68] Misc. Series 6.

nancing the railways of China, and they are exultant enough."[69]
All such signs of this forward movement of German business in
China were noted in the British press. The *Spectator,* indeed,
asserted that in China and Japan "at every turn the British
merchant is now met, and very often routed, by the hitherto unknown German."[70] And very early some bitter things were said
about this intruder.[71]

The next few years saw the Germans sharing very actively
in the development of Far East trading. The extent of their sea
traffic to China and Japan increased from 79,800 tons in
1881-85 to 270,700 tons in 1891-95.[72] It cannot be said that
this growth of German business was as yet a challenge to British
commercial supremacy in the Orient; but it certainly proved a
source of jealousy and annoyance, for although British business
did not stagnate, it failed to expand as rapidly as German.
Moreover, not a few British products were actually crowded
from the markets by competitive German articles. In 1885, for
example, some 83 per cent of the total European import trade
at Singapore came from the United Kingdom, as against 5½
per cent from Germany; ten years later the British percentage
had dropped to 71 and the German had risen to 9½. The
Registrar of Imports and Exports at this great entrepôt, in a
report of 1896, stated "that Germany, in what may be desig-
nated as goods of secondary importance, is rapidly increasing
her exports, and that even in the most important articles Great
Britain has not kept pace with the demands arising from in-

[69] Feb. 2, 1887.
[70] "English, German and Chinese Trade," Aug. 14, 1886.
[71] A writer to the *Times,* signing himself "O," had this to say (Oct. 16,
1886). "There is hardly a single article in the range of English manufactures,
from soap to cotton, and from lucifer matches to Keating's lozenges, which
is not promptly and cleverly counterfeited in Hamburg, and exported to
China for sale by German merchants in any market in which they can get a
foothold by dogging our footsteps. . . . I have always been told, and I think
I have seen some striking cases myself, showing that this is where the shoe
pinches, and that this is the kind of thing that is helping the Germans in
their endeavour to beat us in at least one field of foreign trade."
[72] Misc. Series 443.

creased population, new markets, and new wants."[73] The following notes from an elaborate report of a committee named by the Governor of Hongkong in 1896 to inquire how far foreign imports were displacing British goods, suggest a rather considerable German encroachment upon Britain's eastern markets:[74]

ALKALI.—German goods are preferred to British goods, because they are frequently lower in price, and packed much better. The foreign article is equally suitable and equally adapted to the importer's taste and requirements, as the goods it has displaced. . . . Price for price the importer is in favour of the German article.

ARMS AND AMMUNITION.— . . . Gunpowder comes almost entirely from Germany; English gunpowder is much too dear for the Chinese. . . . The German keg of 25 lbs. costs $2.50, or thereabout, whereas the English is double the price.

BISCUIT AND BREAD.— . . . There is no comparison between the quality and finish of the German and British biscuits. The foreign biscuit is very inferior. . . . The German manufacturer makes a common biscuit; it is not baked well, it is made of cheap flour; but he packs it in fancy tins which suit the Chinaman's taste. . . . Biscuits are an article upon which freight comes very hard from England— 42s. 6d per ton measurement—and they are very bulky, while the German article comes for 35s. per ton.

CAOUTCHOUC MANUFACTURES.—The trade in India-rubber shoes was entirely British a few years ago, but now it is about half German and half British. . . . Were it not for the trade mark the British goods would be knocked out altogether. . . .

CEMENT.—At one time the trade in cement was all English. Latterly, with the exception of that imported for the Government's use, three-quarters of the trade is German, principally and chiefly owing to its being lower in cost, being ground finer than the British, and consequently better suited for use. . . . That is to say, it is more economical than the British article of ordinary make. At the present time the Germans have so flooded the markets with their cements that it is difficult to sell even German cement. . . .

CHEMICAL PRODUCTS AND DYE STUFFS.—The Germans have now got the aniline dye trade to themselves. The British manufacturers have lost their trade, at all events with the East. It is in consequence

[73] Trade of British Empire and Foreign Competition, C.-8449, pp. 315-17.
[74] Ibid., pp. 324-31.

of the Germans being well ahead in chemistry that their manufacturers have secured the trade. . . .

CLOCKS AND WATCHES.—Quantities of German clocks are imported here. . . . There may have been a few English clocks in the olden times, but not now. Hongkong now has a clock factory. It is situated at Wanchai, and is a branch establishment of a German manufactory.

COTTON MANUFACTURES.— . . . More than nine-tenths of the whole of the socks imported into the Colony are of German make. . . . There are hundreds of qualities, and it comes down to this that quality for quality there is no use asking British manufacturers to quote prices. . . .

HABERDASHERY AND MILLINERY.— . . . The German manufacturers put up special machinery for the Indian and Eastern markets, and the consequence is that the trade has gone to them and remains with them, and it is not thought that any British manufacturer could compete against them. It is a very large trade.

There are a great many German needles imported here, and sold at from $3 to $6 per tin of ten thousand, where Kirby's needles are sold at $28 for the same quantity. From 1881 the German article began to appear. The German article was made up exactly like the English. It was packed like the English and had a label, a colourable imitation. . . . Ever since 1881 there must have been a progressive importation of German needles. Now it is a very large trade. . . .

IRON WIRE.—About 25 years ago the wire trade was nearly all of English origin. About 20 years ago it began to shift to the Continent, and now it is almost entirely of German production. The wire they send out here is of excellent quality, fully equal to the best English in finish, of slightly finer gauge than the equivalent size in English. . . .

STEEL, UNWROUGHT.—Bamboo steel is almost all Continental, German. The Scottish manufacturers a few years ago introduced their make, but have been hampered in a great measure by the higher freights charged, otherwise there is no reason why Scottish manufacturers should not successfully compete.

COPPER (MIXED OR YELLOW METAL).—Until 10 years ago the whole import was of British make without exception. The import now of Continental make runs from one-third to one-half of the total import. . . . The Germans give more sheets to the weight. Metal cannot be got out of England at less than 25s. per ton, whereas the German freight is 17s.6d. per ton. . . . The German, who is actually charged 1/8d. per lb. more for his metal, can put it down cheaper than the British merchant. That is a question of freight absolutely. The only reason why the Germans have not the monopoly is that their works are not large enough to overtake the volume of trade. If their works were large enough they would supply the whole of India, which is an immense field for yellow metal, beside Hongkong, Shanghai, and Japan. They cannot keep pace with the demand, and that is how the English manufacturers still manage to get orders.

Woolen Cloths.—In woolen cloths the Germans have knocked the British goods out entirely. The Germans have become adepts in working in cotton with wool. Some samples have been sent home of what is sold here as broad cloths, sold as all wool, and the Yorkshire firms have discovered that they contained a large proportion of cotton, and they have replied that they could not make these cloths at the price.

General Remarks.—The Germans are always bringing things forward for which there is a demand. They appear simple things but there is a considerable amount of business done in them. . . . Relative to the growth of the trade done, the foreigners here get a larger share compared with the trade done now than that done 20 years ago. . . . Nearly the whole growth in exports from the East, so far as regards new articles, is owing practically to the German. He has been the first to see the value of any new article, the first to experiment, the first to send it home, the first to find out what it was worth. With regard to imports he will take up an article that is entirely unknown to the Chinese, and begin to make a market for it. It may be infinitesimal at first, but he pushes and pushes it until it is quite a respectable article to handle. He will take up articles that British merchants would cast aside as too small to trouble with.

In the light of conditions indicated by these notes it is not surprising to find the German trade menace in China quite prominently discussed in Great Britain by 1896. The *Daily Mail*, for example, ran a series of special articles on China in which some very unkind things were said about the Germans in the Far East. "Many of them," it was alleged, "are as unscrupulous as the Japanese in their mode of doing business." These articles rejoiced that England was continuing to lead the field commercially in China, but warned against rivals who were working to destroy her supremacy: "We have a rival who is not only very persevering, but also very unscrupulous. We cannot fight him with his own weapons. Shoddiness and fraud are too dear a price to pay even for commercial success." "Perpetual vigilance and resolution in our commercial policy" were needed to combat Germany and "her designs upon Chinese trade supremacy."[75] A contributor to the *Nineteenth Century* in 1898, surveying the rise of German business in the Far East, bitterly assailed German commercial practices there:

The dignity of commerce suffers at the hands of the Germans. They are shopkeepers, always; merchants, never. . . . Pushfulness is the leading characteristic of the modern German trader. He will push his way into almost any market, but he rarely obtains the entry except at the cost of dignity and sound principles. . . . It is only by giving an undue extension of credit, by "cutting" prices, by selling in any quantities, and generally by descending to the petty ways and details of a shop, that the Teuton can insinuate himself into markets at all, his advent in any numbers being, as a rule, a signal for the subversion of sound commercial principles.[76]

It was probably inevitable that the growing importance of Germany's trade in the Far East should induce the Imperial Government to assert an interest in Chinese affairs and take up a policy of establishing German prestige. A general scramble for economic privileges in the Celestial Empire was precipitated in 1895 by the Chino-Japanese War, and in the succeeding turmoil between China and the Powers important British and German interests clashed. China needed money to pay her war indemnity and in 1896 an Anglo-German syndicate provided a loan of £16,000,000, but not without the German Government first favoring an exclusive German loan of eight millions to take preference over a British loan of equal amount. And all the while

[75] *Vide* especially "The Flowery Land: British Trade Supremacy in the Far East" and "Our Trade With China," Nov. 25, 26, 1896.

[76] Clavell Tripp. "German *vs.* British Trade in the East," vol. 43, 1898.

these arrangements were in progress the German Minister in
China was reported to be seeking a coaling station for Germany
in the Chusan Archipelago, at the mouth of the Yangtze, without
any previous communication with the British Government. By a
treaty of 1846 Great Britain held preferential rights over these
islands, and the Yangtze valley was the chief area of British
economic interests in China. Britain, therefore, reminded China
of her treaty rights and forestalled any German aims in the
Yangtze, but the very suggestion of a German location in that
region left a bad impression in the Foreign Office.[77] Germany's
economic ambitions in China were meanwhile further emphasized
by the departure early in 1897 of an economic expedition, which
was described by the British Consul-General at Frankfort as
"the most important undertaking for the promotion of German
export in 1896." It was supported by the Crefeld silk industry,
the textile interests of Augsburg, the Bremen cotton exchange,
the North German Lloyd, and a large number of smaller industries, with the benevolent coöperation of the Imperial Government. The German Consul at Canton was nominated to lead the
expedition in China.[78]

Far from abandoning the idea of a base in China, Germany
made her sensational leap upon Kiaochow in November, 1897.
The Wilhelmstrasse assured Britain that nothing disagreeable
to her was intended, that Kiaochow was chosen precisely because
it was far removed from regions of special British interest, that
no departure from the open-door principle was contemplated,
and that Kiaochow would be kept open to the commerce of the
world.[79] Nevertheless, the pounce upon Shantung considerably
increased British apprehensions of German action in China.
There was no general denunciation of Germany at this time by
the press, but Lord Salisbury told the German Ambassador that

[77] *British Documents,* I, 328; II, 152-53. For an interesting description of
the value of the Yangtze trade and Britain's position there *vide* "The
Yangtze Valley and its Trade," by Archibald Little, in *Contemporary Review,* Sept., 1898; also Ch. VIII of A. J. Sargent's *Anglo-Chinese Commerce
and Diplomacy,* 1907.

[78] Annual Series 1942.

[79] *British Documents,* I, 330.

his Government's mode of action impressed him "more unfavourably" than its purpose, about which he was almost entirely in the dark.[80] Nor was the British Foreign Office kept informed during the negotiations which led to the German-Chinese Convention of March 6, 1898. What was learned was not very reassuring. In February the British Minister at Peking reported that a Chinese scheme for constructing a railway from Tientsin through Shantung to Chinkiang, with English and American capital, had been strenuously opposed by the German Minister, who let it out that Germany intended Shantung to be commercially a German province. A protest to Berlin then elicited the reply that Germany had only asked for the first offer to be made to German firms in case a railway were built in Shantung; but when the Convention was signed it was seen that the Germans had gathered Shantung into their bag. In addition to the 99 year lease of Kiaochow and sovereign rights in a fifty kilometre zone around the bay, they got exclusive railway and mining privileges in the Shantung peninsula. British surprise was not made less unpleasant when the Chinese Government told Sir Claude MacDonald, the British Minister, that the German Minister had given them to understand that the railway clauses of the Convention had been first communicated to the British Government. The Chinese were at once informed that this statement was absolutely unfounded.[81]

Great Britain's displeasure with Germany's aggressive policy in China is perhaps best evidenced by the famous overture to Russia which Salisbury made in early 1898. Sir Nicolas O'Conor, then Ambassador to Russia, was instructed to ask Count Witte if it would not be possible for England and Russia to "work together in China." Response to the invitation was at first favorable. Sir Nicolas advised Salisbury that Witte was ready to support "what he [Witte] calls England's practical and commercial policy provided that England will not impede Russian ambitions in the north. He regards the Yangtze valley as Eng-

---

[80] *Ibid.*, p. 4.

[81] *Ibid.*, p. 331; text of March 6 Convention in British and Foreign State Papers, XCV, 1105-8.

land's proper sphere of influence, and between us we could hold Germany in check." But the negotiations broke down, for Great Britain wanted a general Asiatic understanding, covering Turkey as well as China, without violating any treaty rights or impairing the territorial integrity of either Empire, whereas Russia sought only a free hand in northern China.[82] Failing to put Russia into the scales against Germany, Britain soon had to seek means for counteracting both, because in the middle of March occurred the Russian seizure of Port Arthur. Britain had been able to secure a new guarantee from China against the alienation of any Yangtze territories, and now she installed herself at Weihaiwei, "as compensation for the advantages given to Russia and Germany." This was a bold counter-thrust against Russia, but since Weihaiwei is situated on the Shantung peninsula the occupation also constituted a warning to Germany. The latter, therefore, was given assurance that England had no intention to injure German interests or to create difficulties for Germany in Shantung, but at the same time the German Ambassador in London was told that England did not recognize the German claim to preferential railway rights in the province.[83]

Altogether the events of 1897-98 served to cast a limelight upon Anglo-German rivalry and especially to excite British distrust. The violent disturbances in China, which the German seizure of Kiaochow was regarded as having started, foreshadowed a new order in the Far East that was to be considerably less favorable to British trading interests. Germany, the chief economic rival, had won a special position for herself, which meant that the German flag would be increasingly conspicuous in Chinese waters, that Germany's voice would be loudly heard in Far East questions, and that the German trader would be more in evidence than ever. "The acquisition of Kiaochow and the efforts which are being directed to the cultivation of German relations in East Asia," observed Sir Charles Oppenheimer, Frankfort Consul-General, "make the development of commerce with China and Japan at present appear especially interesting.

[82] *British Documents*, I, 5-17.
[83] *Ibid.*, p. 331.

. . . The increase of the German export of goods to Eastern Asia has accordingly been rapid and general."[84] And from Hamburg it was reported that "great hopes are entertained in Germany . . . that after the cessation of the present troubles in China, German trade and shipping will experience a considerable development in that country, and more especially in the Yangtze Valley. There are many signs which point to strenuous efforts being made in that direction for pushing on German commerce."[85] By 1900, indeed, the Germans were being pointed out more than ever before as the most formidable danger to Britain's commercial position in the Far East. A *National Review* article found in China

the real commencement of the Teutonic struggle . . . for the naval and colonial as well as the commercial supremacy of the world. . . . Germany's real struggle is not with the Slav, and her fundamental conviction is that in China the work of superseding the British Empire shall begin. There, above all, the relations between the two Powers must resolve themselves into the attempt of two solid bodies to occupy the same place.[86]

The year of 1900, however, saw an attempt on the part of the two rivals to work together. They concerted with the other Powers to suppress the Boxer movement and also sought an accord for defending the "open door" and Chinese territorial integrity. Bülow assured Sir Frank Lascelles, the British Ambassador, in June, that Germany had no selfish interests in China and that

the Germans engaged in commerce in China were convinced of the necessity of working together with the English. The interests of the two countries were identical. They both pursued the policy of the "open door," and although there might be a certain amount of com-

---

[84] Annual Series 2484, Report for 1899.

[85] Annual Series 2628, Report for 1900. For a comparison of British and German export trade to China in these years see Parliamentary Paper, 1906 (131), Return Showing . . . Exports to China, inclusive of Hongkong, from the United Kingdom, Germany, and the United States, for the years 1885 to 1904.

[86] "X: The German Danger in the Far East," Oct., 1900.

mercial rivalry, it was evident that the commerce of both countries
would be increased by friendly understanding and coöperation.[87]

The invitation elicited no response, but later in the summer it
was put forward again. The Kaiser told Lascelles there existed
a general suspicion that England's policy in China was aiming
at special advantages for British commerce to the detriment of
other nations. "On protesting against such an idea," Lascelles
informed Salisbury, "and pointing out that our whole policy
was based on the principle of the Open Door, His Majesty said
that, two years ago, Canada had granted preferential treatment
to Great Britain, and it was not impossible that Australia might
follow her example. If this were the case, England herself might
find it to her interest to depart from the principle of the Open
Door, and this, coupled with the fact that the United States, a
protective Power, had possession of the Philippines, might cause
serious detriment to the commerce of other nations in China.
Now German commercial interests were second and not far inferior to those of England in the valley of the Yangtze, and if
Her Majesty's Government could see their way to give assur-
ances that they would maintain the policy of the Open Door,
they would find the German Government on their side."[88]

The circumspection with which the Foreign Office viewed these
advances from Germany may be seen in the following memorandum drafted by Under Secretary Bertie:[89]

We may be able to arrange a modus vivendi with Germany to tide
over the present crisis, but mere "open door" or "open port" declara-
tions are not likely to satisfy her.

Her pretensions are large, for she starts from the theory that by
her occupation of Kiaochow and her agreement with China respecting
Shantung she has acquired a special status there, and that it is not
open unreservedly to British enterprise, but that the Yangtze region is open unreservedly to German enterprise.

What Germany will claim as her special field will probably be

[87] British Documents, II, 3.
[88] Ibid., p. 9.
[89] Ibid., p. 11. Memorandum dated Sept. 13, 1900.

Shantung and the valley of the Yellow River. We shall have to undertake not to support any British applications in that region.

Germany will further claim that between the Yellow River and the north bank of the Yangtze River the division of good things between British and Germans must be absolutely equal, viz., that every concession granted to an Englishman must be counterpoised by one to a German. On these conditions the German Government may be willing to recognize to Great Britain the same rights in the Yangtze region *south* of that river as Germany claims in Shantung and the Yellow River Valley.

We shall then have to fight out with the French and other Governments, who have not recognized our Yangtze sphere of interest, any claims which we desire to support in the special sphere conceded to us by Germany.

As to making use of Germany to come between the Russians and ourselves, we are not likely to have much success.

There can be no question at present of Germany undertaking the occupation or control of a sufficiently large tract of territory south of Peking for her to be a buffer between Russia and the Yangtze region. If ever she acquires such a position, and if Peking remain then the real capital of China, Russia and Germany will in combination control the Chinese Government to our detriment.

Nevertheless an Anglo-German understanding was realized. September 24, 1900, Count Hatzfeldt, the German Ambassador, presented to Lord Salisbury a proposed draft containing a mutual renunciation of further territorial acquisitions in China and providing for joint opposition to such acquisitions by other Powers, with a special stipulation for the open door in the Yangtze. Salisbury rejoined that Britain could not accept a special stipulation in favor of free trade in the Yangtze, or any other part of China, since "its effect would be held to be, and, in fact, would be, to abandon free trade in the other parts of the Chinese dominions." Salisbury therefore proposed that "in place of a limited reference to the Yangtze, a joint renunciation on our behalf of any special commercial restrictions should be extended to all rivers and ports in China." Hatzfeldt cautioned against using language that would oblige Germany to oppose Russia in Manchuria, and it was at length agreed that the declaration should apply to "all Chinese territory as far as they can exercise influence." The agreement was signed October 16, 1900.[90]

This instrument of coöperation, however, very soon lost its strength. Early in November the Foreign Office heard that the German Government, before turning to England, had sounded Russia with proposals that would have strengthened Germany's position in the Yangtze.[91] This created a bad impression, and then in January the British and German Governments found themselves in disagreement over the method for China to raise the Boxer indemnity money. Soon after that, England sought to invoke the agreement against Russia's forward policy in Manchuria, but without success, for the German Government interpreted the instrument as conferring no obligation on Germany to oppose Russia in Manchuria.[92] This exclusion of Manchuria from the agreement of 1900 provoked from the Duke of Devonshire the remark that it was not worth the paper it was written on. The treaty, indeed, proved almost useless to Britain, and her disappointment in it was not assuaged in the least by the German Chancellor's annoying reference to the "Yangtze Agreement," as though it had a special application to the principal region of British interests.

As for the additional difference growing out of the problem of raising China's indemnity funds, Germany favored an increase in the Chinese customs so that anything in the shape of an international financial control in China might be avoided. Britain, on the other hand, thought such an increase would prove burdensome to trade; and, as Sir Frank Lascelles told Baron von

[90] *Ibid.*, pp. 12-16. Text of agreement also in British and Foreign State Papers, XCII, 31.

[91] *Ibid.*, I, 330-31.

[92] The British Government were of opinion that the agreement did apply to Manchuria, but Lord Lansdowne stated in the house of Lords on March 28 that Germany had made it understood during the negotiations that she did not regard Manchuria as a place where she had influence. Sir Frank Lascelles wrote on March 17: "I am convinced that German Government always understood that the words 'as far as they can exercise influence' were inserted for the purpose of excluding Manchuria from the agreement." *Ibid.*, II, 28.

Richthofen, German Foreign Minister, this would affect chiefly those Powers who had the largest commerce with China, namely, Great Britain and Germany. Instead of sharing these apprehensions, Richthofen held that the duties "could support a very considerable augmentation without in any way hampering trade." Germany, he believed, "had considerable experience in dealing with countries which imposed a very high tariff, such as the United States and the South American Republics, and found that it was quite possible to carry on a large business in spite of such tariffs."[93] In April 1901 Dr. Stuebel, Director of the Colonial Department of the German Foreign Office, went to London and had a series of interviews with Lord Lansdowne and Mr. Bertie, seeking their support for this increase in Chinese customs. His want of success caused considerable disappointment to the German Government, Baron von Richthofen characterizing the British response as "a curt refusal."[94]

Thus the attempted Anglo-German coöperation in China really broke down, and the net result of the activity of the two imperialist rivals was to strengthen their antagonistic positions. Even the military action against the Chinese and the allied evacuation of Shanghai in 1902 were productive of friction.[95] The impression which the whole course of events in China left upon the British Foreign Office may be nicely judged in the following memorandum (January 1, 1907) by the Chief Clerk, Sir Eyre Crowe:[96]

The action of Germany in China has long been distinctly unfriendly to England. In 1895 she tried to obtain from the Chinese Government a coaling station in the Chusan Islands, at the mouth of the Yangtze, without any previous communication with the British Government, whose preferential rights over the group, as established by Treaty, were of course well known. The manner in which Kiaochow was obtained, however unjustifiable it may be considered . . ., did not concern England more than the other Powers

[93] *Ibid.,* II, 21, 31.
[94] *Ibid.,* I, 332; II, 138.
[95] *Vide Times* leader, Feb. 20, 1902, "Germany and China."
[96] *Ibid.,* II, 152-3.

who professed in their Treaties to respect China's integrity and independence. But Germany was not content with the seizure of the harbour, she also planned the absorption of the whole of the large and fertile province of Shantung. The concession of the privileged rights which she wrung from the Chinese Government was obtained owing in no small degree to her official assurance that her claims had the support of England who, needless to say, had never been informed or consulted, and who was, of course, known to be absolutely opposed to stipulations by which, contrary to solemn British treaty rights, it was intended to close a valuable province to British trade and enterprise.

About this time Germany secretly approached Russia with a view to the conclusion of an agreement, by which Germany would have also obtained the much desired foothold on the Yangtze, then considered to be practically a British preserve. These overtures being rejected, Germany wished at least to prevent England from obtaining what she herself had failed to secure. She proposed to the British Cabinet a self-denying agreement stipulating that neither Power should endeavour to obtain any territorial advantages in Chinese dominions, and that if any third Power attempted to do so both should take common action.

The British Government did not conceal their great reluctance to this arrangement, rightly foreseeing that Germany would tacitly exempt from its operation her own designs on Shantung, and also any Russian aggression in Manchuria, whilst England would solemnly give up any chances she might have of establishing on a firm basis her well-known position on the Yangtze. . . . Nevertheless, the policy of conciliating Germany by meeting her expressed wishes once more triumphed, and the Agreement was signed—with the foreseen consequences: Russian aggression in Manchuria was declared to be altogether outside the scope of the stipulations of what the German Chancellor took care to style the "Yangtze" Agreement, as if the terms had referred specially to that restricted area of China, and the German designs on Shantung continue to this day to be tenaciously pursued.

But Germany was not content with the British renunciation of any territorial claims. The underhand and disloyal manoeuvres by which, on the strength of purely fictitious stories of British plans for the seizure of various Chinese places of strategical importance. . . . Germany wrung out of the Peking Court further separate and secret guarantees against alleged British designs, on the occasion of the termination of the joint Anglo-Franco-German occupation of Shanghai, betrayed such an obliquity of mind in dealing with her ostensible friends that Lord Lansdowne characterized it in the most severe terms. . . .

Meanwhile, what of the ebb and flow of trade? There was certainly no visible stagnation of Chinese imports from the United Kingdom. They rose from about ten million pounds in 1894 to more than nineteen millions in 1902, not including the value of goods transshipped from Hongkong, Singapore, or India. Britain continued to lead the field commercially in China, and by a wide margin. China was still buying far more from Britain than from Japan or the United States and more than twice as much as she bought from all Continental Europe (Russia alone excluded). British preponderance over Germany therefore remained enormous. Chinese trade statistics do not distinguish imports of German origin before 1905, but statistics of German exports to China, including Hongkong and Kiaochow, show a total in 1902 of only about two and a half million sterling.[97] It was the rate of increase rather than the growth in volume of Germany's trade in China that seemed ominous. Reference to the import statistics of Japan perhaps gives a more accurate comparative view of the expansion of British and German business in the Far East. Between 1894 and 1902 Japanese purchases from the United Kingdom increased from £4,219,000 to £5,184,000, while those from Germany rose from £791,000 to £2,592,000.[98] Here the absolute as well as the proportionate increase appears greater for Germany than the United Kingdom, although this may not have been true since the figures take no account of British goods imported via Hongkong or any other eastern entrepôt. A trade report from Japan in 1901, however, stated that at the close of the century the aggregate trade of the whole British Empire bore "a less favourable ratio to the whole import trade of Japan than did that of the United Kingdom alone in 1883." Germany's trade in Japan,

[97] Statistical Abstracts for Foreign Countries.
[98] Ibid.

it was pointed out, had in the same period advanced from one-twentieth to one-tenth of the total imports. American business had also gained enormously, but, the report stated, "German trade is and always has been exclusively in articles which compete directly with British productions."[99]

Examination of the trading situation in China and Japan thus suggests that Germany was intensifying the competition which Great Britain faced rather than displacing her. It would certainly be untrue to say that Britain was even beginning to take a general commercial beating in the Far East. In this place and that, of course, she definitely lost ground in certain branches of business, but at other points and in other branches she made prosperous gains. In this connection some developments at Singapore and in the British Straits Settlements Colony ought to be noted. Here the statistics of commerce show a very steady German expansion against a virtual standstill or even decline in the value of United Kingdom trade. The 1894 figures of £3,436,835 for Britain and £319,887 for Germany may be compared with the 1900 figures of £3,289,085 and £732,939.[100] The following observations of an Englishman in Penang attest the changing currents of trade:

Chamberlain's fiscal policy is not making much progress. If only some of the people who vote against it could come abroad . . . they would see what a big hold foreigners have here—especially Germans. Any shop you go into here ask the proprietor where such and such things are obtainable he will reply, "Germany." Everything comes from Germany! All the Chinese shops, of which there are thousands, deal with German firms to the exclusion of English ones.[101]

Moreover, the German invasion of the carrying trade in these waters was very extensive. Something of a sensation was created in 1899-1900 by the transfer of two British lines, operating chiefly between Singapore, Siam and Hongkong, to German ownership and registry. The Holt Line was sold in 1899 and the following year the Scottish Oriental Steamship Company similarly passed into the hands of a German syndicate, with the

[99] Misc. Series 564.
[100] Statistical Abstract for British Colonies.
[101] The *Times,* Feb. 16, 1905.

result that the only two regular lines connecting Bangkok and the nearest British colonies ceased to fly the British flag. A sharp decline consequently appeared at once in British shipping at Bangkok, the number of vessels falling from 396 in 1898 to 151 in 1901; while German vessels entering this port increased from 78 in 1898 to 272 in 1901.[102] That this displacement produced chagrin in England is evident from the following *Times* letter occasioned by the Holt Line sale:

... not only will the British colony of Singapore be dependent on a foreign fleet for practically the whole of its trade with Bangkok (and a large portion of that with the Dutch Islands) but an impetus will be given to German interests, political and commercial, in Siam itself, which it is not easy to gauge accurately, and to the importance of which it is impossible for those who know the East to be indifferent. Such an event will be a severe blow to British prestige and interests, at a time unparalleled in its importance in the history of Siam, and at a time, too, when we are beginning to recognize how competition is narrowing the horizon of our opportunities; and at a stroke of the pen it robs this country of a position which it had laboriously won in open competition with the world, and places in the van a rival power which will avail itself to the very utmost of the opportunity thus surrendered to it. . . .[103]

When, in the following year, the Scottish Oriental Line was also absorbed by the German syndicate the indignant author of this letter again wrote to the *Times*, this time charging that the transactions had been carried through in such secrecy that "everything tends to show that both are the results of the political aims of the German Government in the Far East." It was, he insisted, "idle to pretend to regard with equanimity the passing of the carrying trade from the British to the German flag when it takes place in the wholesale fashion in which it is doing in the Far East."[104] A correspondent of the *Times* at Singapore in 1904 described the transformed business situation. "Things in Singapore are very dull," he reported, "the old people have

[102] Annual Series 2705 and 2898; also Parliamentary Paper Cd. 324, Trade and Shipping of Southeast Asia, Jan., 1901.

[103] Letter of *"Vincere est vivere,"* May 24, 1899.

[104] April 13, 1900.

never seen them as they are now. The Germans are fast buying up the local shipping companies and turning all the British out. . . . Evidently our pioneers have fought for the benefit of the foreigner, who with the assistance of his government is ousting the British out of their hard won heritage. . . . Even in North Borneo the Germans are doing their level best to oust out of the trade the last of the small steamers that fly the British flag there. People at home do not seem to understand all of this and apparently they will not be convinced until it is too late."[105]

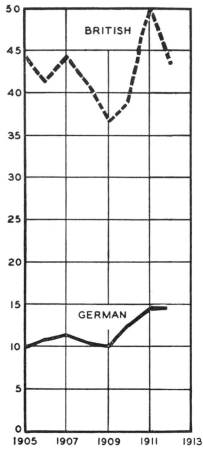

In the remaining years before the War no extraordinary shifts of trade from England to Germany, or vice versa, appear to have taken place in the Far East. Viewed in the large the relative position of the two trades remained fairly constant. Statistical evidence possibly indicates a somewhat steadier increase on the part of German trade, but owing to the enormous growth of Indian exports to China and Japan, and to the lack of import statistics of origin at the great Hongkong entrepôt, it would be hazardous to say that German business in the Far East actually gained at all against British trade after, say, 1902. Far more

CHART 10. IMPORTS INTO CHIEF FAR EASTERN MARKETS FROM UNITED KINGDOM AND GERMANY, 1905-1912, EXPRESSED IN MILLION POUNDS STERLING.

[105] July 26, 1904.

striking than the increase of German commerce was the growth of American and especially Japanese trade; yet even with this, British business continued to hold the dominant position. The Chinese import trade for 1912 will illustrate this: goods received directly from the United Kingdom were surpassed in value only by imports from Japan, although if the Hongkong trade (which can only be estimated) had been reckoned in, Japan would have been a poor second to Great Britain. As for Germany, it would be fair to estimate her trade in China at about one-fourth of Britain's. The tonnage statistics of shipping entered at Chinese ports are also significant: the British total was 38 millions, the Japanese 20, and the German 6.[106] In Japan the relative increase of British and German trade was about the same as in China, and this was true also for Siam and the Straits Settlements. It seems a fair conclusion that however much competition may have been intensified, the last decade before the War saw little if any further German undermining of Great Britain's commercial position in the Far East. The figure on page 190 shows approximately the relative position of the two export trades to the chief Far Eastern markets from 1905 to 1912.[107]

3

In the New World, too, there were important areas of Anglo-German rivalry. Neither Canada nor the United States was untouched by it, but the hottest rivalry was to be discovered in the spacious Latin-American lands to the south, whose markets were of continental proportions, little exploited, and full of promise. The whole vast area of the Caribbean and Central and South America was virtually untouched by modern industry at the opening of the period of acute international trade competi-

[106] Annual Series 5216, Report on Foreign Trade of China (1913) by Commercial Attaché at Peking.

[107] This figure is based on the import statistics of China, Japan, Siam, and Straits Settlements, in the Statistical Abstracts for Foreign Countries and for the British Colonies. Naturally, therefore, it does not represent the total of British and German trade in the Far East, but it may be taken as indicating accurately enough the relative size and relative expansion of British and German commerce.

tion, but its scattered peoples produced huge quantities of food-stuffs and many of the raw materials most needed by industrial nations. The exchange of these for the products of British, American, and European industry was growing into a trade of large dimensions, and the scramble for the lion's share of it became very active in the last two decades of the nineteenth century.

Britain's position here in the decade of the eighties was very commanding. Her chief rivals were America and Germany, the former especially in the Caribbean and Central America, the latter more prominently on the South American continent.[108] But taking the *chief* markets throughout the whole region (the West Indies included), the comparative value of British and German export trade, as late as 1890, was better than four to one;[109] while for South America alone, in 1889, a similar comparison showed figures of £26,326,000 for Britain and £8,396,000 for Germany, with the American trade coming third at £7,010,000.[110] Now Great Britain was not to be thrust out of this leadership in South American markets by either of her two strong rivals, but her lead was to be considerably reduced and its maintenance rendered a good deal more difficult. The British began to feel the sharply competitive edge of German trade in the eighties and to experience its cutting edge severely after 1890, for between 1890 and 1895 their exports to South America dropped from 25 to 20 millions sterling, while those from Germany rose from 7 to 9 millions. This striking shift may have been more apparent than real, owing to the growth of

[108] *Vide* consular references (1885-86) to rising German competition throughout Latin-America given in Appendix I.

[109] Based on British and German export statistics published by Board of Trade in the Statistical Abstracts for the United Kingdom and for Foreign Countries. The markets are those of the British West Indies, British Guiana, British Honduras, Cuba, Porto Rico, Hayti and Santo Domingo, Mexico, the Central American Republics, Colombia, Venezuela, Ecuador, Peru, Chile, Brazil, Uruguay, and Argentina.

[110] *Vide* two useful Parliamentary Papers, Returns Showing British, German, and American Exports to China, Argentina, and All South America, 1885-1906.—1906 (131) and 1907 (351).

direct trading instead of through the United Kingdom entre-pôt;[111] but however that may have been, there was certainly much remarking of the German invasion of British markets in South America. German sea traffic to Brazil increased from 239,800 to 411,000 tons between 1881-85 and 1891-95, while over the same period the traffic to ports south of Brazil grew from 114,900 to 414,000 tons, and the traffic to the western ports of South America shot up from 211,100 to 456,800 tons.[112] This growth was reflected plainly in the consular reports, which contained innumerable notices of the upsurge of German goods. Mr. E. E. Williams called South America the "Happy Hunting Grounds for the German drummer,"[113] and the British news-papers of the nineties published many notices of Germany's advancing trade in this part of the world. A special correspond-ent wrote to the *Times* from Venezuela that there, "as in all other South American Republics, German trade is competing very successfully with British, and German goods are in many cases ousting from the market those of English manufacture."[114] An-other correspondent wrote from Brazil that

the Germans are superseding the British all over the country. For-merly, when I first arrived in this country in 1859, English import houses were established throughout in all the principal sea-coast towns. Now the reverse is the case—the English houses closed, and Germans in their stead. . . . It is a humiliation for a Britisher to see all this.[115]

Such notices as these, together with the observations of consuls (which received frequent publication in the daily press) and the growing national concern for the prosperity of British trade generally, led the *Morning Post*, at the end of 1895, to make the

[111] Exactly the opposite tendency, however, was noted at Trinidad in 1896 by the Collector of Customs.—*Vide* C.-8449, p. 124.

[112] Report on the Maritime Interests of the German Empire, Misc. Series 443.

[113] *Made in Germany*, p. 66.

[114] April 11, 1896.

[115] March 3, 1897. *Vide* also "British and German Competition in Ar-gentine," *Times*, Jan. 25, 1897.

grossly exaggerated statement that the entire trade of South America had come under the control of German merchants.[116]

All this conveyed an utterly fallacious idea of the true position of British and German trade in these markets. The British were not actually being routed by their German rivals, for the statistics of total South American commerce reveal a marked see-sawing tendency. Thus in 1896 the British gained and the Germans lost, in 1897 they both fell back, and in 1898 the British figure again went up while the German dropped. Taking the nineties as a whole German commerce unquestionably went forward very rapidly and, in a measure, at British expense, but its total value was still less than half that of the British at the turn of the century. In certain areas the Germans became very conspicuously established. Venezuela, where German capital went into railways and a government loan, was such a place; yet the situation there was described by the British consul in 1897 thus:

At the present time when the cry is general among Englishmen, about the extent of the increase of German trade to the detriment of British commerce, it might be well to state that although in Venezuela the Germans have a good footing, they cannot be accused of ousting the British for the simple reason that Englishmen have paid very little attention to Venezuela. . . . The largest firms in Venezuela are German and it is quite natural when there is a question of choice they should give preference to their country's manufactures. As opposed to this there is not a single British firm in the whole of Venezuela.[117]

Another such place was Rio Grande do Sul in southern Brazil, where an extensive German colony had arisen. Here also it was natural that German trade should predominate, and at Porto Alegre the Germans gained an almost preponderating share both of the wholesale importing and retail distribution business.[118] The *Times* in 1897 quoted the British consul there as saying that the trade "which was once almost exclusively in the hands of British merchants . . . may be monopolized by German firms, the

[116] Dec. 5, 1895.
[117] Report from Caracas for 1896, Annual Series 1933.
[118] Annual Series 1911 contains good discussion of the influence of this German element in deflecting trade to Germany.

reasons being the number of German emigrants, whole districts in the Southern provinces of Brazil being entirely populated by Germans."[119]

Apart from such exceptional circumstances as in Venezuela and Southern Brazil, a most important reason for British trade losses to Germany in this part of the world seems to have been the remarkable spread of resident German importers, who tended inevitably to cultivate stronger commercial relations with exporting firms in Germany than with those in other countries. The following excerpt from an 1896 Valparaiso report is typical of many consular observations on this fact:

More German importing houses than English have been established here of late years. Though many of the principal houses at Valparaiso are British firms, the German houses now far exceed the English in number, and in the matter of imports this is a question of some importance. . .•. Though both English and German houses often import foreign goods . . . the local merchant is naturally disposed to give preference to the product of his own country . . ., and it may be questioned if the Germans are not making enormous strides as merchants, and in some respects taking the wind out of our sails.[120]

There were other great reasons for the less rapid commercial progress of Great Britain—the familiar ones that have been set forth at length in the third chapter of this study. The Board of Trade sent out a special commissioner, one Mr. T. Worthington, to study the prospects of South American markets in 1897-99, and his reports confirmed the numerous consular criticisms of British trade methods, lack of adaptability, tight credit, and high prices.[121] The *Times* called these reports "far from exhilarating reading,"[122] and the *Daily Telegraph* found in them little that was "agreeable to English readers."[123]

[119] Aug. 25, 1899.
[120] Annual Series 1795.
[121] *Vide* Reports of Commercial Mission to South America, C.-9100, C.-9101, C.-9160, C.-9169, C.-9208. For a discussion of the darker aspects of the situation disclosed by these reports *vide* Agnes Lambert, "Neglecting Our Customers," *Nineteenth Century*, 1899, vol. 45.
[122] Nov. 14, 1898.
[123] Nov. 12, 1898.

But in spite of the unfavorable aspects of the British trade position in South America at the end of the nineteenth century, the succeeding years to 1914 saw no sensational shift toward Germany in the commerce of these markets.[124] The competitive situation undoubtedly became year by year more acute, and this was accentuated by the formidable advance of American goods, but British trade held its own quite well. Imports from Great Britain into Argentina rose from £7,892,009 in 1902 to £21,325,592 in 1912, while the German gain over the same period was from £2,315,240 to £11,735,294. Similarly, the British increase in Brazil was from £5,649,952 to £13,276,091, as compared with a German gain from £2,148,284 to £9,401,970. In Chile the German increase pressed especially hard on British leadership, the comparative figures being £3,062,766 and £1,582,206 in 1902 and £6,515,978 and £5,490,196 in 1912. But in no South American land did the value of German imports rise above the figures for British trade; and even in Venezuela the British increase was greater than the German.[125] The conclusion, therefore, must be that despite the intensification of trade rivalry in South America, Great Britain held her own with rather high success in the years before the war.

In passing from this region one brief glance may be taken at the Central American markets, not because Anglo-German competition raged generally here, but because in one of these countries, Guatemala, a great deal was heard of German economic penetration. The heaviest trade in the Central American Republics in the several decades before the war was enjoyed by the United States, with Great Britain coming second everywhere save in Guatemala. There some heavy investments of German capital in coffee estates, and the presence of several thousand resident Germans explained why imports from Germany *slightly* exceeded those from the United Kingdom. A British trade com-

---

[124] For an interesting description of German commercial progress in South America *vide* A. B. Tulloch, "German Trade in South America," *Nineteenth Century*, 1906, vol. 60.

[125] Based on figures in Statistical Abstracts for United Kingdom and for Foreign Countries.

missioner, Mr. G. T. Milne, studied the Central American markets in 1912-13, and in his very elaborate report to the Board

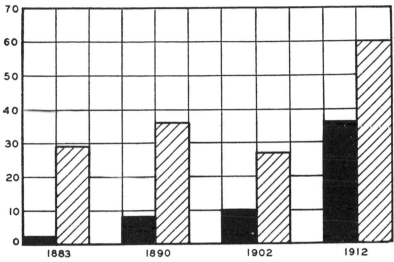

CHART 11. COMPARATIVE TOTAL VALUES OF GERMAN AND BRITISH EXPORT TRADE TO THE MAJOR WEST INDIAN, MEXICAN, CENTRAL AND SOUTH AMERICAN MARKETS IN SELECTED YEARS, EXPRESSED IN MILLION POUNDS STERLING. THE BLACK BAR REPRESENTS GERMAN TRADE AND THE DIAGONALLY LINED BAR REPRESENTS BRITISH TRADE.

of Trade described a situation neither unfavorable to Great Britain nor over-clouded by the German commercial menace.[126]

4

This quantitative survey of the commercial struggle with Germany in overseas markets must conclude with a short inquiry into the trade of the British Colonies and Dominions, whose markets were so important to Great Britain that, at the close of the nineteenth century, they absorbed about thirty per cent of all her exports and were expanding widely. Empire markets, in fact, received almost as much from the United Kingdom as the latter exported to all Continental Europe. How far did Germany cut into this trade?

[126] Report on Conditions and Prospects of British Trade in Central America, Colombia, and Venezuela, Cd. 6969, 1913.

As it has been previously shown, the importance of cultivating colonial markets was increasingly urged in Great Britain from the eighties onward, with the result that special cognizance was taken of the growth of foreign (and especially German) rivalry in overseas British lands. One of Joseph Chamberlain's earliest acts, on going to the Colonial Office in 1895, was to circularize the several Colonial Governments and the India Office for information on this subject; and the result was a large bluebook containing an elaborate survey of trade competition throughout the Empire—a veritable mine of information on colonial markets.[127] The evidence thus assembled showed that the Colonies were steadily increasing that proportion of their imports which came from strictly foreign markets: about one-third of the total colonial imports in 1894 were of non-British origin, whereas this fraction had been only one-fourth ten years earlier. It was also shown that about 38 per cent of all colonial imports were affected by foreign competition in at least some measure. Commenting on the bluebook, the *Times* observed that "the keenest of our competitors in the colonial trade are the United States, Germany, and Belgium, with Japan emerging as a rival in the Far East."[128] The competition, however, was coming more often from Germany than from anywhere else; a rough tabulation of the main facts brought together, in fact, showed more than three times as many instances of German goods displacing British articles as there were instances of American goods (which came next in extent of competition) doing the same.[129] From these reports, and from the agitation of the German trade menace which was very marked at the time, it might seem that German commerce was already thrusting forward very dangerously into the British Empire. Actually, however, Germany's export trade to British Colonies and Dominions was still very small, its value being probably less than five per cent of the United Kingdom's export to colonial markets. "The statistics of the trade of our Colonies and Possessions," wrote the Secretary of the London

[127] Trade of the British Empire and Foreign Competition, C.-8449, 1897.
[128] Leader of September 15, 1897.
[129] Trade of the British Empire, C.-8449, pp. 5-6.

Chamber of Commerce in 1897, "do not indicate any development of direct business relations with foreign countries which
need be considered alarming."[130] In many colonial lands the
German competition was either non-existent or too slight for
notice, and it had only gained important dimensions in Canada,
Australia, Cape Colony, and the Straits Settlements. Only in
those four cases do colonial import statistics show purchases direct from Germany of more than £200,000 a year, and in each
case the United Kingdom trade far exceeded the German. The
following table gives the imports of these four parts of the Em
pire (where German trade was making its way most successfully)
from the United Kingdom and Germany in 1896:[131]

	from United Kingdom £	from Germany £
Canada	6,776,659	1,218,793
Australia	20,252,561	1,574,624
Cape Colony	13,537,064	1,102,088
Straits Settlements	2,364,672	374,411

If comparative figures for the whole Empire were given, the
smallness of the German export trade would appear very striking. India, for example, which was to become a very valuable
market for German goods, bought only £127,000 worth of them
in 1896, as compared with purchases of United Kingdom goods
to the value of more than thirty millions. The Colonial import
statistics, it is true, cannot show the full value of the German
trade, since they do not distinguish the origin of goods from
their ports of shipment; a fair proportion of Germany's trade
reached the Colonies via the United Kingdom, but even when this
is generously allowed for the comparative smallness of the German trade remains.

All this, however, is not to say that Empire trade was unim-

[130] K. B. Murray, "Mr. Chamberlain and Colonial Commerce," *Economic Journal*, vol. 7, 1897. For another very optimistic view of British colonial trade see M. G. Mulhall, "The Trade of the British Colonies," *Contemporary Review*, Nov., 1897.
[131] Statistical Abstract for British Colonies.

portant for Germany. In her struggle to the front in world markets (working on a very narrow margin of profit) no market was sufficiently unimportant to incur her contempt, and in the British Colonies and Dominions the promise of greatly enlarging the volume of trade was very encouraging, especially because (down to 1897) she enjoyed in all of them equal tariff treatment with the United Kingdom.

In the succeeding years, down to 1914, it is hard to discover any important change in Germany's favor in British Empire markets. It is true that the Colonies and Dominions, especially those in Africa, Asia, and Australasia, greatly increased their direct purchases from German houses (becoming highly prized German markets), and that occasional complaints against this competition were heard in these and other British possessions; but it is certainly not true that the United Kingdom's export trade to the Colonies languished or gave way before German rivalry. Nothing is more characteristic of British commercial history in this period than the enormous swelling of Empire trade, and nothing else illustrates so well the continued expansive vitality of United Kingdom exports.[132] More and more the imperialist mood took hold of the commercial classes and eyes were turned to colonial markets. Following Canada's example in 1897 one after another of the self-governing Dominions gave some measure of tariff preference to United Kingdom products, and a powerful movement arose to cement the economic unity of the Empire by establishing a Pan-Brittanic *Zollverein*. The hold of Great Britain upon her colonial markets was most certainly as strong on the eve of the War as it had been twenty years earlier. If a comparison is made of the 1913 British and German imports into those colonial markets where German trade made its strongest showing, the British preponderance appears most overwhelming, as the following table shows:[133]

---

[132] For a somewhat pessimistic view of British trade in colonial markets *vide* J. Holt Schooling, "Our Position in Colonial Markets," *National Review*, 1906, vol. 47.

[133] Statistical Abstracts for British Colonies.

	from United Kingdom	from Germany
	£	£
British India	91,695,158	6,874,708
Straits Settlements	6,175,526	877,739
Ceylon	3,879,975	401,500
British South Africa	25,059,933	3,546,594
Nigeria	4,938,243	811,350
Sierra Leone	1,138,683	174,191
Gold Coast	3,466,351	388,669
Canada	28,521,185	2,921,879
Australia	47,615,561	4,956,834
New Zealand	13,312,193	687,935

The encroachment of German trade upon imperial markets was nevertheless not without its significance in the development of bad blood between Great Britain and Germany. It was a prime factor, or better, a favorite argument in pushing forward the tariff reform movement in England, and, as it will be seen in the last chapter, this issue had a damaging effect upon relations between the two countries. Moreover, there was South Africa.

The intimate relation between commerce and territorial imperialism throughout the huge expanse of Africa (and elsewhere) in which British and German empire-builders began, in the eighties, to vie for position, need hardly be argued; and certainly the story of Anglo-German partition of southern Africa can hardly be retold here. But certain commercial aspects of the rivalry, touching the Transvaal crisis and the question of the Portuguese Colonies, should command attention. By 1890 the territorial disputes of previous years had been resolved and Great Britain and Germany were living as fairly good colonial neighbors in southern and eastern Africa. Neither was satisfied, however, and mutual suspicion and potential sources of conflict still existed. Stretching nearly two thousand miles from German East Africa to Natal and Cape Colony were Portuguese Mozambique and the Boer Republics. These fell under the shadow of British and German economic imperialism in the nineties, at the same time that German trade in British South Africa began to show its competitive edge, and the whole region became an arena of acute rivalry in which fresh and serious difficulties arose. In his report for 1894 the British Consul-General at Hamburg wrote as follows:

In South Africa a satisfactory advance is reported in German commercial progress; and especially is this the case as regards the Transvaal and the Orange Free State. It is confidently anticipated that the time is approaching when Germany will obtain the share, which her position in Europe and her industrial capacities entitle her to in South African trade.[134]

This succinct and colorless statement denoted a situation full of explosive possibilities, created by the collision of British commercial and imperial interests with German economic ambitions.

The impact of German commerce in Portuguese, Boer, and British South Africa was formidable enough by the time of the 1896 Transvaal crisis. Beginning in 1889 the German East Africa Line had set up an active rivalry with British shipping to the ports of the eastern coast. The Reichstag granted a generous subsidy in 1890, and this, together with the effective through-rate system (one fixed transport tariff from inland German manufacturer to ultimate east African destination) not only enabled the line to defeat British competition but also greatly benefited German goods of commerce. All along the coast, therefore, and on into the landlocked Boer states, soon to fall under British dominion, consuls in the early nineties noticed significant increases in German trade and shipping. Special interest attached to the Portuguese port of Lorenzo Marques on Delagoa Bay, the terminus of a railway line which, when completed, would reach into the heart of the Transvaal. "Merchants," it was stated in a trade report for 1890 from Mozambique, "now unanimously consider that this port has established itself as an important one to South-east African development. Although the imports to Delagoa Bay are large, the chief business . . . is the forwarding of goods into the Transvaal. . . . Merchants here look forward to the time when the proposed railway between Delagoa Bay and the Transvaal is to be completed, for

---

[134] Annual Series 1623.

then the trade with the interior will be continuous throughout the year (now a six months trade), and the amount of business done, they think, will be proportionately increased." The same report observed that the previous three years had seen marked increases in the shipping at Lorenzo Marques, and that about ninety per cent of it was British.[135] Several years earlier, however, a concession for the Boer section of the railway line, from Pretoria east to the Portuguese frontier, had been granted by the Transvaal Government to the Netherlands Railway Company, a Dutch-German syndicate, thus establishing an important German interest in a line which promised competition with British communications into the Transvaal from Durban and Cape Town.[136] A fleeting glance at a map of this region reveals at once the superiority of this avenue of access to Transvaal markets.

A rumor at the time (1888) to the effect that German interests were about to get control also of the Delagoa Bay end of the line excited high British apprehensions. Lord Rosebery told the House of Lords it was "a grave and pregnant matter" that the railroad "which gives access to almost the only . . . port on that enormous coast is in danger of falling into hands which, if not hostile, are at any rate unfriendly, and into control which may not merely have an important effect in shutting in our South African dominions, but may have an important bearing on our commerce as a country, and be the means of leading to the imposition of differential and hostile rates on our commerce."[137] Fear of the Boer embracing Germany was already abroad, and from this time onward Britain kept a weather eye open at Lorenzo Marques. The importance which she attached to the Portuguese section of the railway is evident from the fact that the British Government considered buying it; while from the Transvaal a promise was exacted against differential rates in favor of goods imported via Delagoa Bay when the lines were com-

---

[135] Annual Series 855.

[136] Hansard, 3rd. S., vol. 326, p. 144. Statement of Sir James Fergusson, Under-Secretary in Foreign Office.

[137] Ibid., vol. 322, pp. 1466-68.

pleted.[138] The growth of German business at Lorenzo Marques became very active after 1890. By 1892, in fact, the tonnage of German shipping there had reached 54,257 tons as compared with 197,934 tons of British shipping.[139] "The possibilities of developing trade with Johannesburg through Delagoa Bay," wrote the consul there in 1895, "seem to appeal less strongly to British merchants and shipowners than to their German rivals. In a small way at first, but steadily advancing on ever-broadening paths, German manufacturers and German vessels, I will not say supplant British industries and British lines, but certainly enter into a rivalry with them which every year becomes keener, and which every year sees tending to the advantage of the lesser competitor."[140] The situation had already raised international difficulties. Cecil Rhodes in 1893 learned that the Transvaal Government, backed by Germany, was seeking to buy the Delagoa Bay railway from the Portuguese Government; whereupon Great Britain protested at Lisbon. Portugal refused to sell, but the German and Transvaal Governments continued their efforts for some little time. Then in September 1894, a native insurrection, ascribed at Berlin and Lisbon to the intrigues of Mr. Rhodes, broke out at Lorenzo Marques, providing occasion for the landing of British bluejackets to protect the consulate. Germany countered this move by sending two men-of-war to safeguard (as Baron von Marschall stated) "the large German interests involved, both on the coast and in the Transvaal." That British action was under strong suspicion at Berlin is evident from the fact that Count Hatzfeldt, the London Ambassador, took occasion to inform the British Foreign Office that if the Portuguese Colonies in Africa were broken up, Germany could not permit them to become British territory. In December of that year Baron von Marschall told Sir Edward Malet that Germany would object to any British encroachments on the sovereignty of Portugal and the commercial independence of the port or railway. It was plain that this commercial highway into the Trans-

[138] *Ibid.;* also vol. 330, pp. 92-93.
[139] Annual Series 1153.
[140] Annual Series 1760.

vaal could not fall peacefully under either full British or German control.[141]

1895 saw the gathering of darker clouds. Early this year the railway line was opened through to Pretoria, and the occasion was honored by a visit to the Boer capital of a deputation of German naval officers. The Kaiser sent a telegram to President Kruger in which he alluded to the new line "as a means of drawing closer the bonds which connect the two countries." Germany exhibited an ostentatious friendship for the Transvaal Government, and at Pretoria a banquet was held on the Kaiser's birthday, in the course of which President Kruger declared the time had come for establishing the closest friendly relations between the Transvaal and Germany. These were some of the surface indications of more deeply significant developments in German economic penetration of the Transvaal. German exports to this little Boer state had risen from less than £50,000 in 1889 to about £300,000 in 1894, not including goods shipped via England; and the trade was growing prosperously. A large proportion of Transvaal gold-mining shares were in German hands, the new railway had been completed chiefly by German capital, and a host of other German enterprises (some of them directly oppressive to British interests) were now flourishing.[142] These supply the prime reasons for Germany's policy of flirtation at Pretoria and supporting the status quo in the Transvaal against the embracing grasp of British South African imperialism—even dreaming, as the Kaiser certainly did, of a German protectorate.

The status of the Transvaal at the time of these developments that led to the Jameson raid and the Kaiser's famous congratulatory telegram to President Kruger was a somewhat doubtful one: the Boers considered themselves absolutely free under a convention signed at London in 1884, while the British regarded their

[141] A succinct and authoritative summary of the difficulties with Germany over Delagoa Bay and the Transvaal may be found in the Foreign Office memorandum of Mr. J. A. C. Tilley, respecting Anglo-German relations, 1892-1904, written Jan. 5, 1905.—*British Documents,* I, 322-37.

[142] Report of U. S. commercial agent at Weimar quoted in *Times,* May 2, 1896.

republic as being under a quasi-British protectorate. Therefore
the German economic penetration and ostentatious support of
Boer independence took on the appearance of a bold intrusion
into British imperial affairs, of an intrigue against the position
of Britain in South Africa. The following is a British-prepared
catalogue of German offenses written by a contemporary observer in a publication of the highest standing in England:[143]

Germans first appeared in the Transvaal in the comparatively
harmless character of mining financiers. In a list of Rand capitalists
the most striking feature is the large percentage of German names.
. . . As concession hunters they have been unapproachable. Having
got on the right side of the President and the Raad, they had only
to help themselves to whatever they wanted. One monopoly after
another they suggested, engineered through the Raad, floated in
Europe, and are now making fortunes out of both for themselves and
their Boer friends.

One of the best known of a long series of Kruger concessions
is the dynamite monopoly shared by the Nobel Company with Mr.
Lippert of Hamburg. . . . Mr. Lippert was formerly a merchant in
Hamburg with business connections in South Africa. Through them
he had early knowledge of the diamond fields at Kimberley, and again
of the gold fields in the Transvaal. When the question of the dynamite supply was being agitated, he made good use of his influence
at Pretoria, and after a prolonged struggle with rival makers he
and the Nobel Company joined forces. They secured a practically
exclusive right to import dynamite and sell it at exorbitant prices
duly fixed in the concession. . . .

Whiskey is another monopoly among the Boers, and it also
pays toll at Pretoria. This concession is held and exercised by the
Erste Fabrike Hatherley Distillery Company. . . .

The above monopolies are not by any means the finest plums
the Raad has had to distribute. They have been selected as typical
examples because they are best known in this country. Many more
have been financed at home. Waterworks, brickworks, collieries—all
bring grist to the mill, and the Germans are the favoured millers.

[143] W. R. Lawson, "German Intrigues in The Transvaal," *Contemporary
Review*, Feb., 1896. Another interesting and similar view may be seen in
W. H. P. Greswell, "The Germans in South Africa," *Fortnightly Review*,
Feb. 1, 1896.

Contracts for public works go through the same process, and the lion's share of them fall into German hands. In a recent case, the electric lighting of Pretoria, it was announced in the advertisement that no English need apply. That, too, will be "made in Germany." A particularly big plum is now ripening for the punishment of the Uitlanders and the benefit of the Pretoria ring. It is nothing less than a monopoly of the cyanide process in the whole Republic. If it should be realized, the cost of producing gold may be increased by five or ten per cent, but what spoil for the happy family at Pretoria, who will have the enjoyment of the royalties!

But these are not the most embarrassing subjects the Germans have laid hands on. Concessions affect only particular industries, as a rule; a monopolist railway system strangles the whole trade of the country. The Germans have got their hands on that also. Not a mile of railway has been permitted to be built in the Transvaal except by one company, which is now virtually controlled from Berlin. . . .

British protectorates, like other British territories, are as open to foreigners as to Her Majesty's own subjects. They are welcome to settle anywhere, to hold property, to cultivate, to trade, and to make as much money as they honestly can. But it has never been expected outside of the Transvaal Republic that we should allow them to set up iniquitous monopolies against ourselves. The spectacle, we think, cannot be paralleled in any other country of a gang of foreign speculators throttling all the staple industries, controlling the one railway system, and levying toll on the whole community. That more than anything else goaded the Uitlanders into revolt.

There is no need to pass judgment here upon German behavior in the Transvaal, or upon the merits of the Anglo-German quarrel. The point of importance is that this was a clear case of German economic encroachment upon a British imperial preserve, leading to an incident which brought the countries to the brink of war and poisoned their subsequent relations. It would be hard to find a clearer example of economic conflict generating a high political crisis; and this particular crisis, let it be remembered, was the first really violent storm in Anglo-German relations. The British never forgot the Kruger telegram and the angry teeth which Germany bared in 1896; while the Germans learned the lesson that they were impotent against Great Britain overseas without an adequate navy. Nor is there any need for this study to be further detained by subsequent events in South Africa. Germany continued her commercial penetration there, but backed down politically in the Transvaal; and rivalry was blunted in 1898 by the Anglo-German convention dividing the Portuguese Colonies into spheres of interest, against the day when they might slip from Portugal's nerveless grasp. In this arrangement the Delagoa Bay section of Mozambique was earmarked for Great Britain.[144] In 1899 came the secret Anglo-Portuguese treaty of London renewing the historic alliance, with a British guarantee for the integrity of Portuguese Colonies; and then followed the Boer War and the political consolidation of British South Africa. Germany remained a trade rival through all the markets of this region, but she did not challenge the British politically again.

It was not only by expanding her export trade and bidding for economic privileges that Germany made her business power felt disagreeably in several important regions of the British Empire. It will be recalled that the tremendous growth of the German beet-sugar industry was primarily responsible for deflating the prosperity of the cane-sugar plantations of the British West Indies in which large sums of United Kingdom capital were invested. A somewhat parallel case was that of the indigo growers in India whose ruin was encompassed by the German manufacturers of artificial indigo. This industry arose in the nineties, and in 1897 the artificial product was placed on the market by the Badische Anilin Soda Fabrik of Ludwigshaven, then the largest color works in the world, at a price capable of competing with the natural article. The India plantations, in which some five million sterling was invested, came face to face with a chemically pure indigo, and the effect upon their prosperity was immediate.

A special *Times* article in 1899 said, "It almost seems as if the calamity which has overtaken the sugar growers of the West

<hr />

[144] *British Documents*, I, 44-48.

Indies in competition with the beet sugar industry of Germany now impends over the indigo growers of Bengal, and that the existence of another British industry is in peril."[145] A Marseilles consular report for 1900 thus described the introduction of the German product in France:

German competition in artificial indigo has already decreased the demand for natural indigo by at least 10 per cent at the close of the first year's operation of the German manufacturers in France. This proportion is bound to increase with the output of artificial indigo. The artificial dye already regulates prices. The small crops of last year would have justified a rise in prices of natural indigo, but owing to the artificial produce put on the market this has not taken place. . . . It must be confessed that the outlook for Indian growers of indigo appears black.[146]

The decline of the market for the natural product was not arrested, and British interests had to take the blow thus delivered. Writing in 1909 a distinguished German economist summed up the story of indigo:

It was one of the great staples of India and had been the important means of placing the raw material production of the Indian Empire on a basis of money exchange. At the beginning of the nineties the total crop of indigo was estimated from $20,000,000 to $25,000,000, with both culture and trade almost exclusively in British hands. But in Germany science progressed, the output of coke wonderfully increased with the spreading iron works, and the new nation acquired the raw material for manufacturing coal-tar dyes. Today the Germans by chemical processes make three-quarters of all the indigo used in the world. The total yield of indigo in India has meanwhile fallen to a quarter of its former amount. Since 1903 England has imported from Germany more indigo annually than her average yearly purchase from Calcutta in the years 1881-96.[147]

[145] "A Threatened Industry," Oct. 4, 1899. *Vide* also another article, "Indigo a Threatened Industry," Dec. 26, 1899, and letters to the *Times,* Oct. 11, 19, 23, 25, 31, 1899, and April 24, 1900.

[146] Annual Series 2668; *vide* also 1901 Marseilles report No. 2855, and 1900 report from Frankfort-am-Main, No. 2680.

[147] G. von Schulze-Gaevernitz, "England and Germany—Peace or War," *American Review of Reviews,* Nov., 1909.

Sugar and indigo were two conspicuous instances of imperial business interests undermined by Germany. There were undoubtedly others, and one more may be alluded to: the deflation of the diamond market by gems from German Southwest Africa. From about 1870 onward almost the whole of the world's diamond-mining industry was confined to South Africa, where the great British firm of de Beers largely controlled production. Diamonds made up almost 20 per cent of the total value of exports from the Union of South Africa prior to the war, 5,503,861 carats worth more than twelve million pounds being sent out in 1913. Now the years of 1908 to 1913 saw a sensational output of diamonds from the Lüderitzbucht fields in German Southwest Africa. An insignificant production of 39,375 carats in 1908 shot up in 1913 to 1,570,000 carats, or better than one-fifth of the South African export. "The output of diamonds for the year 1913," observed a 1914 consular report, "was over 575,000 carats more than the output for 1912, a greater increase than any other single year has to show."[148] This was an important cause for a severe depression of the market in 1913. An Amsterdam consular report described the supply of German diamonds placed on the market as "practically unlimited," and said the situation was "most critical on account of the contract made by the German Regie with a consortium at Antwerp that the latter should accept during 1913 a million carats."[149] This was more than the market could possibly absorb, so that in yet another important branch of imperial business the Germans appeared as authors of the over-production evil.

5

The fifth and final section of this chapter will deal with the shipping rivalry. The menace which the German merchant marine offered to the prosperity and world leadership of the British maritime carrying trade loomed up at the close of the century. Signs of it appeared somewhat earlier, it is true, but

[148] Annual Series 5352.
[149] Annual Series 5315.

Germany's future hardly "lay upon the water" until about 1900. During the last two decades of the nineteenth century British shipping appears to have weathered the tightening competition more successfully than did British industrial and trading interests;[150] it and banking were indubitably the strongest branches of the nation's business.

As late as 1894 a competent observer, writing in the *Contemporary Review,* surveyed the carrying trade of the world and said: "The British flag at present holds the same preponderance on sea that the Phoenicians enjoyed in early times, and this preponderance is increasing."[151] Even in the middle of 1895, when the German trade menace was large upon the English horizon, a *Times* leader confidently observed: "Looking at the place which our mercantile marine holds in comparison with the merchant service of other countries, there is solid ground for satisfaction."[152] Such optimistic views were fully supported by reference to the tonnage statistics of the leading maritime trading nations.[153] Between 1870 and 1900 the merchant navy of the United Kingdom had increased nearly four million tons, while Germany had only added a million tons to her mercantile fleet.

Nevertheless, evidences of a developing duel with Germany in the shipping world were by this time numerous enough. The Germans made strenuous efforts in the nineties to free their shipping from dependence on British builders and British materials.[154] "Even in shipbuilding," a writer in the *Nineteenth Century* asserted in 1896 ". . . our position is threatened; only the other day there was launched from a German yard a first class ar-

[150] A Foreign Office official, Mr. H. Farnall, told the Select Committee on Steamship Subsidies in 1901 that the consular reports did not find fault with British navigation in the same way they did with British traders.— Report, 1901, p. 51. This was a completely true observation.

[151] M. G. Mulhall, "The Carrying Trade of the World," Dec., 1894.

[152] Leader of Aug. 28, 1895.

[153] Accounts of Papers on Shipping give these figures for 1900:

	U.K.	Germany	France
Total tonnage	9,304,108	1,941,645	1,037,727
Steam tonnage	7,207,610	1,347,875	527,551

[154] *Times* articles, Nov. 25, 1895; July 14, 1898; Dec. 25, 1900.

moured battle-ship, perfect it is said to be in every detail, and the Kaiser's delight was quite justified. Had any one prophesied twenty years ago such an event as this he would have been laughed at."[155] A report from the Commercial Attaché at Berlin in 1897 dwelt at length upon recent extension of German ship-building, pointing attention to the splendid new yards and docking accommodations at Hamburg, Bremen, Elbing, Danzig, and Stettin—"great works which can carry out all possible demands on their resources." Hamburg in 1896 had built a floating dock of 17,000 tons' lifting power, which made it no longer necessary for even the largest ships to go to England; while at Bremen a dock was in process of construction capable of lifting ships of 20,000 tons.[156] Besides all this, an ominous growth in the size of the German merchant marine had taken place since the early eighties, and the ship-subsidy policy of the German Government was being extended. This had been instituted in 1885 with a grant to the North German Lloyd (in the guise of a postal sub-vention) of £85,000 per year for a direct steamer line to the Far East, and another of £115,000 for a direct line to Australia. In 1890 an annual subsidy of £45,000 was conferred upon the German East Africa Line; in 1893 the Lloyd got £5,000 more for its Far East service, and in 1898 an additional £75,000; three years later the East Africa subsidy was enlarged fifty per cent. So that at the beginning of the twentieth century some £347,500 (exclusive of payments for carriage of trans-atlantic mails) was being spent annually by the German Government to aid shipping lines which were sharply competitive with British com-panies.[157] Moreover, by this time the German system of through-rate shipments from place of manufacture to ultimate destina-

[155] B. H. Thwaite, "The Commercial War Between England and Germany," Dec., 1896.

[156] Miscellaneous Series 443.

[157] Commercial No. 4, 1901; *supra* Ch. II; Meeker, *History of Shipping Subsidies*, pp. 82-95; Report of Select Committee on Steamship Subsidies, 1902, XXV. Comparatively, German subsidies were not large. France paid three times as much, and British grants, too, were much larger, although only for postal and Admiralty purposes, trade considerations being virtually excluded.—Report of Committee, 1901, p. 313; 1902, VII, XXIV.

tion (a great boon to the Levant and East Africa lines) had been in operation to the Near East and East Africa for a decade. Also, it may be noted, in 1897 Germany launched the *Kaiser Wilhelm der Grosse*, then the fastest steamer on the seas,[158] and three years later came the *Deutschland*, which was even faster. (The British did not regain the Atlantic ribbon until the launching of the *Mauretania* and *Lusitania* in 1907.) Such developments could hardly fail to excite fears in England lest even the powerful shipping industry totter from its supremacy under the impact of Germany's blows. "For Germany's merchant marine," warned the *Daily Mail* in 1898, "is increasing at a rate that would be alarming if English people could ever be alarmed."[159]

In the early years of the twentieth century British shipping faced a serious crisis, and something resembling panic was created in the country by news of what appeared to be very serious reverses to the national maritime trading supremacy. The increase of subsidized foreign competition and the purchase by foreigners of a number of British lines were the causes of this. Danger lurked especially from two quarters: Germany and the United States. The Imperial German Government in 1898 and 1901 had considerably increased its subsidy payments, and in America a formidable movement for subsidy legislation had got under way. One bombshell after another exploded between 1899 and 1902. Three British-owned lines in the Far East (the East India, Holt, and Scottish Oriental) passed into German hands, while the Hamburg America Company absorbed the Atlas Line operating between New York and the West Indies.[160] Then in April, 1902, the sensational news of the Morgan Trust was given to the world. The American financial wizard had formed a powerful combination of At-

[158] A *Saturday Review* article, "British Shipping and Foreign Competition," May 22, 1897, said at this time: "The competition of foreign with British ships . . . is becoming every day more severe. . . . Germany launched the other day a vessel designed to outsteam the best two steamers now in the Atlantic trade, and not long before sent to Australia the largest steamer that has ever crossed the equator."

[159] Leader of Jan. 27, 1898.

[160] Report of Committee on S. S. Subsidies, 1902, XVIII.

lantic lines (most of them British), including the Leyland, Atlantic Transport, American, Dominion and White Star. The Morgan idea was to bring the whole Atlantic service into a single organization, toward which end a traffic agreement was entered into with the two great German lines and an unsuccessful attempt was made to draw in the Cunard Company.[161]

The press in these days abounded in letters and articles of warning, alarm, and dismay. It was characteristic of the time that a writer in the *Fortnightly Review* should discuss the question, "Will England Last the Century?" and declare that

even in the case of German shipping British owners cannot stand against the power of the subsidy. For the Far East alone the annual subventions voted by the Reichstag . . . amount to more than a quarter million sterling. From Singapore to Shanghai British lines of steamers and British shipyards are passing to German ownership and the German flag.[162]

A contributor to the *Shipping World* was convinced that "Our position as shipbuilders and shipowners is being attacked from every quarter."[163] The future, according to a *Westminster Review* contributor, "only offers a vista of declining prosperity,"[164] and another writer in the same journal pronounced British shipping "doomed."[165] The *Times* complained bitterly that the competitive German lines, because of their subsidies, had their Government as a partner, with the result that they

cut into our trade anywhere, working at a loss. Having gained a footing without a shadow of risk, they can afterwards raise their prices to paying point. If a British company again tries to compete, they drop at once below cost price without any injury to their shareholders.[166]

The grave concern in official circles was shown in the appointment of a Parliamentary Select Committee in 1901-02 to hear

[161] Huldermann in Ch. V gives an excellent account of the formation of the Morgan Trust and the role of the German lines.

[162] Jan. 1, 1901.

[163] E. R. J., "Our Foreign Competitors," Jan. 1, 1902.

[164] Yolet Capel, "England's Peril," Feb. 1, 1902.

[165] P. Barry, "Doomed British Shipping," July, 1902.

[166] Leader of May 29, 1902.

evidence and report upon the question of how far the foreign subsidies were damaging Britain.[167] The *malaise* of the shipping business was revealed at length in this array of testimony; and even so orthodox an economic liberal as the venerable Board of Trade statistician, Sir Robert Giffen, was convinced that "something must be done, and soon, to prevent the diminution of progress in our mercantile marine, since our first line of defense is seriously endangered by it." He expressed the view that the German mercantile fleet had been able to make its remarkable progress simply because of Government subsidies, and was quoted as saying that "subsidized steamers which are really part of the German navy are being nursed on the internal business of the British Empire." Such an opinion from Sir Robert Giffen, of all men, the *Times* thought calculated to make "a profound impression upon public opinion in this country . . . the maritime preponderance of the Empire, as far as merchant shipping is concerned, is threatening to become a thing of the past."[168]

The frequent charges made in England to the effect that the German merchant marine was largely the creature of state subsidies drew fire from German shipping circles. Albert Ballin vehemently denied this upon several occasions,[169] and as a matter of fact he was right. The report of the Select Committee took no exaggerated view of subsidies and their effects; as compared with skill and industry, it was found, subsidies were a relatively minor factor in the recent development of foreign shipping trades. France, it was shown, paid far more than Germany in subsidies and bounties, although French shipping could boast of no such progress as German companies had achieved. The actual sums disbursed by the German Government were relatively small; but other important favors, such as reser-

---

[167] A very large part of the evidence taken had to do with German shipping, especially to East Africa, the Levant, and the Far East. Plainly the chief danger espied at the time was German shipping.

[168] June 7, 1902; *vide* also *Daily Chronicle* and *Pall Mall Gazette* of same day.

[169] Ballin's letter to *Times*, August 31, 1901, and report of an address by him in Germany, the *Times*, June 13, 1902.

vation of the coasting trade, tariff exemption for shipbuilding materials, and preferential railway rates on shipbuilding materials and goods for export over German lines, were granted. "Merchant shipping in England," the Committee stated, "has not the Government at its back in the same way merchant shipping has in Germany. . . . There not only the Government, but the Kaiser himself, takes the most active steps in pushing German trade."[170] But the Committee was very far from denying that the essential factors in German progress were skill and excellence of service. Only one certain case of German success due directly to subsidies, in fact, could be cited: the German East Africa line.[171] Nevertheless it was hard to kill the idea in England that the German merchant marine lived on subsidies paid by a Government thirsting for world power. The error in this view only emphasized the danger in the German shipping rivalry.

The reaction in England to the Morgan Trust is of special interest here even though that threatening movement came from America rather than Germany. Albert Ballin was intimately concerned with the whole process of forming the combine and had negotiated the traffic agreement with the German lines. Just before public announcement of the great trust was made he wrote:

In compliance with the wishes emanating from prominent British quarters, the whole transaction will be represented in the light of a big Anglo-American "community of interest" agreement; and the fact that it virtually concedes to the United States the control of the North Atlantic shipping business will be kept in the background, as far as it is possible to do so.[172]

That is exactly the way in which the announcement was communicated to the British public.[173] Thus the *Times* treated it as an economy measure, in which the British constitution of the sev-

[170] Report, XXIV.
[171] Report, XXVI.
[172] Huldermann, p. 59.
[173] *Times* and other papers, April 19, 1902 also *Shipping World* for May 14, 1902.

eral companies joining the trust would be carefully safeguarded at the same time that closer alliance was made between American and British business interests. When, a little later, the combine's traffic agreement with the German lines became known, the *Times* remarked (not without some satisfaction) that the Germans had been forced into a corner.[174] The Germans, however, did not see themselves maneuvered into any such position. Ballin was entirely satisfied and had no difficulty in securing the consent of the North German Lloyd and the hearty approval of the Kaiser. "What makes people in England feel most uncomfortable," Ballin wrote in his diary (June 5, 1902), "is not the passing of the various shipping companies into American hands, but the fact that the German companies have done so well over the deal."[175] In Germany the Morgan Trust seems to have been represented as a severe blow to British shipping, and emphasis was placed upon the success of the German lines in maintaining their independence; which provoked the *Times* to charge the Germans with seeking to poison Anglo-American friendship. The subtle German idea, according to the *Times*, was this: if England could be goaded into adopting a hostile attitude toward the Morgan combine a breach would be made in "the very stronghold of Anglo-American friendship—namely in the world of business"—and if she could be further tempted into taking reprisals there would be, instead of a community of interest on the Atlantic, a regular shipping war between England and America.

In such a struggle all the old ill feeling and jealousy between America and England . . . would very soon be revived, and Germany would not merely be able to play her favourite rôle of *tertius gaudens,* but would be the first to reap direct political and commercial benefits from this estrangement.[176]

What truth, if any, there was in this accusation, it does not seem possible to judge. One thing seems certain, however, that the German lines made no dictated surrender to an Anglo-American combination. The real line of battle was drawn between

[174] Leader of May 27, 1902.
[175] Huldermann, pp. 54-61.
[176] May 22, 1902, leader and Vienna dispatch.

the Morgan Trust and the German lines on the one side and the powerful Cunard Company on the other.

Anglo-German shipping rivalry, which had thus assumed the proportions of a national economic crisis in the early years of the twentieth century, did not abate; although Britain certainly recovered from the alarmist mood of those times. The prophets of doom were confounded by the unflagging expansion of British shipping that took place in the last decade before the war. In these years, despite the very striking progress of German shipping, it is hard to detect any sure signs of British decline. Throughout the ports of the world, now crowded with great vessels of many different national flags, Britain was still the undisputed leader in 1914. Her monopolistic supremacy had been reduced to leadership, but however hard was the competition faced on this or that route, she was still far above challenge if the totality of her shipping is considered. The figure given here shows the comparative measures of the growth of British and German steamship tonnage from 1902 to 1912;[177] plainly there was nothing in the statistics of merchant shipping to discomfort England. An-

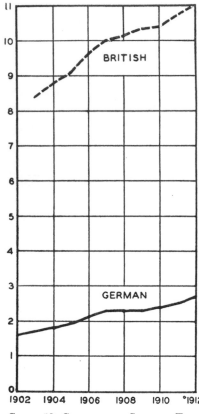

CHART 12. COMPARATIVE STEAMER TONNAGE OF BRITISH AND GERMAN MERCHANT NAVIES, 1902-1912, EXPRESSED IN MILLION TONS.

[177] Based on figures given in Statistical Abstract for Foreign Countries. It need hardly be said that German shipping was far ahead of all other national carrying trades for the second position.

218

other view of the situation in the large may be got by contrasting the relative tonnage of the two national carrying
trades in a select list of the world's chief ports, and such an
inquiry does not even hint at the passing of British shipping
business to Germany.[178] It is probably not too much to say
that British shipping withstood German and world competition more successfully than any other major department of
the national economic life. In certain specific rivalries German lines of course gained business that British companies
wanted, especially in the trade to East Africa, the Levant
and the Far East, and in the transatlantic passenger service
(the German lines gained the lion's share of this last) ;[179]
but in world shipping considered as a whole the British yielded
little or nothing to the Germans. At the end of 1912 a *Times*
leader could say exultantly:

We know something of the determination with which Germany
has of late years set herself to build up a great merchant fleet,
of the energy and enterprise of Japan, and of the wonderful progress
made by certain other nations. Yet the British tonnage is more than
four times that of Germany, more than nine times that of France,
and more than fourteen times that of Japan; and to the shipping
of these countries may be added that of Norway . . . and Italy
and Holland, and the aggregate of the six . . . is but two-thirds
that of Britain. . . . At a time when so much is being said of
the inroads which other nations are making on British commercial
supremacy—when, from so many quarters we are being told that,
as a nation, we cannot stand the pace of modern competition—it
is worth pausing to consider these figures. . . . For it must be
clearly understood that our preëminence on the sea is not, as it
were, a mere stationary superiority—a thing established long
ago which is gradually vanishing before the enterprise of our
rivals.[180]

[178] For such a comparison *vide* Appendix III.

[179] In 1912 the North German Lloyd carried 168,723 passengers from
Europe to New York, the Hamburg-America 137,076, the Cunard 110,018,
and the White Star 71,063.—*Vide* leader, "North Atlantic Rivalry," in
Shipping Gazette and Lloyd's List, Jan. 31, 1913.

[180] Leader of Dec. 13, 1912.

It would be impossible, in these few pages, to describe the various competitions, rate wars, etc., in which British and German lines engaged during the period of this study, but notice may well be taken of a few facts which pointed to a sharpening of rivalries and provided the occasion for a new flurry of alarm in England on the very eve of the war.

Trouble brewed in the North Atlantic Shipping Conference (a traffic pool embracing all the chief transatlantic lines then held together by a set of agreements made in 1908); and it had its origin in the competition for the profitable emigrant carrying trade to the New World—a bone of contention by no means new at the time. The two great German lines had grown prosperous in this business and had long striven by every possible means to direct emigrants from central and eastern Europe to German ports and German lines; this had long been against the interest of the Cunard Mediterranean service from Hungary. Now early in 1913 the competitive situation was intensified. The Canadian Pacific quit the Atlantic Conference and opened a direct service between Trieste and Canada, to which the Germans replied by placing enough steamers at the service of a small Austrian line to enable it to run a rival direct line to Montreal. Very quickly the quarrel spread from the Adriatic. "A disturbing element," commented the *Shipping Gazette*, "has been introduced into the North Atlantic Passenger Conference, an organization which, if report speaks truly, was previously not working with absolute harmony."[181]

There was, in fact, another aggressive line demanding more elbow room. The Hamburg-American Company had been enormously increasing its capacities. The great *Imperator*, the world's largest ship, had been launched in 1912, and the company was carrying on an extensive building program including the *Vaterland* (1913) and the *Bismarck* (1914). Ballin's firm, therefore, in 1913 pressed the Conference for a larger quota of continental passenger traffic, to which the North German Lloyd

[181] Article, "North Atlantic Rivalry," Jan. 31, 1913; *vide* also another, "The Canadian-German Battle," in issue of Feb. 14.

naturally objected; so that the end of the year found the two great German companies at loggerheads and the Atlantic pool threatened with disruption. All existing Conference agreements were due to expire January 31, 1914, and a general rate war thus loomed on the near horizon. "By all appearances," said the *Shipping Gazette,* "we are at the commencement of a struggle which may have disturbing consequences."[182] "One thing at all events is clear," observed the *Shipping World.* "The Hamburg Company, in obtaining a free hand, and through its action having caused the Conference agreements for the time being to be suspended, has at the same time given the British lines freedom of action." It was therefore broadly hinted that if Ballin reached for too much there would be retaliation by one or two of the leading British lines.[183] In February steps to avert a general shipping war were taken by the conclusion of a general community-of-interest agreement between the German lines,[184] after which they presented a united front in the negotiations for reconstituting the Conference. These stretched out over the spring and reached no satisfactory conclusion, the chief difficulties being the position of the Canadian Pacific and Cunard companies in the Mediterranean. The problem of the pool, in fact, resolved itself primarily into an Anglo-German dispute. A final meeting of the lines at Cologne on May 1, after failing to discover a formula, adjourned to August 5. So that when war supervened, although a general rate-slashing had been held in abeyance, the Atlantic pool had not yet been reconstituted.[185] When it is recalled that the White Star and Cunard Companies had put the *Olympic* and *Aquitania* to sea in the same years that saw the launching of the giant Hamburg liners, that the Atlantic pool was virtually disrupted, and that the world was slipping in 1914 into another economic depression it seems plain enough that a

---

[182] *Ibid.,* "The German Lines Quarrel," Dec. 26, 1913.
[183] Jan. 28, 1914.
[184] *Shipping World,* Feb. 25.
[185] *Shipping World* for March 25 and May 6; details given in *Times,* Jan. 26-28; Feb. 2-4; 11-24; March 9-21; April 23, May 2.

bitter shipping war upon the Atlantic was just in the offing when August 1 came.

But this does not exhaust the symptoms of intensified rivalry on the eve of the War. It was an ominous sign when in 1913 a curious fall in British shipping at Antwerp occurred simultaneously with a sharp rise in Germany's tonnage;[186] and in October of that year the new Emden harbor, which it was hoped would come to rival Rotterdam and Antwerp, was opened by the Prussian Government.[187] Sir Francis Oppenheimer, British commercial attaché at Berlin, in his 1914 report dwelt upon the increased dangers of German competition, now "rapidly becoming ubiquitous." "It may be safely expected," he wrote, "that as a result of the combination between the North German Lloyd and the Hamburg-America Line it will in future become possible for these two concerns to pursue the traditional policy of spanning the globe with a purely German set of services with ever greater energy because the friendly working agreement between the old rivals will lead to a great saving of expense."[188]

The Woermann Line, chief German competitor in the trade to West Africa, in 1914 enlarged its fleet and increased the frequency of its sailings from Hamburg and Rotterdam.[189] The Rickmers Line of Hamburg about the same time established a regular fortnightly steamer service between Hamburg-Antwerp and Roumania;[190] and soon afterwards the Hamburg-America established a new line between New York and the ports of the Near East. *The Board of Trade Journal* remarked significantly that "a considerable part of the cargo carried between America and the Near East has been carried hitherto in British ships with trans-shipments in United Kingdom or Dutch ports."[191] All these developments were indeed competitive thrusts into fields of British shipping enterprise.

In the Far East the same signs were manifest. The Rickmers

---

[186] Antwerp report, Annual Series 5274; *Shipping World*, June 3, 1914.
[187] *Vide* Annual Series 5414.
[188] Annual Series 5404.
[189] *Board of Trade Journal*, Jan. 29; *Times*, June 15.
[190] *Board of Trade Journal*, March 12.
[191] *Ibid.*, March 26.

Line was crowding out the British flag at Vladivostok, according to the consul there, who wrote in 1914:

It would be pleasant to think that the growing export trade from this new country would be likely to ensure a more frequent appearance of the British flag in Russian Far Eastern waters. This is, unfortunately, not to be anticipated, for the Rickmers Line . . . have ensured to themselves the carriage of the regular trade both ways. For years past ten or twelve British ships have been chartered every year for the trade between Hamburg, Antwerp, Liverpool, Vladivostok and Nicolaievsk. During 1913 this number abruptly fell to three . . . the growing freight has been transferred to the German flag. In fact, United Kingdom shipowners have lost touch with the Russian Far East just at the moment when it was likely to provide a stable and reliable trade both outwards and homewards.[192]

In 1914 the Rickmers Company enlarged its Far East service and began a freight rate war with rival British lines.[193] Meanwhile a new subsidy bill was being placed before the Reichstag, which, although proposing to drop certain existing subventions to Far East services, provided for new grants to German shipping lines in Australasia.[194] The bill remained before the Reichstag until the coming of the War, and while it was being watched with interest in Great Britain announcement was made that the North German Lloyd and German-Austrian companies had decided to open a direct service between continental Europe and New Zealand. This news created an excited reaction in England, where the move was viewed as a bold and significant intrusion into British imperial shipping trade.[195]

From these scattered and varied facts it should be abundantly plain that the Anglo-German rivalry in ships was getting considerably hotter as the spring of 1914 passed into summer.

[192] *Ibid.*, Feb. 26, 1914; Annual Series 5259.

[193] *Board of Trade Journal*, May 14, 1914; *Times*, June 6, 9.

[194] *Board of Trade Journal*, April 30; *Shipping World*, May 6, 1914.

[195] *Times*, May 29-June 15; *infra* Ch. VI; the shipping press was less excited than the regular newspapers, however. "In invading this trade," said the *Shipping Gazette*, "there seems reason to believe that they will not be acting without regard to the claims of British lines . . . or, indeed, under conditions which will be wholly unacceptable to those lines."—Article, "German Shipping Competition," June 5, 1914.

Chapter VI
NATIONAL ALARM

"I HAVE often thought," remarked Lord Salisbury, "how strange is the contrast between men in their individual and in their collective capacities. The individual Briton is the boldest, the most disregarding man as to danger you can find anywhere on earth. He never expects that evil is coming upon him or doubts his power to resist it. The collective Briton, however, is as timorous as a woman; he sees danger everywhere. If any nation increases its exports for a single year, the downfall of British trade is at hand. If any nation finds an outlet for its trade in some new or unexplored portion of the world, instead of rejoicing at the amount of natural resources which is proclaimed for human industry, he says there is a rival to whom our fall will be due."[1] These words were spoken by the great Prime Minister in an address to the annual dinner of the Associated Chambers of Commerce on March 10, 1897, and they were occasioned by a recent and extraordinary outburst in the country of commercial fear and jealousy of Germany. It will be the purpose of this chapter to take some measure of this outburst and the subsequent course of national alarm over German commerce down to 1914.

It has previously been shown that British fears of Germany as a dangerous commercial rival were first manifested plainly in the middle eighties.[2] Certain organs and individuals in those years saw a menace to national prosperity and business supremacy in the progress of German industry and the expansion of the German export trade. But it cannot be said that a really widespread national alarm over German trade existed before the nineties. Alarmist views were officially discouraged, and even

[1] Quoted by Henry Birchenough in "Do Foreign Annexations Injure British Trade?" *The Nineteenth Century*, vol. 41, 1897, p. 993.
[2] *Supra* Ch. II.

denied,[3] while Free Trade orthodoxy steadily made light of the idea that the economic expansion of any foreign nation could possibly react unfavorably on British business. Fear of Germany was therefore quite commonly dismissed as a protectionist's nightmare. That view, however, weakened a good deal in the next decade when the rate of German commercial progress was considerably accelerated. Hard times, the evident stagnation of some British industries, the increased quantities of German goods sold in England, the widened area of world competition, the rise of German shipping, the many voices raised against the German peril, all conspired to produce a high measure of national apprehension. Germany, by 1896, was singled out in the popular mind as England's deadly commercial rival, at the same time that her political and diplomatic policies and interests diverged sensationally from those of Great Britain.

This fear of German commerce permeated the national controversy over tariff reform, and, like that controversy, it appeared chiefly in years of trade depression. Protectionist opinion, which aimed vaguely at the creation of a commercial federation or imperial *Zollverein* in the British Empire, and which, to attain that end, urged a tariff on foreign imports, was inclined to see a very grave danger in Germany and to trumpet warning after warning to the country. Even Cobdenite opinion was now less inclined to minimize the German peril, and raised a loud demand

[3] Sir Robert Giffen, perhaps the most influential and authoritative economist among Free Traders, in a special report to the Board of Trade in 1888, wrote: "The popular impression given by some consular reports that German trade is gaining ground everywhere at the expense of British trade would appear to be largely due to the fact that there are no consular reports from British possessions, and partly to the fact that prominence is naturally given to minor countries in these consular reports. . . . The iteration of particular facts from many little places as to German competition, while the larger trades are not reported on, produces the illusion that the trade of the United Kingdom is giving way at every point, whereas the actual facts stated are entirely different. The particular facts stated are in all cases important in their own place, but the inference as to the general course which English export trade is taking is too hasty."—*Foreign Trade: Statistical Tables Relating to The Progress of the Foreign Trade of the United Kingdom and of Other Countries, in Recent Years: With Report to the Board of Trade Thereon.* C.-5297, 1888, p. 9.

for more individual initiative, more education, and more effective trade methods, as weapons with which to combat it. The gravest questions that can face a vigorous modern nation were staring Britain in the face after 1890. Industrial progress appeared to have halted and economic decay to have set in. Productive capital was fleeing the country, and the increasing margin of imports over exports was regarded uneasily. "A great many people," remarked the *Times*, "have on these grounds worked themselves into a state of acute apprehension. They argue that if we import and consume more goods than we send out . . . British industry must be languishing, British trade must be decaying, and this unhappy country must be living like a starved camel on its own hump."[4] Those who were chiefly concerned for the continued productive energy and capacity of the country pessimistically foresaw a day when England would be a land populated only by a few millionaires and a proletariat of hired retainers. J. A. Hobson wrote in 1891 that if the country declined to protect itself against the alienation of capital,

another century may see England the retreat for the old age of a small aristocracy of millionaires, who will have made their money where labour was cheapest, and return to spend it where life is pleasantest. No productive work will be possible in England, but such labour as is required for personal service will be procurable at a cheap rate, owing to the reluctance of labour to keep pace with the migration of capital.[5]

[4] Leader of Jan. 18, 1899.

[5] "Can England Keep Her Commerce?" *National Review,* vol. 17, 1891. The migration of capital from England to lands better suited for production was very much discussed in the nineties and after, and constituted the most powerful argument for the advocates of Tariff Reform. The outlook of the early nineties is very well shown in Mr. A. Williamson's *British Industries and Foreign Competition,* 1894. He gives (pp. 204-10) a number of instances of British industries foresaking England for the Continent and America, because of tariffs and cheaper production costs. He quotes Mr. Porter, of the American Tariff Commission, as follows: "I found shoddy manufacturers from Batby and Dewsbury established in Aachen, Prussia; Lancashire and Scottish spinners in Rouen: Leicestershire hosiery manufacturers in Saxony; Yorkshire wool-combing establishments in Rheims; Dundee jute mills in Dunkerque; all-wool stuff manufacturers in Roubaix; English iron and steel mills in Belgium; and English woolen mills in Hol-

Such a view was very frequently heard (and with the day of ruin more imminent than a century hence!) in the last decade of the nineteenth century—barely twenty years after the peak of England's supremacy! The modern business world works fast revolutions. Now this fear of economic ruin coincided with the termination of what remained of Anglo-German cordiality and the uncomfortable realization of the country's dangerous political isolation. So that the *fin de siècle* found England questioning doubtfully her economic and political security, all the while her social and economic institutions were being challenged by the rising tide of socialism. All these circumstances conspired to shake the confidence of the nation, and to make it especially apprehensive of that Power which not only offered imperialist rivalry in Asia and Africa but represented a collectivist challenge to individualistic business and a threat of ruin to British industry and commerce.

The great panic did not burst, however, until the middle of the decade. At the beginning of the nineties little was being heard of the German commercial peril, for the very natural reason that the years of 1889-1891 were a period of business revival. It was also at this time that Germany's "new course" was signalized by the 1890 Convention with England, which, in reaffirming official cordiality and reducing temporarily imperialist rivalry, doubtless had some influence in silencing the voice of commercial fear and jealousy. Germany, moreover, did not appear at this time to be going forward so rapidly;[6] she was meeting with those trade obstacles in Europe which induced her at length to modify

---

land. Removing English capital to the Continent has secured a profitable home market, while England was near with widely open ports to serve as a 'dumping ground,' to unload surplus goods, made by foreign labour, superintended by English skill. In this way the English markets are swamped, and her labour undersold."

[6] A *Times* article of Oct. 6, 1891, for example (occasioned by the annual reports of the German chambers of commerce), showed how far behind Britain Germany still stood in the extent of her export trade; and "the conclusions," it was observed, "is that the hope hitherto entertained in Germany, of overtaking the trade of Great Britain, which has centuries of strenuous labour and struggle behind it, must soon be surrendered."

her fiscal policy. It is, therefore, hardly surprising to find the British press giving scant notice to the German danger.[7] Little attention, in fact, seems to have been paid in England to that Continental tariff revolution inaugurated by the Caprivi Conventions, which was a prelude to new large German gains in European markets. "England has certainly nothing of which to complain," said the *Morning Post* in referring to the treaties. "This country will assuredly not suffer, and it is quite possible that she may benefit. . . . We may look on as independent and interested spectators at the very important experiment which is being tried in Continental Europe."[8] The *Times,* still loyal to Free Trade, was inclined to welcome the new tariff conventions, although not without perceiving the dangers to Britain should the commercial alliances of Central Europe grow into a protectionist *Zollverein;* in which case it would be "far from clear that . . . this country and other nations lying outside the magic circles would not meet with as little mercy as the McKinley tariff dealt out to them."[9] The country for the most part, however, in so far as it showed an interest in the new order of tariffs, viewed it as a vindication of liberal commercial policy and a promise of benefit to Great Britain.[10]

[7] Expressions of alarm were rare, but not entirely absent; e.g., one "H. W. W.," writing in the *Westminster Review* in 1891, said: "Then there is our commercial rivalry—never greater, unfortunately, or threatening to grow to still more formidable proportions, than just now, at the moment chosen for a rapprochement. To what exent that rivalry has been sharpened since Germany laid herself out for a deliberately competitive commercial policy, probably few people in England are fully aware. But it deserves to be pointed out, while we are looking for a liberal effusion of good-will, to what degree our commerce with Germany has become aggressively competitive and overlapping, whereas our trade with France, Russia, and other countries is certainly far more dovetailing and mutually complemental. Cottons, machinery, hardware, coals, the trans-atlantic trade—above all, the trade with the Far East—in all these Germany has ranged herself specifically against us. . . ."—"England and Germany," vol. 136, 1891, pp. 650-64.

[8] Dec. 9, 1891.

[9] Dec. 8, 1891.

[10] "I do not say that they are free trade treaties," said Sir Michael Hicks-Beach, President of the Board of Trade, "but in some important particulars they are a step in that direction."—Hansard, 4th S., vol. 1, pp. 112-13, Feb. 9, 1892.

The trade revival of 1889-91 ended as usual in the return of severe depression. A slow-up in late 1891 opened a period of hard times which ran through all the following year. The McKinley tariff and political and fiscal troubles in South America and Australia were regarded as the principal causes for the slackening of commerce. 1893 was another bad year, and although 1894 was somewhat better, not until 1896-97 was trade again very active. "Not even the most confident of optimists can pretend that we are in a flourishing condition," observed the *Times* in early 1895, ". . . Foreign competition tends to become more and more acute in Europe, and to attain to very formidable dimensions in the Far East."[11] Now Germany, too, went through severe depression in these years, and her tariff war with Russia down to 1894 made it necessary for her to seek trade more energetically in other markets, thus intensifying her competition with Great Britain. The narrowing of the Russian and American markets undoubtedly served to throw British and German business against each other more violently in other parts of the world. Germany's pressure upon the British home and colonial markets increased, and her new commercial treaties with European neighbors conferred greater advantage on her than on Great Britain. Moreover, the depression in Germany appeared to relax earlier and more rapidly than in England, a fact which perhaps excited some commercial jealousy. Given this set of circumstances, the stage was set in England for a revival of the tariff-reform issue, new demands for the government to help business, and the reappearance of the German trade menace.

2

As the depressed state of trade lengthened out toward 1896 the symptoms of commercial apprehension of Germany began to manifest themselves very distinctly. Exactly when and where they were first to be discerned it is hardly possible to say, but after a virtual absence since the later eighties they became evident enough by 1893. Newspaper items of information about

[11] March 14, 1895.

commercial competition in all parts of the world became more conspicuous. The progress of German industry and the advance of Germany in the export market took on a much increased news value in the British press; and all references to German success were grist for the mill of tariff reformers. Such books as A. Williamson's *British Industries and Foreign Competition* (1894) signalized the growing attention of the British mind to the serious problem of foreign rivalry, and more and more the idea took root that foreign competition was everywhere chiefly German competition. "Germany," wrote the *Times'* Berlin correspondent in 1895, "is by far the most dangerous of our industrial competitors at the present moment all the world over, and one cannot but regret that the influence of German competition upon British industry has not yet received the full amount of official attention which the magnitude of the interests at stake deserves."[12]

Official circles certainly were slow to apprehend the situation. The disposition of the Liberal Government, especially before Mr. Gladstone's retirement, was to pay no attention whatever to the recrudescing German trade peril, save perhaps to minimize it. In the spring of 1894 the Board of Trade issued a Bluebook calculated to allay all fear of Germany. Sir Robert Giffen undertook an inquiry into the comparative progress of British and foreign commerce since 1884, and his analysis of official statistics resulted in a very optimistic report.[13] His figures indicated a ten per cent increase in British exports as compared with only five per cent increase in German exports, over a ten-year period. In the more distant countries, he argued, the major share of trade was still in British hands, while even in Europe he declared the British position to be sound. Sir Robert, in fact, could discover "no weakening in the hold of the United Kingdom [in comparison with its chief competitors] upon either the import or export trade of the world." His report was an

[12] Berlin dispatch, Nov. 25, 1895.

[13] *Foreign Trade: Statistical Tables Relating to the Progress of the Foreign Trade of the United Kingdom, and of Other Foreign Countries,* with Report to the Board of Trade Thereon. C.-7349, 1894.

excellent example of official optimism, Cobdenite certainty that nothing could be basically wrong with a nation adhering to free-trade principles, and the misleading possibilities of statistics.[14] Sir Robert formulated his conclusion about Germany by looking at the figures of trade for 1890-92, years when that country was finding its productive capacity cramped by too narrow markets. He did not guess that Germany was on the eve of the great 1895-96 expansion. Giffen was a high authority, however, and his report drew wide press notice. A *Times* leader analyzed it and declared "the impression regarding the supposed growth of German trade" was erroneous. A *Daily News* leader of course voiced the same view; while even the *Morning Post*, although refusing to accept the report as "absolutely conclusive," admitted that "as far as it goes it proves that, whilst there is a general expansion of business all over the world, the advance of Germany in comparison with England is not by any means so great as is commonly supposed."[15]

The German trade menace was not to be dispelled, however, by Sir Robert Giffen's statistical studies. It went on gathering fresh strength through 1894-95, as the press continued to cite evidences of German gains the while British commerce languished. It is impossible to present here the multiplicity of notices referring directly or indirectly to the increase of German competition, but it may be said that a search at random through the files of the *Times* in these years demonstrates plainly that the attention of the British nation was repeatedly summoned to the forward march of German business in scores of threatening directions.

Inevitably, official circles became penetrated by the uneasiness growing up in the commercial and industrial class; and the Salisbury Government, formed in 1895, displayed an attitude toward the problems of foreign trade competition which was

---

[14] For another highly optimistic view at this time, based entirely on statistics, see A. W. Flux: "The Commercial Supremacy of Great Britain," *Economic Journal,* 1894, vol. 4, pp. 457-67, 595-605.

[15] May 4, 5, 1894.

strikingly different from that of its predecessors.[16] The Chamberlain policies now began to unfold themselves. Joseph Chamberlain was the best representative of that type of statesman which the age of commercial and imperialist rivalry called to power, and his ascendancy marks a conspicuous departure from that official laissez-faire indifference toward commerce which was so long a time dying in Great Britain. Entering the Colonial Office in 1895, he began at once to seek the restoration of commercial prosperity through the exploitation of colonial markets and to infuse the Government with the spirit of neo-mercantilism. "All the great offices of state," he told a Birmingham audience in 1896, "are occupied with commercial affairs. The Foreign Office and the Agricultural Office are chiefly engaged in finding new markets and defending old ones. The War Office and the Admiralty Office are mostly engaged in preparations for the defense of these markets and for the protection of our commerce. . . . It is not too much to say that that Government does most to deserve the popular approval which does most to increase our trade and to settle it on a firm foundation."[17] What Mr. Chamberlain did in 1895, which should be noted here, was to institute a survey of British trade and foreign competition throughout the whole of the Empire. Stating his object to be the securing of "as large a share as possible of the mutual trade of the United Kingdom and the Colonies for British producers and manufacturers," he circularized the Colonial Governments (November 28) for elaborate information on "the extent to which . . . foreign imports of any kind have displaced, or are displacing, similar British goods and the causes of such displacement."[18] The circular also asked for samples and patterns of foreign-made articles taking the place of British goods; and arrangements were effected with the London Chamber of Commerce for exhibiting the samples in

[16] *Vide* an interesting article, "Foreign Office Assistance to Trade," in *Morning Post*, Dec. 5, 1895.

[17] Report of speech in *Times*, Nov. 14, 1896.

[18] *Trade of the British Empire and Foreign Competition*, 1897, C.-8449, p. 16.

the United Kingdom. "The despatch," remarked the *Chamber of Commerce Journal,* "marks an important epoch in the economic history of this country, as it indicates the official abandonment of laissez-faire, and also the official recognition of the fact that foreign competition is to be taken into serious considera-tion."[19] No specific reference to German goods was made in Mr. Chamberlain's letter to the Colonial Governors, but there can be no doubt that the pressure of German competition largely explains his move. No other world-wide competition had as yet come to appear serious, and the results of the survey were to show Germany as the principal rival in imperial markets.

The Colonial Office was thus awakening to the German danger on the eve of the great alarm of 1896, and the Foreign Office was urged to imitate its example. "If it be necessary, as it undoubtedly is," declared the *Morning Post,* "to gather in-formation from the Colonies of the various openings for British trade, it is even more urgent that no effort be spared to procure the same news with regard to our foreign trade." Attention was drawn to the progress of Germans and others in the Far East, and, as for the new world, "it is not too much to say that the entire trade of South America is under the control of German merchants." Therefore, it was necessary to draw a closer relationship between consuls and diplomatists and the great English centers of commerce, "for there is still much to be done in the way of obtaining information as to the possibilities of trade in foreign countries."[20] The *Chamber of Commerce Journal* voiced the same opinion and demand; and early in January the Foreign Office began to take steps toward secur-ing a greater commercial usefulness from its agents.[21] Such

[19] Quoted in *Correspondence Respecting Diplomatic and Consular Assistance to Trade,* C.-8432 (Commercial No. 5, 1897).

[20] Leader of Dec. 5. *Vide* also special article of same date, "Foreign Office Assistance to Trade."

[21] *Vide* Correspondence Respecting Diplomatic and Consular Assistance to Trade, C.-8432, 1897. Some results of this were summarized in a *Times* article, "British Consuls and Foreign Trade," Dec. 11, 1896. The new mer-cantilist spirit in the Foreign Office under Salisbury and Curzon is most ex-cellently illustrated in some words of Curzon in 1898 to the Associated

action in these two great offices of state testify unmistakably to the increased official cognizance of the German trade rivalry. International commercial competition had become one of the livest topics of the day by the beginning of 1896, and no other competitors of Britain seemed half so tenacious and ubiquitous as the Germans. Even the Government was waking up.

Meanwhile, the United Kingdom producing community was exhibiting a notable sensitiveness toward German encroachments in the home market. Since the adoption of the Merchandise Marks Act of 1887, the stamp "made in Germany" had become increasingly familiar in Great Britain, and the country gradually came to recognize how large a quantity of German manufactures it had long been buying. Coinciding with a period of slack trade, when German pressure on the British market was increasing, the discovery was quite disagreeable. It created in some quarters a certain measure of nervousness which was quick to resent the slightest inroad upon British production, and quick to accuse Germans of "unfair" trade tactics, such as dumping, forging trade marks, conniving at violations of the Merchandise Marks Act, copying English models, and purposely striking at English trades by exporting prison-made goods.

The Parliamentary Debates for 1893 and succeeding years abounded with manifestations of this sensitiveness. Frequent questions were asked concerning the purchase of German paper and pencils for Government offices, German iron exports to the United Kingdom, Admiralty purchases of lifeboats from Ger-

---

Chamber of Commerce: "Time was, I believe, when the Foreign Office regarded the Associated Chamber of Commerce with some tinge of suspicion, and when the feelings of the Associated Chambers of Commerce, on their part, towards the Foreign Office were not those of altogether unclouded affection or esteem. But happily those days are past. . . . I hope that both the Foreign Office and the Chambers of Commerce will continue to regard themselves as joint partners in the great firm of the British Empire Company."—*Times,* March 17, 1898.—A good summary of the increased interest and attention given to trade questions by the Foreign Office may be seen in an article, "Government and Foreign Trade," *Chamber of Commerce Journal,* July 16, 1896.

many, and the sale of German knives, whips, cards, and bottles represented as of British manufacture.[22] The charge was frequently made that the Merchandise Marks Act was inadequately enforced against German goods, and this was the reason why Colonel C. E. Howard Vincent strove to secure legislation requiring all imported goods to bear a mark of origin. Such a bill came to second reading on May 2, 1894. In support of it Vincent declared "that in Scotland German cutlery was being sold at English prices and under English names." Another Member told the House how a large Birmingham firm had declined an order for goods on which a certain mark was to be placed, whereupon the order was given to a German agent in the same street. "It was executed abroad, the goods were imported without a mark, in Birmingham they were marked with a mark to which they were not entitled, and they were then sent to Singapore as English-made goods."[23] Although the Vincent bill and other efforts to get similar legislation uniformly failed, attention did not cease being directed to alleged evasions of the Merchandise Marks Act by German goods. The real culprit in these cases was, of course, the importer in Great Britain (perhaps a German, to be sure) rather than the German manufacturer, but they added weight to the multiplying evidence of German competition, and strengthened the popular notion that the Germans were infected with commercial dishonesty.

The principal voice in Parliament for expression of these grievances was that of Colonel Vincent, who sat for Sheffield, an industrial center which had long nursed a grudge against German cutlery. Vincent was a founder of the United Empire Trade League which sprang up in the nineties to agitate for tariff reform, and he held the leadership of a small group in Parliament which steadily attacked unrestricted freedom of

[22] For instances, *vide:* Hansard, 4th S., vol. 8, pp. 239, 1026-27, 1698; vol. 9, pp. 977-78; vol. 10, pp. 18-20, 25-26, 62 ff.; vol. 13, pp. 764-65; vol. 14, pp. 1270; vol. 15, pp. 1338-39; vol. 24, pp. 41-42, 1272-73; vol. 26, p. 243; vol. 28, pp. 1222-24; vol. 29, pp. 346-47, 389-91, 421. These are all in 1893 and 1894.

[23] *Ibid.,* vol. 24, pp. 186-97.

imports. To cocksure Cobdenites, Vincent and his allies were rather ludicrous men, excited over German birthday anniversary cards and slate pencils, and warning the nation of industrial ruin because Bavarian lead pencils were to be found on the table of the House of Commons. But they were probably closer to a true realization of the country's position in world industry than were those who scoffed at their economic heresies.

Most illustrative of this uneasiness in the producing community was the cry which went up in 1894 against German prison-made goods. Early in February one R. A. Toleith, of the *Manchester Examiner and Times*, informed the Foreign Office that German prisoners were making cotton goods and that the bales were "fraudulently stamped with the names of Manchester firms."[24] Lord Rosebery at once instructed Sir Edward Malet at Berlin to inquire into this. Meanwhile, early in March, a Birmingham trade journal (*The Hardwareman*) published the report of an agent whom it had sent to Germany and who charged that German convicts were engaged in making, from English models, various articles (some twenty kinds were enumerated) "for the English market." These revelations quickly inspired questions in Parliament which continued through the 1894 session.[25] The brush makers seem to have been most affected by the unwelcome importations. In fact, a Dublin Member told the House early in 1895 "that the brush makers in Great Britain and Ireland complain that their trade is injured and almost paralyzed by the enormous importation of brushes made by convicts in German gaols," and referred to a "petition presented by the employees of the North Dublin Brush Company, containing 150 signatures, praying for the prohibition of the importation of manufactured goods produced wholly or in part by convict labour."[26]

[24] Reports from Her Majesty's Representatives on Prison Labour. C.-7550, 1894, Doc. No. 1.

[25] *Vide:* Hansard, vol. 22, pp. 42, 1103-4, 1158-59; vol. 23, pp. 1079, 1096, 1586-87; vol. 24, pp. 375-76, 766-67; vol. 26, p. 9, vol. 27, pp. 545-46, 1240; vol. 28, pp. 1211-12.

[26] *Ibid.*, vol. 30, pp. 287-90.

When the questions were first raised, the Board of Trade possessed no information at all about imported prison goods, and was disposed to view the complaints lightly. No prohibitory legislation existed, and the Government was reluctant to frame any. A bill introduced on May 9 by Colonel Vincent and bearing the names of eleven other Members failed to get a second reading. But an inquiry was undertaken through the Foreign Office, and the results of this were embodied in a Parliamentary paper laid before the House in the closing days of the 1894 session.[27] The most enlightening part of this was a report drafted by the Berlin Embassy giving details of the "contract" labor system in German prisons, but offering no clue whatever to the destination of the goods produced.[28] That the affair stirred up some official resentment in Germany was evident from a published communication of Baron von Marschall to Sir Edward Malet, in which he insinuated that "certain articles in Manchester and Birmingham papers . . . make such unfair attacks upon German industry that the conviction is forced upon one that the whole agitation has very different objects than to ascertain the truth."[29]

In the fall of 1894 the Trades Union Congress adopted a resolution against imported prison goods, and when Parliament reconvened in 1895 the question was brought forward again. It occasioned a short but lively debate in the House of Commons on February 19.[30] Colonel Vincent presented a motion that "it is incumbent upon Her Majesty's Government . . . at once to take steps to restrict the importation of goods made in foreign prisons." He recited the complaints at some length, drawing upon the material in the Parliamentary paper of the previous session. The full charge now (although by no means

---

[27] Reports, etc., C.-7550, referred to above.

[28] There was not a shred of evidence in the reports from Germany that *prison authorities* were guilty of sending goods, falsely marked or otherwise, to England. The articles were disposed of by concessionaire contractors, and where they were sent could not be ascertained.

[29] Document No. 18.

[30] Hansard, vol. 30, pp. 1135-79.

warranted in the reports from Germany) was that more than 44,000 German convicts and felons were competing with British production in sixteen staple trades. Joseph Chamberlain made a strong speech in support of Vincent's motion. "The Germans," he said, "have actually sent over to this country for models of English manufactures, and they are making them in their prisons. At the present time they are making about 20 different articles in various branches of industry; so that after they have contrived to ruin the brush trade they will go into many other trades." Keir Hardie, John Morley, and A. J. Balfour also joined the debate, which served to air the grievance against German prison goods as it had not been aired before. Mr. Bryce, President of the Board of Trade, said he could not find in the reports from Germany "any evidence whatever that any British industry suffered from prison labour," and argued that no measure of prohibition could be effectively carried out. The House, however, adopted the motion without a division.[31]

As a result, the Board of Trade instituted a Departmental Committee of investigation which completed a lengthy report in early September.[32] This document was a disappointment to those who had led the agitation for a prohibitory law, since it recommended that nothing be done. The Committee concluded that British trade was not being injured *generally* by foreign prison goods, and as for the brush makers (the chief complainants) the report declared:

. . . though it is true that a certain number of foreign prison-made brushes are imported into England, there is no proof that this importation affects our brush trade, as a whole, detrimentally. . . .The evidence as to the large importation of foreign prison-made brushes principally rested on the inference drawn by witnesses that they must be prison-made because of their cheapness.[33]

[31] There was considerable press applause for this, especially in leaders in the *Times* and *Morning Post,* Feb. 20, and the *Daily Telegraph,* Feb. 21.

[32] Report of the Departmental Committee on the Importation into the United Kingdom of Foreign Prison-Made Goods. C.-7902, 1895.

[33] Report, p. 10.

The report indicates rather convincingly that the cry against German prison goods arose from the general uneasiness and apprehension of German commerce rather than from any actual damage done to British trades. Although it was a rebuff to Colonel Vincent and other Members demanding legislation, it did not quiet them; and their pressure for action continued until the Salisbury Government sought an international understanding for the suppression of the traffic,[34] and, failing that, accepted a prohibitory measure in 1897.

All the manifold symptoms of apprehension among British producers, obviously, cannot be set down here, but some illustrations of the fear of German competition in the iron trade may be allowed. These were to be discerned not only in special trade publications, but in the general newspaper press. An excellent example may be seen in a long and prominently placed article, "Decay of the Iron Industry," appearing in the *Times* of September 18, 1894. The writer declared that "very serious apprehensions have been aroused by the circumstances of the iron industry of the United Kingdom, more especially in view of the progress made by competitive countries." In commercial circles it was now quite a common thing to hear the iron trade spoken of as a manufacture that had ceased to make progress and was doomed to gradual decay. Belgian and German competition, especially the latter, were largely the cause for this. "It will probably be among the things not generally known," the article stated, "that more German iron is imported into Great Britain than into any other country except Switzerland, and in the latter case the iron was probably largely in transit for Italy and other countries, while in our own country it had come to stay." The German practice of selling abroad at cheaper prices than in the protected home market, it was said,

has been a sore point for a number of years past—the more so that the case becomes worse instead of better. . . . The whole ques-

[34] *Vide:* Correspondence between the Board of Trade and the Foreign Office and Between the Foreign Office and Certain of Her Majesty's Representatives Abroad on the Subject of Foreign Prison-Made Goods, 1897. C.-8339.

tion has, in short, entered upon the phase and assumed the dimensions of a pretty little quarrel, and has tended to strain somewhat the usual seemingly cordial relations of the metallurgists of the two countries.[35]

Attention was drawn to the special advantages conferred upon German exporters of iron by the State Railways and to the easy access to the English market provided by the newly opened Manchester Ship Canal. "Apart, however, from these special conditions affecting the German competition," the writer went on to say, "there can be no doubt that the iron trade of that country has of late years greatly improved its competitive position in reference to the iron and steel industries generally, and that it now menaces the prosperity of the English iron trade to a larger extent than has ever happened in the past."[36]

This was the reason why a deputation of employers and workmen went to the Continent in 1895 to visit German and Belgian iron and steel industries. They sought an explanation for the successful progress of these competitive plants, and what they learned must have been to many little short of startling. Their report, published in January, 1896, showed that English manufacturers stood at considerable disadvantage in respect of railway and shipping charges, royalty rents, and wages; and it pointed to more enterprise and business tact on the part of Continental industries. In Germany it was shown how much greater was the care taken to give the rank and file of men sound technical education, while young men of special promise were even sent to technical colleges for several years of study at the expense of their employers. The consequence was that the German manufacturers had the great advantage of employing a body of men who thoroughly understood the tech-

[35] A leading article of the same issue asserted that this practice "has done, and is doing, mischief to the interests of the British manufacturer, and has contributed to bring a great branch of our industry into a condition which may be called precarious, if not perilous."

[36] For a more optimistic and possibly sounder view, *vide* the article, "Competition in the Iron Trade," in *Iron and Steel Trades Journal* for Sept. 28, 1895.

nique of their work. The report also suggested that the German firms exhibited greater enterprise in organizing syndicates for extending foreign business, while the syndicates formed to regulate prices and production were believed to be helpful to manufacturers in competing against the British. The report appears to have been a very frank statement of the serious outlook for this section of British industry, and if the full eclipse of that industry was not envisaged, the passing of its historic leadership was surely revealed as never before.[37] The following was the *Hardware Trade Journal's* comment on the report:

It has for some years past been evident, even to the most casual observer, that Germany especially, and one or two others of the Continental nations to less marked a degree, have been competing against this country with conspicuous success in all the leading markets of the world in respect to the supply of iron and steel. But only those who have gone more deeply into the question are aware of the serious nature of this competition. . . . It is something more than humiliating to confess . . . that our former and oft-repeated boast that the iron industry is one which is pre-eminently British in character has no longer any existence in fact, and that our much-vaunted resources in the natural proximity and abundant supplies of ores and fuel, to say nothing of the excellent quality of skilled labour, are no longer of any avail.[38]

The time of the report's appearance is significant. The Colonial and Foreign Offices, under Chamberlain, Salisbury and Curzon, were manifestly stirred by Germany's commercial advance at precisely this time. And German *Weltpolitik*—politico-commercial in its meaning—had just collided violently with British imperialism. The world was reverberating with the shock of the Transvaal crisis, which signalized so dramatically the

[37] The Iron and Steel Industries of Belgium and Germany: Report of the Delegation Organized by the British Iron Trade Association. London, 1896. Good analyses of the report in *Daily Telegraph* and *Times,* Jan. 20. See also *Saturday Review* article, "German Competition," Jan. 25, 1896, vol. 81, pp. 91-92. A careful review of the report is that by D. F. Schloss in the *Economic Journal,* 1896, vol. 6, pp. 265-68. The press notices of this report were many and wide.

[38] Issue of Jan. 31, 1896.

end of Anglo-German cordiality. Almost simultaneously with the news of the Kruger telegram the British nation was learning that one of its great staple industries, on which the economic strength of England had largely been reared, was imperiled by German rivalry. How greatly this fact contributed to exciting the "made in Germany" alarm of 1896 it would not be easy to exaggerate.

It may also be noted here that the visit of the British iron-trade deputation had itself stirred up an unfortunate little quarrel in 1895. The *Times* of August 15 published a special article describing the visit, and pointing out that, "contrary to what was generally expected, the employers on the Continent threw little or no difficulty in the way of the delegation's seeing over their works." The reception at German plants was praised as exceptionally cordial, every question propounded having been freely and fully answered and references even allowed to the books of firms. This article raised a storm in the German press which rang with charges of British trickery. It was asserted that at all German establishments the English deputation had said their chief object was to get material for their struggle against trade unions, inspection of works being only secondary. The *Kölnische Zeitung* caustically branded the English visitors as "not gentlemanlike," and declared: "In the future . . . we shall be more cautious and distrustful in our relations with the English." The *Berlin Neueste Nachrichten* expressed the view that, however strong national selfishness might be in England, there were still people who must be offended by the behavior of their countrymen, who had allowed their zeal for outstripping competitors to extinguish considerations of probity. The *Börsen Courier* reproduced the whole *Times* article and confessed its loss for words to express suitably its opinion of the British delegation's conduct.[39] These charges, which seem quite without real foundation, were indignantly denied by authoritative voices in the Iron Trade Association, and steps were taken to vindicate

[39] Summary of German press comment in *Times* despatch from Berlin, Aug. 17, 1895.

the honor of the delegates.[40] Acrimonious exchanges soon evapor-
ated from the press, but not without having added a measure
of bitterness to the spirit of competition.

One more striking illustration of the rising complaint against
German trade in England was the cry of the cheaper tailoring
interests heard in 1895. This found choice expression in an
article in the June number of the *New Review,* wherein it was
declared that cheap ready-made clothes from Germany were
depressing thousands of London workers to ruin.[41] The annual
national outlay of a million and a half pounds for these goods
was described as an "odious" fact, and there were bitter words
for the German enterprise of buying up Britain's worn-out
woolens to return them regenerated into shoddy garments. This
article illustrates so well that mixture of admiration, scorn,
envy, bitterness, fear, and indignation toward the Germans that
it may justifiably be quoted at some length:

. . . Perhaps the birth of the trade may be traced back to those
golden years that followed on the Franco-Prussian War; when,
enriched by French milliards, the country started a mercantile
marine, drew up a code of equality of tariffs for the several states,
and sent out her young men to acquire not only the language of
her neighbours but also an insight into their commercial secrets.
Where the English clerk would have starved, the frugal German
could save money, and appear respectably dressed, obsequiously
polite, and invariably punctual. His employer recognized these
virtues as of great price; "but, all the while," to quote a recognized authority, the British Consul-General at Hamburg, "Hans
Meyer had a note-book in one pocket and a pair of folding scissors
in the other. He entered in the one the addresses of all his principal's customers, with the prices at which the goods were shipped
to Rio, to Morocco, to Tokio, or anywhere else, and with the
scissors he secured one square inch of each as a sample. When
he got home, he raised a few thousand marks in his family, married

[40] *Vide* letter of Benj. Hingley, of Board of Management of Iron Trade
Association, to *Times,* Aug. 20; also statement of J. S. Jeans, head of delegation, in *Times,* Aug. 23; also resolution adopted by delegation and published in *Times,* Sept. 12.
[41] Mary F. Billington: "Tailor-Made in Germany," vol. 12, 1895, pp. 631-40.

a girl with a few thousand more, and set up to compete with his former principals. . . . It was not only cotton that he learnt to imitate. He marked the types of serge and cloth in demand and wear in this country, and he began to compete in these also, sparing not tact, nor zeal, nor attention to minor details. A characteristic illustration is furnished from Hamburg, which for some years has been rising into eminence as a rival to Dundee in the raw jute trade. Even as with the finer fabrics, the manufacturers resolved to carry the industry beyond the elementary stage, and to turn out sacks and the like, like finished workmen. By the offer of a shilling a week more than could be earned in the trade at the mouth of the Tay, some fifty Scots girls were induced to export themselves to the mouth of the Elbe. They stayed for over a year; and in the course of that sojourn many of them 'fell' and had children. Meanwhile, the German hands were mastering their methods, and when there was no more to be learned of them, they were turned out: the most, in their utter destitution, to beg a passage home; and all to find on their arrival that the demand for made-up jute was falling off, and wages going down. In the same way, the German exporter comes very early to the manufacturing centers here, and buys a piece of all the promising novelties in woolens. With these he hastens to the Fatherland. Specimen jackets are made up from the materials thus secured, and these he submits to his customers. They are pleased with the value, and they give their orders. Then he sends the stuff to be copied at Aachen; and this is done quite cheaply, and quite closely enough for the retail market. Thus it is not only the London sempstress who suffers, but the weaver as well, to say nothing of vast subsidiary interests in the matters of braids, trimmings, linings, sewing silks, and buttons."

3

Enough has been said above to show the preparation of the public mind for the 1896 alarm, which may now be examined in some detail. January, the month of the Transvaal crisis, saw the appearance in the pages of the *New Review* of the first installment of Ernest E. Williams' *Made in Germany*, which continued in successive monthly articles until June, after which it was issued in cheap popular book form.[42] The timely publication of this work insured it increasing attention, month by month, until by midsummer it had grown into an important national event. Simultaneously, other public organs caught the fever and opened their columns to articles bearing upon the German economic menace. Resentment at Germany's attitude in the Transvaal crisis found expression in a number of attacks on German goods throughout the Midlands, the newspapers publishing many letters (which seem to have been not entirely unheeded) urging a boycott of German goods.[43] Renewed complaints against the infiltration of Germans into the United Kingdom, at a time of slack employment, made their appearance.[44] A writer in the *National Review* for February analyzed their manifold occupations and declared it to be "the plain truth that the English people have good cause to complain of the endless and increasing invasion of Germans."[45] Violent attacks upon the German commercial penetration of South Africa appeared the same month in the *Contemporary* and *Fortnightly Reviews*. "We are reminded," asserted the *Fortnightly* contributor, "of the old story of the Hanse Cities and the merchants of the Steelyard over again. In the old days of the Tudors, enterprising Germans of the Free Towns came over to London, and availing themselves of our insular supineness, began . . . to filch away British trade from under the very noses of British merchants in London. . . . History repeats itself, and there is an historical lesson in the proceedings of these merchants of the Steelyard which it would be wise to lay to heart now."[46]

---

[42] *New Review,* vol. 14, pp. 14-28, 113-27, 253-68, 376-91, 492-506, 636-50. These articles, plus some additional matter, were published in single volume in July.

[43] *Hardware Trade Journal* (Sheffield Despatch), Jan. 31, 1896.

[44] *Vide* two-column article on Germans in England, *Times,* Jan. 14, 1896.

[45] Arthur Shadwell: "The German Colony in London," vol. 26, pp. 798-810.

[46] W. H. P. Greswell: "The Germans in South Africa," vol. 65, p. 209 *et seq.; vide* also W. R. Lawson: "German Intrigues in the Transvaal," *Contemporary Review,* vol. 69, pp. 229 ff.

Another contributor in the same issue of the *Fortnightly* pointed out that the Germans

have led a very hard fight with our people, whom, thanks to our own supineness and the lack of an imperial Zollverein, they are gradually ousting out of the principal markets of the world, in the same way in which their clerks, tradesmen, and waiters are driving Englishmen across the seas where they will find German competition again.[47]

The *Hardware Trade Journal* in February published a leading article on the German trade peril in the industries represented by that organ. "Hardware is a sufficiently elastic term, and comprises a variety of branches, from tinned tacks to battleships," it was stated, "but from one end of the scale to another we find that we are confronted by a competition that is none the less serious even where it may be least apparent. If we start with the largest class, there is no more comfort to be obtained than if we reverse the process. In either case there is evidence of the same pushing, indomitable growth of rivalry."[48] In the March number of the *Westminster Review*, a contributor, alarmed for the home market, proposed the formation of "A Society for the Maintenance of the Supremacy of British Trade," which would promote the patronage of home industries; for "the encroachment of German competition upon the trade of these Islands," he asserted, "has increased of late years to such an extent that it is important seriously to consider any practical means whereby its progress may be stemmed."[49]

But the most famous and sensational piece of alarmist literature was Ernest Williams' book, a trumpet blast to awaken his countrymen, because, as he said, "the industrial glory of England is departing and England does not know it." The little book was vigorously written, offered a powerful argument buttressed by statistics and excerpts from consular reports and trade journals; and it became overnight, so to speak, the chief text for those who perceived the country's supine drifting in

[47] "Genosse Aegir": "A Lesson in German," vol. 65.
[48] "Made in Germany," Feb. 29, 1896.
[49] George Newcomen: "Made in Germany and How to Avoid It," vol. 145, pp. 276-79.

the modern industrial and commercial world. "For Germany," Williams admonished, "has entered into a deliberate and deadly rivalry with her, and is battling with might and main for the extinction of her supremacy. . . . An industrial development, unparalleled, save in England a century ago, is now her portion. A gigantic commercial state is arising to menace our prosperity, and contend with us for the trade of the world."[50] The English market and the world market were surveyed, and almost everywhere German business was found to be menacing that of Britain. Iron and Steel manufactures, ships, hardware, machines, textiles, chemicals, toys, glass, cement, leather goods, paper and pasteboard, musical instruments, and printing, in all these trades Williams discovered the Germans accomplishing a progress deadly in its effects on British trade. It was "but too clear . . . that on all hands England's industrial supremacy is tottering to its fall and that this result is largely German work."[51] The temper of the book showed very little malice towards Germany, although the familiar accusations of unscrupulous imitation and trade-mark piracy were put forward. As a socialist, Williams had much praise for German efficiency, education, and intelligent organization of national economic life; and he advised England to abandon laissez-faire, as the Germans had done, in order to maintain her position in world business.

Mr. Williams' alarmist views shook England as no similar piece of writing had yet done. The press of the summer of 1896 was full of *Made in Germany*. The book was widely reviewed and occasioned numberless editorial leaders, special articles, and letters from readers. The Cobdenite press tended, of course, to deride the book as just another Protectionist pamphlet, and, although not seriously challenging the author's body of facts, to ridicule his mercantilist proposals. For example, the strongly Free Trade *Spectator* gave disdainfully brief notice to the work, but acknowledged that "beyond all question, Mr. Williams' book calls for serious attention."[52] It was, indeed, impossible to make

[50] Williams, *op. cit.*, pp. 1, 8, 10.

[51] *Ibid.*, p. 44.

[52] Vol. 77, p. 710. The *Iron and Steel Trades Journal* sharply denied his alarmist views (Aug. 8, 1896).

a successful assault upon the factual substance of the book. What he had to say, of course, had (as must be evident) been said before, but never with such force and to so wide an audience. "There is a great deal of luck about writing books, as about everything else," commented the *Saturday Review*, " . . . everything Mr. Williams tells us we have been told before. Mr. Williams has but collected skillfully and industriously information that has been published piecemeal for many years past. . . . Mr. Williams, however, has had the cleverness to hit upon a telling title, and—this is where the luck comes in—he published at a moment when the Emperor of Germany had succeeded in exciting all the latent prejudice of England against a trade rival."[53]

Lord Rosebery, perhaps somewhat inadvertently, made himself what the liberal *Westminster Gazette* called "the vehicle of a flaming advertisement" of the book in a speech at Epsom on July 24. He used it as a text for exhorting England to raise her technical education to the German level, and in doing so he sounded gravely a warning against the growth of German trade.[54] The Epsom speech provided a topic for a great many leading articles in the press, and seems to have pitched the German trade menace into the forefront among questions of the hour.[55] "Lord Rosebery and the author of 'Made in Germany' are both to be congratulated on the speech made by the former . . . at Epsom," remarked the *National Observer*, pointing out that although Mr. Williams was an alarmist he had told the important truth. "The facts as they stand are undoubtedly disquieting," commented the conservative *Standard;* and the liberal *Daily Chronicle* declared it "high time some leader of opinion called public attention conspicuously to the extraor-

---

[53] "The Fetish of Free Trade," July 25, vol. 82, pp. 85-6.

[54] Reports of speech in *Standard* and *Times,* July 25.

[55] *Vide* especially leaders in *Standard, Daily Chronicle, Daily News, Westminster Gazette,* of July 25, and *Manchester Guardian* July 27; also, "Made in Germany," *The Speaker,* Aug. 1, vol. 14, pp. 109-10; article of same title in *National Observer,* Aug. 1, vol. 16, p. 321; and "Lord Rosebery's Economic Despair," *Spectator,* Aug. 1, vol. 77, pp. 137-8.

dinary inroads made by Germany during recent years upon our trade—a subject which British consuls, all over the world, have emphasized in vain throughout hundreds of reports." There followed then a rush of articles and letters in a large section of the press. It was Williams' book and Lord Rosebery's Epsom speech that gave the signal for the hysteria of that summer. And right in the midst of it—greatly contributing to it, indeed— came the opening in London of an exhibition of the foreign competitive goods which Mr. Chamberlain had begun to collect from the Colonies. The display was greeted in the press by an excited outburst of astonishment and chagrin which greatly increased the clamor over the German peril.[56]

The contribution of the newspapers to the alarm must have been very great. The whole metropolitan press of London gave space to the subject, especially the *Daily Chronicle* and the young and aggressively imperialist *Daily Mail*. A series of special articles entitled "The Truth about German Competition" appeared in the *Chronicle* in August. They were quite judiciously written, but reached the conclusion that German competition was very serious in iron, steel, and textiles—that it was, indeed, "fraught with considerable danger to two of our staple industries." British trade, it was held, when all allowance was made for the different positions of the two competitors, was in a less healthy condition than that of Germany. The weight of these articles in the public mind must have been especially great in the light of the fact that the *Chronicle* was one of the two largest liberal papers in London and that the other, the *Daily News*, reflected the general tendency of the liberal press to deride the German danger as a nightmare of tariff reformers.[57] Thus the *Saturday Review* observed:

The official organ of English Liberalism [*Daily News*] having demonstrated to its own complete satisfaction that the increased

[56] Leaders in *Daily Telegraph* and *Daily News, Evening Globe, Standard*, Aug. 25; *Times, Morning Post,* and *Daily Mail*, August 26; *Pall Mall Gazette,* Aug. 31, 1896.

[57] August 24, 25, 26. The *Chronicle* itself editorially took a more optimistic view than was expressed in the special articles. *Vide* leader of Aug. 24.

importation of German goods into England and the Colonies is an incalculable blessing, it is refreshing to turn to the columns of the junior organ, there to find German competition dealt with after a fashion of less acute imbecility. We rejoice that the *Daily Chronicle* is helping to quicken the minds of Englishmen concerning this great peril.[58]

But no public organ did so much to aggravate the panic as the youthful and truculent *Daily Mail*, less than a year old but forging rapidly to the front and destined within two years to be the largest morning daily in the United Kingdom. It had made its début during the Transvaal crisis, and was anti-German from birth.[59] But although vigorously imperialist and proclaiming its first aim to be the "maintenance of British prestige in all parts of the world," and although keenly interested in the conditions of trade, it launched no agitation against the German commercial peril until August. Then, however, a series of one-column daily articles by Gilbert Burgess, entitled "Germany as She Is," were published very prominently from August 17 to September 5, contemporaneously with those in the *Chronicle*. A leader of August 17 explained that the articles were occasioned by Williams' book and Lord Rosebery's exhortation, and expressed the hope that public interest might be concentrated upon this matter, "not with any desire to merely fan the popular prejudice against things 'made in Germany,' but in hope that a timely awakening and some prompt measures of precaution may avert a more serious decline in our commercial supremacy." The initial article was entitled "A First View of Our Commercial Enemy," and declared "we are slowly awakening to the fact that a far greater peril than a conflict . . . of arms with Germany awaits us." The fourth was called "Scourges for the British Back," and number six, which treated of the growth of Essen, Crefeld, and Chemnitz, was headed "Towns That Injure England." The final article, "A last Look Around," gave warning that the Germans were no longer mak-

---

[58] "The German Menace," August 29, vol. 82, pp. 208-9.

[59] Its view of Germany was well revealed in a leader of Jan. 20, referring to "Turkey, Germany and other semi-civilised countries."

ing headway by cheap imitation and stealing trade marks, but by skillful adaptability and sound manufacturing progress. These articles, vividly written and disseminated throughout the enormous mass of *Daily Mail* readers, must be ranked with Williams' book as an incitement to public apprehension.

Among the influential weekly journals the *Saturday Review* was conspicuously alive to the German trade peril. The renewed attack on the British sugar trade occasioned by the increased German sugar bounties here received important notice. The new German bounties were bitterly complained against, August 15, in an article by Mr. Williams, appealing for countervailing duties. This matter was, of course, one of the outstanding items in the bill of grievances against Germany at the moment. "Germany," wrote Williams in this connection, "is likely to serve us in commerce as a quarter of a century ago she served France before Sedan. . . . Defeat has already begun to overtake us, and while the supremacy of our big industries is visibly tottering, others less big, but yet important, have capitulated. The worst instance is sugar."[60] Soon after this, the *Saturday Review* congratulated the *Daily Chronicle* upon its valuable revelations, and appealed anew for an imperial commercial union: "The German menace will then loom less balefully on our industrial horizon."[61] An article of September 5 described the rising peril of competitive German coal, which was "making headway to our detriment."[62] Two weeks later there appeared a contemptuous but admonitory fling at German silks,[63] and in the issue of September 26 Mr. Williams appeared again to analyze the suffering glass industry and find its ailments due largely to German competition.[64]

Relatively little of the 1896 alarm was manifested in Parliament. Colonel Vincent's familiar questions, of course, were not

[60] "Beetroot and Bounties," vol. 82, pp. 156-57. The correspondence department of the *Saturday Review* fairly bristled at this time with complaints against the German bounties.

[61] Article cited above.

[62] "British and Foreign Coal," vol. 82, pp. 249-50.

[63] "The Decline of the Silk Trade," *ibid.*, p. 306.

[64] "Our Flourishing Glass Industry," *ibid.*, pp. 335-36.

lacking; several times during the session he complained against German cocoa butter and scolded the Stationery Office for buying Bavarian pencils. The Foreign Office was urged to enlarge its assistance to trade abroad, and a demand was raised for an inquiry into the working of the Merchandise Marks Act, "as affecting British trade and shipping and the advertisement it gives to foreign goods, resulting to some extent in the shipping trade of Hamburg already taking precedence over Liverpool." The German sugar bounties several times were the subject of anxious questions in Parliament, as was the unexpected appearance of Westphalian coal in the London market. On August 7, when the German scare was at its height, Colonel Vincent asked for a national inquiry into Great Britain's trade position. Had Parliament not adjourned in August a great deal more about the threatening character of German trade doubtless would have been heard at Westminster.[65]

Meanwhile, attempts to banish the alarm were both numerous and vociferous. The stale dogma of Free Traders that England's prosperity was to be measured by the growth of imports and not by the decline of exports was given endless restatement in the liberal press. The stagnant condition of the export trade was questioned, and some organs argued that increased imports from Germany, far from being harmful, were beneficial to Great Britain. Thus a leading liberal oracle, the *Manchester Guardian*, held that the sale of cheap foreign manufactures in England economized the resources of every British household and left so much the more money to be spent on articles of British production. "The Germans," it was stated, "are in this way our benefactors, and last year they supplied to us sugar to the extent of nearly £9,400,000 at less than its cost, not to speak of other articles outside the class of food products. . . . It is a fatal delusion to imagine that the industrial and commercial progress of one nation means the destruction of the trade and manufactures of another. And certainly there is

[65] Hansard: vol. 37, p. 850; vol. 39, pp. 45, 1239; vol. 41, pp. 65, 215, 1553; vol. 42, pp. 53-54, 521; vol. 43, pp. 676-77, 1701-2; vol. 44, pp. 112-13.

nothing in the statistics quoted by Lord Rosebery which can justify the conclusion that the industrial preëminence of this country is departing. Other nations are advancing and so are we, but their gain does not necessarily mean our loss."[66] The *Daily News* likewise argued that if exports declined while imports increased, it only indicated that Great Britain was driving a better bargain with the rest of the world. "No free trader," it was maintained, "can seriously contend that the importation of German goods into this country is a misfortune."[67] The *News* also published a series of articles (contemporaneous with the excited Burgess articles in the *Daily Mail*) entitled: "Our German Rivals. Are They Cutting Us Out?"[68] These reached the conclusion that there was no foundation in fact for the current alarm. A similar point of view was reflected by the *Spectator*, which ridiculed Lord Rosebery for "succumbing before the *pons asinorum* of economics," and argued that the more Germany sold in England and elsewhere the better it was for England.[69]

It is very much worth observing that a strain of contempt and disparagement was often to be discerned in the expression of anti-alarmist views. There seems to have been a temptation to dismiss the German trade menace by saying that German sharp practices could have no permanent success, that German goods were trashy and worthless, and that German business was unsound. Thus the *Daily News*, while minimizing the German peril, paid it the tribute of a denunciatory fling at "trash or shoddy," with the admonition that "the triumph of sharp practice is apt to be ephemeral."[70] The *Pall Mall Gazette* characterized the Chamberlain exhibit of competitive German goods from the British colonies as

a collection which the Englishman sees with mingled feelings of pride and disgust . . . it is nothing less than disgusting to know that

[66] Leader of July 27.
[67] Leader of July 25.
[68] *Vide* issues of Aug. 18, 25, 27, Sept. 7.
[69] Aug. 1, vol. 77, pp. 137-38.
[70] Aug. 26.

the inhabitants of the West Indies, Christians, highminded niggers, cultured and intellectual half-breeds, ladies and gentlemen enjoying the inestimable advantages of living under an ennobling and elevated British rule, should not merely be so utterly lost to any sense of patriotism, to any conception of gratitude, but should be so entirely devoid of taste and even the common housekeeping qualities of marketing as to buy such terrible rubbish. One can feel very sorry for the unfortunate Germans who are driven by stern commercial necessity to degrade themselves and their inferior machinery by making such goods.[71]

To a large section of British opinion the people who resorted to tariffs, bounties, kartels, subsidies, reduced freight for exports, etc., had bad commercial manners and morals and worked on unsound principles. The liberal *Spectator* spoke of a "seamy side" to German trade activity.

Much of it is far from genuine, being galvanized into unhealthy vigour by the artificial stimulus of bounties, cheap freights for exports, and other such measures by which the German tax-payer is bled so that the trader may supply other nations with cheap goods. Moreover, much of this trade is carried on at an infinitesimal profit, or even at a loss, in the hope of driving competitors out of the market. Hence it is that the Germans, in spite of the expanding figures of their commerce, remain a poor people, and hence their politics are a series of unseemly squabbles for state assistance to various industries.[72]

The anti-alarmists, at the height of the scare, received ammunition from a Board of Trade Blue Book, issued August 25.[73] This continued, without interpretation, the series of official statistical tables which had been laid ten years earlier before the Royal Commission on the Depression of Trade. These tables certainly did not reveal Great Britain in so desperate a state as the Cassandras of 1896 pictured her, and the *Daily News* interpreted them to show that there was no German danger at all. "The German bogey disappears with the light," it declared

[71] Aug. 31, 1896.
[72] Aug. 1, vol. 77, pp. 137-38.
[73] Comparative Trade Statistics, C.-8211.

exultantly, ". . . this Blue Book destroys all reason for panic or even for apprehension."[74] The *Westminster Gazette* likewise exploited the tables to argue against any cause for alarm, although confessing regretfully: "We do not suppose that any statistics issued by the Board of Trade will avail to kill the panic about things 'made in Germany.' " The *Gazette* then went on to warn against the development of

that least amiable trait of the commercial character—a continuous jealousy and suspiciousness of other people's prosperity. . . . The perpetual whine that somebody else is getting on faster than we are (which is generally not true) is neither dignified nor courageous, and not at all in keeping with that proud and silent going ahead which used to be thought a British characteristic.[75]

The *Chronicle* naturally noticed the Blue Book in a leader, but read it rather differently from the other liberal organs. The book, it was felt, lent "some countenance to the cry of foreign competition," and the figures, if not "sensational," for that very reason perhaps betokened "a more real and lasting danger."[76]

The "made in Germany" scare as a prominent public phenomenon in 1896 was a kind of midsummer madness, and after the August-September crescendo it quieted down greatly. The press gave no great notice to it during the fall,[77] and Joseph Chamberlain in November drew laughter from the Birmingham Chamber of Commerce when he referred to it in an address. "On the whole," he assured his audience, ". . . there is substantially no change of the slightest importance in the relative proportion of German and British trade."[78] A fortnight

[74] Aug. 26.
[75] Aug. 26.
[76] Aug. 26.
[77] For some significant articles in the periodical press for the fall see: *New Review*—E. E. Williams, "The Case for Sugar" (Oct.) and "My Critics" (Nov.), vol. 15, pp. 410-21, 596-610; *Nineteenth Century*—B. H. Thwaite, "The Commercial War Between England and Germany" (Dec.), vol. 40, p. 925 *et seq.; Westminster Review*—J. J. Rose-Soley, "English and German Interests in Samoa" (Sept.), vol. 46, pp. 277-95; *Saturday Review* —"The Voice of The Sluggard" (Nov. 28), vol. 82, pp. 558-59.
[78] *Times*, Nov. 14.

later the President of the Board of Trade, C. T. Ritchie, spoke
at Croydon on the gratifying state of trade and scouted all
alarm over German competition.[79] Such pronouncements were
greeted with applause in the *Daily News* and other organs
which had been making light of the German peril, and with silence
by those which had fomented apprehension. By this time a
vigorous business revival plainly was in progress and the Country's optimism was returning; under such conditions the German menace seemed to vanish. The *Saturday Review* observed
somewhat bitterly at the end of November:

English statesmen and economists were aroused a few months ago
to a consideration of the German menace. They were startled a bit
at first, opened one eye, and turned over. Now they are somnolently
muttering that they have been called too soon. . . . Mr. Chamberlain,
Mr. Goschen, and Mr. Balfour are now voicing in chorus the sluggard's complaint. "You have called us too soon," says Mr. Balfour;
"Sheffield can still make very fine armour-plates." "Let us sleep
again," the press echoes obsequiously; "we will forget the German
scare."[80]

Meanwhile the Board of Trade had been pursuing an inquiry.
This was completed and published in January, 1897, when
business was again active and fears of competition were sink-
ing away.[81] The report was given in cautious and restrained
words, calculated to show Britain's position in the most favorable light possible.[82] The economic orthodoxy of the Board of
Trade officials guarded against giving ammunition or encourage-

[79] *Daily News,* Nov. 26.

[80] Article cited, Nov. 28.

[81] The report of certain members of the former Royal Commission on
Technical Education in January served to emphasize again the matter of
German competition. There was considerable press comment and the con-
sensus of opinion was that England should take some hints from Germany
in education and business methods. *Vide Manchester Guardian, Times, Daily
Telegraph, Daily Chronicle,* and *Standard* (all leading articles), Jan. 20,
1897.

[82] British and Foreign Trade Memorandum, C.-8322. Inquiry made by Sir
Courtenay Boyle and Sir Robert Giffen. *Vide* excellent analysis of report
in *Times,* Jan. 29, 1897.

ment to tariff reformers, and the report was consequently hailed as a vindication of those voices which had decried the recent wave of fright. Mr. Ritchie found the results of the inquiry very satisfactory, with nothing to warrant fear.[83] "If fact can ever kill fiction," declared the *Daily News* triumphantly, "then Sir Courtenay Boyle's Memorandum on British and Foreign Trade . . . ought finally to kill the 'made in Germany' scare."[84] The *Times* thought that, if the outlook was not all that could be wished, it was "at least much better than the public are often assured it is. . . . There is no sign of substantial displacement of England by any of her commercial rivals."[85] Such organs as the *Morning Post, Daily Mail,* and *Daily Chronicle,* which had sung in the alarmist chorus, failed to honor the Blue Book with leading articles, either because it seemed to convict them of having been unduly excited or, more probably, because the passing of the scare had diminished public interest in the subject of German rivalry. The Memorandum, cautiously orthodox though it was, certainly could be read also to defend the grounds for alarm. E. E. Williams insisted in the *Saturday Review* that Sir Courtenay Boyle had not disposed of the case for German competition, but had only "shrunk from the full and obvious deductions which his own figures require." He had "but fulfilled the Moabite Prophet's rôle—he went out to curse the Charlatan and the Quack, and he has ended by coming very near blessing him altogether . . . he was called to curse the 'foolish German Scare' and he has blessed it."[86] But the country's disposition to listen to Mr. Williams had changed by 1897.

[83] Report of address to Wolverhampton Chamber of Commerce in *Manchester Guardian,* Jan. 28, and also in the *Times*. "These figures," he said, "sufficiently dispose of any alarm about German invasion of the home market that may be founded upon the abundance of Bavarian pencils, Nuremberg Christmas cards, and smoker's knickknacks, which, in spite of all that is said about German schools of art, so richly deserve the charge of woodenness brought against them."

[84] Feb. 2.

[85] Jan. 30.

[86] "Sir Courtenay Boyle's Report," Feb. 6, vol. 83, pp. 137-38.

Fear of German trade simply could not live and grow when times were good again. Although echoes of 1896 were heard occasionally in the succeeding year, the prophets of woe could not get the ear of the nation when business continued prosperous. The press abounded rather in exultant observations upon the return of lively trade. A writer in the August *Contemporary Review* proclaimed an "annus mirabilis" in which the sum total of British imports and exports reached a record high level. "In twenty years," he could assert, "the trade of the British Empire has increased in greater ratio than that of the world in general. . . . Under these circumstances it is impossible to regard the condition of British trade as other than highly satisfactory."[87] Scores of similar expressions of exultant optimism might be shown, and in such an atmosphere the German peril for the time being almost faded away. "So long as the shadow of trade depression hung over this country," wrote Prof. A. W. Flux in the March *Economic Journal*, "the controversy as to the relative progress of German and British trade excited no small interest in all classes of the community. Now that we are able to welcome more assured signs of trade revival, it may be expected that, for a time, the outcry in relation to foreign competition will be less audible."[88] And Mr. Williams, writing several years later, acknowledged that "even some who had backed me hesitated and admitted that I was probably too pessimistic and my statements exaggerated." The wave of trade expansion "seemed to the casual observer a refutation of all the doleful prophecies, and did have the effect of banishing most of the apprehensions which had been aroused."[89] A *Times* article of 1902, looking back upon the 1896 alarm, described it as "that bewilderment which is always excited by incomprehensible facts with importance of the first magnitude," and from which

[87] M. G. Mulhall, "Twenty Years of British Trade," vol. 73, p. 213 *et seq.*
[88] "British Trade and Foreign Competition," vol. 7, pp. 34-35.
[89] "Made in Germany—Five Years later," *National Review,* Sept. 1901, vol. 38, pp. 130-44.

there sprang, as usual, a tendency to overrate and to misinterpret. It is no exaggeration to say that "the German danger" spread dismay and alarm through a considerable section of mercantile Britain. It was distorted and exaggerated in those newspapers which are given to sensationalism; it was impressed into the service of those who believe the best way to rouse their country is to send a shudder through its nerves.[90]

By the time anxiety about foreign competition was again current the German peril was partially neutralized by the looming up of a similar American menace. This latter, indeed, followed very rapidly in the wake of the former. As early as March, 1897, a contributor to the *Westminster Review*, without decrying the German threat, sought "to direct attention to other and equally formidable sources against which we have to contend, to wit, the United States of America."[91] There, it was pointed out, was a power speaking the same language, emulating the same practices, endowed with the same British talents of ingenuity and enterprise, and now competing with Britain all over the globe. This was one of the earliest notices given to the rising commercial portent in the new world, and within a very few years a veritable "made in America" scare swept over the country. "The chimera 'made in Germany,'" observed a writer in the same journal for January 1899, "appears as though it were about to yield to the new bogey 'made in the United States.'"[92] "The twentieth century," prophesied a writer in the *Fortnightly Review* about the same time, "will witness an unparalleled contest between Great Britain and America for the commercial sovereignty of the seas."[93] The *National Review* for June 1899 published an article entitled "Our American Competitors," which dealt with evidence of American rivalry in the engineering trade. "Considerable fear," it was said, "has been expressed that one of our most vital industries is leaving

[90] "German vs. British Trade," April 4, 1902.
[91] G. Gibbon, "Made in Other Countries," vol. 147, pp. 310-16.
[92] Mark Warren, "The Ascendancy of the United States Export Trade and Its Significance," vol. 151, pp. 28-37.
[93] E. Taylor, "The Commercial Sovereignty of the Seas," vol. 71, p. 284 *et seq.*

us."[94] E. E. Williams, in 1901, looking back over the five years since the publication of his famous book, found that a more powerful rival than Germany had arisen. The industrial competition of the United States five years earlier he likened to the "hand-breadth cloud upon the horizon"; but now America was coming forward more rapidly and formidably than Germany, and her production threatened "to flow in a deluge over the markets of the world."[95] J. A. Hobson expressed the same view in the *Fortnightly* for March 1902. "We have reason to fear," he thought, "less perhaps of Germany, though her competition will be serious, than from America. . . . Still behind us, she is coming up with a pace which is really formidable. . . . America, indeed, makes no concealment of her intentions to dispute with Great Britain her economic supremacy."[96]

4

In the years following 1896 no outburst of public alarm over German trade comparable to the excited clamor of 1896 is to be discovered, although that is not to say that Germany ceased to be feared commercially or that her trade competition became less formidable and intensive. The German peril remained, but the fact of it became simply one of those disagreeable realities which English business had to accept and seek to adjust itself to in a dynamic world. Moreover, to many in Britain it became apparent that however great Germany might become commercially it did not follow necessarily that England must be brought to economic ruin. They could see that in the new century their own trade was going along fairly well, giving way before Germany, to be sure, in Continental markets, but expanding more widely overseas. British business on the whole was as active

---

[94] Vol. 33, pp. 568-80.

[95] *National Review* article cited above, vol. 38, pp. 130-44.

[96] "The Approaching Abandonment of Free Trade," vol. 77, pp. 435-36. A vivid account of the American menace may be seen also in F. A. McKenzie: *The American Invaders,* London, 1902, parts of which appeared in articles in *Daily Mail,* June 6 ff., 1901. Interesting also is a *Times* leader, "American Trade Competition," Sept. 15, 1900.

and prosperous as Germany in the dozen-odd years preceding 1914. As it has elsewhere been remarked, the continuous read-justments of trade and industry to the exigencies of a growingly competitive world ironed out many of the frictions between British and German commerce which had existed in the nineties. New sources and areas of friction, however, developed and com-manded notice, and the impact of American commerce on world markets intensified world (and therefore Anglo-German) trade rivalry. The ceaseless march of Germans through the markets of the world continued to arrest the close attention of a nation whose commercial leadership grew steadily more restricted; pub-lic organs continued to remind England of the keenness of German economic competition, so that it was never forgotten, nor even temporarily lost sight of in years of exceptional pros-perity. An examination of the press and parliamentary debates makes it very plain that all through these years there was a fixed recognition of acute German trade rivalry. Everybody knew it, everybody took the fact for granted. To shout warn-ings about it was to sound an old cry which all had heard long ago. It was impossible to raise again such an outburst of ex-cited alarm as had accompanied the original discovery. The truth seems to be that the British nation steadily grew more and more acutely, at the same time less noisily, aware of the relentless commercial struggle with Germany.

Certain definite matters, clearly visible and understandable to all, from time to time served to galvanize anew the latent fear and to focus attention prominently upon the economic antag-onism. There was the shipping scare of 1899-1902 which threw into relief German shipping subsidies and German absorption of several British lines, exciting apprehension over the possible foundering of Britain's maritime carrying trade. This was soon followed by the excited agitation against the Bagdad Railway, a clear issue revealing to England so plainly how German busi-ness expansion might well lead to a thrust at the security of the British Empire.[97] Almost simultaneously with this there came

[97] *Supra* Ch. V.

to the front the quarrel with Germany over the Canadian tariff preference, the Chamberlain tariff reform program, and the likelihood of an Anglo-German tariff war.[98] The agitation for tariff reform was a major issue in the election of 1906 and it centered national attention, perhaps as never before, on the German trade danger. During this agitation the nation was treated to another dramatic spectacle of German *Weltpolitik*— the first Moroccan crisis—and it need hardly be said that all manifestations of German *Weltpolitik* contained commercial threats, which were more clearly perceivable when dramatized at Pretoria, Kiao-Chau, Venezuela, Tangier, Teheran, and Agadir. The defeat of the tariff reformers in 1906 was followed soon by Germany's bid for a voice in the Persian question (on the grounds of commercial interest) and the sensational emergence of the navy peril, an outgrowth primarily of commercial and imperialistic rivalry. The Bagdad Railway problem also came forward again to remain a serious issue between Britain and Germany down to the eve of the War. And in the midst of these difficulties came (in 1909-10) a heated revival of the tariff reform issue. All of these matters kept Anglo-German relations difficult, and advertised the antagonism; and all of them not only were related either directly or indirectly to commercial rivalry, but served to keep the public mind aware of the ceaseless economic competition and to excite complaints against it. One does not have to read the pre-war British press very extensively to catch something of the nervous spirit of alarm and jealousy of German economic success which pervaded those years. Some words of Mr. Ramsay Macdonald in the House of Commons in 1911 suggest how lively it was. "We must cease," he said, "all these irritating and pettifogging criticisms regarding German economic advance. Germany is going to increase her markets. Germany is going to increase her trade and commerce. Germany is going to be a more and more effective competitor with us in world markets. We had better in a scientific and calm frame of mind regard that, than constantly lose our tempers,

[98] *Infra* Ch. VII.

and very often throw common sense behind us and engage in foolish, windy and cant phrases about Germany being the enemy."[99]

It will be worth while to say something here of the chief newspapers on the eve of the War, not only to illustrate this state of nerves, but because they indicate a decided quickening of the alarmist temper in 1914. After the tariff reform agitation of 1909-10, and during the economic recovery that followed it, not a great deal (comparatively) was heard of the German commercial peril. But business activity began to slow down again in late 1913, and the western world appeared to be going into another period of sluggish trade. Germany especially appeared to be in serious need of larger markets, and her efforts to secure them were played up sensationally in the British press.

A Reuter dispatch from Berlin early in February 1914 announced the projected formation under Albert Ballin's leadership of an organization to coördinate all efforts for the promotion of German foreign trade. "German Company for World Commerce—Herr Ballin Leads a Great Movement,"—so ran the caption on the first page of the *Daily Chronicle*. "Germany and the World's Trade—Herr Ballin's Scheme—Foreign Press to be Captured,"—such were the headlines over a prominent *Times* article, which described the project as a concerted movement of German shippers, bankers, and industrialists to secure from the press throughout the world a more favorable view of German commerce. "The aim of the organizer of the Association for World Trade and of the journalistic enterprise that appears to be linked with it," it was asserted, "is evidently to extend and intensify the influence over the press of the world which the various press bureaux maintained by the German Government have in the past striven not unsuccessfully to do."[100] Nothing further was heard of this scheme for a little while, but

[99] Hansard, 4th S., vol. 21, p. 100. Feb. 6, 1911.
[100] *Vide* especially *Daily Chronicle, Standard,* and *Times,* for Feb. 6, 7. War came before this scheme was in operation.

it served to bring the German trade peril forward once again in the newspapers.

In the middle of February the alarming news was blazoned across the papers that the Southeastern and Chatham Railway had ordered ten locomotives from a German firm. "German Engines for a British Railway" was the black-faced headline over an article given the most conspicuous position of the day in the *Daily Telegraph* for February 18. Equal prominence was given to the news by the *Evening Globe,* which declared this order to be the first of its kind that Germans had secured in England; and the announcement inspired a number of leading articles.[101] Following closely upon this press sensation came news that some London gas companies had placed orders in Germany for a million tons of coal, which was a relatively huge quantity. This report was undoubtedly much exaggerated, the truth having probably been that the companies were merely raising the German bogey to get more favorable contracts from British coal sellers.[102] But here, nevertheless, was the substance for additional alarmist writing in the press. "German competition," declared a prominent article in the *Daily Telegraph,* "appears to have broken out in a fresh place. Our coal trade has now been thrown into a flutter by the announcement that the London gas companies have placed orders in Germany for a round million tons. Doubtless this will be the subject of eager discussion for months to come. Its significance is emphasized by the fact of an English railway having contracted for a considerable number of German locomotives."[103]

Doubtless this startling invasion of German locomotives and coal served to give news value to all reports from Germany bearing upon commercial matters. A series of very interesting dispatches from Berlin appeared in the *Times* for February 23,

[101] Especially interesting was an article, "British Railways and Foreign Orders," in *Morning Post,* Feb. 23, deploring the diversion of orders for rolling stocks to German makers.
[102] *Vide Colliery Guardian,* Feb. 20, and *Coal Merchant and Shipper* for Feb. 21.
[103] Feb. 24.

24, 25, captioned "Germany and the World's Trade," "The Politics of Commerce," "Germany's Trade Ambitions." They told of the postponement of the formation of Herr Ballin's above-mentioned scheme, but reported the institution of a new *Weltwirtschaftliche Gesellschaft* to study the history and condition of world commerce, and the founding of a new Institute of Sea Traffic and World Commerce, at Kiel, in the presence of Prince Henry of Prussia and a large number of naval officers. "The organization of these societies," wrote the *Times* correspondent, "is . . . the outcome of a fresh movement towards commercial and possibly even naval expansion." This news provided a timely occasion for the appearance in the *Daily Mail* of a prominently placed article by its Berlin correspondent, Frederick William Wile.[104] This was something of a journalistic sensation, disseminated as it was amongst the million readers of Northcliffe's lively morning daily, so that it may well receive important notice here. Englishmen, Wile insisted, should prepare for a German trade campaign "designed to put all previous efforts into the shade." Within two months Ballin's German Association for World Commerce, "inspired by the Kaiser and backed by millions of money," was to take the field "to wage in the Fatherland's name the most prodigious war of trade conquest of modern times." And then came the following:

The German Association for World Commerce is not to be the stereotyped trade booming syndicate of tradition. It has nothing to sell. It represents no special branches. It is to be as impersonal as the German Government itself, of which, in fact, it will practically be an adjunct. Its mission is to spread far and wide the gospel of German trade, to fight its advance guard actions, and to blaze the way for an army of occupation in territory where German commerce has either had no foothold at all or a precarious one. Its scouts are . . . to hunt down ceaselessly the slanders by which it is claimed British and French rivals are systematically obstructing the development of German business. They are to be the organs of an Intelligence Department as vigilant as that maintained by the Headquarters Staff in time of war. On the strength of their

[104] "Germany's Bid for World Trade," Feb. 25.

observations the disposition of the Fatherland's new business army will be based. . . .

This stupendous scheme has special significance for Great Britain, of further-reaching importance than the eventual capture by Düsseldorf and Chemnitz of orders which once went to Sheffield and Manchester. The president of the German Export League once told me that the Reichstag is always good for an extra dread-nought or two if Admiral von Tirpitz can justify the Estimates on the ground of "defense of German trade." Europe has been educated to believe that the armada which the Kaiser and "our magnificent von Tirpitz" have built is for the protection of Germany's golden sea-borne commerce. To Little Navyites, good at multiplication, I leave it to figure out how long Germany will remain content with a high seas fleet of forty-one dreadnoughts held necessary for export and import trade worth £1,040,000,000—the present figure—when the German Association for World Commerce has raised the total to £2,080,000,000. That is the modest ambition it sets for itself.

If the German trade peril subsided a little as the winter wore on, it mounted again to the newspaper headlines late in the spring as a result of new developments in the shipping world. Dismay and consternation were produced by the news that the German lines intended to open a direct steamer service between Continental Europe and New Zealand. It was pointed out in the *Times* that this move would cost the port of London an annual trade of 100,000 tons—cargo which had hitherto been brought to the Thames in both British and German bottoms, had passed through the London docks and been shipped to New Zealand in British ships. "In future London will lose that entrepôt trade," it was said regretfully. "The merchandise will be consigned direct from the Continent." The German intrusion into the New Zealand shipping trade, following so closely on the announcement of the Hamburg-America and North German Lloyd community-of-interest agreement, seemed a clear indication of the forward movement in German shipping which that combination had promised. Thus the *Times* viewed it as the "latest incident in a German campaign for a larger share of the world's shipping. Those who are in a good position to judge the real meanings of the moves that are being made have no doubt that the campaign will be conducted on a great and systematic scale. There is really no trade in which British owners must not expect the keenest competition in the future." Some of the headlines over the *Times'* articles dealing with the proposed German line reflect very clearly the excited reaction to the enterprise in Great Britain, e.g., "World's Shipping— International Fight for Supremacy," "German Shipping Ethics —Invasion of New Zealand—An Aggressive Policy." Some unpleasant exchanges on this subject took place between the newspapers of the two countries, while an unsuccessful attempt on the part of British and German shipping men to reach an agreement only emphasized the Anglo-German crossed interests. And it should be added that there were appearing in the British press simultaneously conspicuous notices of plans for further extensions of German shipping—to South America, to Canada, to Persia, to West Africa.[105]

Thousands of newspaper readers must indeed have received the impression that the Germans were attacking the British lines on all seas, for the *Times* was not alone in playing up the news of German shipping developments. The *Pall Mall Gazette* declared that the estimated loss of trade at London which would follow the opening of the German line to New Zealand was "the least important consequence likely to flow from this new development of the German bid for supremacy on the sea." The imperial consequences would be far graver than the commercial, and hope was expressed that New Zealand would find a way to counter the German move by some sort of preference to British shipping. Another day the *Gazette* appealed for a union of British shippers against foreign rivalry, emphasizing "that the retention of our supremacy in the carrying trade is a matter of imperial concern."[106] The *Daily Mail*, of course, was conspicuous in exploiting the flurry of excitement, one of its major contributions being the publication of a most interesting inter-

[105] *Vide Times,* May 29-June 15.
[106] June 2, 4.

view with Sir Owen Philipps, chairman of the Royal Mail Steam Packet Company. The New Zealand development Sir Owen regarded as only an incident in a worldwide state of affairs, and he thought it would be well if the interest it had aroused served to draw attention to the world situation. "On every trade route in the world," he said, "in every great commercial port you will find German ships. They are the only formidable rivals British shipping has to face. They have practically captured the trade on the west coast of America and to Brazil and the Argentine. . . . The fight for world supremacy is being waged by German ships and British ships in every ocean." He then went on to contrast the solidarity of German shipping interests with the relatively disintegrated condition of British lines, and to recommend British combination for defense.[107]

In view of the fact that late in May a fusion between two powerful British lines running to Far Eastern and Australian waters (the Peninsular and Oriental and the British India Steam Navigation) had been announced, accompanied by a rumor that the purpose of the amalgamation was to counteract the growth of German shipping in these waters—and in view, also, of the fact that the direct German line to Australia had not been prospering (the German Government had, indeed, proposed that the Reichstag discontinue the subsidy to this line), one gets the impression that the press greatly magnified the significance of the German intrusion into the New Zealand trade. The *Manchester Guardian*, always unruffled by the German menace, spoke of "a quite unnecessary stir,"[108] and the shipping press itself showed much the same attitude. Lloyd's *Shipping Gazette* could see no serious menace in the German venture, and even suggested that Sir Owen Philipps' observations were "for the most part pitched in too pessimistic a key." This organ raised the question of "whether it is not possible to overstate the perils of German rivalry. We have a very high opinion of German ability as exemplified in steamship progress,

[107] *Daily Mail*, June 4. There appeared another alarmist article entitled "The Fight for South American Trade" in the same issue.
[108] "German Shipping Competition," June 5.

but we are not going to abandon the belief that our own steam-ship owners are quite as able and quite as successful."[109]

Echoes of the alarmist cry were still reverberating in the press when fresh warnings about German shipping were published before the nation. The *Times* of June 20 announced that the German Government had decided after all to continue and even to enlarge the Australian subsidy; this the *Times* correspondent called "a deliberate challenge." Three days later came a prom-inent notice of the plan of the Kosmos Line of Hamburg for opening a line of steamers between New York and the western ports of South America as soon as the Panama Canal was opened. Simultaneously the *Times* published the news that a lead-ing shipowner was "seriously thinking of placing an order for a large cargo steamer, representing a value of about £100,000, with German yards." He had received tenders from a number of British shipbuilding companies, it was said, but the German prices were lower. This announcement, accompanied by some observations from the anonymous shipowner on the higher effi-ciency of German tonnage, was news of sufficient importance to occasion a leading article in the *Times*. Public attention to Anglo-German shipping rivalry at this time must have been quickened also by news of the launching of Hamburg-American liner *Bismarck,* the world's largest ship, and by the fact that more than a hundred members of the Berlin Association of Mer-chants and Manufacturers were being entertained in England by the London Chamber of Commerce. Dr. Paul Dernburg, for-mer German Colonial Secretary, in a luncheon address, used the occasion to speak reassuringly of the shipping competition, promising "on good authority that whenever . . . differences arose in the future they would be settled and arranged in the most friendly spirit, giving due weight to the interests at stake on both sides."[110] This was certainly pouring oil on troubled waters, for, as the *Shipping Gazette* remarked, very much had been "made of the German bogey," and the claim of the German lines for a share in the New Zealand trade had been "discussed

[109] "Briton and Teuton," June 12.
[110] *Times,* June 23.

in some newspapers as if it were a matter of life and death to our flag."[111]

The German menace in the shipping world thus continued to be displayed before British eyes on into July 1914. A multitude of items, large and small, kept appearing in the great newspapers, notably the *Times* and *Daily Mail*, and of them one more striking sample may be given. The *Daily Mail* for July 6 printed an article from its Berlin correspondent under bold headlines—"German Shipping Move. Plans to Gain the Trade of Australasia"; and with this appeared a leading article which read in part as follows:

By a stroke of the pen the German Government has rendered possible the great German assault on British trade with Australia and New Zealand. . . . The Government has increased its subsidy to the North German Lloyd and German Australian Steamship Companies by £142,000 a year. Thus furnished with the sinews of war, the two companies are putting forth a special effort . . . to wrest from British shipping the 100,000 tons of German freight now forwarded to New Zealand via England. We should be underestimating the perspicacity of the Germans did we suppose that their efforts would end there. Already the hope is expressed in Bremen that the Government subsidy will be further increased and fixed for a definite number of years to offer increasingly strong opposition to foreign competition in the Australasian trade. . . . German shippers have their eye on this young country, with its immense and undeveloped capacity for expansion. With their wonted foresight and ably supported by their far-seeing Government, they are determined to create opportunities for increased trading which they will afterwards seize. Until the British Government realize how hopelessly handicapped British shipping must be in its fight with its heavily subsidized rival there is every likelihood that the German shipping leaders will obtain in the Australian trade the increasingly important position they have already gained on every other trade route of the world.

From all this it should be abundantly plain that right on the eve of the Great War the British public was being loudly re-

---

[111] Issue of June 26.

minded through the press of a new German commercial peril in one of the few remaining fields of British leadership. And the intimate relationship between shipping expansion and the enlargement of that naval power which had become Great Britain's nightmare was stated very plainly. At the same time that the Bagdad Railway Convention of June 1914 was resolving one of the great economic issues which had poisoned Anglo-German relations (this Convention did not engage public attention at all), the press was in a flutter over German shipping and the British nation was experiencing another wave of fright at German business expansion. Indeed, on July 25 a huge journalistic sensation was sprung by the *Daily Mail* with the announcement that the Dutch Government had granted a concession for a "private harbour" near Rotterdam to the Vulcan Shipbuilding Company. It was almost breathlessly stated that this concern, dominated by August Thyssen, worked in the closest conjunction with the German Government, had built dreadnoughts at Hamburg and Stettin, and that its new port would be available for the largest ships. Further, it was broadly hinted that this would make an admirable German naval base. The article was captioned: "A German Coup—Harbour in Holland—Only 115 Miles from England—A 'Private' Scheme—Grave Misgivings." The other papers for the most part ignored this astounding news, and two days later the *Daily Mail* printed a brief notice to the effect that the concession was to be used for commercial purposes only, that Herr Thyssen already owned a similar "base" at Caen, in Normandy, as well as docks and harbor facilities in India, Brazil, and on the Black Sea. But the Northcliffe organ did not cease to exploit the alarm which its first announcement must have created, for on July 28 it published a letter from "Dutch Business Correspondent" calling attention to the dangers to England in the Thyssen concession; and on the same day appeared a prominent special article by Frederick William Wile on "King Thyssen, the German Who Bought a Port in Holland." Thyssen, wrote Wile,

holds advanced views on the underlying cause of "bad blood" between England and Germany. He declares that naval rivalry is an effect and not a cause of Anglo-German antagonisms, which spring primarily and exclusively from commercial competition. . . . He boldly proclaims that England cannot hope for quarter from Germany in the struggle for the world's markets.

The day this appeared Austria declared war on Serbia, and whatever threat to England there was in the Thyssen concession was obscured by the war clouds that gathered over the whole of Europe. Another week and Great Britain drew her sword against Germany in defense of Belgian neutrality, but it is worth remembering that she had very recently been much alarmed at Germany for rather different reasons. And, as will be shown elsewhere in this study, the Germans were not very long in Belgium before men in England were talking frankly, yes patriotically, of the glorious opportunity for stripping Germany of her trade, her colonies, and her ships.

Chapter VII

THE TRADE QUESTION AND BRITAIN'S GERMAN POLICY

IT WILL be the aim of this concluding chapter to suggest the degree to which Great Britain's commercial rivalry with the people of the German Empire contributed to shaping Britain's policy toward that Power. To raise and seek to answer this question involves serious risk of failure, or at least inadequacy; for every student of history knows that the direct influence of economic circumstances on political policies and enterprises is not always easy to discern and very seldom easy to prove completely. No one, so far as the writer of this work is informed, has yet given a full and accurate answer to the question; but many loose assertions have abounded, especially during the War, and also in the many studies dealing with the genesis of the War which continue to flow from the press.

There was a widespread opinion in Germany during the War that the British had engineered a sinister conspiracy for the destruction of a commercial rival: the nation of shopkeepers had embarked upon a Carthaginian policy of ruining a prosperous and threatening business competitor. Such an idea of British policy, indeed, antedated the outbreak of the war by some few years. Some writers devised an economic interpretation of Britain's moves as soon as Germany's "encirclement" became manifest. Writing in 1909 Dr. Gerhardt von Schulze-Gaevernitz charged that back of the excited British masses stood a group of leaders "deliberately inflaming public opinion to the danger point." Their reasoning was that

German industrial progress is overtaking that of England with giant strides. It has gradually amassed those stupendous aggregations of capital that first rivaled the individual capitalism of England and then grew to American dimensions. The day is now not far distant when the economic power of Germany will equal that of England, mistress of the world and still its leading creditor. Then the two-power standard for her navy will have become financially impossible. With purely economic development British sea dominion must pass away—melt under the very sunshine of peace. Today, perhaps—but not tomorrow—new Germany, rising, can be struck to earth by a mailed fist. Thence comes for England, while she still has power in her hands, the great temptation to a "preventive war." By blockade and privateering they think that German trade . . . would be all but destroyed and German wares crowded out of the markets of the world."[1]

The late Dr. Gustave Stresemann, a man of very penetrating intelligence and extensive knowledge of the modern business world, was one of the many who voiced this German conviction again and again in wartime speeches: England made war upon Germany *"propter invidiam."* It was argued, indeed, that war on Germany began with the Merchandise Marks Act of 1887, was continued in the Patent Law of 1907, and came at length to arms in 1914, the Great War being simply the last form of the economic struggle against Germany.[2] The ex-Kaiser, in his memoirs, insinuated the same charge;[3] and that the wartime view still lingers in the German mind is well known, although the progress made by German scholars in the study of the origins of the War has gone far toward banishing it. They have done much to vindicate their country of the awful guilt charged against her, and to build a case against the Entente Powers, but they have not been able to sustain the charge that the War was peculiarly the outcome of calculating British trade jealousy. None of the great collections of published diplomatic documents has given nourishment to the allegation, and it has therefore largely disappeared from serious writings on the *Kriegschuldfrage.*

In general, the view of German investigators is that of Erich

[1] "England and Germany—Peace or War?" *American Review of Reviews,* November, 1909; *vide* also C. S. Goldman, "A German View of the Anglo-German Problem," *Nineteenth Century,* vol. 65, 1909.

[2] Rochus von Rheinbaben, *Stresemann: The Man and the Statesman,* pp. 100-101.

[3] William II: *My Memoirs, 1878-1918,* London, 1922, pp. 298-99.

Brandenburg, to wit, that as far as it is now possible to determine, no responsible person in England actually wanted the War, and that the view widely spread in Germany that Great Britain instigated the war in order to check the rapidly growing economic competition of Germany is therefore untenable.[4] Professor A. F. Pribram, the distinguished Austrian authority on the origins of the War, has recently reviewed the policies of England with the Continental Powers over the period 1871-1914, and, if his virtual ignoring of the trade competition issue be indicative of his estimate of its importance in shaping British policy, plainly he attaches little or no importance to it.[5] A recent and remarkable book on British policy by Professor Hermann Kantorowicz emphatically denies the wartime German doctrine that British policy was the expression of commercial envy. His argument is a strong one, even though it suffers somewhat from a pronounced anglophil bias. He points to the fact that Britain did not abandon Free Trade and thus open national economic warfare with Germany (apparently not realizing how strong the drift in that direction was), and to the fact that the British Documents on the Origins of the War ("although the most intimate plans are laid bare in them") "talk of quite other things than economic war aims against Germany." These are the principal circumstances which lead him to the conclusion "that there is nothing, absolutely nothing, in the notion that Trade Envy was the motive of English policy."[6]

British writings on the causes of the War, both the memoirs of statesmen and scholarly studies, have given very little attention to the trade question as a factor in British policy toward Germany. Asquith and Loreburn, for example, ignored it entirely in their volumes, and so did Churchill. Grey paid it the honor of a denial. "Some Germans," he wrote, "cannot under-

[4] Brandenburg, *Vom Bismarck zum Weltkriege,* p. 444, Berlin, 1924. (Eng. Trans.)

[5] Pribram, *England and the International Policy of the European Great Powers, 1871-1914,* 1931.

[6] Kantorowicz, *The Spirit of British Policy,* 1932, pp. 371-81. Trans. from *Der Geist der Englischen Politik und das Gespenst der Einkreisung Deutschlands,* Berlin, 1929.

stand why we went into the War, because the motive that impelled us is something outside their perception. Because that is so, because they cannot see the real motive, they invent reasons other than the true one, to account for British action. One of these motives very generally attributed to us is that of industrial rivalry and commercial jealousy of Germany. It is the reverse of the truth. Our great industrial sections, especially Lancashire, were most averse to war. Trade was good, industry wanted to be undisturbed."[7] Among British scholars, likewise, there has been a strong tendency either to ignore the commercial question or deny that it had much to do with shaping the official British attitude toward Germany. The distinguished Mr. Gooch, for example, in his excellent history of the years 1878 to 1919, wrote at length on Anglo-German rivalry but gave disdainfully scant notice to the commercial conflict.[8] This seems to be typical of British works on the origins of the War. They have been chiefly based on the great collections of diplomatic documents and memoirs, which contain very little on the subject of trade but very much about navies and the balance of power. The latter, therefore, are viewed as the great determining factors in British policy toward Germany.

But it is the conviction of this writer that too exclusive attention to the mass of diplomatic documents has been paid generally by scholars seeking to explain the genesis of the War. Professor S. B. Fay has observed:

If one reads the diplomatic correspondence of the years before the War, one is struck by the relatively slight importance which is given to these economic rivalries which haunt so largely the mind of the average business man and newspaper editor. It is not so much questions of economic rivalry as those of prestige, boundaries, armies and navies, the Balance of Power, and possible shiftings in the system of alliances, which provoke reams of diplomatic correspondence and raise the temperature in Foreign Offices to the danger point.[9]

[7] *Twenty-five Years*, I, 325.
[8] G. P. Gooch, *History of Modern Europe*, 1923.
[9] Sidney B. Fay, *The Origins of the World War*, I, 46.

It may be admitted that this observation is largely true, but far from eliminating the importance of economic rivalries (as Professor Fay evidently seeks to do in his otherwise excellent volumes), it merely indicates the limitations of diplomatic documents as materials for study. Ministers and diplomats do not discuss general conditions of economic competition, but the specific issues arising out of those general conditions; to neglect or minimize the latter is to fall short of a thorough understanding of basic forces in international antagonisms.

But let not what has been said be taken as prefatory to an insistence upon a strictly economic interpretation of England's German policy. During the preparation of this study the writer has been led, certainly, to regard the German commercial rivalry as a powerful shaping factor in English national policy, but he has also been impressed with equal force by the potency in international relations of the elusive factor of national psychology. A steady interplay goes on between economic circumstances and the public mind, and what the latter thinks the former to be may well have a more decisive influence upon national policy than what the former in reality are. This is especially true in states where the government is quickly responsive to public opinion, and Great Britain was such a state. No evidence whatever has been unearthed to indicate or even to excite a rational suspicion of a conspiracy of interests in Britain to reduce Germany for purposes of economic gain. The talk of seizing German markets and driving German ships from the seas which was heard so soon after the War broke out might seem to indicate some hidden calculating purpose in the decision to draw the sword,[10] but there is no sign of such a motive in published diplomatic documents. Nor is there any evidence that the violently anti-German press was the voice of British economic interests that stood to gain by Germany's ruin, although it is true that the organs most hostile to Germany (such as the *Daily Mail*, the *Times*, the *National Review*, and the *Fortnightly Review*) played up the German trade peril more conspicuously than did the *Man-*

[10] *Vide* Appendix III.

chester Guardian, the *Daily News,* or the *Westminster Gazette.*
But it was only natural that the nationalist-mercantilist organs
should see German rivalry differently from the way it appeared
to the liberal Cobdenite press. That a few leading journals were
loud in their warnings to the nation is not the slightest warrant
for insinuating that they wanted or worked for war with
Germany.

The attitude of the various trade journals toward Germany
must have reflected fairly well the view of the business community, and it is significant that they were not only well disposed
toward Germany, for the most part, but even were inclined to
regard the German trade peril less seriously than the general
newspaper press viewed it. Thus the *Chemical Trades Journal,*
which spoke for a branch of industry that suffered especially
from German competition, declared in 1908:

At a period when mischief mongers appear to be so busy with their
self-appointed task of sowing discord among the great nations, a
serious duty rests on those who have been trained in the more
responsible schools of science and industry, and a wholesome cor-
rective may usefully be applied by those journals which are representative of applied science and commerce. . . . Racial enmity
does not flourish in the atmosphere of science, technology, and
commerce. There are, undoubtedly, both "firebrands" and a "yellow
press" on each side of the North Sea, but we cannot think that
there is any real sympathy in scientific and commercial circles
with the periodical foolish attempts to foment international enmity,
and we especially welcome the recent signs of Anglo-German friendship. Rivals in commerce we may be; but the powerful bond of
science should prevent us from ever finding ourselves antagonists
on the "stricken field."[11]

The *Shipping World* about the same time strongly denounced
the idea of an "inevitable" war between England and Germany:
"There is no reason, no excuse, not even a plausible pretext in
justification of this horrible 'inevitable war'. Each country is
the other's best customer, we have a common origin, kindred

[11] Leading article, "Anglo-German Relations," March 21, 1908.

aspirations and tastes . . . "[12] In the spring of 1914, when shipping rivalry was growing more intense, this same journal rejoiced in the signs of an improvement in Anglo-German political relations.[13] There can be no doubt but that the trade journals, on the whole, bear out Sir Edward Grey's statement that British business wanted no disturbance of the peace.[14]

Had then the German trade rivalry nothing whatever to do with Great Britain's going to war with Germany? Hardly. It was the soil out of which the great questions at issue between the two nations grew. It was a source of fear for alarmists to exploit, and it gave nourishment to suspicion, jealousy, and hatred. It was a powerful excitant of Germanophobia, which inevitably made its force felt throughout the highest political circles, and therefore it may rightly be viewed as a basic cause for the anti-German orientation of British world policy. This can be clearly shown.

2

Unless one holds a deterministic view of history (which this writer completely disavows) no war can be said to be inevitable. But it is a commonplace that nothing can make a war so nearly certain as a widespread belief in its inevitability, that it lies— to use Bismarck's famous words—in "the logic of history." Now the idea of an ultimate and virtually inevitable conflict with Germany was most assuredly born in Great Britain, and it appears to have sprung in large measure from a recognition of Germany's rivalry in commerce.

As has been previously shown, before 1900 there were two periods in which the emergence of German trade competition was especially noticed in England: roughly, the years of 1884-88 and

[12] Leading article, "No Inevitable War," Aug. 19, 1908.

[13] Leading article, "Anglo-German Friendship," April 8, 1914.

[14] It is significant that in February, 1910, at the height of election excitement when tariff reform and anti-Germanism were being violently agitated, the Anglo-German Section of the London Chamber of Commerce was formed. A number of speeches were heard at the occasion emphasizing the solidarity of Anglo-German business interests and scouting all talk of war, etc. *Vide* account of this, and accompanying leader on "Anglo-German Relations," in *Chamber of Commerce Journal*, March, 1910.

1894-98. It was not mere coincidence that these periods were also featured by strained relations between the British and German governments. The African colonial dispute and the Transvaal crisis were imperialist conflicts essentially commercial in their origin, although that is not the whole point to be made here. What must also be emphasized is that the emergence of the German trade rivalry in the eighties was a subject of considerable public interest, disposing the popular mind (which British governments cannot ignore) to take particular notice of all German enterprise. Thus there was a distinct tendency in Britain to magnify the significance of Germany's bid for colonies in Africa. Moreover, the Bismarck-Granville embroglio dramatized the rising competition in world commerce, enhanced the news value of all information relating to German economic expansion, and riveted British attention upon the neighbor across the North Sea. Very much the same may be said of the Transvaal crisis. British commercial apprehensions of Germany, after a lull in the early nineties, were undergoing a lively reawakening by 1895; so that fear and jealousy of German business were again stalking the land when the Kaiser sent the Kruger telegram and brought Anglo-German relations to the brink of war. Here again mere reference to the subtle relation between the political quarrel and the business conflicts in the Transvaal does not exhaust the significance which the event has for this study. Once more the German trade menace was dramatized before British eyes, and the incident helped to bring on the most acute attack of nerves the British nation has as yet suffered from the portent of German commerce. There were violent expressions of business jealousy, and every piece even of the most remotely alarming news about German business was magnified by the anti-German mood of 1896.[15] One cannot read the press of that year

[15] Sir Charles Oppenheimer, British Consul-General at Frankfort, in his report for 1896 included the following significant quotation from a German chamber of commerce report: "We regret . . . that with a friendly nation of close origin, with whom we are united by many similar views and interests, our progress in this field (commerce), expected by her, has led to an excited state of feeling that is endangering the reciprocal sympathies of both peoples."—Annual Series, 1942.

without perceiving how much the Transvaal crisis helped to advertise the "made in Germany" peril. The enemy stood revealed in a clear light, and the ultimate consequences of economic warfare were suspected. Englishmen began to feel that this formidable commercial rival was also a political enemy who even dreamed of sea power; and as this was the time when theories of economic determinism in history were being popularized, the idea of an inevitable war with Germany began to take hold of the public mind. The idea found its clearest and strongest expression in 1897 in the famous *"Germania esse delendam"* article in the *Saturday Review:*

. . . in Europe there are two great, irreconcilable opposing forces, two great nations who would make the whole world their province, and who would levy from it the tribute of commerce. England, with her long history of successful aggression, with her marvellous conviction that in pursuing her own interests she is spreading light among nations dwelling in darkness, and Germany, bone of the same bone, blood of the same blood, with a lesser will force, but perhaps with a keener intelligence, compete in every corner of the globe. In the Transvaal, at the Cape, in Central Africa, in India and the East, in the islands of the Southern Sea, and in the far Northwest, wherever—and where has it not—the flag has followed the Bible and trade has followed the flag, there the German bagman is struggling with the English pedlar. Is there a mine to exploit, a railway to build, a native to convert from breadfruit to tinned meat, from temperance to trade gin, the German and the Englishman are struggling to be first. A million petty disputes build up the greatest cause of war the world has ever seen. If Germany were extinguished tomorrow, the day after tomorrow there is not an Englishman in the world who would not be the richer. Nations have fought for years over a city or a right of succession; must they not fight for two hundred and fifty million pounds of yearly commerce?[16]

That this often-quoted article represented a universal or as yet even very widespread opinion is, of course, not true. But the fact that one of the great weeklies (albeit of declining influence)

[16] "England and Germany," Sept. 11, 1897.

should voice such views makes it plain that the idea had taken important hold on some British minds. A few more years passed —those turbulent, exciting *fin-de-siécle* years—and the fixed idea of Germany as the standing, permanent enemy took very deep root in England. The German pounce upon China, the rupture of the Anglo-German commercial treaty of 1865, the 1900 Naval Law, the German press attacks during the Boer War, the ill-fated Anglo-German coöperation against Venezuela, and the acquisition of the Bagdad Railway concession, filled the years between the Transvaal crisis and the Anglo-French Entente. There took place that significant reorientation of British foreign policy and the laying of the foundations of the Triple Entente partnership which led in time to Germany's undoing. By 1904 the enmity of Germany was a fixed idea in the British public mind; and it remained an unshaken and insuperable obstacle to any far-reaching accord between the two nations.[17] There is no need for this study to trace the steps in the revolution of the British official attitude towards Germany accomplished between 1896 and 1904; but it is important to insist that this fixed idea, which gradually attained an ascendancy over the British mind and the British government as well, most certainly had one of its principal roots of origin and sources of nourishment in commercial apprehension. It was not an unconventional view to which J. Ellis Barker gave expression in 1908:

Fate has placed Great Britain and Germany in the same reciprocal position into which it put Rome and Carthage two thousand years ago. Germany wishes to possess that which Great Britain wishes to keep, and it is difficult to see how, under the circumstances, a collision between the two countries can be avoided. Germany has entered upon the same line of business as Great Britain, and the consequence is that almost every profit to Germany means a loss to Great Britain, and almost every profit to Great Britain means a loss to Germany.[18]

[17] Caroline E. Playne has best described this fixed idea of Germany as the standing enemy in Chapter VII of her *The Pre-War Mind in Britain,* London, 1928.

[18] "The Foreign Policy of William II," *Nineteenth Century,* vol. 63.

3

One of the major issues in British public life between the close of the Boer War and the outbreak of war with Germany was the proposal for abandoning Free Trade and establishing a system of preferential tariffs within the British Empire. The pressure of world trade competition at length wore down much of the Cobdenites' resistance and, as the imperialist mood gained increased ascendancy over the British mind, tariff reformers managed to get a hearing before the country. The nineties were filled with demands for a return to mercantilist policies as weapons of defense in the neo-mercantilist world, and the popular discovery of so many goods "made in Germany," on sale in the United Kingdom and throughout the Empire, contributed powerfully to the movement for tariff reform. That this movement should take an anti-German direction was inevitable, since Germany was England's greatest trade competitor; and it was frankly admitted that a fiscal revolution in the British Empire would deal a most severe blow to German commercial prosperity. Great Britain was the most valuable customer Germany had, and the freedom of access which German business enjoyed in the markets of the United Kingdom and the British colonies and dominions were privileges which it could not well afford to lose.[19] This was not so evident in the nineties, when the Caprivi treaties were obtaining greater elbow room for German trade in Continental markets, but after 1900, when Continental tariffs were going up and German business was feeling again the need for wider markets, the immense advantage of commercial liberty throughout the British Empire came to be seen clearly. As early as 1900, indeed, E. E. Williams wrote that Germany was

becoming abjectly dependent upon the markets of the British Empire. Already, by the institution of the Canadian preference, German traders have begun to shiver with apprehension; and Canada's

[19] In discussing the Anglo-German flirtation of 1899 a *Times* leader (Oct. 27, 1899) observed that "the great commercial and industrial classes of Germany . . . fully realize how large a share of their prosperity they owe to the protection and liberty conferred upon them all over the world under the British flag."

example is going to be followed more widely. It can be followed to any extent, and quite easily to such an extent as would bring Germany to her knees, pleading for our clemency.[20]

The first step in this direction, taken in 1897 when Canada extended preferential treatment to United Kingdom goods, had most important consequences: Germany retaliated upon Canadian goods and charged that the Canadian tariff had violated the commercial treaty of 1865 between England and the German Zollverein. The treaty had, indeed, been broken, since it obligated the whole British Empire to accord most-favored-nation treatment to German goods; and the result was that Great Britain denounced the treaty.[21] No substitute trade convention was afterwards negotiated, and although the German Government continued to give most-favored-nation treatment to the United Kingdom by an annual ordinance of the Bundesrath, commercial relations between the two countries lacked a secure basis.[22] If at any time Great Britain had adopted protection the German Government could have immediately rescinded the Bundesrath ordinance. A tariff war between England and Germany would probably have followed a victory by the British protectionists, and because of the prominence of the fiscal question in Britain after 1900 this cloud hung continuously over Anglo-German relations. Difficult as these were, the estrangement between England and Germany would certainly have been very much greater had a tariff war come about.

In such a contest the Germans doubtless would have got the worse of it, since there was no obvious way in which they could have retaliated very effectively against the formation of a Pan-Brittanic Zollverein, the markets of Britain and her Empire being a great deal more valuable to German business than the

[20] "The Economic Revolution in Germany," *National Review,* Aug., 1900.
[21] *Vide* Correspondence With Governments of Belgium and Germany as to Their Commercial Relations with Great Britain and British Colonies.— Cd. 1630, 1903. Also an excellent review of the Canadian-German tariff quarrel in a *Times* leading article, July 14, 1903.
[22] *Vide* discussion of this in House of Lords, May 30, 1905, by Viscount Ridley and Lord Lansdowne, Hansard, 4th Series, vol. 147, pp. 211-18.

German market was to British firms. So that in this situation lay unquestionably one of the great dynamic reasons for Germany's vigorous navalism and imperialism: to guard against the closing of British markets, or at least to reduce the force of the blow if and when it fell. So long as Germany remained at all dependent for her commercial prosperity on the British free-trade system her economic life was precarious, and this was realized increasingly all over Europe in the years before the War. A random search of the newspapers of this period, especially in 1903-6 and 1909-10, very quickly reveals how great was German concern over the outcome of the British tariff reform issue. It is true that the percentage of Germany's total exports absorbed by the British Empire on the eve of 1914 was less than in 1900, but it was nevertheless great enough for the closing or narrowing of British markets to have inflicted heavy losses on German business. Moreover, with a reformed fiscal policy Great Britain might well have been able (because of her larger markets) to bargain more successfully than Germany in the making of new commercial treaties. There was a wide opinion that the conclusion of a Pan-Brittanic customs union would lead rapidly to a decline in German prosperity and the transfer of many German industries to Great Britain; a kind of economic strangulation thus would be Germany's fate, unless she was strong enough to keep economic doors open, make her navy feared, and acquire sufficient colonies.[23]

Upon this question of British tariff reform, which obviously had arisen largely out of Anglo-German trade competition, depended much that was fundamentally decisive for Anglo-German relations. The pressure of German business on British markets drove Britain towards protection and imperial preference, while the drift towards tariff reform stimulated German navalism and imperialism. These in turn steadily heightened British alarm. The situation became a vicious circle from which the only escape might have been an effective economic entente.[24] So shrewd and

[23] Cf. J. Ellis Barker, *Modern Germany*, 1912, 3d., Ch. XXXI.

[24] Such ideas were of course frequently discussed. *Vide Times* article, Nov. 24, 1911, "The Price of German Friendship." A Member of Parliament,

informed an observer as Albert Ballin, managing director of the Hamburg-American Line, was convinced that no formula for Anglo-German friendship was possible as long as there existed the danger that Britain would shut the door of her markets against Germany. In the informal overtures for an Anglo-German rapprochment between Ballin and Sir Ernest Cassel in July 1909, when the naval question was being dangerously agitated, this fundamental condition was discussed, and Ballin insisted that the British retention of free trade was absolutely necessary for any secure agreement.[25]

The tariff question was the source of many bitter and dangerous recriminations. Upward revisions in the German duties (a new general tariff with increased duties was adopted in 1902) of course excited displeasure in Great Britain,[26] but this was as nothing compared with the bitterness generated by the British tariff-reform movement. During this agitation there were countless attacks upon Germany, which further poisoned the atmosphere breathed by the British public and steadily fired anew the bitter press war between the two countries. Proponents of the movement made constant attacks on German "dumping," accused the Germans of meddling in British affairs to prevent the enactment of tariffs, and played upon the fears of patriots for the security of England and the Empire. Joseph Chamberlain, speaking at Birmingham in 1903, violently attacked Germany for her retaliation against the Canadian preference, characterizing German policy in this matter as one of "dictation and interference."

The German newspapers [he said] frankly explain that this is a policy of reprisal; and that it is intended to deter other Colonies

---

one Mr. Bigland, about the same time advocated that the time had come for the Foreign Secretary to ask ten British business men to meet ten German business men in conference, to clear up the business difficulties between the two nations and effect some form of tariff reciprocity.—Hansard, 5th S., vol. 32, pp. 2646-48.

[25] Ballin's report to Kaiser, Huldermann, *op. cit.,* pp. 146-51.

[26] A *Times* leader, Oct. 2, 1901, characterized the new German tariff proposals as a "determined and carefully calculated attack projected upon the interests of British . . . producers."

from giving to us the same advantage. Therefore it is not merely punishment inflicted by Germany upon Canada but it is a threat to South Africa, to Australia and to New Zealand; and this policy . . . is justified by the belief that we are so wedded to our fiscal system that we cannot interfere, that we cannot defend our Colonies, and that in fact any one of them which attempts to establish any kind of special relations with us does so at her own risk. In my mind that is putting us in a rather humiliating position. I do not like it at all.[27]

Soon after this a blue book containing the correspondence that had passed between the Foreign Office and the Wilhelmstrasse on the Canadian tariff question was issued, and this revealed that Germany had hinted she might withdraw most-favored-nation treatment from both the United Kingdom and the Colonies if she were discriminated against in important parts of the British Empire. "This," asserted the *Times* indignantly, "is a very direct menace, couched in diplomatic language, that if Great Britain does not take steps to prevent her Colonies from giving any preference to her goods, then Germany will punish not only the erring Colonies, but Great Britain herself. . . . The main point is that Germany, relying upon our inability to retaliate, threatened interference with the internal affairs of the Empire, which extends beyond the commercial sphere, and is calculated to exert a serious and obstructive influence upon the political consolidation at which we aim."[28] J. Ellis Barker, in the *Nineteenth Century*, charged Germany with having "deliberately endeavoured to drive a wedge between Great Britain and our Colonies, and to prevent the unification of the British Empire."[29] Such expressions, reaching the public ear when it was still ringing with the violent press attacks upon the Bagdad Railway, must have heightened considerably the anti-German mood.

Throughout 1904 and 1905 attacks upon German "dumping"

[27] Report of speech in *Times,* May 16, 1903.
[28] Leader of July 14, 1903.
[29] "The Future of Anglo-German Relations," vol. 59, April, 1906; the same charge was launched in the *Fortnightly Review* ("The Foreign Policy of Germany," by * * *), vol. 78, 1905.

in England were widely made, and the cry was listened to because these were years of severe trade depression.[30] In the General Election of 1906, which was fought largely on the issue of tariff reform, Tory papers and speakers exploited the cry to extreme limits. England rang with denunciations of "cheap foreign goods" (popularly believed to be mostly German goods); and Germany's natural hope that England would not quit Free Trade was flung in the face of the Liberals, in an attempt to identify protectionism with patriotism.

The repercussion of this election agitation in high politics is hinted at in some words of M. Gabriel Hanotaux, ex-Foreign Minister of France, written in early 1906. He singled out Anglo-German commercial rivalry as the great disturbing condition in the world and an omen of impending war:

An unforeseen incident will give rise to a general conflict. Each of the two governments knows that it must be prepared for that event, and they are preparing for it. Perhaps one of them tomorrow will consider it to its advantage to hasten its advent. It is that apprehension which weighs upon the world.[31]

An upswing of the business cycle in 1906 robbed the Protectionist claims of much of their effectiveness and helped the Liberals to return to power as defenders of Britain's established fiscal policy;[32] but the same sort of clamor, only far more intense, featured the election of January 1910. Trade had gone

[30] A characteristic example of this was Mr. Bonar Law's speech in the House of Commons, Feb. 9, 1904.—Hansard 4th Series, vol. 129, pp. 782-83. *Vide* also Mr. Chaplin's speech, Feb. 11, 1904, *ibid.*, pp. 1058-59.

[31] *Times,* March 31, 1906. In September R. B. Haldane had an interesting talk with the Kaiser and von Tschirschky about the Chamberlain program, the election, and the possibility of war over trade.—Diary of his visit, *British Documents,* III, 379-80.

[32] The Free Trade victory at this election was by no means clear or emphatic, for tariff reform was not the sole issue. In 1907 the London Chamber of Commerce adopted a resolution for tariff reform, and the *Pall Mall Gazette* was probably near the truth in stating: "There can be no controversy as to the general attitude of the business community. British employers and British workmen are alike beginning to 'see the lie of the land' as the mists of electioneering nonsense are rolled back from the horizon."— Leader of April 11, 1907.

down in another slump in 1908-9, and although recovery was setting in by election time the Conservatives appealed again to the tariff issue. This was the election in which the Asquith Government went to the country fighting the House of Lords for Mr. Lloyd George's budget, and the Conservatives preferred to emphasize other issues. Naval rivalry with Germany had just produced a serious war scare, so that national alarm was running almost as high as the political passions stirred up by the House of Lords and budget questions. The Conservatives, therefore, sought to capitalize the trade depression and the navy peril; so that while the Liberals assailed the Lords the Tories patriotically declaimed against the German menace. "The specious but shallow appeal to anti-foreign prejudices on which the protectionists trade," commented the *Westminster Gazette*, "is one of the misfortunes of this controversy, and the facile manner in which leading newspapers and responsible public men have lent themselves to it is greatly to be deplored."[33] A most striking example of Tory pandering to anti-Germanism was a speech made by Mr. Balfour, the Conservative leader, at Hanley, early in January. He declared,

Go about at this moment, if you will, and consult the statesmen and diplomatists of the lesser powers, and I am perfectly confident that you will find among them an absolute unanimity of opinion that a struggle sooner or later between this country and Germany is inevitable. I don't agree with them, but that is their opinion . . . they have come to the conclusion, I believe utterly wrongly, that we are not alive to our responsibilities, and that therefore we are destined to succumb in some great contest . . . to a country which does face facts, which is alive to its responsibility, and which talks little and does much. So far has this depreciatory view of the virility of the manhood of Great Britain gone that I have known of Germans—not connected with the Government, but men of position and character, engaged in great affairs—who, if you talk to them of the adoption of tariff reform by this country, actually have the audacity to say, "Do you suppose we should ever allow Great Britain to adopt tariff reform?" I don't press private and irresponsible conversations more than they ought to be pressed,

[33] Leader of Jan. 20, 1906.

but the idea that any man of education and character outside this country should have the audacity to say that Great Britain is not to settle its own taxation according to its own ideas makes my blood boil.[34]

Mr. Balfour was of course sharply attacked for this kind of campaigning by the Liberal press. "We dislike bringing the terms of political morality into political controversy," said the *Manchester Guardian* caustically, "but if political speeches are ever immoral, the passages in Mr. Balfour's speech . . . were— immoral not because they suppress the facts while affecting to do homage to them, or because they are evasive and equivocatory, but because they are not unwilling to subvert the foundations of international amity for the remote chance of catching stray votes."[35] The *Daily Chronicle* charged him with "joining in the attempt to create a war scare over Germany in order to cloak the revolutionary conduct of the Peers," and said his speech had aroused "universal indignation."[36] The *Westminster Gazette* rebuked him sharply for trying to exploit for party advantage the Anglo-German antagonism—"the most delicate question of international politics." "He has known Germans of high position," said the *Gazette*, "who say that Great Britain shall not be

---

[34] *Daily Mail* report of speech, Jan. 5, 1910. This speech of Balfour's lends credibility to a memoir of Countess Seherr-Thoss, daughter of Henry White, the American diplomat, which Allan Nevins presents in his biography of White. The Countess recorded a conversation which she overheard in March 1907 between her father and Mr. Balfour. "We are probably fools," remarked Balfour somewhat lightly, "not to find a reason for declaring war on Germany before she builds too many ships and takes away our trade." White expressed his amazement at the contemplation of "anything so immoral as provoking a war against a harmless nation" which had as good a right to a navy as Britain; to which Balfour replied that competing against Germany meant lowering the British standard of living, and that "it would be simpler for us to have a war." When the Countess recorded this does not appear, so that the complete accuracy of the memoir may well be doubted.— Henry White, *Thirty Years of American Diplomacy*, New York, 1930, pp. 257-58.

[35] Jan. 5, 1910. For an excellent, although hostile description of the tariff reformers' campaign methods *vide* article, "The New Protectionism," *Manchester Guardian*, Jan. 6.

[36] Jan. 6, 1910.

'allowed' to adopt Tariff Reform, and, though of course they do not represent their Government, their talk has made his blood boil. And then, with parenthetic disclaimers which his audience will discount, he contrives to get a good deal of scare talk into the language without, as he thinks, committing himself."[37] But Mr. Balfour was not rebuked by such organs as the *Times*, the *Morning Post*, the *Pall Mall Gazette*, the *Daily Telegraph*, or the *Daily Mail*, all of which were now protectionist and very anti-German. "It is impossible," said the Northcliffe organ, "to exaggerate the gravity and significance of Mr. Balfour's words."[38] And the *Morning Post* in a leading article quoted a letter from a resident British manufacturer in Germany as follows:

Balfour said some one had told him that if we adopted Tariff Reform it would mean war between Germany and us. That is just what a German manufacturer from C—— told me the other day. He said: "We do not so much mind about your little island, but your country is the door through which we export our goods throughout the British Empire, and we shall never allow it to be shut in our face."

The view of this manufacturer, the *Post* pointed out, was merely an amplification of Mr. Balfour's statements, so that it was "impossible to doubt that this attitude is adopted by certain Germans of position."[39] The columns of the *Morning Post* were opened wide during the campaign to articles and comments from the German press and German individuals showing the alarm with which Germans would regard a victory for tariff reform. The *Daily Telegraph*, too, gave much space to "Our Lost Trade," showing how Germany especially invaded and seized British markets. And the *Pall Mall Gazette* for January 11 published a cartoon showing Asquith, Churchill, and Lloyd George teaching John Bull to "curtsey nicely to the pretty gentleman"—the Kaiser.

It would, indeed, be hardly possible to exaggerate the degree to which Germany was discussed and warned against in the

[37] Jan. 5, 1910.
[38] *Daily Mail*, Jan. 7, 1910.
[39] Jan. 12, 1910.

excited election atmosphere. While one speaker or paper pointed to Germany's economic successes as a result of her protectionism and urged England to learn a lesson from her, another was accusing Germany of trying to thwart a reformation of British fiscal policy, even suggesting that her naval building was designed for the ultimate purpose of keeping the British economic door open. "Our German friends," said the *Daily Chronicle*, "ought to feel very much flattered by the conduct of the present British election."[40] The excitement persisted well into the year without any subsidence of the anti-German mood. Albert Ballin was in London that spring and described the situation to the Kaiser as follows:

Tariff Reform and a Zollverein with the Colonies are the catchwords that are on everybody's lips, and the anti-German feeling is so strong that it is scarcely possible to discuss matters with one's oldest friends, because the people over here have turned mad and talk of nothing but the next war and the protective policy of the future.[41]

The tariff question thus was one of the stones upon which the knife of Anglo-German antagonism was sharpened. As a standing threat of a tariff war, it was a serious obstacle to any lasting accord with Germany; and moreover, it called out innumerable utterances which planted more firmly than ever in the British mind the fixed idea of German enmity. This had the inevitable effect of stiffening the official policy of linking Britain with the anti-German powers on the Continent. Finally, tariff reform even suggested itself as a weapon with which to liberate England from the hazards of German naval and imperialist rivalry, for the idea got abroad that the adoption of protection by Great Britain would so cripple Germany economically that she would have to abandon all hope of disputing British supremacy. "English industries will flourish again," wrote J. Ellis Barker in 1912, "and Germany will no longer financially be able to dispute Great Britain's naval supremacy. A strong tariff will pay for a strong fleet, and enable us to preserve our

[40] Jan. 13, 1910.
[41] Huldermann, *op. cit.*, p. 160.

292

independence, wealth, and Empire. The latent resources of Great Britain and her Colonies are ample. All that Great Britain desires is to preserve and develop her country and possessions. All that she may desire from Germany she can obtain by means of a tariff. Therefore, a strong tariff will make an Anglo-German war senseless on the part of Great Britain and impossible on the part of Germany, whose resources will be crippled when Great Britain introduces Protection."[42]

4

Germany's commercial rivalry with Great Britain has been called the "soil out of which the great questions at issue between the two nations grew." What were these questions? Before 1900 there were the colonial troubles in Africa, the tilt in the Transvaal, the Samoan question, the German advance upon China, and the divergence of policy in Turkey. All of these obviously were either outgrowths of or intimately bound up with clashing economic ambitions. After 1900 the chief British grievances against Germany were the Bagdad Railway, the German intrusion into Persia, what appeared to be German bullying of France (the Moroccan question, of course), German expansionist symptoms and tendencies upon the Continent, and, finally and chiefly, the growth of the German navy. The roots of all these problems, too, lay embedded in German economic progress, ambition, and rivalry with Great Britain. The Bagdad Railway, as has been seen, began as an innocent German business enterprise and became the heart of a German interest that helped to turn the Turks against England and seemed to threaten British imperial security in Asia. From Bagdad German influence crept into Persia, at a moment disconcerting to Great Britain, and, as we have seen, the motive was trade. The other questions of German domination in Europe and the naval rivalry, it is plain from the British diplomatic documents, were the great decisive factors in the anti-German orientation of British policy. Let us consider the relation of these to the economic rivalry.

[42] Barker, *op. cit.*, p. 756.

It has been shown in the fourth chapter of this study that Germany's commercial conquests (at British expense) were heaviest in Continental Europe, that Germany succeeded in obtaining a powerful grip on Dutch, Belgian, Danish, and Russian markets, indeed, on all the markets of countries contiguous to herself (even France). In this expansion there was surely suggested an economic basis for the realization of the grandiose European ambitions of the Pan-German League—that notorious group of patriots whose fame so far outstripped their actual influence upon German national policy. A *Daily Mail* article, entitled "Germany's Rapid Progress, Increasing Wealth and Prosperity," published in 1906, may be used to illustrate how this expansion appeared to endanger England. After drawing attention to the mounting figures of Germany's trade with her neighbors the article said:

In view of these figures it is interesting to speculate on the future of Germany. Outside the Empire there are 16,000,000 people of German race in Central Europe, who must gravitate towards Germany. Here are all the elements of a military empire, with 80,000,000 citizens of homogeneous nationality—a stronger empire than Napoleon ever dreamed of.[43]

This was, of course, the avowed program of the Pan-German League—this and the economic unification of all central Europe under German hegemony. The trade significance of that ambition was estimated about this time by Mr. Reginald Tower in a report to Sir Edward Grey from Munich:

An extension of the German Zollverein over Belgium and Holland, Switzerland as well as Austria-Hungary with Bosnia and Herzegovina would cover an area of 1,322,238 kilometres, with more than 108 million inhabitants. . . . The inclusion of Roumania would add the entire Danube to the basins of the Rhine, Elbe, and Oder. The Mid-European Zollverein would thus be assured on the North Sea, on the Baltic, on the Adriatic, and the Black Sea, and geographically a territory with the most favourable opportunities for trade would be offered.[44]

[43] Sept. 16, 1906.
[44] *British Documents*, III, 352-55.

It is all very well to recall that the German Government did not draw its policies from the Pan-German League, but that does not dispose of the fact that in England there was a genuine fear that German economic expansion might prepare the way for Continental domination. "It is of course true," commented Sir Eyre Crowe in a minute on the above-quoted document, "that the Pan-German aspirations to dominion over the Low Countries and over the Adriatic are openly disavowed by all responsible people in Germany, but it would be foolish to doubt that if and when a favourable opportunity presented itself for realizing such political aspirations in whole or in part, the opportunity would be seized by the German Government with all its wonted energy." The well-known ability of the Germans to assert their influence by means of economic penetration lent considerable substance to such apprehensions.

Especially ominous to Great Britain was the sweeping commercial success realized by the Germans in the Dutch and Belgian Netherlands. A view of the trade statistics and a knowledge of what German economic penetration might signify made it appear that the tentacles of an ambitious military and naval power were being silently wrapped about the North Sea ports opposite the Thames mouth. It is safe to say that in no other part of the world did German commercial penetration suggest so directly a threat to British security.

Toward the end of the Boer War, during which Holland had naturally been strongly Anglophobe, British attention began to be drawn to the possibility of an inclusion of Holland within the German state system. An outstanding sample of literature on this matter was a book by one *"Vigilans sed Aequus,"* which appeared in 1903 and obtained wide notice. The author described the nature of German writings on the subject of Anglo-German relations, with particular reference to Germany's expansionist ambitions.[45] A *Times* leader, commenting on this work, admitted that it would be unjust to regard

[45] *German Ambitions, as They Affect Britain and the United States of America.* London, 1903. Prominently reviewed in *Times Literary Supplement*, June 5, 1903.

the views proclaimed in it as embodying the settled opinions and aims of the German people, but yet advised that "they are the views of a large and influential section." "The remedies which Germany is urged to adopt against the threatened ruin of her commerce by the exclusive trade policies of England, America, and Russia," the leader went on to say, "are, of course, whole-sale conquest and the extension of her own Zollverein. . . . Holland is particularly selected as a field for German expansion. That country has the double recommendation of affording 'the best Continental sally-port against England' and of possessing colonies, which are valuable in themselves and which command all-important positions in the immediate neighbourhood of Singapore and also in that of the new Isthmian canal. Holland is accordingly invited to enter into a close commercial union with her neighbours, who would grant her, in return, their protection and the 'rational social legislation' which Germans enjoy. But there is no concealment as to the nature of this step. It is merely a stage to the ultimate goal of incorporation."[46]

A multitude of reminders of the German danger in the Netherlands continued to appear, as, for example, a long *Times* account (in 1905) of an article in M. Clemenceau's *L'Aurore*, telling of the German commercial conquest and political designs on Antwerp.[47] The British Minister at Brussels, Sir A. Hardinge, in his annual report for 1906 on Belgium, made some observations which one may be sure did not pass unnoticed at the Foreign Office. He said in part:

Of late years the growing power of Germany has made her, what France formerly was, the supposed aspirant to hegemony in Western and Central Europe, and the avowed desire of the Pan-Germanists to absorb Holland, and at least Flemish Belgium, including Antwerp, has led the Belgians, in common with other small peoples, to regard her expansion with some anxiety. Her commercial activity, especially

---

[46] June 3, 1903.
[47] Nov. 7, 1905. *Vide* also P. J. Troelstra, "Will Holland be Germanized?" *National Review*, 1905, vol. 45; J. E. Barker, "The Absorption of Holland by Germany," *Nineteenth Century*, 1906, vol. 60, and *ibid.*, Yves Guyot, "*Le Pangermanisme, La Hollande et La Belgique.*"

at Antwerp, where there are now 40,000 Germans settled, and where the foreign trade once monopolized by England has passed mainly into German hands, is believed by many of them to portend future dangers to the maintenance of Belgian independence. . . . In its commercial and economic aspects the growth of German interests in the Low Countries is in a great measure the result of the immense development of German industry, especially in Westphalia and Rhenish Prussia, during the last twenty years, and of the export of its products through Rotterdam and Antwerp; but this increase of commercial activity has been certainly used by German patriotic expansionists in promoting German political influence. I have been assured that for many years past German clerks from Hamburg, Bremen, and other ports are encouraged and receive financial assistance from German patriotic societies to seek engagements in Belgian business houses in Antwerp, where their industry, linguistic knowledge, and thoroughness as workers make them sought after at nominal wages, and, indeed, often for nothing, and are often helped, after mastering the local ropes, to set up small businesses (which soon increase and expand) of their own; that the leading German merchants have greatly strengthened themselves matrimonially, as well as commercially, with the great commercial families of Antwerp; and that the Pan-Germanists have systematically encouraged and subsidized the Flemish movement, of which Antwerp is the center, with its Teutonism and antagonism to France. All this is believed to be deliberately planned with a view to the increase of German political as well as commercial influence, and with the object of rendering Antwerp as completely German a city as Johannesburg under Boer rule was a British one.[48]

In the light of this report, and of the fact that the French in 1907 warned the British Government against German designs on the Low Countries, it is certain that a genuine apprehension from this quarter developed in the Foreign Office. How grave this fear was it does not seem possible to say, since the subject is very little touched upon in the British documents so far published. Sir Frank Lascelles, the Berlin ambassador down to 1908,

[48] *British Documents*, III, 202-3. It may be noted, however, that Hardinge acknowledged that his acquaintance with Belgium and Antwerp were insufficient to enable him to state "with any certainty what solid ground exists for all these fears."

strove to banish such apprehensions of Germany, writing to Grey in 1907 that the Dutch "live too close to Germany to believe that she ever needed the suppression of smaller states to attain her development"; but it is well known that Lascelles' germanophil opinions were strongly discounted at the Foreign Office.[49]

Whatever may have been the measure of official fear, it is certain that on the eve of the war the vision of the Germans in control of the Dutch and Belgian North Sea ports was being conjured up very clearly and ominously before the British nation. Sir Rowland Blennerhassett, writing on "The Vital Question" in the *Fortnightly Review* in 1907, insisted that Germany would be forced to acquire new harbors for her growing navy or give up her overseas ambitions. "These harbours," he declared, "should also serve her industrial centers, which are for the most part connected with the Rhine. The great harbours where the main streams of the Rhine reach the ocean are Antwerp and Rotterdam. Many grave and influential Germans hold that it does not correspond with the fitness of things that the mouths of the noble river associated with many romantic legends and stirring memories, as well as connected with German material prosperity, should be in the hands of an extremely inferior power. It must, moreover, not be forgotten that reconstituted Germany is the heir of the old Empire, and that the Low Countries formed part of that Empire. . . . The moral forces . . . keeping Holland from Germany are becoming steadily weaker. On the other hand, the acquisition of Holland by Germany involves a change so great in the balance of naval power that England, in order to keep her supremacy at sea, will have to increase her Navy to an extent which, in view of the actual burdens, Imperial and Municipal, is serious to contemplate. Even under present conditions Germany aims at supremacy in the North Sea, which England cannot permit consistently with her practical independence. Unless, therefore, the latter maintains her Navy in such strength as to render her present position

[49] *Ibid.*, VI, 9, 14, 85-86.

at sea absolutely impregnable, the question of the North Sea will inevitably be settled by blood and iron, like the Prussian and Austrian struggle for the hegemony of Germany in 1866."[50] In the 1912 edition of his widely noticed *Modern Germany*, J. Ellis Barker pointed out that Antwerp and Rotterdam were now more important harbors for Germany than Hamburg, because of the tremendous growth of Rhenish and Westphalian industry. "It appears," he wrote, "that by far the greatest and most valuable part of Germany's trade is not carried on via Hamburg and Bremen as is usually believed, but via Rotterdam, Amsterdam, and Antwerp, and that the foreign trade carried on across the Dutch frontier grows proportionately far more quickly than the general foreign trade of Germany." These Low Country ports were, therefore, "in the same position in which Lancashire would be if Liverpool and the Manchester Ship Canal were possessed by a foreign country." The German project for extending the Ems-Dortmund Canal to the Rhine and developing the port of Emden, Barker described as a scheme for the economic coercion of Holland (by diverting traffic from Rotterdam) into some kind of an *Anschluss* with Germany. "The absorption of Holland," he went on to say, "would permanently threaten the safety of England." Therefore the acquisition would not come unless a chance for it arose in a general European war. The outlook in 1912, as Barker pictured it, was that Germany would seek "gradually to strengthen her hold upon Holland and to swallow that country by degrees. An economic arrangement between Germany and Holland may lead to a customs union, to a railway union, to the introduction of uniform coinage . . . and Holland may become German almost unnoticed. . . . In view of Germany's record, it seems natural to conclude that she will continue her triumphant progress, and many influential Dutchmen believe that the absorption of their country by Germany is inevitable, that this consummation is merely a question of time."[51] Such views got a wide hearing before the country. The *National Re-*

[50] July, 1907.
[51] Barker, *op. cit.*, Ch. IV.

view, for instance, in the fall of 1913 published several prominent articles, based on Barker's book, describing the expansionist pressure of Germany on the Netherlands.[52] "I say it deliberately and sorrowfully today," wrote Frederick Harrison in 1913, "England, Europe, civilization is in imminent peril from German expansion. . . . Belgium, northern France, Holland, either one or all may be the object of assault; or in the case of the Low Countries, of practical control without actual war . . . this is what the effective leaders of German policy are maturing today, and within five, seven, ten years may be able to force upon their Emperor and their nation."[53]

If Germany's economic advance was thus a basic circumstance giving rise to English fears of a German Continental domination, it is even clearer how intimate was the relation between trading rivalry and the critical naval question—undoubtedly the most serious problem in pre-war European international politics. That issue synthesized and epitomized in high politics all the various threads of Anglo-German antagonism. "Rightly or wrongly," wrote Sir Edward Grey in 1908, "a great part of the world has come of late years to concentrate upon the relations between England and Germany, to look to them for the chief indication of whether the peace of the world is likely to be disturbed, and to estimate this by their rivalry in naval expenditures."[54] No one familiar with British navalism would minimize the gravity of the situation in which Britain saw a German challenge to her maritime ascendancy. The *British Documents on the Origin of the War* show nothing more clearly than the fact that this was the decisive question in Anglo-German relations after 1900. The British Government stood committed to the famous "Two-Power Standard" and found it necessary to make enormous increases in the naval estimates, which, despite the terrific burden on Treasury and

[52] *"Weltpolitik,"* September-October, 1913.

[53] *English Review,* Jan., 1913.

[54] Memorandum of Aug. 6, 1908, given to King Edward and Sir Charles Hardinge for their conversations with the Kaiser at Kronberg. *British Documents,* VI, 173-74.

taxpayers, were approved almost unanimously by the country. Maritime supremacy was a cardinal doctrine in the national credo, and no serious opinion in the country even considered a retreat from it. The universal view was that for England this was a matter of life and death. Englishmen were far from challenging Germany's right to judge of her own naval needs, but it was axiomatic that no matter how far she carried her program England would maintain her established superiority, the national conviction being that to fail in this would entail the absolute ruin of the country. "History," declared the *Times* (voicing the universal credo), "teaches us that the great naval powers of the world have been successively those which possessed a flourishing and generally a preponderant maritime commerce and that those powers which have neglected to provide this commerce with an adequate defense upon the seas have always lost it in the end."[55] The generation that read so eagerly the works of Admiral Mahan knew very well that the necessity for a navy sprang from the existence of overseas trade and shipping.

The relation between commerce and navies need hardly be argued, although it may be useful to observe that it consisted of more than the argument of admirals that the growth of commerce necessitates steadily increased naval protection. If navies did no more than police the seas, the fleets of Britain, patrolling a free-trade empire and everywhere defending commercial liberty and the "open door," might have served to defend German as well as British maritime trade. Most Englishmen, indeed, since they regarded their country as the defender of commercial liberty and the independence of nations, were entirely convinced that it was best for the whole world that England should rule the seas. But navies do more than protect commerce; they also promote it. They are weapons of national imperialism for the realization of commercial aims. They create prestige, which, in regions such as the Persian Gulf and the Far East, for example, was often rewarded with economic privileges. The prestige of the British Navy was a very great asset to British trad-

[55] Leader of Jan. 24, 1906.

301

ing firms all over the world, and Germany naturally became eager to exploit her own prestige in the same way and for the same reasons. Especially intimate was the relation between national merchant carrying trade and naval expansion. The mercantilist view was that each nourishes the other. The huge British mercantile marine was both a nursery for seamen and a reserve arm of national maritime defense; so the conviction was strong that a weakening of it would weaken British naval protection. Moreover, the great navy was an important factor in the continued prosperity of the shipbuilding industry.

The same views were held and exploited in Germany. "It has been the experience of all ages," said the Government to the Reichstag in 1897, "that Navy and mercantile marine must work together and that they are so closely connected that any neglect of the one will have a correspondingly evil effect on the other.[56] The stock argument of the German Admiralty was that of trade defense and trade promotion. "It is indispensable to the continued prosperity of the Empire," declared an Admiralty publication of 1906, "to maintain and increase the economic relations of Germany with foreign countries, especially those across the seas, and to induce German labor and German capital to seek employment in overseas directions. This is the true function of the development of maritime interests in the widest sense of the words, and its due discharge under adequate protection and support . . . demands the continuous attention of the state."[57] The Berlin Correspondent of the *Times*, in 1914, suggested the economic significance of the German navy very accurately when he wrote that German shipping leaders "have always recognized that naval strength and shipping go hand in hand and that for their purposes there is not much difference between promoting a navy to 'protect' trade and promoting trade for a navy to protect."[58]

* * * * * * *

[56] Misc. Series 443. Précis of statement to Reichstag, Nov. 30, 1897, in connection with German navy bill.

[57] This work, *Die Entwicklung der deutschen Seeinteressen im letzten Jahrzehnt,* was comprehensively analyzed in *Times*, April 23, 1906.

[58] Berlin Dispatch, June 11, 1914.

In view of the foregoing, can it be seriously denied that the growth of German trade and its competition with that of Great Britain was *a*, perhaps even *the* basic cause for the anti-German orientation of British world policy? Is it not plain that the issues which divided these nations arose from and were nourished by this world set of economic circumstances? Is it not plain that the German commercial rivalry bred resentment, jealousy, and fear in England? And are not these sentiments the main ingredients of hatred? Who would deny that a dislike of Germany, rising indeed to the level of hatred, was widespread in pre-war England? The press reeked of it, and the published British diplomatic documents conceal it very unsuccessfully under the forms and conventions of diplomatic language. Professor Kantorowicz has declared that his sole surprise in reading these documents was finding in them a detestation of German policy—"a detestation which often causes the German reader to be transfixed with horror."[59] The world's greatest industrial, commercial, maritime trading power found a deadly enemy in its most successful economic rival—is it conceivable that this enmity did not spring mainly from that rivalry?

Any number of contemporary observers might be summoned to testify to British jealousy and resentment against Germany's economic advance—men such as Ramsay Macdonald, Norman Angell, Keir Hardie, H. G. Wells, and a host of others. "You might sink the German navy," declared Hardie in the House of Commons in 1911, "but the invasion of the German trader would still continue, and it is the German trader who is being resented. All this preparation to beat Germany is intended to cripple the German trader, and prevent him encroaching on our market . . . all this outcry against Germany is based solely and exclusively upon the fact, let the reason be what it may, that the German trader is encroaching more and more on the markets of the world which have hitherto been believed to be the monopoly of the British trader."[60] An overstatement? Undoubtedly. It would be a grave historical error to ignore British

[59] *Op. cit.*, p. 381.
[60] Parliamentary Debates, 5th S., V. 22, pp. 1925-26.

dislike of German militarism and political institutions, disapproval of German diplomatic methods, distaste for German manners, and distrust of German political ambitions, as factors in building the mountain of Germanophobia in Great Britain. But it is surely quite reasonable to doubt whether Englishmen would have seen so much to detest in Germany had the commercial rivalry been nonexistent. The spirit of commercialism had come to penetrate the British nation very deeply, and under its deteriorating influence, jealousy, fear, and hatred found freer play. The British Government may stand acquitted of making war for the ends of trade, but that the anti-German orientation of the British mind and British world policy sprang chiefly from the great economic competition seems incontrovertibly proved.

APPENDIX I

THE following is a compilation of selected statements and information taken from the replies to a questionnaire sent out by the Foreign Office to H. M. Diplomatic and Consular Officers, in 1885, to ascertain what impediments to British trade existed in the various regions of the world and what diversions of British trade to competitive nations had taken place. The complete replies were all published in the Report of the Royal Commission on the Depression of Trade and Industry (Reports of Commissioners, 1886, vols. 9, 10, 11).

WESTERN EUROPE

Lisbon, Portugal, December, 1885.—"The Germans are of late years underselling English manufacturers in the Lisbon market in many articles, the principal of these being woolens and hardware, refined sugar and rice, and there has been no doubt some transfer of our trade to Belgium and some to France, though in far less degree in these latter cases than in that of Germany."—vol, 10, p. 276.

Barcelona, Spain, November, 1885.—"The special impediments to the extension of trade between Great Britain and this district are the customs laws, the high port dues charged . . .; the competition created by the favourable differential tariff to Germany and France, and the maladministration of the law."—vol. 10, p. 320.

Malaga, Spain, November, 1885.—"France and Germany have doubtless profited considerably by the unfair treatment to which England is subjected under the present Spanish tariff and have already got in more than the thin edge, since, no doubt, a large portion of goods formerly obtained from England, such as machinery, hardware, cutlery, earthenware, glass and porcelain, linen, cotton and cloth textiles, and certain goods of inferior quality are now imported from those countries to replace those which were formerly obtained from England."—vol. 10, pp. 320-21.

Cadiz, Spain, December, 1885.—"A large portion of the import trade from Great Britain has been transferred to France, Germany and Belgium. Large orders for manufactured iron have been executed in those countries, which have strengthened their position by increasing direct steam communications with their ports, thus indirectly injuriously affecting British shipping interests also."—vol. 10, p. 323.

Corunna, Spain, November, 1885.—"The following branches of trade formerly imported from Great Britain have almost all been transferred to Germany, France and Belgium: machinery, railway material, steel rails, bridges, cranes and kindred manufactures."—vol. 10, p. 323.

Bilbao, Spain, November, 1885.—"Many articles, such as linen, yarns, cloths, cutlery, hardware, steel, railway plant, machinery, rails, beer, etc., that formerly were almost exclusively obtained from England, are now to a very large extent imported from other countries, such as Germany, Belgium and France."—vol. 10, p. 324.

Rouen, France, December, 1885.—"The spun cotton yarns, previously sent here from Great Britain, are to a considerable extent now supplied from Switzerland."—vol. 10, p. 148.

Antwerp, Belgium, January, 1886.—"The gradual progress made by native manufactures in most branches of industry, some of which had hitherto been supplied principally by England, is a fact of considerable importance in connexion with this inquiry. The progress referred to applies especially to certain kinds of machinery and iron manufactures, as also to manufactures of wool and yarn, certain descriptions of which are now in a position to compete with British products in our own markets. The frequent strikes which have occurred of late years in Great Britain have been the means of encouraging foreign competition; quite independently of this, however, the progress of continental commerce and industry tends to displace ours in Belgian as well as in other markets. British manufactures, however, still retain their supremacy in some particular branches, such as woolen fabrics, cutlery, agricultural implements, sanitary engineering products, paper, and various qualities of hardware and pottery, all of which command a higher price than the corresponding Belgian products. Should it appear, however, that the trade in British commodities shows a tendency to decline, it is satisfactory to note that a direct trade has been springing up of late between Belgium and various British colonies. So marked has been this movement that some of the principal steamship companies have found it to their interest to send their large ocean steamers

306

to Antwerp to compete for Belgian and other Continental produce for export, chiefly to the East."—vol. 11. p. 459.

Brussels, Belgium, January, 1886.—"A few years since there was imported from England to this district a considerable quantity of iron piping and tubes, but this branch of trade appears now to be almost entirely in the hands of the Germans. This district is also now very largely supplied by Germany with felt hats, which at one time was almost exclusively an English import. The amount of boots and shoes and uppers, which a few years since were imported in a considerable quantity from England, has considerably fallen off, and the trade in this branch seems to have fallen into French hands; a great many are also now manufactured here. Germany seems to be competing closely with most English imports, as well as with the productions of this country, and it is complained that Germany is ruining many Belgian industries."—vol. 11, p. 461.

The Hague, Holland, December, 1885.—"Germany is stated to compete successfully in this country, as regards machinery and the cheaper kinds of carpets, with British manufacturers, whilst native industry now supplies the home markets to a great extent with flannels, blankets, etc., which were formerly imported chiefly from Great Britain."—vol. 10, p. 260.

Berlin, Germany, February, 1886.—The depression of English trade to Germany was attributed chiefly to the German tariff. The Berlin Consul-General drew attention to the direct importation, rather than by way of England, of several colonial goods, and to the displacement of British manufactures by German goods. The Hamburg Consul-General called attention to the displacement of English by German products, and stated that Colonial goods were now coming in large quantities direct to Hamburg, instead of by way of England, a movement which, he said, was likely to increase. The Frankfort Consul-General cited the displacement by German goods of the products of Bradford, Manchester, Sheffield and Birmingham, and pointed to the competition offered by the German chemical industry. The Düsseldorf Consul mentioned rolled iron girders imported from Belgium in preference to English products. The Stettin and Königsberg Consuls also stressed the advance of the home trade which was displacing British imported goods. The latter also called attention to the growth of direct imports at the expense of the British entrepot trade.—vol. 10, pp. 157-199.

Munich, Bavaria, March, 1886.—"The chief impediments to the extension of commercial relations between Bavaria and Great Britain are . . . the high freight costs charged upon all articles of trade; and . . . the increasing duties upon goods imported into Germany, and which duties are unmistakably intended to hamper the introduction of English products. . . . But it may be remarked that English goods, being invariably superior in workmanship and durability, supposing them to be of equal quality and cost, are preferred to the wares produced in Bavaria. This predilection for English goods, unfortunately, has led to a very large trade in bad imitations, which, though bearing little or no resemblance to the original save in price, are gradually driving English goods from German markets. The German imperial law with regard to trade marks is necessarily in force in Bavaria, and has in some degree counteracted the prevailing practice of disposing of spurious goods under fictitious and better names. Notwithstanding this law, however, the imitation of foreign, and especially of English, goods is carried on to a large extent. They are brought into the market in such a form which enables them to evade the law. . . . British commerce with this country, and indeed with the rest of Germany, has certainly diminished within the last ten years, but the cause of this decrease must be attributed less to the quality of goods exported by England than to the progress made by German manufacturers. . . . It is barely to be hoped, therefore, that the ground lost by England in its commercial relations with this part of Germany will easily be recovered."—vol. 11, pp. 443-44.

SCANDINAVIAN EUROPE

Copenhagen, Denmark, December, 1885.—"Considerable quantities of the iron and steel which in former years were got from England are now bought by the consumers here in the German markets, the only reason being that they can buy a better article for the same money; in other words, they can buy steel or iron plates cheaper in Germany than in England, when regard is paid to the quality."—vol. 10, p. 114.

Stockholm, Sweden, December, 1885.—"A considerable amount of the import trade from Great Britain in iron and manufactured goods has passed over to Germany and Belgium, especially machinery and textiles. Sweden has also imported of late years cotton and pork direct from America, thus diminishing the transit trade of Great Britain in these articles."—vol. 10, p. 329.

Gothenburg, Sweden, December, 1885.—"No transfer has taken place from this district to other countries of trade . . . of Great Britain, excepting that lines of Swedish steamers now regularly ply between this port direct to the principal ports of Holland, Belgium, France, Spain, and Portugal, all such trade having previously passed through British ports, while the Germans have lately opened up a direct line of steamers between this port and German ports to the United States of America, taking and bringing back passengers and produce which likewise hitherto passed through British ports."—vol. 10, pp. 332-33.

CENTRAL EUROPE

Berne, Switzerland, December, 1885.—"It is a matter of no uncertainty that England's most formidable rival in Swiss commerce is the German Empire, whose trade with this country has enormously increased since 1870. In some branches, indeed, it has almost completely ousted British manufactures."—vol. 10, p. 347.

Rome, Italy, December, 1885.—The Secretary of the Rome Embassy offered some reasons for the decreased demand for certain manufactures in the Italian markets, and pointed out certain obstacles to British trade. He cited the rise of North Italian industry, assisted by the protective tariff, and foreign competition, especially German, now assisted by the new St. Gothard Railway, as among the chief difficulties to be met with in the Italian market. He wrote in part: "The most serious competition would appear to come from Germany, and to exist in the less bulky articles of trade, such as crockery, glass, cutlery, hardware, chemicals, surgical instruments, earthenware and fancy goods generally. In these articles France, Belgium, Switzerland and Austria also manage to undersell Great Britain, but in a lesser degree than Germany does. The reason for this successful foreign competition would seem to be a higher standard of technical education, greater activity in the employment of commercial travellers speaking Italian, greater attention paid to the wants of the Italian market, greater facilities for delivery and for payment, and above all the advantage of shorter distances afforded by the St. Gothard Railway. . . . All the consular reports in speaking of foreign and especially of German

309

competition draw attention to the absence in Italy of British commercial travellers. Surprise has constantly been expressed to me during my inquiries, by Government officials, professional men, merchants and shop-keepers that Italy and Rome should be so neglected by British commercial travellers, whilst German travellers are everywhere, and by their intelligence, activity and pertinacity secure quantities of orders no matter how small. These German travellers, I am informed, all speak Italian, having generally served as clerks in houses of business where they are content with the smallest salaries, seeking compensation in knowledge of the language and of the business."—vol. 10, pp. 207-9.

Rome, Italy, December, 1885.—"Terms for payment by British manufacturers are also an impediment as regards British trade. Importers find great facilities with manufacturers of other countries, Germans particularly, who allow credit up to six months, and even more. German manufacturers take up any small order, while British manufacturers don't care for small orders, which must go through wholesale merchants, and prices are dearer that way. German and French manufacturers are more in connexion with importers than are British manufacturers. They send round numbers of commercial travellers who consult their wishes and communicate with them in Italian or French. German business houses even correspond in Italian."—vol. 10, pp. 245-46.

Milan, Italy, December, 1885.—"British manufacturers could considerably augment their trade within the Milan district and in Italy generally if, instead of trusting their business generally to a single representative, they employed their own travellers who should be well acquainted with the Italian language. This system has been largely adopted by German houses, and I am informed that there are twenty or more German travellers to one British."— vol. 10, p. 208.

Genoa, Italy, December, 1885.—"A good many transfers of trade have taken place within the last twenty years. In the first place colonials, cotton and petroleum, up to about that time used to come, for the greater part from England, whereas they now come from their places of origin direct. . . . Then the opening of the Saint Gothard route has brought certain qualities of German iron down even as far as Genoa, and brings a quantity of iron and coal as far south as Milan, and both German and Swiss cotton and woolen goods are favoured by that route in their competition with us for so much of this market as native industry has still left open."—vol. 10, p. 241.

Leghorn, Italy, December, 1885.—"In cotton prints England has . . . lost ground, partly owing to native production, but also in great measure to the introduction of German and Austrian fabrics, which are able to compete with ours, both as regards price and taste in designs. Germany is also taking the lead in velvets and now furnishes a larger amount than England, their dyes, particularly black, being preferred here."—vol. 10, p. 247.

Naples, Italy, December, 1885. "A good deal of the British iron trade has been diverted to Belgium and Germany and to local manufacturers."—vol. 10, p. 247.

Palermo, Sicily, December, 1885.—"German and Swiss goods introduced through the northern land frontiers of Italy are being brought into competition with our direct trade with this island. The opening of the St. Gothard tunnel has facilitated German importations, which may, in the course of time, materially injure British trade, and if the Germans, by a better system of education of the lower classes and harder labour, can produce the same article cheaper than we can, the facilities of transit being equal, our trade must necessarily give way to theirs, particularly when it is fostered by commercial travellers who frequent the place."—vol. 10, p. 249.

Massina, Italy, December, 1885.—Here was reported a considerable transfer of British trade to other countries. The British earthenware trade was "almost extinct," being replaced by German, French, and Italian products. Woolen cloth was now coming largely from Germany, and cutlery and hardware were almost wholly of German importation. Alkaloids, chemicals and medicines were now coming largely from Stuttgart and Leipzig instead of England.—vol. 10, p. 251.

Catania, Italy, December, 1885.—"Germany and Italy have absorbed a part of British trade, which would otherwise have been imported from Great Britain into this district."—vol. 10, p. 252.

Vienna, Austria, December, 1885.—The Secretary of the Embassy reported a great increase in Austrian industry and a falling off in British imports, due to the protective tariff. "It may fairly be stated that Germany and Switzerland, owing to their being neighbouring countries with less expense for freights, have taken over a considerable portion of our imports; also Belgium."—vol. 10, pp. 101-3.

Buda Pesth, Hungary, January, 1886.—"Articles formerly imported from England are made in Austria, and to a lesser degree imported from Germany. . . . Generally speaking the depression of British trade in Hungary has not yet reached its climax, and in all probability it will before long be restricted to articles of the finest descriptions which the industries of Austria and Germany are not as yet capable of producing. . . . The principal causes of the recent depression of British trade with Hungary are to be found, especially in regard to the textile industry, in the increased import duties imposed by the Austro-Hungarian tariff revision in 1882. Under shelter of the raised duties new factories in Austria have been called into existence, while older ones have been enlarged and their operations extended. The products of these now have the command of the Hungarian market. Another reason why the importation of textiles has decreased is to be traced to the development of the industry of Germany, which is able to compete in point of quality with that of England, while owing to propinquity and to cheap railway tariffs it is placed in an advantageous position. In regard to iron and steel goods, and to machinery, the influence of the increased duties has been sensible, but here again the development of Austrian and German, and to a lesser degree of Hungarian industry, has obviously affected British trade."—vol. 10, pp. 105-7.

Serajevo, Bosnia, December, 1885.—"Cotton yarn used to come exclusively from England, and the yearly importation was estimated at about 1,600 to 2,000 tons. Now only one superior kind is imported, and of that not more than 100 tons. Some raw articles of commerce which formerly came from England now come from Germany and Switzerland, but in very small quantities."—vol. 10, p. 103.

EASTERN EUROPE

St. Petersburg, Russia, January, 1886.—"An increase of importation from Germany and Belgium of some sorts of iron, tin plates and machinery has been latterly observable in the Russian customs returns, and these articles are beginning to compete successfully in the Russian markets with British products of a similar character."—vol. 10, p. 294.

Ekaterinoslav, Russia, January, 1886.—"The most marked transfer is that of some kinds of agricultural machinery to America;

bar and rod iron to Belgium. Hardware is now to a large extent received from Belgium, Austria, and Germany, also agricultural machinery from the two last named countries. Domestic utensils, bedsteads, enamelled ware, agricultural implements, iron, steel, crockery, chemicals, and cement are now more extensively made in Russia and Poland; indeed there has been a general improvement in home trade manufactures; and linen and woolen goods, cloth, etc., are now received from Poland, St. Petersburg, and Moscow."—vol. 10, p. 299.

Warsaw, Poland, January, 1886.—"A good many articles, especially in the iron, metal and textile branches, formerly imported from Great Britain, are now supplanted by German goods, because the latter are cheaper. However, British articles in the same branches are still in demand, a proof of which is that German makers are often obliged to stamp and label their goods with English trade marks and inscriptions."—vol. 10, p. 302.

Nicolaiev, Russia, January, 1886.—"The hardware and metal trades have suffered considerably, owing to the competition offered by Germany, France and Belgium, which countries have supplied cheap imitations of English goods. Now Russia herself is largely supplying her own markets with not only hardware and cutlery, but also cloth, linen, carpets, cotton goods, cement, agricultural implements, and machinery, which formerly were supplied by Great Britain."—vol. 10, p. 305.

Odessa, Russia, December, 1885.—"A general tendency is experienced in the substitution of German for English manufactures, often sold, especially so in the case of hardware, under English trade marks and names. The Germans are able to produce a cheap article which, although inferior to the English article, meets with ready purchasers on account of its cheapness."—vol. 10, p. 307.

Bucharest, Rumania, November, 1885.—It was stated that the British were losing their hold upon the Rumanian trade to Austrians and Germans, who gave more extended credit and enjoyed better transport facilities. It was further stated that the British did not study the market closely enough, and did not manufacture the cheap goods desired in Rumania. Since the opening of the Suez Canal a considerable portion of colonial goods were diverted from Great Britain to Genoa and Marseilles, and recently Austria and Germany had entered into strong competition with Great Britain for this trade. Sugar had been almost wholly diverted to Germany and Austria-Hungary, and Belgium was supplying rails, iron girders, bridge work, railway materials, etc., which were formerly supplied by Great Britain. Ploughs which formerly came from England and Buda Pesth now came from Germany, and likewise a certain class of engineers' tools.—vol. 10, pp. 281-88.

Sofia, Bulgaria, November, 1885.—Here a Russian competition in cotton goods which had sprung up during the past three or four years was noted.—vol. 10, pp. 108-10.

Athens, Greece, February, 1886.—"Woolen cloths, soft goods, iron, hardware, machinery, glassware and pottery, which were formerly chiefly imported from the United Kingdom come now exclusively from Germany, Belgium and France. Germany and Belgium have at present most of the iron trade; the 'merchant' iron and girders, formerly brought in large quantities from England, come now chiefly from Belgium, and almost all of the narrow gauge railways in course of construction in Greece are imported from Germany, where, I am told, a small bounty is paid by the Government on the exportation of such articles, enabling the German manufacturers to undersell English firms in the same trade. A great deal of machinery and small hardware is likewise imported from Germany. . . . As regards the transfer of British trade to Germany, our greatest rival in Greece, it has been brought about by reason of cheaper costs of production, greater facilities of transport from German industrial centers to Trieste, and the low rates of freight . . . of the Austro-Hungarian Steamship Company; the establishment in Germany of 'forwarding agencies' which undertake to forward goods direct from the manufactory to the importer at fixed rates, all expenses included, so the latter knows exactly what any article will cost him on delivery; and, lastly by reason of what I can only call the 'conservatism' of the British manufacturer, who does not move with the times, or sufficiently consult the taste and wishes of the foreign customers. The British manufacturer does not understand that he is no longer the 'boss,' so to speak, of the manufactory industries of the world, and that of late years other countries can, and do, produce an article almost, if not quite, as good as his, at a lower price and more suitable as a rule to the tastes of the nation for which it is destined. If you ask an English manufacturer to alter the shape of an article to suit the requirements of foreign markets, he is full of excuses and generally refuses the request, and there is no doubt that the sale of many articles formerly purchased in the United Kingdom has, from this dislike of any change on the part of the British manufacturer, passed to other countries. The German manufacturer, on the other hand, has no prejudices; if he finds that an article of a certain shape, etc., can command a ready sale in any particular country, he makes it, however foreign it may be to his own taste or wants."—vol. 10. pp. 204-5.

Crete, January, 1886.—"Austrian and German trades are increasing on a larger proportion than those of all other nations, in consequence of the direct communications which exist between Trieste and this island by means of the steamers of the Austro-Hungarian Lloyd. The example of German and Austrian manufacturers of sending samples with the prices at which goods could be delivered here, if followed, would tend to promote the extension of British trade, as it does that of those two countries. . . . It may be foreseen that important transfers are likely to take place on such of the cotton and woolen fabrics as may be manufactured at equal prices in Germany and Austria, both of which countries, being in closer proximity than Great Britain, can send here their products at a lower expense." —vol. 10, p. 361.

Philippopolis, Turkish Roumelia, November, 1885.—"British trade holds the first rank in the province, and . . . has remained fairly steady during the last five years, the only decline being in common hardware and cheaper articles of cutlery, where Austrian and German wares, by lower prices and long credits, have succeeded in displacing them."—vol. 10, p. 336.

Salonica, Turkey, January, 1886.—"An important feature in the trade of Salonica is the growing increase in the importation of Belgian manufactures, some of which, such as iron, copper, starch, candles and glassware, affording better prices, are able to compete successfully with similar goods from England. Hardware is now greatly imported from Solingen, in Germany, being much cheaper than British, although much inferior. In order to compete British manufacturers must make lower class goods."—vol. 10, p. 367.

Constantinople, January, 1886.—"In cotton yarns, grey goods and prints, Manchester still retains the large bulk of the trade, but Switzerland and Italy have been supplying Turkey red yarns, and French and Austrian cotton prints are gradually working their way

315

into the market. The woolen goods of Austria and Germany are being successfully brought into competition with Yorkshire fabrics, and ready made clothing has passed into the hands of Austria. In hardware, cutlery, and small wares, Germany, Austria, and Italy have nearly superseded Birmingham and Sheffield. In the item of paper, Italy and Austria have monopolized the trade; British window glass is superseded by that of Belgium, and glassware and crockery are now imported from Austria and France, and Italian silks have replaced those of England in the Ottoman market. . . . British trade is not increasing in due proportion to the trade of foreign countries."—vol. 10, p. 353.

COUNTRIES ADJACENT TO EUROPE

Angora, Turkey, December, 1885.—"The import of articles of clothing, glass and hardware has to the extent of 25 per cent passed from the hands of British dealers into those of Austrian and Swiss. Fifteen years ago clothing of English manufacture was largely imported, but has been almost entirely replaced by Austrian articles which are sought after on account of their cheapness."—vol. 10, p. 359.

Beirut, Syria, December, 1885.—"Germany and Switzerland both compete to a small extent with Manchester in supplying cotton goods. Whereas formerly this trade was entirely in the hands of Manchester firms, these two countries now have found it possible to supply cotton handkerchiefs, some woolen goods, and red cotton twist at a rate which enable them to compete successfully in the sale of these articles. The last named article is, however, English twist dyed in Germany, German manufacturers being able to dye more cheaply than English. But this competition is not very serious, and does not in any way threaten the supremacy at present maintained by Manchester, the percentage of foreign cotton goods sold here being very small indeed."—vol. 10, p. 359.

Trebizond, December, 1885.—"The following transfer of formerly British imports is taking place: English steel, silk stuffs and velveteens, are being superseded by Austrian and Italian; coffee and sugar by French and Austrian; spirits by American, Austrian, French and Russian, crockery and glass by Austrian and German."—vol. 11, p. 486.

Alexandria, Egypt, January, 1886.—The consul here reported

"Sheffield and Birmingham trade diverted to Germany."—vol. 10, pp. 119-124.

Cairo, Egypt, December, 1885.—"In cutlery a slight transfer has taken place in favour of Germany. German goods are often introduced with imitated English trade marks and names."—vol. 10, pp. 119-24.

Tripoli, December, 1885.—"Many articles hitherto imported through Malta from England, such as drugs, earthenware, glass, hardware, etc., are now mostly brought from France, Italy, and Germany."—vol. 10, p. 373.

Tunis, December, 1885.—"The iron trade has been transferred from England to Belgium. The transfer, which dates from 1881, is all but complete. The causes are two-fold, first and mainly the cheaper rates of freight from Antwerp to Tunis, and secondly, the cheapness in first cost."—vol. 10, p. 351.

Morocco, January, 1886.—"Within the last three or four years Germany has been endeavouring to develop a trade with Morocco, and appears to be succeeding in introducing German goods into the country, particularly cloth and hardware. She may possibly draw to herself a portion of the trade hitherto in our hands, but it is not anticipated that any serious damage will be done to British trade by her competition."—vol. 10, pp. 254-55.

Balearic Islands, January, 1886.—Some transfer in the collier trade was reported. Coal formerly came in English bottoms, but now foreign vessels were coming into competition, especially Spanish sailing vessels from the northern ports. Also there was reported "slight competition in the importation of German machinery."—vol. 10, pp. 324-25.

Canary Islands, November, 1885.—"The beer import trade, which was formerly almost entirely from England, is now to a very great extent supplied by Germany; English beer, as a rule being considered too expensive to allow a profit, especially bottled beer." — vol. 10, p. 325.

The Azores, December, 1885.—"During the past 15 years cotton and woolen manufactured goods as well as hardware have been imported from Germany and America to the detriment of similar importations from Great Britain."—vol. 10, p. 281.

Madeira, November, 1885.—"No actual transfer to other countries of any particular branch of British trade has taken place; but

Hamburg is now competing with England for the supply of various articles, such as stationery, fancy work, lamps, cigars, etc., which were formerly imported from Great Britain."—vol. 10, p. 280.

NORTH AND SOUTH AMERICA

Washington, D.C., January, 1886.—"British trade has suffered . . . but no extensive transfer of trade to other countries is shown, although it is true that at New Orleans and Galveston French and German houses are supplanting the British, the latter not meeting American requirements. . . . The tariff is shown to be the only impediment to British trade."—vol. 10, p. 381.

New Orleans, December, 1885.—"This district was French, was Spanish, is cosmopolitan. It became committed to Continental markets, and as there are now next to no British importers, our import trade does not have a fair chance. The little we have had during my experience has dwindled and gone into French and German hands, owing (in the case of iron wares) to neglect in 'putting up' and marking the goods, and in other respects to want of enterprise. I think that if British merchants and manufacturers would allow themselves to disregard preconceived opinions, and to learn that conditions of supply and demand have changed, they might extend their trade."—vol. 10, pp. 411-12.

Mexico, January, 1886.—"It is only too evident that the commercial supremacy the Americans have already wrested from our countrymen will, before long, become so absolute, as practically to exclude a large portion of British goods from this market. It remains to be proved whether the British commercial world is content to submit quietly and without an effort to be driven from a market, which, though insignificant, comparatively speaking, is unquestionably destined, ere long, by its geographical position, by the extent of its territory, and by the density of its population, to be one of the most important, if not the most important, of the Spanish American Republics."—vol. 11, pp. 67-8.

Nicaragua, January, 1886.—The consul here wrote of "the introduction from the United States of high class cotton goods, and from Germany of low class cotton or woolen goods and hardware. The English brands of beer have been entirely superseded by the light classes of beer, imported from the United States and Germany."—vol. 11, p. 63.

318

Costa Rica, December, 1885.—Some transfers of British trade were here reported: "the trade with the United States of America and Germany is increasing, especially in such articles as long knives, axes, shovels, American cloth, unbleached cottons, fruits, sewing machines, saddlery, toys, etc."—vol. 11, p. 63.

Caracas, Venezuela, January, 1886.—"In order to contend with rivals of other nationalities British merchants or manufacturers should send out agents making it their business, besides advertising goods, to study carefully the requirements of the consumer which are often of so whimsical and trivial a nature in themselves as to pass entirely unheeded by the British manufacturer. To illustrate again my meaning I must mention that when travelling through Central America a few years ago I put up at an Englishman's house. In his 'store' I observed a vast stock of machetes, a kind of cutlass used by the natives, some of British but most of German manufacture. On inquiring which was preferred, I was told 'the German unquestionably' on account of the peculiarity of design, quite unimportant in itself, which happened to be the fashion of the moment, although the discarded British article was superior in quality."—vol. 10, p. 420.

Caracas, Venezuela, November, 1885.—"A fair amount of manufactured goods and hardware, which were exclusively imported from Great Britain into Venezuela, are now introduced from the United States and Germany."—vol. 10, p. 422.

La Guaira, Venezuela, January, 1886.—"In the dry goods line and in beer I believe some of the business formerly done with the United Kingdom has been transferred to Germany and even to the United States, although in a much smaller scale; principally owing to most of the mercantile houses of the kind here being German, and German goods, if inferior, being cheaper."—vol. 10, p. 421.

Puerto Cabello, Venezuela, December, 1885.—"The importation of dry goods from the United States and of iron ware from Germany has increased in the last five or ten years, as these goods come to stand cheaper imported from those countries, and though in quality generally inferior to the English manufactures, are preferable for our markets at present, on account of the general poverty."—vol. 10, p. 422.

Cuidad Bolivar, Venezuela, December, 1885.—"I consider that a transfer in the trade of dry goods, hardware, and some other articles

. . . has taken place from the United Kingdom to Germany, France and the United States. In the case of Germany particularly this is not to be wondered at, as the principal merchants of this place are all German."—vol. 10, p. 423.

Maracaibo, Venezuela, December, 1885.—"The United States of America receive today most of the exports of this consular district . . . and consequently control a great deal of the imports. Germany also, and France, and other nationalities, are trying to do the same. A few years past we had from 40 to 50 arrivals of steamers under the British flag, and some twenty sailing vessels displayed the colours of Great Britain; no more steamers are coming, and occasionally only one or two sailing vessels are seen; other European flags, especially the German, are constantly seen in our harbour."—vol. 10, p. 425.

Guayaquil, Ecuador, November, 1885.—"It may justly be stated that the principal commerce of the country is carried on with Great Britain. In the export business a considerable amount of cocoa, which in previous years always went to the London market, has been diverted to Hamburg, on account, it is stated, of better prices ruling there, and of a lower rate of expense. Nearly the whole of the ivory nut trade has been diverted to the same port, due to the large increase in the consumption in Germany of that article. It is also to be noted that the carrying trade in sailing vessels has been almost entirely monopolized by German sailing vessels, owing to their being generally of more conveniently small size than the average of British vessels; but at the same time it must be observed that the principal part of the carrying trade of the Republic is performed by steamers, and these are all British vessels. An attempt has been made to bring American prints into competition with those of Manchester, but this has not succeeded. There is no doubt that the establishment of agencies for British manufactories, properly supplied with samples, etc., would have a good effect in stimulating trade, but considering the slow increase of population no large extension could be looked for."—vol. 11, p. 470.

Buenos Aires, May, 1886.—"It would . . . appear that during the period . . . (1876-1886) the ordinary trade of the country has increased 128 per cent, and the proportion corresponding to Great Britain has advanced . . . 141 per cent. Some of the other nations have, however, increased in larger ratio. Germany, Belgium, and the United States have about quadrupled; France . . . just doubled her trade, and it would have been greater but for the recent establishment of direct German lines of steamers, many German goods having formerly been imported via France."—vol. 11, p. 59.

Uruguay, November, 1885.—"Iron girders and fencing wire were formerly imported from England, but now are brought from Belgium. This change has been the result not so much of quality as of price."—vol. 10, p. 419.

Peru, December, 1885.—"The severest competition which British trade in Peru has to anticipate is with regard to American and German hardware, and German and French woolens."—vol. 10, pp. 267-8.

THE FAR EAST

Reports from China, 1885-86.—No evidence of any serious German competition nor of any transfer of British trade to other countries is indicated, but the consul at Taiwan reported: "More petty articles of German origin are imported than formerly, mostly window glass, cheap soaps, patent medicines, pacotille and shoddy of all kinds." The consul at Hankow wrote: "There is a general belief that German needles and buttons and Japanese matches are driving the British from the field," although this was not stated for a certainty. From Chinkiang came this statement: "American drills and American sheetings are coming into favour here, but their imports remain less than that of English goods of the same kind. In matches, Germany, Norway and Japan share the trade with Bryant and May's English goods of the same kind."—vol. 11, pp. 463-71.

Tokyo, Japan, February, 1886.—"There has been for several years past a determined and energetic effort to push German trade all over the East, by shipping cheaper imitations of British goods. In woolens this is specially noticeable. Belgium, also, has successfully competed as regards iron, a large proportion of Japan's importation of that metal being now of Belgian make, though I understand that the pigs from which the iron is refined are usually English, shipped from the eastern coast to Belgium, and there worked up, as the sea freight from England to Antwerp is very low and the scale of wages prevailing in Belgium considerably under that in England. Pig iron can be shipped in this way from England, and after having been manufactured in Belgium ultimately exported at a lower cost than similar manufactures can from England direct. I hear,

321

however, from a trustworthy source, that a mutual arrangement has been recently concluded between the leading iron and steel manufacturers in England, Germany, and Belgium by which ruinous competition between them will in future be avoided, and a pro-rata distribution secured between them of all eastern business in those staples. The terms of the arrangement are, I understand, that all orders from eastern countries shall be divided, irrespective of the nationality of the manufacturer to whom they are given in the first instance, between the countries I have mentioned, in proportion of five tenths to England, three tenths to Germany and two tenths to Belgium. As to the causes of the falling off of British trade, it must be borne in mind that London has ceased to be the distributing center of the silk trade; that the Continent of Europe is supplying itself direct with various productions of this country, instead of buying in London; that Belgian ore can undersell English, and that Bombay and India generally is competing for the trade in yarns. Germany and France also now share with England Japan's shipbuilding orders, while the former supplies nearly all her war material. The business of furnishing Japan with rails and rolling stock of railways, previously transacted by England alone, has likewise been in part transferred to Germany, and the same is true of many other manufactured goods. In addition to this competition, Japan is gradually manufacturing for herself cotton yarns to a small extent, and various piece goods. Manufacturers in England are accustomed to large orders, to established markets, and to no very marked change in the tastes of consumers. German manufacturers, on the other hand, do not disregard small orders; they are eager to meet the tastes of the market and adapt themselves with greater readiness to the varying capricious needs of the Japanese for manufactured cotton and woolens, etc., etc., than do the mill owners of Great Britain, who rather despise a small trade, and will not alter their productions to suit a demand that does not offer a certainty of extensive future business. In this way British manufacturers have lost some trade that would otherwise have gone to them, as for instance, mousselines de laine. These goods are made entirely of wool, which may be considered specially an English staple article, yet until the last three years almost all the mousselines sold in Japan were of French manufacture, and now they are divided between France and Germany, the latter country making the cheaper inferior kind.

Hardly a piece comes from Great Britain. . . . English manufacturers will, undoubtedly, have to give in the future a closer attention to the wants of the smaller foreign countries in order to retain the position they have hitherto occupied, against the competition of Continental Europe, and England will also, before many years, have to meet a new competition in China and Japan, due to the investment of European capital in various manufacturing directions in Asia, and she will likewise have to bear in mind that both in China and Japan labor is very cheap; that the price of coal in many places is low, and that there seems no reason why many articles of large consumption hitherto imported from abroad should not be made in Japan. British merchants had, some months ago, some reason to complain of official influence being brought to bear to promote German commercial interests in Japan. Government contracts were given to German firms, and there can be no doubt that there have been cases where this class of business has been influenced to the detriment of the British merchant. On the whole, however, British merchants have not much to complain of on this score; they have probably enjoyed a fair share of these favours in the past, and if they take the same amount of trouble as the Germans do they may likewise secure them in the future. To obtain Government business and contracts necessitates, however, much activity. It requires frequent intercourse with the Japanese, and demands great forbearance and the exercise of much patience and good temper. There are individual Englishmen in Yokohama who are not one whit behind the merchants of other nationalities in the exercise of these qualities, but many are content to work on the old lines, and do not seem to keep up with all the progressive movements in Japan, and thus find themselves at a disadvantage in business transactions with the Japanese."—vol. 11, pp. 472-73.

Kanagawa, Japan, December, 1885.—"A certain proportion of British trade has been diverted during the past six years to Germany, and also the United States."—vol. 11, p. 475.

Hyogo, Japan, December, 1885.—"Probably some transfer has taken place to German and French steamers of the carrying trade between this port and Continental Europe, but I am not of opinion that this will be found to have resulted in a diminution of the total of the British carrying trade. In imports, under metals . . . the imports of British nail rod iron has been to some extent supplanted by the importation of French and Belgian. . . . Further, a transfer has, undoubtedly, taken place from British to German firms in the importation of iron, machinery and plant, on Government orders; and, as a consequence of that, partly also on private business in these articles. The articles imported remain mostly of English origin, only the intermediary being different."—vol. 11, p. 477.

Nagasaki, Japan, December, 1885.—"There is no doubt that a large portion of the produce, which 15 years ago or less went first to London and was thence distributed, has since been shipped in increased quantities direct to ports on the Continent of Europe and more recently to America. In this connection I may mention having been informed that the heavy dock charges to which goods are subjected in London as compared with America and Continental ports makes it very disadvantageous to merchants to ship to the former." —vol. 11, p. 478.

Bangkok, Siam, February, 1886.—"The trade in piece goods has to some extent been transferred to India and to Switzerland. In the case of the Indian piece goods a particular pattern of cloth of a very cheap make was manufactured to suit the native dress, and to a great extent it took the place of cloth previously brought from England. In the case of the Swiss cloth it would seem that its cheapness secured it a market. It appears to be a mistake to suppose that in the eastern markets cloth is objected to solely on account of any inferiority in the quality arising from excessive sizing, for, as a fact, cheapness is the most important consideration; quality is only of secondary importance. No doubt many articles manufactured on the continent have supplanted those of British manufacture entirely because of their greater cheapness. The market is quite content with the inferior article, and as yet desires no better. . . . Australian and Japanese coals have to a considerable extent replaced coal from England, these coals, though inferior in quality, being much cheaper than the English. Machinery from the Continent of Europe has also to some extent replaced that formerly obtained from England. It is to be feared that British manufacturers do not adapt their goods as much as some foreign manufacturers do to the requirements of the native market."—vol. 11, p. 483.

APPENDIX II

THE GREAT OPPORTUNITY IN 1914

ALTHOUGH conscious, purposeful motives for breaking an economic rival were absent from the British decision in 1914 to go to war with Germany, it is none the less true that once the war was entered upon the nation and Government were quick to apprehend the splendid opportunity for delivering a mortal blow to German commerce.

The immediate effect of the outbreak of the war on British business was, of course, the closing of the Stock Exchange and a paralyzing halt of business operations. If the routes of trade were closed Britain faced starvation and ruin. But in a few days the outlook underwent an optimistic transformation. "If we keep command of the sea, what is going to happen?" asked Mr. Bonar Law in the House of Commons on August 6. "It all depends on that . . . after all the total amount of our exports to all the European countries which are now at war is only a small part of our total exports. . . . We shall have free trade, if the sea routes are maintained, with the colonies and with the whole of the American continent, and, unfortunately for them, both our allies and our enemies will not be competing with us in those markets. Look at it as a problem, and I think we have a right to believe, not that trade will be good, but that it will be much more nearly normal than is generally believed."[1] There were many other reassuring expressions of opinion. The *Hardware Trade Journal* made haste to remind its readers that the country's trade had actually benefited from past Continental wars, and its Birmingham correspondent wrote significantly: "For losses in some directions there will be compensations, at least as long as the engineering and manufacturing trades have any call to make upon iron-masters. The bitter cry of the Midlands against German and Belgian 'dumping' will be silenced for a time."[2] The *Chemical Trades Journal* likewise was early in pointing to the optimistic aspects of the situation. "The purchasing power of the world will be diminished," it observed, "but many orders that would in the

[1] Parliamentary Debates, 4th. S., vol. 65, p. 2088.
[2] Issue of Aug. 7.

ordinary course have gone to the Continent will be diverted to this country."[3]

This last was the note which, by the end of the third week in August, resounded throughout the press. The early success of the navy in driving German ships to cover and the war-risk insurance extended to merchant vessels by the Government strengthened public confidence, and the eyes of the nation were opened to the supreme opportunity which the war offered for recapturing lost markets. In scores of journals it was recalled how the Germans had long engaged in successful rivalry with Britain, had edged her out of countless markets—and now the moment had come to undo all that. The destruction of German trade and the replacement of German with British goods became a great patriotic endeavor.

The Board of Trade, the Foreign and Colonial Offices turned their attention quickly to the problem of substituting British for German orders and contracts in all parts of the world. "This war," declared the *Daily Telegraph* two weeks after Britain's entry into it, "provides our business men with such an opportunity as has never come their way before . . . there is no reason why we should not permanently seize for this country a large proportion of Germany's export trade. . . . Practically the whole of the German trade with the British Dominions should fall to our commerce at a stroke, and British manufacturers ought to be able to hold their own with the United States in the sharp competition for German trade with the Far East and South America."[4] The *Daily Mail* and the *Pall Mall Gazette* likewise pointed out eagerly the rare opportunity before the British nation. A special article in the former, entitled "Trade We Can Take from Germany," appeared August 18, and declared that "at the present crisis in the affairs of nations there is and will be opened the rarest opportunity for a new prosperity." Two days later a *Daily Mail* leader stated: "They [British manufacturers] have now, if they will only seize it, an unequalled opportunity to show that they can be as resourceful, thorough, and adaptable as their rival. They ought at once to explore every one of the new avenues of trade that war has opened up to them. They ought to conduct an immediate investigation into every article of German make that has won for itself a position in the British market, and

[3] Issue of Aug. 8.
[4] Leader of Aug. 19.

see that it is replaced by a British article equally good. Now is the time not only to lessen the immediate pressure of unemployment but also to lay the foundations of a vaster trade than even this country has ever known."[5] The *Pall Mall Gazette* of August 19 congratulated the Government offices for working in coöperation to obtain the fullest information as to the goods which Germany and Austria had been exporting to foreign and neutral markets. "The sending of these things," it was observed, "has ceased with the war, and . . . the English manufacturer has now the first opportunity he has ever possessed of getting the trade in his own hands. . . . If we rise to the occasion, British trade should see a period of tremendous prosperity . . . , and should be supreme not only in the home market but in the whole area of business." "Get back the trade" was the caption over another *Pall Mall Gazette* leader for August 21 which declared, " 'We are out for German trade and we are determined to get it.' This remark, made with great emphasis by a manufacturer's representative at the office of the Commercial Intelligence Branch of the Board of Trade today, indicates the determination that is felt throughout the country to 'get back the trade' from Germany. Manufacturers and their agents are beseiging the offices from morning till night. Nothing like it has ever been known in the history of the Board of Trade."

The *Morning Post* and the *Times* joined in the cry for capturing Germany's commerce. The former argued that since Great Britain was fighting the Germans on sea and on land there was no reason why the struggle should not be extended to trade: "Just as the nation showed a united front and approved of the war, so it is ready to make the attempt to turn Germany and Austria-Hungary out of those neutral markets where their prosperity has been built up largely at the expense of Great Britain."[6] The *Times,* beginning August 19, ran a series of special articles captioned "War on German Trade," and day after day for several weeks drew conspicuous attention to the markets open for attack in the Far East, Africa, Europe, the New World, and the British Colonies, to the fine opportunity for recapturing the chemical industry, and to the excellent openings now for the engineering and electrical trades.

The same vision of great commercial opportunity was caught by

[5] Aug. 21.
[6] Aug. 20.

the various trade journals. "Is there not a chance here for British machinery to come by its own?" asked the *Colliery Guardian.* "British-made pumps, steel props, electrical appliances, etc., etc., are every whit as good as the German equivalents with which they have had to compete in the past. . . . All over the world, in British possessions and the lands of friendly powers, mining is still being carried on without intermission, and mine owners who have had German machinery in the past must perforce turn elsewhere. They may go to America, but why not to Great Britain?"[7] Germany, the *Hardware Trade Journal* observed, had called the tune and therefore would have to pay the piper, not only in colonial acres but in commerce; so an appeal was made for "a policy of push—and a very strong push—in markets hitherto more or less sacred to the subjects of the Kaiser."[8] The war for England was not two weeks old before the *Chemical Trades Journal* declared very frankly: "It is undeniable that Germany's export trade, alone among the other great nations of the world, has developed in a much greater ratio than has our own, and in many foreign markets Germany has constituted our most formidable competitor. This is an essential point that must be borne in mind. As Germany's export business from the present time on to the end of the war is crippled absolutely, it follows that those countries which hitherto obtained a large proportion of their supplies from that source must of necessity turn elsewhere in order to meet their demands, and British manufacturers must see to it that *their* products are the ones consumed. Once this business is secured there need not be the slightest fear of much of it being lost again to Germany, for that country, through her unprecedented arrogance, has irretrievably lost that prestige and esteem and respect which previously were undoubtedly hers."[9] A week later this journal declared that the chemical trade, more than any other section of industry, stood to derive great benefit from the European upheaval; a full-page advertisement was published urging manufacturers to realize the enormous amount of colonial and foreign trade done by Germany. "This," it was stated, "is all open to our people now, as the whole world is not going to stop on account of a war in Europe. . . . This knowledge should spur us on to a pace we have never attained before.

[7] Aug. 21.
[8] Aug. 14.
[9] Aug. 15.

. . . All new trade we do now we shall keep forever. The manufacturer's part in this war is to gain new trade, and new trade means
new power, and new power in the hands of the United Kingdom will
always mean peace rather than annoyance and aggressiveness."[10]

These few characteristic expressions of the commercial mind are
enough to show that the idealistic crusade for bleeding Belgium,
the sanctity of treaties, and the independence of small nationalities,
did not close the shrewd business eye of the country.

[10] Aug. 22.

APPENDIX III

THE table below shows the comparative tonnage of British (United Kingdom) and German shipping entered at several ports of the world in 1900 and 1913. The table has been constructed from the returns given in various consular reports (Annual Series) and in the Statistical Abstract for the United Kingdom.

	1900	1913
ALL U. K. PORTS		
British	32,864,524	46,602,920
German	2,582,769	9,073,855
HAMBURG		
British	2,779,688	4,095,480
German	4,282,751	8,637,297
BREMEN		
British	501,620	1,125,325
German	1,807,245	3,490,198
ANTWERP		
British	3,210,678	6,173,231
German	1,584,708	4,510,522
ROTTERDAM		
British	?	7,080,848
German	?	4,236,342
LE HAVRE		
British	974,833	1,699,404
German	400,134	712,394
CHERBOURG		
British	?	1,891,236
German	?	2,296,990
LISBON		
British*	5,680,262	2,230,068
German*	1,835,803	2,042,288
MARSEILLES		
British	1,531,663	2,498,020
German	80,675	691,421

* All Portuguese ports for 1900.

	1900	*1913*
GENOA		
British	991,729	1,454,337
German	605,535	938,603
NAPLES		
British	650,404	2,111,138
German	743,145	1,594,051
CONSTANTINOPLE		
British	4,220,562	6,436,505†
German	273,173	867,192†
THROUGH SUEZ CANAL		
British	5,605,421	12,052,484
German	1,466,391	3,352,287
SHANGHAI		
British‡	2,479,727	3,881,472
German‡	531,079	820,732
YOKOHAMA		
British	856,684	1,509,105
German	258,615	406,309
BUENOS AIRES		
British	1,066,474	3,052,410§
German	310,910	804,160§
NEW YORK		
British‖	3,933,644	6,571,342
German	1,699,929	3,012,583

† Straits traffic for 1913.
‡ Steamers only.
§ Figures for 1912 (steamers only).
‖ British figures include colonial vessels.

BIBLIOGRAPHY

THE following materials were used in the preparation of this study:

I. ANNUAL PUBLICATIONS

Annual Register.

Annual Statement of the Trade of the United Kingdom (Parl. Papers).

Annual Statement of the Navigation and Shipping of the United Kingdom (Parl. Papers).

Accounts Relating to the Trade and Commerce of Certain Foreign Countries and British Possessions (Parl. Papers).

British and Foreign State Papers.

Hansard's Parliamentary Debates.

Public General Statutes.

Statistical Abstract for the United Kingdom (Parl. Papers).

Statistical Abstract for the Several British Colonies, Possessions and Protectorates (Parl. Papers).

Statistical Abstract for Foreign Countries (Parl. Papers).

Statistical Abstract for the British Empire. 1903 ff. (Parl. Papers).

Statistisches Jahrbuch für das deutsche Reich. (Berlin).

Tables Showing the Progress of Merchant Shipping in the United Kingdom and the Principal Maritime Countries (Parl. Papers).

II. COMMERCIAL REPORTS

(These are all in the volumes of Parliamentary Papers. There are two series: those before and those after 1886. The former have been cited according to the volumes of Accounts and Papers in which they are to be found, the latter by their individual numbers. The Roman numerals refer to the volumes of Parliamentary Papers as arranged by the House of Commons Library, are used in the official indices, and will most readily enable one to search down a given paper.)

Old Series

> Accounts & Papers, 1872, vols. 22-23. lvii-lviii.
>   " " " , 1873, vols. 26-28. lxiv-lxvi.
>   " " " , 1874, vols. 31-34. lxv-lxviii.

Accounts & Papers, 1875, vols. 33-37. lxxiv-lxxviii.
"   "   "   , 1876, vols. 32-35. lxxiii-lxxvi.
"   "   "   , 1877, vols. 33-36. lxxxi-lxxxiv.
"   "   "   , 1878, vols. 27-31. lxxii-lxxvi.
"   "   "   , 1878-9, vols. 28-32. lxix-lxxiii.
"   "   "   , 1880, vols. 33-36. lxxii-lxxv.
"   "   "   , 1881, vols. 33-35. lxxxix-xci.
"   "   "   , 1882, vols. 33-36. lxix-lxxii.
"   "   "   , 1883, vols. 34-38. lxxi-lxxv.
"   "   "   , 1884, vols. 33-37. lxxix-lxxxiii.
"   "   "   , 1884-5, vols. 32-37. lxxvi-lxxxi.
"   "   "   , 1886, vols. 28-30. lxv-lxvii.

New Series

(*Explanatory note:* These are in two classifications—(1) Annual and (2). Miscellaneous Series of Diplomatic and Consular Reports. Each has a special number (shown here at the left), and more than five thousand of them were published between 1886 and 1914. No attempt has been made to list all that have been used; of the Annual Series only those appear below to which specific footnote reference has been made.)

ANNUAL

14 Shanghai.	1887.lxxxiii.
50 Königsberg.	1887.lxxxiv.
56 Crete.	1887.lxxxvi.
70 Eastern Roumelia.	1887.lxxxvi.
130 Christiania.	1887.lxxxv.
152 Corunna.	1887.lxxxvi.
176 Servia.	1887.lxxxvi.
189 Nice.	1887.lxxxiv.
239 Sicily.	1888.ci.
245 Venice.	1888.ci.
274 Barcelona.	1888.ciii.
308 Genoa.	1888.ci.
329 Corunna.	1888.ciii.
379 Frankfort-am-Main.	1888.ci.
440 Christiania.	1888.cii.
447 St. Petersburg.	1889.lxxx.
534 Servia.	1889.lxxx.

573	Frankfort-am-Main	1889.lxxviii.
614	Japan	1890.lxxvi.
700	Portugal	1890.lxxvi.
729	San Domingo	1890.lxxvii.
765	Bavaria	1890.lxxv.
855	Mozambique	1890-1.lxxxvii.
1082	Frankfort-am-Main	1892.lxxxii.
1099	Constantinople	1892.lxxxiv.
1153	Lorenzo Marques	1893.xcv.
1308	Oporto	1893.xcv.
1362	Cyclades	1894.lxxxvi.
1384	Constantinople	1894.lxxxviii.
1439	Odessa	1894.lxxxvii.
1448	Bulgaria	1894.lxxxv.
1591	Greece	1895.xcviii.
1609	Roumania	1895.xcix.
1623	Hamburg	1895.xcviii.
1632	Japan	1896.lxxxvii.
1682	Patras	1896.lxxxvi.
1683	La Rochelle	1896.lxxxv.
1699	Cherbourg	1896.lxxxv.
1700	Leghorn	1896.lxxxvi.
1720	Cyclades	1896.lxxxvi.
1740	Shanghai	1896.lxxxv.
1752	Frankfort-am-Main	1896.lxxxvi.
1760	Mozambique	1896.lxxxviii.
1763	Cephalonia	1896.lxxxvi.
1775	Galatz	1896.lxxxviii.
1826	Bulgaria	1897.lxxxix.
1911	Rio Grande do sul	1897.lxxxix.
1933	Venezuela	1897.xciv.
1942	Frankfort-am-Main	1897.xci.
2099	Serbia	1898.xcviii.
2034	Le Havre	1898.xcv.
2040	Berlin	1898.vcvi.
2062	Stockholm	1898.xcix.
2068	Piraeus	1898.xcvi.
2100	Galatz	1898.xcviii.
2122	Frankfort-am-Main	1898.xcvi.

2484	Frankfort-am-Main	1900.xciii.
2493	Bulgaria	1900.xcii.
2524	South Italy	1900.xciv.
2553	Serbia	1901.lxxxiv.
2569	La Rochelle	1901.lxxxii.
2577	Amsterdam	1901.lxxxiii.
2628	Hamburg	1901.lxxxii.
2650	Constantinople	1901.lxxxv.
2668	Marseilles	1901.lxxxii.
2680	Frankfort-am-Main	1901.lxxxii.
2705	Siam	1902.cx.
2813	Constantinople	1902.cx.
2851	Frankfort-am-Main	1902.cvii.
2855	Marseilles	1902.cvii.
2857	Bohemia	1902.cv.
2898	Bangkok	1902.cx.
2950	Constantinople	1903.lxxix.
3064	Northern Portugal	1903.lxxviii.
3140	Constantinople	1904.ci.
3183	Northern Portugal	1904.c.
3277	Odessa	1905.xcii.
3329	Serbia	1905.xcii.
3441	Moscow	1905.xcii.
3533	Constantinople	1906.cxxviii.
3776	Constantinople	1907.xciii.
3948	Amsterdam	1908.cxiv.
3951	Bushire	1908.cxiv.
4126	Stockholm	1908.cxvi.
4283	Düsseldorf	1909.xcv.
4325	Frankfort-am-Main	1909.xcv.
4530	Canton, China	1910.xcvii.
4609	Bulgaria	1911.xc.
4643	Oporto	1911.xcv.
4659	Bordeaux	1911.xci.
4668	Corfu	1911.xciii.
4677	Roumania	1911.xcv.
4689	Lisbon	1911.xcv.
4786	Rio de Janeiro	1911.xc.
4797	Salonica	1911.xcvi.

4817	Bulgaria	1911.xc.
4836	Rome	1912-13.xcvii.
5081	Norway	1913.lxxi.
5216	China	1914.xc.
5225	Bagdad	1914.xcv.
5227	Riga	1914.xciv.
5233	Poland	1914.xciv.
5259	Vladivostok	1914.xciv.
5261	Persia	1914.xciii.
5265	Portugal	1914.xciii.
5274	Antwerp	1914.lxxxix.
5307	Wuchow, China	1914.xc.
5310	Rome	1914.xcii.
5315	Rotterdam	1914.xciii.
5326	Roumania	1914.xciv.
5328	St. Petersburg	1914.xciv.
5329	Warsaw	1914.xciv.
5352	German S.W. Africa	1914.xci.
5354	Finland	1914.xciv.
5369	Basra, Turkey	1914.xcv.
5404	Berlin	1914-16.lxxii.
5414	Hamburg	1914-16.lxxii.

MISCELLANEOUS

1. Notes from H. M. Consul General at Odessa on a Visit to Kieff. 1887.lxxxii.
4. Report on Gotha Exhibition of European Manufactures Used in China. 1887.lxxxii.
6. Report on Exhibitions of European Manufactures Used in China. 1887.lxxxii.
8. Openings for British Enterprise in Catalonia. 1887.lxxxii.
23. Conditions of Trade in Saxony. 1887.lxxxii.
34. Means for Developing British Trade in Chile. 1887.lxxxii.
37. Development of Industries and Manufactures of European Russia. 1887.lxxxii.
226. Roumanian Trade, 1881-90. 1892.lxxx.
237. Progress of Trade of Hamburg. 1892.lxxix.
328. Report on Treaty of Commerce between Russia and Germany. 1894.lxxxix.

329. Same title as No. 328. 1894.lxxxix.
340. Germany's Commercial Relations with Foreign Countries. 1895. cii.
391. Commercial Relations of Great Britain and Egypt. 1896.lxxxiv.
398. The Port and Railway of Lorenzo Marques. 1896.lxxxiv.
417. The Economic and Financial Situation in Italy. 1897.lxxxviii.
419. German Competition with British Manufactures in the Netherlands. 1897.lxxxviii.
436. German Trade in 1897 as Compared with British Trade. 1898. xciii.
443. The Maritime Interests of the German Empire. 1898.xciii.
449. Suggestions for Development of British Trade with Italy. 1898.xciii.
458. Trade of Central and Southern Asia. 1898.xci.
462. German Imports and Exports of Iron, Hardware, Implements, Machines, in 1896-97. 1898.xciii.
479. Extent and Character of Trade between Hamburg and Africa. 1899.xcvii.
489. British and Westphalian Coal at Hamburg. 1899.xcvii.
490. Development of Commercial, Industrial, Maritime and Traffic Interests in Germany, 1871-1898. 1899.xcvii.
499. Suggestions for Development of British Trade with Italy. 1899.xcvii.
509. British Trade with Switzerland. 1899.xcvii.
536. German Subsidized Mail Steamers to South Africa. 1900.xci.
542. British Trade with Switzerland. 1900.xci.
543. The Commerce of The Netherlands. 1900.xci.
557. British Trade in Egypt, 1895-1900. 1901.lxxx.
561. Chemical Instruction in Germany and Growth and Present Condition of German Chemical Industries. 1901.lxxx.
564. Notes on Trade of Japan, 1872-1900. 1902.ciii.
568. Suggestions for British Traders with Turkey in Asia. 1902.ciii.
574. The Prussian Railways. 1902.ciii.
575. German Iron Trade for 1900-01. 1902.ciii.
613. The Projected Rhine-Neckar-Danube Ship Canal. 1904.xcvi.
622. German Machinery Import and Export Trade and Industry. 1905.lxxxvi.
624. Memorandum on German Cement. 1905.lxxxvi.
642. German Paper Industry and Export Trade. 1906.cxxii.

653. German Ceramic Industries and German Export Trade in Ceramic Products. 1906.cxxii.
662. Mexican Imports from United Kingdom and Germany. 1907. lxxxvii.
681. New Scheme of Belgian Government for Extension of Port of Antwerp. 1912-13.xciv.

III. MISCELLANEOUS PARLIAMENTARY PAPERS
(listed chronologically)

Report of C. M. Kennedy on International Congress of Commerce and Industry at Brussels, 1880. vol. 33, Accounts and Papers, 1880.lxxii.

Report of Select Committee on Sugar Industries. vol. 5, Reports of Committees, 1880.xii.

Correspondence Respecting Diplomatic and Consular Assistance to Trade. Commercial No. 16, 1886.lx.

Report of Royal Commission on Depression of Trade and Industry. vols. 9-11, Reports of Commissioners, 1886. xxi-xxiii.

Special Report from Select Committee on Merchandise Marks Act (1862) Amendment Bill. Reports of Committees, vol. 4, 1887.x.

Foreign Trade: Statistical Tables Relating to the Progress of Foreign Trade of United Kingdom and Other Foreign Countries in Recent Years: with Report to Board of Trade Thereon, by R. Giffen. (c.-5297), 1888.xciii.

Report of Sir Robert Giffen to Board of Trade on the Progress of the Sugar Trade. 1889.lxxii.

Foreign Trade: Statistical Tables Relating to Progress of Foreign trade of United Kingdom and of Other Countries, with Report to Board of Trade Thereon, by Sir Robert Giffen. (c. 17439), 1894. lxxx.

Reports from H. M. Representatives in Certain Foreign Countries on Prison Labour. Commercial No. 8 (c. 7550), 1894.xc.

Report of Departmental Committee on Importation into United Kingdom of Foreign Prison-made Goods. (c.-7092), 1895. lxxxviii.

Comparative Trade Statistics. Tables Showing Progress of British Trade and Production, 1854-1895. (c.-8211), 1896.lxxvi.

Trade of British Empire and Foreign Competition. Despatch from

V. PRINCIPAL SIGNED PERIODICAL ARTICLES

Adams, Brooks: The International Struggle for Life. *Fortnightly Review*, 1899, vol. 71.

Asiaticus: The Rise and Fall of the Indigo Industry in India. *Economic Journal*, 1912, vol. 22.

Baden-Powell, G.: The Expansion of Germany. *Nineteenth Century*, 1884, vol. 16.

Baden-Powell, G.: The Doom of Cane Sugar. *Fortnightly Review*, 1897, vol. 67.

Baden-Powell, G.: Imperial Free Trade. *Ibid.*

Barker, J. Ellis (ex-O. Eltzbacher): Is Great Britain Living on Her Capital? *Contemporary Review*, 1901, vol. 80.

Barker, J. Ellis: The Economic Decay of Great Britain. *Ibid.*, 1901, vols. 79, 80.

Barker, J. Ellis: The Fiscal Policy of Germany. *Nineteenth Century*, 1903, vol. 54.

Barker, J. Ellis: The Fiscal Controversy—Some Noticeable Facts and Extracts. *Ibid.*

Barker, J. Ellis: German Colonial Ambitions and Anglo-Saxon Interests. *Fortnightly Review*, 1903, vol. 79.

Barker, J. Ellis: The Chemical Industry of Germany. *Contemporary Review*, 1904, vol. 85.

Barker, J. Ellis: The Lesson of the German Water-Ways. *Ibid.*, 1904, vol. 86.

Barker, J. Ellis: The Future of Anglo-German Relations. *Nineteenth Century*, 1906, vol. 59.

Barker, J. Ellis: The Absorption of Holland by Germany. *Ibid.*, 1906, vol. 60.

Barker, J. Ellis: The Future of Great Britain. *Ibid.*, 1906, vol. 60.

Barker, J. Ellis: Will the British Empire Stand or Fall? *Ibid.*, 1907, vol. 61.

Barker, J. Ellis: England, Germany, and the Baltic. *Ibid.*, 1907, vol. 62.

Barker, J. Ellis: The Foreign Policy of William II. *Ibid.*, 1908, vol. 63.

Barker, J. Ellis: The Naval Policy of Germany. *Ibid.*

Barker, J. Ellis: The Triple Entente and the Triple Alliance. *Ibid.*, 1908, vol. 64.

Mr. Chamberlain to Governors of Colonies and Replies Thereto. (c.-8449), 1897.lxi.

Correspondence between Board of Trade and Foreign Office and between Foreign Office and H. M. Representatives Abroad on Subject of Foreign Prison-made Goods. (c.-8339), 1897.lxxxviii.

Correspondence Respecting Diplomatic and Consular Assistance to British Trade Abroad. Commercial No. 5 (c.-8432), 1897. lxxxviii.

British and Foreign Trade Memorandum. (c.-8322), 1897.lxxxiii.

Foreign Trade Competition: Opinions of H. M. Diplomatic and Consular Officers on British Trade Methods. (c.-9078), 1899. xcvi.

Commercial Mission to South America. Reports of Mr. T. Worthington, Special Board of Trade Commissioner to inquire into conditions and prospects of British Trade in South America. (c.-9100, 9101, 9160, 9161, 9298), 1899.xcvi.

Reports from H. M. Representatives Abroad respecting Bounties on Shipbuilding. Commercial No. 4 (cd.-596), 1901.lxxx.

Return of Trade, Shipping, etc., of French Indo-China, Siam, Straits Settlements, Malay Federated States, and British and Dutch Possessions in East Indian Archipelago. (cd.-342), 1900. lxxxvii.

Report from Select Committee on Steamship Subsidies. 1901.vii and 1902.ix.

Return of Correspondent with British Firms as to Competition (in India) between German and British Locomotives. 1902.lxxi.

Correspondence relating to Brussels Sugar Conference, and Despatch from British Delegates Enclosing Copy of Convention signed March 5, 1902. (cd.-940, 1003, 1013), 1902.civ.

Return of Number and Tonnage of Vessels Sold from United Kingdom Ownership under British Flag to Foreign Ownership under Foreign Flags, 1875-1902. 1900.lxiii.

British and Foreign Trade and Industry. Memoranda, Statistical Tables and Charts Prepared in the Board of Trade with Reference to Various Matters Bearing on British and Foreign Trade and Industrial Conditions. (cd. 1761), 1903.lxvii.

Correspondence with Governments of Belgium and Germany respecting their Commercial Relations with Great Britain and British Colonies. (cd. 1630), 1903.lxxv.

Commercial Mission to South Africa. Report received from **Mr.**
Henry Birchenough, Special Board of Trade Commissioner to
inquire into and report on Present Position and Future Prospects of British Trade in South Africa. (cd. 1844), 1904.lxi.

British and Foreign Trade and Industry. Second series of Memoranda, etc., Prepared in Board of Trade Respecting British
and Foreign Trade and Industrial Conditions. (cd. 2337), 1904.
lxxxiv.

Report by H. W. McLean, Special Board of Trade Commissioner,
on Conditions and Prospects of British Trade in Persia. (cd.
2146), 1904.xcv.

Reports on Tariff Wars between Certain European States. Commercial No. 1, (cd. 1938), 1904.xcv.

Return Showing Exports of British, German, and American Exports
to China, Argentina, and All South America, 1885-1906. 1907.
lxxxi.

British Trade in Australia. Report upon the Conditions and Prospects of British Trade in Australia by Advisory Committee in
Commercial Intelligence Department of Board of Trade. 1907.
lvi.

Report to Board of Trade on Conditions and Prospects of British
Trade in New Zealand. (cd. 3867), 1908.lxxiii.

Coal Statistics. Tables Showing Production, Consumption, Import
and Export of Coal, etc., in British Empire and Principal
Foreign Countries, 1883 ff. 1908.xcvi.

British and Foreign Trade and Industry. Statistical Tables and
Charts relating to British and Foreign Trade and Industry, in
continuation of cd. 1761, of 1903, and cd. 2337, of 1904, with
additions. (cd. 4954), 1909.cii.

Report of Royal Commission on Shipping Rings. 1909. xlvii-xlviii.

Report on Conditions and Prospects of British Trade in Central
America, Colombia, and Venezuela. (cd. 6969), 1913.lxviii.

IV. NEWSPAPER AND PERIODICAL PRESS

DAILY NEWSPAPERS
Daily Chronicle
Daily Express
Daily Mail
Daily News

Daily Telegraph
Evening Globe
Manchester Guardian
Morning Post
Pall Mall Gazette
Standard
Times
Westminster Gazette

REVIEWS, WEEKLIES, PERIODICALS, ETC.
Contemporary Review
Economic Journal
Economic Review
Edinburgh Review
English Review
Fortnightly Review
Fraser's Magazine
Journal of Society of Arts
Macmillan's Magazine
The Nation
National Review
National Observer
New Review
Nineteenth Century and After
Quarterly Review
Saturday Review
The Speaker
Spectator
Westminster Review

TRADE AND BUSINESS PUBLICATIONS
Board of Trade Journal (official)
Chamber of Commerce Journal (pub. by London (
Chemical Trades Journal.
Coal Merchant and Shipper
Colliery Guardian
Hardware Trade Journal
Iron and Coal Trades Review
Iron and Steel Trades Journal
Shipping Gazette and Lloyd's List (daily p
Shipping World

Barker, J. Ellis: Anglo-German Differences and Sir Edward Grey. *Fortnightly Review,* 1912, vol. 91.

Barry, P.: Doomed British Shipping. *Westminster Review,* 1902, vol. 158.

Barth, Theodore: England and Germany. *Contemporary Review,* 1900, vol. 77.

Bashford, J. L : The German Mercantile Marine. *Fortnightly Review,* 1903, vol. 79.

Battine, Cecil: How to Postpone an Anglo-German War. *Ibid.,* 1912, vol. 91.

Bedford, Rudolph: Germany in the Pacific. *Macmillan's Magazine,* 1907, vol. 1.

Bellairs, Carlyon: The Cobden Club and the Navy. *National Review,* 1907, vol. 49.

Bernstein, Edouard: The Growth of German Exports. *Contemporary Review,* 1903, vol. 84.

Billington, Mary F.: Tailor-Made in Germany. *New Review,* 1895, vol. 12.

Birchenough, Henry: Do Foreign Annexations Injure British Trade? *Nineteenth Century,* 1897, vol. 41.

Birchenough, Henry: The Expansion of Germany. *Ibid.,* 1898, vol. 43.

Birchenough, Henry: Lord Rosebery on the Dangers to British Trade. *Ibid.,* 1900, vol. 48.

Blennerhassett, Rowland: The German March to the Persian Gulf. *National Review,* 1903, vol. 41.

Blennerhassett, Rowland: The Vital Question. *Fortnightly Review,* 1907, vol. 82.

Boulger, D. C.: British Distrust of Germany. *Nineteenth Century,* 1906, vol. 59.

Brailsford, H. N.: Germany and the Balance of Power. *Contemporary Review,* 1912, vol. 102.

Brand, W. F.: England and Germany. *Westminster Review,* 1910, vol. 174.

Brand, W. F.: Is Britain Going Down Hill? *Ibid.,* 1911, vol. 176.

Briscoe, George: Eastern Competition and Western Trade. *Ibid.,* 1897, vol. 147.

Brooks, Sidney: England, Germany, and Common Sense. *Fortnightly Review,* 1912, vol. 91.

Browne, Benj. C.: Our American Competitors. *National Review,* 1899, vol. 33.

Buxton, Noel: England and Germany. *Contemporary Review,* 1911, vol. 100.

Byng, G.: Fiscal Problems of Today. *Fortnightly Review,* 1902, vol. 78.

Calchas: Will Germany Fail? *Ibid.,* 1901, vol. 75.

Calchas: Will England Last The Century? *Ibid.*

Calchas: The Ocean Trust and National Policy. *Ibid.,* 1902, vol. 77.

Calchas: German Light on German Policy. *Ibid.,* 1902, vol. 78.

Calchas: The New German Intrigue: A Note of Warning. *Ibid.,* 1904, vol. 82.

Capel, Yolet: England's Peril. *Westminster Review,* 1902, vol. 71.

Clarke, G. S.: Germany as a Naval Power. *Nineteenth Century,* 1899, vol. 45.

Colmer, J. G.: An Imperial Customs Union. *Economic Journal,* 1896, vol. 6.

Constantinople: German Finance in Turkey. *National Review,* 1906-7, vol. 48.

Cox, Harold: West Indian Sugar. *Economic Journal,* 1897, vol. 7.

Cripps, C. A.: Competition and Free Trade. *National Review,* 1887-8, vol. 10.

Cross, J. W.: British Trade in 1898. A Warning Note. *Nineteenth Century,* 1899, vol. 45.

Crozier, John B.: Free Trade or Protection for England. *Fortnightly Review,* 1902, vol. 77.

Crozier, John B.: How to Ruin a Free Trade Nation. *Ibid.,* 1902, vol. 78.

Curzon, George N.: Destinies of the Far East. *National Review,* 1893, vol. 21.

Dawkins, C. E.: The German Abroad. *National Review,* 1885, vol. 5.

Dawson, W. H.: Germany's Commercial Progress. *Economic Journal,* 1901, vol. 11.

Dillon, E. J.: The Commercial Needs of the Empire. *Contemporary Review,* 1902, vol. 81.

Dillon, E. J.: Germany's Foreign Policy. *Fortnightly Review,* 1896, vol. 60.

Dillon, E. J.: The Bagdad Railway. *Contemporary Review*, 1903, vol. 83.

Delbrück, Hans: The Price of an English-German Entente. *Ibid.*, 1911, vol. 99.

Drage, Geoffrey: The Progress of British Imperialism. *Fortnightly Review*, 1906, vol. 86.

Durham, Geoffrey: The Foreign Trade of Great Britain and Germany. *Contemporary Review*, 1910, vol 98.

Earle, E. M.: The Secret Anglo-German Convention of 1914 regarding Asiatic Turkey. *Political Science Quarterly*, New York, 1923, vol. 38.

Elkind, Louis: Germany's Commercial Relations. *Fortnightly Review*, 1906, vol. 80.

Ellinger, Barnard: Thirty Years Export Trade. *Economic Review*, 1902, vol. 12.

Findlay, J. J.: The Genesis of the German Clerk. *Fortnightly Review*, 1899, vol. 72.

Fleming, Owen: The New German Tariffs. *Economic Review*, 1905, vol. 15.

Flux, A. W.: The Commercial Supremacy of Great Britain. *Economic Journal*, 1894, vol. 4.

Flux, A. W.: British Trade and German Competition. *Economic Journal*, 1897, vol. 7.

Flux, A. W.: Our Foreign Trade Rivals. *Economic Review*, 1898, vol. 8.

Flux, A. W.: The Commercial Supremacy of Great Britain. *Economic Journal*, 1899, vol. 9.

Flux, A. W.: Britain's Place in Foreign Markets. *Economic Journal*, 1904, vol. 14.

Fraser, H. D. J.: The Peaceful Penetration of Germany into Belgium. *Westminster Review*, 1909, vol. 172.

Fraser, Lovat: The Position in the Persian Gulf. *National Review*, 1907, vol. 50.

Fraser, Lovat: Why Help the Baghdad Railway? *National Review*, 1911, vol. 57.

Fraser, Lovat: The Baron and His Baghdad Railway. *National Review*, 1912, vol. 59.

Garvin, J. L.: The Future of Tariff Reform. *National Review*, 1906-7, vol. 48.

Genosse Aegir: A Lesson in German. *Fortnightly Review,* 1896, vol. 65.

German Resident: Some Candid Impressions of England. *National Review,* 1905, vol. 45.

Gibbins, H. de B.: Made in Germany and How to Stop It. *Fortnightly Review,* 1899, vol. 71.

Gibbon, G.: Made in Other Countries. *Westminister Review,* 1897, vol. 147.

Giffen, Robert: Trade Depression and Low Prices. *Contemporary Review,* 1885, vol. 47.

Giffen, Robert: Our Trade Prosperity and the Outlook. *Economic Journal,* 1900, vol. 10.

Giraud, A.: A New German Empire: The Story of the Baghdad Railway. *Nineteenth Century,* 1914, vol. 75.

Goldman, C. S.: A German View of the Anglo-German Problem. *Ibid.,* 1909, vol. 65.

Gray, Albert: False Marking of Merchandise. *New Review,* 1890, vol. 3.

Greenwood, Frederick: The Cry for New Markets. *Nineteenth Century,* 1899, vol. 45.

Greswell, W. H. P.: The Germans in South Africa. *Fortnightly Review,* 1896, vol. 59.

Guyot, Yves: Le Pangermanisme, la Hollande et la Belgique. *Nineteenth Century,* 1906, vol. 60.

Gwinner, Arthur v.: The Baghdad Railway and the Question of British Participation. *Nineteenth Century,* 1909, vol. 65.

Haldane, J. R.: The Tariff in the Struggle for Markets. *Westminster Review,* 1910, vol. 173.

Halle, E. v.: The Rise and Tendencies of German Transatlantic Enterprise. *Economic Journal,* 1907, vol. 17.

Hallett, H. S.: Western Nations and Eastern Markets. *Nineteenth Century,* 1894, vol. 35.

Hallett, H. S.: British Trade and the Integrity of China. *Fortnightly Review,* 1898, vol. 69.

Hamilton, Angus: The Question of Persia. *Fortnightly Review,* 1907, vol. 82.

Harris, W. J.: A Reply to Lord Randolph Churchill. *National Review,* 1887, vol. 10.

Harrison, Frederick: 1913. *English Review,* 1913, vol. 13.

Herzfeld, A. G.: Our Falling Trade. *Westminster Review,* 1898, vol. 150.

Hewins, W. A. S.: The Influence of the New German Commercial Treaties on British Industries. *National Review,* 1905, vol. 45.

Hobson, J. A.: Can England Keep Her Commerce? *Ibid.,* 1891, vol. 17.

Hobson, J. A.: The Approaching Abandonment of Free Trade. *Fortnightly Review,* 1902, vol. 77.

Hodgson, H. M.: The Economic Crisis in Germany. *Contemporary Review,* 1902, vol. 81.

Howell, G.: The State of English Trade. *Fortnightly Review,* 1887, vol. 47.

Hozier, H. M.: England's Real Peril. *Macmillan's Magazine,* 1888, vol. 58.

Hurd, A.: England's Peril—Invasion or Starvation. *Fortnightly Review,* 1910, vol. 87.

Ignotus: England and Germany. *Fortnightly Review,* 1901, vol. 75.

Jennings, L. J.: Trade League Against England. *Nineteenth Century,* 1890, vol. 28.

Johnston, Sir H.: German Views of an Anglo-German Understanding. *Ibid.,* 1910, vol. 68.

Johnston, Sir H.: The Need of an Anglo-German Understanding. *Ibid.,* 1911, vol. 69.

Kershaw, J. B.: The Future of British Trade. *Fortnightly Review,* 1897, vol. 68.

Lambert, Agnes: Neglecting Our Customers. *Nineteenth Century,* 1898-99, vols. 44, 45.

Lascelles, Frank: Thoughts on the Anglo-German Problem. *Contemporary Review,* 1912, vol. 101.

Law, Andrew Bonar: Tariff Reform and the Cotton Trade. *National Review,* 1910, vol. 56.

Lawrence, Joseph: British Patent Laws and Their Relation to Industrial Employment. *National Review,* 1906-7, vol. 48.

Lawson, W. R.: German Intrigues in the Transvaal. *Contemporary Review,* 1896, vol. 69.

Lethbridge, Roper: Is an Imperial Fiscal Policy Possible? *National Review,* 1885, vol. 5.

Leyd, E.: Causes of Decline in Commerce of Great Britain. *Journal of Society of Arts,* 1878, vol. 26.

Little, Archibald: The Yangtze Valley and Its Trade. *Contemporary Review,* 1898, vol. 74.

Loftus, A.: England and Commercial Unity with the Colonies. *Nineteenth Century,* 1893, vol. 33.

Lord, Walter Frewen: The Lost Empire of England. *Ibid.,* 1909, vol. 65.

Low, Sidney: The Decline of Cobdenism. *Ibid.,* 1896, vol. 40.

Lynch, H. F.: The Baghdad Railway: The New Conventions. *Fortnightly Review,* 1911, vol. 89.

MacColl, Malcolm: Russia, Germany, and Britain. *Ibid.,* 1902, vol. 77.

Magnus, Philip: Trade and Training in Germany. *National Review,* 1897, vol. 29.

Magnus, Philip: Schools of Commerce. *Contemporary Review,* 1887, vol. 52.

Mahan, A. T.: The Persian Gulf and International Relations. *National Review,* 1902-3, vol. 40.

Mann, J. S.: Mr. Balfour and Economic Fact. *Contemporary Review,* 1903, vol. 84.

Mijatovich, Chedo: Pan-Germanism. *Fortnightly Review,* 1907, vol. 81.

Money, L. G. Chiozza: Tariff Reform: Ten Years After. *Contemporary Review,* 1913, vol. 103.

Morgan-Browne, H.: Is Great Britain Falling into Economic Decay? *Ibid.,* 1901, vol. 80.

Morgan-Browne, H.: But Are We Decaying? *Ibid.,* 1901, vol 79.

Mulhall, M. G.: Ten Years of National Growth. *Contemporary Review,* 1886, vol. 50.

Muhall, M. G.: The Carrying Trade of the World. *Ibid.,* 1894, vol. 66.

Mulhall, M. G.: The Trade of the British Colonies. *Ibid.,* 1897, vol. 72.

Mulhall, M. G.: Twenty Years of British Trade. *Ibid.,* 1897, vol. 73.

Mulhall, M. G.: Imports and Exports of 40 Years. *Ibid.,* 1900, vol. 77.

Mulhall, M. G.: Forty Years of British Trade. *Contemporary Review,* 1900, vol. 77.

Murray, Kenric B.: Commercial Museums. *Ibid.,* 1887, vol. 51.

Murray, Kenric B.: Mr. Chamberlain and Colonial Commerce. *Economic Journal,* 1897, vol. 7.

Murray, S. L.: The Deflection of Our Export Trade in Time of War. *Nineteenth Century,* 1913, vol. 74.

Newcomen, George: Made in Germany and How to Avoid it. *Westminster Review,* 1896, vol. 145.

O'Connor, T. A.: The Baghdad Railway. *Fortnightly Review,* 1914, vol. 95.

O'Neill, Aeneas: Six German Opinions on the Naval Situation. *Nineteenth Century,* 1909, vol. 65.

Palgrave, R. H. I.: Colonial Friends and Foreign Rivals. *National Review,* 1904, vol. 42.

Parker, A.: The Bagdad Railway Negotiations. *Quarterly Review,* Oct., 1917.

Pears, Edwin: The Bagdad Railway. *Contemporary Review,* 1908, vol. 94.

Peart-Robinson, W.: Our Colonies and Free Trade. *Westminster Review,* 1894, vol. 141.

Politicus: Baron Marschall and Anglo-German Differences. *Fortnightly Review,* 1912, vol. 91.

Ritortus: The Imperialism of British Trade. *Contemporary Review,* 1899, vol. 76.

Roberts, A. W.: Low Prices and Hostile Tariffs. *National Review,* 1885-6, vol. 6.

Robertson, Edmund: The Shipping Combine and the British Flag. *Nineteenth Century,* 1902, vol. 51.

Rose-Soley, J. J.: English and German Interests in Samoa. *Westminster Review,* 1896, vol. 46.

Round, J. H.: The Protectionist Revival. *National Review,* 1895, vol. 25.

Salmon, Edward: From Cobden to Chamberlain. *Fortnightly Review,* 1896, vol. 65.

Salmon, Edward: The Business of Empire. *Ibid.,* 1902, vol. 77.

Salmon, Edward: England After the War. *Fortnightly Review,* 1902, vol. 78.

Schooling, J. H.: British Shipping. *Ibid.,* 1902, vol. 77.

Schooling, J. H.: Our Position in Foreign Markets. *National Review,* 1906, vol. 47.

Schooling, J. H.: Our Position in Colonial Markets. *National Review,* 1906, vol. 47.

Schulze-Gaevernitz, G. v.: England and Germany—Peace or War? *American Review of Reviews,* 1909, vol. 40.

Schuster, George: The Patents and Designs Act of 1907. *Economic Journal,* 1909, vol. 19.

Shadwell, Arthur: The German Colony in London. *National Review,* 1896, vol. 20.

Smith, F. E.: Tariff Reform. *Fortnightly Review,* 1912, vol. 92.

Spender, J. A.: Great Britain and Germany. *Fortnightly Review,* 1905, vol. 78.

Stout, Robert: Australasia—Her Resources and Foreign Trade. *Contemporary Review,* 1900, vol. 78.

Taylor, Benj.: The Commercial Sovereignty of the Seas. *Fortnightly Review,* 1899, vol. 71.

Taylor, Benj.: The Struggle for Industrial Supremacy. *Fortnightly Review,* 1900, vol. 73.

Taylor, Benj.: The Maritime Expansion of America. *Fortnightly Review,* 1901, vol. 76.

Taylor, Benj.: Sugar and the Convention. *Fortnightly Review,* 1902, vol. 77.

Taylor, Benj.: British and American Shipping. *Nineteenth Century,* 1902, vol. 52.

Taylor, Benj.: Aspects of Tariff Reform. *Fortnightly Review,* 1910, vol. 88.

Thwaite, B. H.: The Commercial War between England and Germany. *Nineteenth Century,* 1896, vol. 40.

Tripp, Clavell: German versus British Trade in the East. *Ibid.,* 1898, vol. 43.

Troelstra, P. J.: Will Holland be Germanized? *National Review,* 1905, vol. 45.

Tryon, G. C.: Commercial Strategy and the Loss of Neutral Markets. *National Review,* 1905, vol. 45.

Tulloch, Major, A. B.: German Trade in South America. *Nineteenth Century,* 1906, vol. 60.

Turner, W.: International Commercial Competition. *Westminster Review,* 1912, vol. 178.

Vidi: Bismarckianism in Business. *National Review,* 1909, vol. 52.

Vincent, C. E. Howard: False Marking of Merchandise. *New Review*, 1890, vol. 3.

W., H. W.: England and Germany. *Westminster Review*, 1891, vol. 136.

Waechter, Sir Max: England, Germany and the Peace of Europe. *Fortnightly Review*, 1913, vol. 93.

Warren, Mark: The Ascendancy of the United States Export Trade. *Westminster Review*, 1899, vol. 151.

Warren, Mark: The Trade of The Great Nations. *Contemporary Review*, 1903, vol. 83.

Warren, Mark: The Trade of the Empire. *Ibid.*, 1903, vol. 84.

Watchman: Some New Facts About German Commercial Tactics. *National Review*, 1910, vol. 55.

Watchman: Weltpolitik. *Ibid.*, 1913-14, vol. 62.

Wells, David, A.: The Great Depression. *Contemporary Review*, 1887, vol. 52.

Wilson, A. J.: British Trade. *Fraser's Magazine*, 1876, vol. 94.

Wile, F. W.: German Colonization in Brazil. *Fortnightly Review*, 1906, vol. 79.

Williams, E. E.: Made in Germany (six articles, January to June). *New Review*, 1896, vol. 14.

Williams, E. E.: Beetroot and Bounties. *Saturday Review*, Aug. 15, 1896, vol. 82.

Williams, E. E.: My Critics. *New Review*, 1896, vol. 15.

Williams, E. E.: The Case for Sugar. *New Review*, 1896, vol. 15.

Williams, E. E.: Our Flourishing Glass Industry. *Saturday Review*, Sept. 26, 1896.

Williams, E. E.: The Economic Revolution in Germany. *National Review*, 1900, vol. 35.

Williams, E. E.: Made in Germany—Five Years Later. *Ibid.*, 1901, vol. 38.

Wilson, H. W.: A National Tariff for Defense. *Ibid.*, 1904, vol. 42.

Whitman, Sidney: England and Germany at Constantinople. *Fortnightly Review*, 1907, vol. 81.

Whitman, Sidney: The Anglo-German Mirage. *Ibid.*, 1912, vol. 92.

X: The German Danger in the Far East. *National Review*, 1900, vol. 36.

X: The Focus of Asiatic Policy. *Ibid.*, 1901, vol. 37.

Young, Sir F.: Commercial Union of the Empire. *Nineteenth Century,* 1896, vol. 40.

————: The Foreign Policy of Germany. *Fortnightly Review,* 1905, vol. 78.

VI. BOOKS

Andrillon, H.: *L'Expansion de l'Allemagne.* Paris, 1914.

Armitage-Smith, G.: *The Free Trade Movement and its Results.* London, 1898. 2nd. ed. 1903.

Artifex and Opifex: *Causes of Decay in a British Industry.* London, 1907.

Ashley, P.: *Modern Tariff History.* London, 1904. 3rd. ed., 1920.

Ashley, W. J.: *British Industries.* London, 1903.

Ashley, W. J.: *The Tariff Problem.* London, 1903. 4th. ed. 1920.

Asquith, H. H.: *The Genesis of the War.* London, 1923.

Bakeless, J.: *The Economic Causes of Modern War.* New York, 1921.

Barker, J. Ellis: *Modern Germany.* London, 1905. 3rd. ed. 1912.

Barker, J. Ellis.: *Great and Greater Britain.* London, 1910.

Barker, J. Ellis: *Drifting.* London, 1901.

Barker, J. Ellis: *Tariff Reform.* London, 1909.

Bassett, H. H.: *British Commerce: A Modern Survey.* London, 1913.

Bastable, C. F.: *The Commerce of Nations.* London, 1891. 9th. ed., 1923.

Berard, Victor: *British Imperialism and Commercial Supremacy.* Trans. from French. London, 1906.

Blackmore, E.: *The British Mercantile Marine.* London, 1897.

Bowley, A. L.: *Short Account of England's Foreign Trade in the Nineteenth Century.* London, 1903.

Brandenburg, Erich: *Von Bismarck zum Weltkrieg.* Berlin, 1924. English Trans., London, 1927.

Burgis, Edwin: *Perils to British Trade.* London, 1895.

Burnley, J.: *The Story of British Trade and Industry.* London, 1904.

Chamberlain, Joseph: *Imperial Union and Tariff Reform.* London, 1903.

Clapham, J. H.: *An Economic History of Modern Britain.* Vol. I. London, 1926.

Cox, Harold: *The United Kingdom and its Trade.* London and N.Y., 1902.

Cunningham, W.: *The Free Trade Movement.* London, 1904.

Cunningham, W.: *The Case Against Free Trade.* London, 1911.

Cunningham, W.: *Growth of English Industry and Commerce in Modern Times*. vol. 2. London, 5th. ed., 1912.

Drage, Geoffrey: *The Imperial Organization of Trade*. London, 1911.

Earle, E. M.: *Turkey, the Great Powers, and the Bagdad Railway*. New York., 1923.

Farrer, J. A.: *England under Edward VII*. London, 1922.

Fay, Sidney B.: *The Origins of the World War*. Vol. I. New York, 1928.

Feis, Herbert: *Europe the World's Banker, 1871-1914*. New Haven, 1930.

Fuchs, C. J.: *The Trade Policy of Great Britain and Her Colonies since 1860*. London, 1905.

Gastrell, W.H. S.: *Our Trade in the World in Relation to Foreign Competition*. London, 1897.

Gibbins, H. de B.: *Economic and Industrial Progress of the Century*. London, 1903.

Gooch, G. P.: *History of Modern Europe, 1878-1919*. New York, 1923.

Gooch, G. P., and Temperley, H. W. V.: *British Documents on the Origins of the War, 1898-1914*. Vols. I-VII, XI. London, 1924-1932.

Gretton, R. H.: *A Modern History of the English People*. 3 vols. London, 1913, 1929.

Grey, Viscount: *Twenty-Five Years*. 2 vols. New York, 1925.

Halevy, Eli: *A History of the English People in 1895-1905*. Trans. from French. London, 1929.

Hauser, Henri: *Germany's Commercial Grip on the World*. Trans. from French. New York, 1918.

Helfferich, Karl: *Germany's Economic Progress and National Wealth, 1888-1913*. New York, 1914.

Hobson, C. K.: *The Export of Capital*. London, 1914.

Hobson, J. A.: *The German Panic*. (Cobden Club pamphlet) London, 1913.

Hohenzollern, Wilhelm: *My Memoirs, 1878-1919*. London, 1922.

Huldermann, Bernhard: *Albert Ballin*. London, 1922.

Hurd, A., and Castle, H.: *German Sea Power, Its Rise, Progress and Economic Basis*. London, 1913.

Iron and Steel Industries of Germany and Belgium: Report of Delegation Organized by British Iron Trade Association, London, 1896.

Jenks, L. A.: *The Migration of British Capital to 1875*. New York, 1927.

Kantorowicz, Hermann: *The Spirit of German Policy*. Trans. from German. London and New York, 1931.

Kirkaldy, A.: *British Shipping*. London, 1914.

Levi, Leone: *History of British Commerce*. London, 1880.

Loreburn, Earl: *How the War Came*. London, 1919.

McKenzie, F. A.: *The American Invaders*. London, 1902.

Medley, G. W.: *The Reciprocity Craze*. (Cobden Club pamphlet) London, 1881.

Meeker, Royal: *History of Shipping Subsidies*. Publications of American Economic Association, 1905.

Moon, P. T.: *Imperialism and World Politics*. New York, 1926.

Nevins, Allen: *Henry White, Thirty Years of American Diplomacy*. New York, 1930.

Page, William: *Commerce and Industry*. 2 vols. London, 1919.

Perris, G. H.: *Germany and the German Emperor*. London, 1912.

Perris, G. H.: *The Industrial History of Modern England*. London, 1914.

Playne, Caroline E.: *The Pre-War Mind in Britain*. London, 1928.

Pogson, G. A.: *Germany and Its Trade*. London, 1903.

Pribram, A. F.: *England and the International Policy of the European Great Powers, 1871-1914*. Oxford, 1931.

Price, L. L.: *Short History of English Commerce and Industry*. London, 1900.

Rheinbaben, Rochus v.: *Stresemann the Man and the Statesman*. Trans. from German. New York, 1929.

Rogers, J. E. T.: *Industrial and Commercial History of England*. London, 1892.

Root, J. W.: *Trade Relations of the British Empire*. Liverpool, 1903.

Sargent, A. J.: *Anglo-Chinese Commerce and Diplomacy*. Oxford, 1907.

Schierbrand, Wolf v.: *Germany. The Welding of a World Power*. New York, 1902.

Schmitt, Bernadotte: *England and Germany, 1740-1916*. Princeton, 1916.

Schulze-Gaevernitz, G. v.: *Britischer Imperialismus und Englischer Freihandel zu Beginn des zwanzigsten Jahrhunderts.* Leipzig, 1906.

Schulze-Gaevernitz, G. v.: *England und Deutschland.* Freiburg, 1908.

Seligman, E. R. A.: *An Economic Interpretation of the War.* New York, 1915.

Shadwell, Arthur: *Industrial Efficiency. A Comparative Study of Industrial Life in England, Germany, and America.* 2 vols. London, 1906. 2nd. ed., 1909.

Slater, G. W.: *The Making of Modern England.* New York, 1915 ed.

Smart, W.: *The Return to Protection.* London, 1904.

Thorp, Willard L.: *Business Annals.* Publications of National Bureau of Economic Research, No. 8. New York, 1926.

Townsend, M. H.: *The Origins of Modern German Colonialism.* New York, 1921.

Townsend, M. H.: *The Rise and Fall of the German Colonial Empire.* New York, 1929.

Tryon, G. C.: *Tariff Reform.* London, 1909.

Veritas: *The German Empire of Today.* London, 1902.

Vigilans sed Aequus: *German Ambitions as They Affect Britain and the United States.* London, 1903.

Wallace, D. M.: *Russia.* New York, 1877 ed.

Walter, S.: *The Meaning of Tariff Reform.* London, 1910.

Wertheimer, M. S.: *The Pan-German League, 1890-1914.* New York, 1924.

Whelpley, J. D.: *The Trade of the World.* New York, 1911.

Williams, E. E.: *Made in Germany.* London, 1896.

Williamson, A.: *British Industries and Foreign Competition.* London, 1894.

INDEX